GROUP CARE OF CHILDREN
Transitions Toward the Year 2000

edited by
EDWIN A. BALCERZAK

Child Welfare League of America
Washington, D.C.

3-27-95

CHILD WELFARE LEAGUE OF AMERICA, INC.
440 First Street, NW, Suite 310, Washington, DC 20001-2085

CURRENT PRINTING (last digit)
10 9 8 7 6 5 4 3 2 1

Cover design by Anita Crouch

Text design by Rose Jacobowitz

Printed in the United States of America

ISBN 0-87868-287-2

THIS BOOK IS DEDICATED TO the late Morris Fritz Mayer, who was a colleague, a friend, a mentor, a teacher, and even at times a father figure. Fritz was a committed and tireless worker in behalf of troubled children. He impressed upon me his concern about the quality of children's services, especially group care. His level of devotion to these issues was one to which all people concerned about children should aspire.

This book is also dedicated to all the children who need help, and to the organizations that help them. The importance of children must never be slighted, and our investment in them must never waver. Organizations should always wonder whether they are doing enough, well enough, and whether what they are doing moves children toward self-reliance and productivity in our society.

Contents

Acknowledgments

W HEN I WAS ASKED TO PUT TOGETHER this volume for the Child Welfare League of America, I accepted without fully grasping what the assignment should entail. As time wore on, I understood better the responsibility of offering the field a volume of sound ideas to help its readers make the transition to the year 2000.

The initial papers for the book were drawn from the 120 presentations given at the CWLA Group Care Conference in Houston, in February 1986. Since all presenters could not submit their papers for consideration, additional papers on important subjects were sought from others. Despite the comprehensiveness afforded by the papers this volume comprises, it cannot be said that all possible topics were dealt with; perhaps that is never possible. We hope, however, that we have touched the main bases on the way to home plate.

One of my goals in this book was to provide for the possibility of extending new knowledge by acquainting people with each other. The contributors' list therefore includes addresses at the time of publication; the authors would welcome hearing from readers.

I was aided in my assignment by an outstanding group of ad hoc advisers who met with me from time to time to give their advice and counsel, review papers, and raise important questions about the book's content areas. Their advice was indispensable, and I would like to express my appreciation to them: Bob Barker, Sam Berman, Nan Dale, Joan DiLeonardi, Tim Fitzharris, Don Harris, Dick Pancost, and Jim Whittaker. I am also grateful for the support and help of Sue Brite, the Child Welfare League's director of publications; her unwavering assistance and friendship were important ingredients in getting the job done. Finally, I would like to acknowledge the support of my wife, Kathie, who encouraged me unflinchingly in the unhappy moments when the prospects of completing the book seemed slim.

Introduction

The Context of Group Care

EDWIN A. BALCERZAK

W HAT IS THE PLACE OF GROUP CARE in today's society? What must the field of group care do to regain its status in a society that came to view it as a placement of last resort, and, worse, destructive of family life? If there is a place for it, what must that be, and what must it become in the future? How does the field take charge of its own destiny? Can the field address the forces of society that shape the public policy that affects it? What kind of children are in need of group care, and what services will be effective in helping them? How can the services be delivered efficiently? How do group care agencies engage parents who themselves may be fragile and without hope? How do we help children to go home, find permanent surrogate families for them, or establish them as independent persons? How essential is it to develop a spectrum of services and a continuum of care? And, most especially, how do organizations better serve children of different cultural or ethnic backgrounds?

These and other current issues and questions facing group care and child welfare have not arisen suddenly but have evolved over time in the fabric of society. Moreover, they have been accelerating, as a comparison with the Child Welfare League of America's Group Care Conference over a decade ago will show.[a]

[a]*Group Care of Children: Crossroads and Transitions.* Morris Fritz Mayer, Leon H. Richman, and Edwin A. Balcerzak. New York, Child Welfare League of America, 1977.

3

What are the changes in American society affecting group care? Social attitudes and a shift in economic thinking have created one level of effect on public social policy. Slow economic growth, the soaring national debt, the trade imbalance, and the decline of the industrial base in the United States have all sharpened the focus on near-term profitability; that is, emphasis on short-term gain. The belief that the individual has complete control over his or her own destiny has been rekindled and is a preemptive argument against social programs. Changes in federal policy about domestic spending, a decrease in federal dollars to states and cities, and an emphasis on local control and states' rights are the by-products of these trends. In the public policy arena, the idea of large-scale social investment in human service programs has been abandoned by the federal government. The legislative intent designating "the least restrictive environment" has been reinterpreted to be "the least expensive alternative." With each fiscal year the focus of public policy seems to be narrowing to the children most severely in need, instead of expanding intervention in the early problem stages. Consequences of these changes have been a decline in, and more restrictive funding for, group care, along with a greater emphasis on more accountability and better results in shorter periods of time. What has largely been ignored is that the children coming to group care have greater problems than was true earlier and have usually failed out of a weak foster family care system.

The interplay between social attitudes, economic issues, public policy, and the demographic changes in America has yielded a number of curious paradoxes that bear directly and indirectly on group care. First, there is a spark of recognition but little action on the great need for social investment in children, despite the fact that as a group they are a declining cohort in the population, and the necessity for them to be highly educated in order to take their places in a technologically oriented work force. Second, the policy of investment in medical technology, especially for premature and low birthweight infants, has saved children but has failed to recognize that many such children are the product of the lack of adequate free or low-cost prenatal care among poor mothers, and that preventive care is more cost-effective per capita over the life of the child. Third, the policy of storing surplus food on the basis of cost alone does not recognize that the nutritional needs of poor children first need to be satisfied before they can learn in school and grow and develop into the productive citizens the nation will require in the future.

Fourth, although it is known that early intervention and preventive strategies are more cost-effective in health care, children needing out-of-home care are generally not referred for residential treatment until they are very seriously emotionally disturbed. These children have to fail out of less restrictive and less intensive programs. Even then, these children are eligible only for inpatient psychiatric care and only for a brief period of time. By then the problems are usually long-standing and difficult to resolve. The free-enterprise response to this paradox is the development of single-service, profit-making psychiatric units for children and adolescents. These entities lack aftercare and do little family work but subscribe to the payment mechanism perfectly. Finally, despite cutbacks in funding and more restrictive placement policies and new services like in-home treatment, the number of children needing group care has not diminished significantly, and the cooperation between the four human service providers—mental health, child welfare, juvenile justice, and education—has not improved. Financial considerations and strict adherence to service eligibility criteria get in the way of services to meet the needs of children. This situation gives credence to the Procrustean-bed mentality that rivals the belief the Greek myth must have received in ancient times.

The consequences of these paradoxes have had many implications for group care. In addition to the severity and magnitude of presenting problems of children and the severe deficits they manifest, parents too often have serious deficiencies. This critical problem must be addressed if children are to return home as quickly as possible. The provision of diverse need-meeting services to multiproblem children is often impeded by the unwillingness of the four human service providers to pay for a share of the services necessary.

The demographic picture in America has also changed since the 1970s and has had an effect on group care service delivery. Along with disposable goods have come disposable relationships. The divorce rate has nearly doubled over the past decade, with no reversals in sight. An ever-increasing number of children are growing up in single-parent households and in new emerging lifestyles such as stepfamilies and joint custody agreements. Many of the children in these circumstances live in poverty, may be neglected or abused, have problems in school or with the juvenile authorities, and bear the scars of family discontinuity. Shelters for the homeless dispossessed by economic problems are now seeing two-parent families with children in addition to the single-parent families and battered spouses. Social attitudes about relationships, a greater inward directedness, and a lack of hope about the future characterize and surround the children of today. The dropout rate among high school students in many urban cities approaches 50 percent. Drug and alcohol abuse and teenage pregnancy are not decreasing and remain as problems needing real solutions. The child or adolescent who comes into group care today is different from the child of ten years ago. Today's child is more clearly a product of the society and family structure.

How has the field of group care been responding to these forces and demographic changes? Residential group care has become more adaptive to changing conditions. There are fewer and fewer single-service group care organizations. The number of large congregate institutions has diminished. Some group care agencies that failed to change have failed to survive. For many that waited too long, the process of change—downsizing, program shifts, mandated staff reductions, staff realignment and retraining—has become painful economically and professionally; change was externally directed rather than internally developed and nourished. And many group care agencies have diversified and created new programs as both a child-care service strategy and a means to healthy survival. The development of a spectrum of services and a continuum of care within many group care agencies has become normative in the last ten years, as organizations have recognized changes in the societal landscape of America.

Even more extraordinary are the interagency arrangements for the least restrictive environment. Paradoxically, however, funding bodies have tended to see these organizations as single-service, out-of-home care institutions, rather than as multi-service organizations seeking to provide continuity in a relationship to children and their families through the interplay of a variety of services that follow the child and family as their needs change, somewhat like the HMO model of managed health care. This innovation has not, as yet, been widely accepted by public funding bodies.

The importance of coalitions, and formal associations of group care coalitions, in communities, states, provinces, and large metropolitan areas in North America is a positive force in the development of better services for children and their families. In addition to being strong advocates in social policy arenas for children's services and for greater congruence between needs and access to the continuum of care, these organizations have improved programs through stronger standards of practice, access to new sources of funding, public education, greater interaction with parents and children in the community, and improved information about service effectiveness. The efforts of the CWLA Task Force on Out-of-Home Care toward a unified policy statement on group care constitute a strategy to create rallying points and more congruity for the field of group care. All of these dynamics for change must continue the development of new models of care, research on service effectiveness, and the dissemination of new knowledge from a variety of fields of service.

Despite the problems of working with more difficult, multiproblem parents, as well as multiproblem children, work with families and new ways of working with parents are beginning to spread. There are notable efforts to move organizations from "child-saving" to creating safe and secure child-and-family environments. Parents are playing new roles in agencies' pursuit of these goals.

The future of group care is solidly in the hands of all those who care deeply about children, for they are the future of society itself. It is rooted in providing the highest quality of services to children and their families and a spectrum of services and a continuity of care as their needs change. It is based in a philosophy of flexibility and an abhorrence of the rigidity that comes from years of doing something in just one way. As the authors and programs presented in this volume so incisively demonstrate, it lies in a willingness to risk, to work with children and families in new ways of responding to their complicated needs.

Part 1

Children in Group Care

1

Trends in Residential Group Care: 1966–1981

THOMAS M. YOUNG
MARTHA M. DORE
DONNELL M. PAPPENFORT

THE ORGANIZED PROVISION OF RESIDENTIAL GROUP CARE for children and youth changed markedly during the period 1966 to 1981. Changes in sources and methods of financing group care; new legislation promoting deinstitutionalization, normalization, and permanency planning; and the implementation of more family-oriented treatment philosophies all influenced the provision of residential group care during this period.[1]

This paper describes some of the changes in residential group care that occurred between 1966 and 1981. It focuses on changes over time in the numbers and kinds of facilities, by auspices and by size; changes in the numbers and selected characteristics of the children in care and their average length of stay; and changes in the complexity of the facilities' programs. When appropriate, we discuss what may have brought about these changes. The paper concludes with the question of what the trends identified here might imply for the future of residential group care.

Sources of Data

The information reported here was obtained through two research efforts, both carried out at the University of Chicago. The first is the National Survey of Residential Child Care, the full results of which were published in seven volumes, as *A Census of Children's Residential Institutions in the United States, Puerto Rico, and the Virgin Islands: 1966.*[2] The second is the National Survey of Residential Group Care, conducted from September 1981, through June 1982, from which some of the data are here being published for the first time.[3]

The data for 1981 pertain to nine types of residential group care facilities for children (persons under 21 years of age) considered to be:

> Dependent and neglected
>
> Delinquent
>
> Emotionally disturbed
>
> Mentally ill
>
> In need of services due to pregnancy
>
> In need of services due to use of an illegal substance
>
> In need of supervision (sometimes referred to as "status offenders")
>
> In need of temporary shelter or emergency care
>
> In need of detention[4]

The categories for which information is available from 1966 differ in two ways. First, specialized facilities for substance-abusing children did not exist in 1966. Second, facilities for status offenders in 1966 had not become differentiated from those for delinquents to the extent that is true today. Instead, they both were part of a category then referred to as facilities for predelinquent and delinquent children. When possible, data from facilities for delinquents and facilities for status offenders have been added together in the tables that follow, for comparison with 1966.[5]

In both surveys, the classification of each facility was made by its director in response to a question about the current primary function of the facility. Functions in addition to the primary one were also recorded, and these are discussed in the section on functional complexity of the facilities.

Facilities and Children: Numbers by Type of Care

During the 15 years between the two surveys, the total number of residential group care facilities for children increased, but the number of children living in them declined. In both 1966 and 1981, the numbers of children are based on the number in residence at each facility on the day they completed the questionnaire mailed to them. In 1966, 2,318 facilities reported a total of 155,905 children in care. In 1981, 3,914 facilities reported a total of 125,323. For both points in time, Table 1 gives the number of facilities by their primary function; Table 2 gives the number of children living in them on the day they responded to the survey.

In both tables, the categories of facilities have been listed in a way that permits comparison among the fields of child welfare, juvenile justice, and mental health. For example, in Table 1, the only increase in child welfare facilities occurs in the category of temporary shelter. There were fewer facilities for children considered dependent and neglected in 1981 than in 1966 and many fewer facilities for pregnant adolescents. In contrast, all three kinds of juvenile justice facilities—those for children considered delinquent or status offenders and those for temporary detention—were more numerous in 1981 than in 1966. Mental health facilities—those for children considered emotionally disturbed, and those providing

TABLE 1

Number of Facilities by Type: 1966 and 1981

Type of Facility	Number of Facilities			
	1966		1981	
	n	(%)	n	(%)
Dependent and neglected	955	(41)	907	(23)
Pregnant adolescents	201	(9)	100	(3)
Temporary shelter	54	(2)	351	(9)
Delinquent	414	(18)	840	(21)
Status offenders	a		227	(6)
Detention	242	(10)	378	(10)
Substance abuse	a		62	(2)
Emotionally disturbed	307	(13)	680	(17)
Psychiatric	145	(6)	369	(9)
Total	2,318	(99*)	3,914	(100)

aNot recognized as a type of facility in 1966
*Figures do not equal 100 percent due to rounding

TABLE 2

Number of Children and Youth, 1966 and 1981,
by Type of Facility

	Number of Children and Youth			
Type of Facility	1966		1981	
	n	(%)	n	(%)
Dependent and neglected	60,459	(39)	24,533	(20)
Pregnant adolescents	5,835	(4)	1,676	(1)
Temporary shelter	1,832	(1)	3,893	(3)
Delinquent	55,000	(35)	40,335	(32)
Status offenders	a		4,754	(4)
Detention	10,875	(7)	15,423	(12)
Substance abuse	a		1,629	(1)
Emotionally disturbed	13,876	(9)	20,397	(16)
Psychiatric	8,028	(5)	12,683	(10)
Total	155,905	(100)	125,323	(99)*

aNot recognized as a type of facility in 1966
*Figures do not equal 100 percent due to rounding

psychiatric inpatient care for children—also were more numerous in 1981 than in 1966.

These changes in the number of facilities, however, do not provide a complete description of the transformation that took place in the provision of residential group care during the 15-year period under discussion. For that we have to examine the data for number of children in residence given in Table 2. There we see, for example, that the modest decrease in facilities for children considered dependent and neglected involved a substantial decrease in the number of children living in facilities of this kind.

By contrast, the opposite pattern appears within the field of juvenile justice. There the increase in number of facilities for children considered delinquent or status offenders was accompanied by a decline in the number of children. Interestingly, in both fields of practice the increases in numbers of temporary care facilities— for shelter and detention—also were accompanied by substantial increases in number of children living in them. In all categories of the mental health group, the substantial increases in number of facilities were accompanied by substantial increases in number of children reported in residence. Overall, then, the growth sectors in residential group care during this period, at least as measured by number of children, were in temporary shelter and detention care and in the mental health facilities.

Children in Care by Auspices

The changes in the organized provision of residential group care for children that occurred between 1966 and 1981 involved much more than the growth and decline in number of facilities and their residents, as just described. There also were substantial changes in the distribution of children by auspices of the facilities in which they were placed. Table 3 summarizes those changes.

Overall, facilities operating under Catholic auspices showed the largest decrease in the number of children in residence (− 18,697), followed by those operated by agencies of State government (− 13,796) and those under Protestant auspices (− 8,267). The general pattern of decreases for most categories of auspices is offset by a substantial increase in number of children living in facilities operating under Secular (private, not-for-profit) auspices (+ 8,731) and those operating under Proprietary (for-profit) auspices (+ 3,372). The large decline in number of children living in facilities for the dependent and neglected (− 35,926), was concentrated in facilities operating under Catholic (− 16,262) and Protestant (− 8,521) auspices. Facilities operating under State (− 3,886) or Local (− 3,992) governmental auspices also show decreases but not of the magnitude shown for facilities operating under private sectarian auspices.

The reductions in number of children in facilities for pregnant adolescents occurred primarily in facilities operating under Secular, Protestant, and Catholic auspices. In contrast, the increases in number of children living in temporary shelter care were concentrated among facilities operating under Secular auspices, public auspices (both State and Local), and those operating under Protestant auspices. The decline in number of children living in facilities for children considered delinquent or status offenders (− 9,911) took a less uniform pattern by auspices. Facilities operating under Protestant, Secular, and Proprietary auspices actually show increases (+ 438,

TABLE 3

Auspices of Facilities, 1966 and 1981: Changes in Number
of Children and Youth, by Type

Type of Facility

Auspices	Total All Types	Dependent and Neglected	Pregnant Adolescent	Temporary Shelter	(Pre)Delinquent — Delinquent	Status Offender	Detention	Substance[a] Abuse	Emotionally Disturbed	Psychiatric
Public										
State	−13,796	−3,886	−18	+156	−11,602		+3,061	+314	−1,568	−253
Local	−1,763	−3,992	+26	+325	−433		+1,900	+38	+142	+231
Private										
Protestant	−8,267	−8,521	−1,588	+299	+438		+8	+102	+666	+329
Catholic	−18,697	−16,262	−633	−125	−2,319		+3	+21	+113	+505
Jewish	−162	−7	−12	−31	−23		0	0	−34	−55
Secular	+8,731	−3,235	−1,867	+1,403	+3,732		−438	+982	+6,504	+1,650
Proprietary	+3,372	−23	−67	+34	+296		+14	+172	+698	+2,248
Total of Children	−30,582	−35,926	−4,159	+2,061	−9,911		+4,548	+1,629	+6,521	+4,655

[a]Not used as a category in 1966

+3,732, and +296, respectively) that offset substantial reductions in the number of children living in facilities operating under State auspices (−11,602). Facilities operating under the auspices of Local government also show a decrease (−433). The pattern of decreases for the publicly operated, longer-term care facilities in the juvenile justice group is in contrast to the pattern of increases for publicly operated temporary detention facilities. Both state (+3,061) and locally (+1,900) operated facilities showed increases in numbers in residence.

Within the mental health group, there were substantial increases for numbers living in facilities operating under Secular and Proprietary auspices. The largest occurred for facilities for children considered emotionally disturbed operating under Secular auspices (+6,504) and for psychiatric facilities operating under Proprietary auspices (+2,248). The decrease in numbers within this group were concentrated in State-operated facilities for children considered emotionally disturbed (−1,568) and those providing psychiatric care (−253).

Although the surveys that collected these data could not also study why these changes occurred, there are several plausible explanations. The reductions in numbers living in State-operated facilities for longer-term care (those for children considered dependent and neglected, delinquent, status offenders, emotionally disturbed, or psychiatric facilities) probably reflect policies promoting permanency planning in child welfare, deinstitutionalization and diversion to community-based care in juvenile corrections, and community-based services in the children's mental health field. The increases in numbers in facilities operating under Secular and Proprietary auspices suggest, however, that perhaps some of the deinstitutionalization of State-operated facilities in those categories was accomplished through purchasing residential group care from providers operating under private auspices. Another explanation for the increases in numbers living in Secular and Proprietary facilities might be that those facilities have been admitting more privately insured children. It should be noted, however, that the largest decrease by auspices—the decrease of 18,697 children living in facilities operating under Catholic auspices—is the least amenable to explanation at the present time.

The increases in numbers living in publicly operated detention facilities are probably due to an increase in federal funds to state and local governments for the construction of such facilities. These funds were made available, at least in part, to reduce the use of adult jails for detaining juveniles.[6] A related explanation might account for the increases in numbers living in publicly operated temporary shelters; that is, it may be that some state and local governments constructed temporary shelters for temporary care of status offenders. These shelters enabled them to comply with federal regulations requiring different custodial arrangements for status offenders and delinquents, and thus they remained eligible to receive federal funds.

Perhaps a cautionary note should be inserted here. Although we can neither confirm nor refute these hypotheses, many of them appear consistent with the changes in numbers of children in residential group care by type of facility and auspices. The data we are discussing were collected by two separate surveys carried out 15 years apart, however, not from a longitudinal study. Many of the facilities that responded in 1966 were no longer in existence in 1981, and many more facilities were established some time after 1966. So, while the juxtaposition of data from 1966 with comparable data from 1981 in these tables makes it tempting to speculate about systematic relationships among fields of care or types of facilities used, the two surveys were not carried out to examine the factual bases for such speculations. Still, the data from them do suggest that further research to study some of these relationships might produce important information for those who provide and finance such care.[7]

Size of Facilities

Another major change in residential group care that took place during the 15-year period under consideration was a reduction in the average size of facilities. Table 4 presents the relevant information.

In general, the average number of children in residence per facility declined from 67 in 1966 to 32 in 1981, and the pattern of decline occurred for all types of facilities, although to varying degrees. The decline in average size of facilities for children considered delinquent or predelinquent (status offenders) is the most noticeable—from 133 to 42. Typically, these facilities were by far

TABLE 4

Average Number of Children and Youth, 1966
and 1981, by Type of Facility

Type of Facility	Average Size	
	1966	1981
Dependent and neglected	63	27
Pregnant adolescents	29	17
Temporary shelter	34	11
Delinquent and predelinquent	133	42
Detention	45	41
Substance abuse	a	26
Emotionally disturbed	45	30
Psychiatric	55	34
Total All Facilities	67	32

[a]Not recognized as type of facility in 1966

the largest in 1966. Among the other longer-term care facilities, those for children considered dependent and neglected declined in average size from 63 children per facility in 1966 to 27 in 1981. Facilities for children considered emotionally disturbed and those providing psychiatric care also declined in average size. Among the short-term care facilities, temporary shelters became much smaller, typically, while those for detention care did not.

Averages, of course, emphasize certain facts at the expense of others. In this instance, they do not reveal what may be the most significant change that has taken place in residential group care over the past years: namely, the increase in number of smaller facilities. Two-thirds of the facilities responding to the survey in 1981 reported having 25 or fewer residents. Fifteen years ago, only 36 percent of those responding were of that size. The main trend over the past 15 years regarding size has been the replacement, so to speak, of facilities with 50 or more residents by facilities with ten or fewer.

Space does not permit here the detailed examination of changes in the average size of facilities by both type and auspices. A summary statement can be made, however. The trend toward smaller facilities is impressive, but large facilities remain, particularly in juvenile justice. There also remain large private facilities for children considered dependent and neglected, emotionally disturbed, and mentally ill. Large numbers of children in residential group care still continue to live in big facilities. At the time of the survey, three-fourths of the children in public facilities lived in facilities with more than 50 residents, most of them in detention or in the longer-term facilities for delinquents. Among privately operated facilities, two-fifths of the children lived in facilities with more than 50 residents, most in facilities for children considered dependent and neglected or emotionally disturbed. Although the number of children involved is much smaller, substantial proportions of those in both publicly and privately operated psychiatric care lived in larger facilities.

One of the main findings of the 1966 survey was that size served as an indicator of resources. The larger facilities tended to have smaller ratios of staff members to residents, provide services to smaller proportions of the children, and make available less adequate living arrangements than did facilities with fewer residents. We have not yet had the opportunity to examine the correlates of size in the data for 1981 to see if the relationships continue to exist now that so many residential group care facilities are, on the average, smaller. But we know from conversations with many of the directors of the facilities surveyed that the influence of size on the quality of care they can provide continues to be a concern. One more recent development that has made this relationship more complex is that a number of the newer, smaller facilities are members of a group or chain of six or seven facilities—all operated by a larger agency with central responsibility for the physical plants, staffing, and services provided the residents of all of them.

Average Length of Stay

In addition to shifts over time in the distribution of children by type and auspices of facilities, and the proliferation of newer, smaller facilities, a third major change in the field was a reduction in average length of stay of the children in residential group care. Table 5 summarizes the responses for both 1966 and 1981 by showing the percentage of facilities in each category according to four

TABLE 5

Average Length of Stay, 1966 and 1981: Percentage of Facilities

Length of Stay	Total All Types		Dependent and Neglected		Pregnant Adolescent		Temporary Shelter		Delinquent (Pre)		Delinquent		Status Offender		Detention		Substance Abuse		Emotionally Disturbed		Psychiatric	
	1966	1981	1966	1981	1966	1981	1966	1981	1966	1981	1966	1981	1966	1981	1966	1981	1966	1981	1966	1981	1966	1981
Less than one month	11	19	1	3	3	2	28	82	1	NA	NA	3	NA	8	86	88	NA	5	0	a	0	10
One month up to one year	31	48	14	33	97	92	59	16	62	NA	NA	82	NA	74	14	11	NA	74	10	39	36	63
One year up to two years	20	21	19	31	0	6	6	1	28	NA	NA	12	NA	14	0	a	NA	15	44	47	24	18
Two years or longer	38	12	66	33	a	0	7	a	9	NA	NA	3	NA	4	0	a	NA	6	46	14	40	9
Total	100	100	100	100	100	100	100	99*	100	NA	NA	100	NA	100	100	99*	NA	100	100	100	100	100
Base Numbers	2,290	3,816	937	876	201	95	54	337	410	NA	NA	819	NA	221	242	372	NA	61	302	668	144	366

aLess than 1 percent
*Figures do not equal 100 percent due to rounding

intervals for average length of stay: less than one month; one month up to one year; one year up to two years; and two years or longer. Every category of care for which a comparison could be made—with two exceptions—reported briefer average lengths of stay in 1981 than they had 15 years earlier. (The exceptions are facilities for pregnant adolescents and for detention care.) Psychiatric in-patient units as a group experienced the sharpest reduction in averages.

The general pattern of reduction in average stays reported for 1981 compared to 1966 is most pronounced for certain categories of care at certain intervals. For example, 66 percent of the facilities for children considered dependent and neglected in 1966 reported average stays of two years or longer. By 1981, the percentage of facilities reporting average stays of that duration had declined to 33 percent. Corresponding increases in the percentage of facilities reporting shorter average stays for their residents in 1981 can be seen in the first three intervals.

A similar pattern can be seen among facilities for delinquents and predelinquents in 1966 and those for delinquents and status offenders in 1981, except that for this category of care the decline occurs in the third interval (one year up to two years). The corresponding increases occur in the first and second intervals. Among facilities for children considered emotionally disturbed and those providing psychiatric care, the largest reductions occur in the "two years or longer" interval, and the corresponding increases occur in the "one month up to one year" interval.

Temporary shelters follow the pattern of decline in average stays but with the changes occurring, for the most part, in the first two intervals. So too, generally, do detention facilities, except that a small number of facilities in that category reported average stays of one year or more in 1981 when none did so in 1966. The only category that does not follow the overall pattern of decline in average stays (smaller percentages in 1981 for the longer-term intervals and larger percentages in the shorter-term intervals) is that of facilities for pregnant adolescents.

The reason for the reduced average stays (or, for facilities for pregnant adolescents, the increased stays) were not pursued in the survey. But we might speculate, as we did for the changes over time in the number of children in residence, that the reasons might be different for the different types of facilities. Facilities for children considered dependent and neglected, for example, may have reduced the length of their residents' stays in response to public policies emphasizing permanency planning and the use of foster family homes as less restrictive placement alternatives. Those for children considered delinquent or status offenders may have reduced their residents' average stays in response to policies emphasizing use of community-based programs as alternatives to incarceration and in response to efforts to control overcrowding in juvenile correctional facilities. Those for children considered emotionally disturbed and those providing psychiatric care may have reduced their residents' average stays due to the increased availability of (nonresidential) special education and day treatment programs and curtailments in duration of insurance coverage for residential treatment and psychiatric hospitalization. Those for temporary shelter and detention may have changed to shorter stays following implementation of policies promoting increased frequency of judicial and administrative reviews of all admissions to such facilities. Those for pregnant adolescents may have changed to longer average stays as a result of increased efforts to help adolescent parents keep their babies rather than put them up for adoption.

Degree of Disturbance and Types of Problems Among Residents

Table 6 presents information for both years about the perceived level of emotional disturbance or behavior problems of children in residence. The question was worded: "Among the children/youth currently in residence in your facility, about what proportion would you classify at each of the following levels of emotional disturbance or disordered behavior?" Respondents entered proportions for each of the four categories: severe, moderate, mild, none.[8]

In 1966 the collective judgment of residential group care staffs, in all types of facilities throughout the country, was that 75 percent of their children were emotionally disturbed or exhibited disordered behavior to some degree. By 1981 that proportion had increased to 86 percent, or 107,000 children.

Most of that increase occurred for children living in facilities for the dependent and neglected, and in temporary shelters—the

TABLE 6
Level of Emotional Disturbance or Behavior Problem, 1966 and 1981: Percentage of Children and Youth

Level	Total All Types		Dependent and Neglected		Pregnant Adolescent		Temporary Shelter		(Pre) Delinquent		Delinquent		Status Offender		Detention		Substance Abuse		Emotionally Disturbed		Psychiatric	
	1966	1981	1966	1981	1966	1981	1966	1981	1966	1981	1966	1981	1966	1981	1966	1981	1966	1981	1966	1981	1966	1981
Some degree of emotional disturbance or behavior problem	75	86	55	76	76	79	60	79	87	NA	NA	84	NA	90	79	80	NA	86	96	98	98	99
Severe	14	22	4	8	5	9	4	9	16	NA	NA	17	NA	13	18	14	NA	16	28	35	57	59
Moderate	32	36	21	30	27	32	28	32	40	NA	NA	36	NA	46	33	31	NA	40	47	47	33	33
Mild	29	28	29	38	45	39	28	38	31	NA	NA	31	NA	31	29	35	NA	30	21	17	8	7
No particular emotional disturbance or behavior problem	25	14	45	24	24	21	40	21	13	NA	NA	16	NA	10	21	20	NA	14	4	2	2	1
Base Numbers	147,090	124,457	56,648	24,412	5,258	1,676	1,717	3,887	51,765			40,128	4,718		10,187	15,186	1,424		13,597	20,381	7,918	12,645

two categories of care with the smallest percentages in 1966. For all other types of facilities in that year, the percentages had already reached nearly 80 percent, or more, and remained stable through 1981.

The stability extended as well to the distributions by degrees of disturbance or behavior problems—mild, moderate, and severe. Psychiatric inpatient units for children and facilities for the emotionally disturbed reported children with emotional disturbances in proportions exceeding those for other types of facilities. In 1981, 99 percent of the children in psychiatric units were considered disturbed, 59 percent severely so. Facilities specifically for children considered emotionally disturbed reported that 98 percent of their children had emotional problems. They classified their children as severely disturbed less frequently than did psychiatric units, but reported a larger proportion as severely disturbed than they had in 1966.

The juvenile justice facilities reported smaller proportions. In 1981, 17 percent of the children in facilities for delinquents were considered severely disturbed, as were 13 percent in facilities for status offenders. (These figures cannot be compared directly with those for 1966.) Fourteen percent of the children in detention were considered severely disturbed, a modest decline from 1966.

The percentage of children and youth considered moderately disturbed increased for all three of the categories of facilities in the child welfare group, but remained unchanged for facilities in the mental health group.

Problems, Conditions, or Patterns of Behavior

Some understanding of what may have influenced the directors' perceptions of disturbance can be obtained from an additional question asked in 1981. The question provided a list of 17 problems, conditions, or patterns of behavior and asked the director to estimate the proportions of children in care having each. The aggregate responses are in Table 7.

Overall, large proportions of children with three characteristics—family problems, problematic peer relationships, and depression—were reported from every type of facility except those for detention. Similarly, children who had been abused made up a

TABLE 7

Problems, Conditions, or Patterns of Behavior, 1981: Percent of Children and Youth, by Type of Problem

	Total All Types	Dependent and Neglected	Pregnant Adolescent	Temporary Shelter	Type of Facility Delinquent	Status Offender	Detention	Substance Abuse	Emotionally Disturbed	Psychiatric
Violent to self/suicidal	14	7	6	9	13	11	16	18	13	28
Violent toward others	27	14	6	16	33	17	36	18	26	33
Abused	40	46	39	49	38	45	23	41	51	34
Depressed	48	43	50	49	45	57	40	61	60	55
Peer relationships	60	51	55	49	60	61	45	68	75	74
Family problems	74	80	71	81	72	85	55	76	80	77
Problems regarding property	42	22	14	22	63	33	53	43	35	29
Disruptive behavior	51	37	28	48	57	78	54	65	54	46
Accused and adjudicated delinquent	51	15	8	20	90	38	89	46	25	17

Learning and perceptual problems	38	31	21	27	39	34	33	22	50	45
Chronic physical illness	9	7	6	7	9	8	11	6	8	10
Mentally retarded	9	6	8	7	10	6	8	2	10	12
Thought disorders	17	9	8	10	15	11	14	7	22	36
Drug or alcohol abuse	7	6	6	5	8	8	9	3	6	9
Problems beyond control of family	16	24	18	15	13	15	16	20	16	13
Sexuality	18	13	86	20	18	21	15	25	19	17
Total %	100	100	100	100	100	100	100	100	100	100
Base Numbers	116	22,937	1,453	3,692	37,606	3,734	14,027	1,495	19,116	12,292
No answer	9	1,596	223[a]	201	2,729	1,020[a]	1,396	134	1,281	391
Total of Children	125	24,533	1,676	3,893	40,335	4,754	15,423	1,629	20,397	12,683

Note: Columns do not equal 100 percent: individuals may have more than one problem, condition, or pattern of behavior.

[a]Exceeds 10 percent of children and youth

third or more of the total number in care in each type of facility, again with the exception of detention. Children with learning and perceptual problems made up one-fifth or more in every type of facility, with the largest proportions occurring in facilities for children considered emotionally disturbed, those providing psychiatric care, and those for delinquents.

Children who had been violent to themselves were concentrated in facilities within the mental health group and especially in those providing psychiatric care. Children who had been violent toward others were concentrated in both the mental health facilities and in those for delinquents and temporary detention, while those children with problems regarding the destruction of other people's property were concentrated in facilities for delinquents and those for temporary detention. Some children who had been violent toward themselves, or toward others or their property, were, however, reported in facilities of every type.

Thus, while some types of facilities reported higher proportions of certain problems, conditions, or patterns of behavior than others for their residents, what is most striking is the large proportion of several problems, conditions, or patterns of behavior reported for children in each type of facility. The proportions of children presenting learning and perceptual difficulties and disruptive behavior patterns, who have been abused, who are depressed and have problematic peer and family relationships are substantial in nearly every type of facility. These figures suggest that providing residential group care and treatment is a complex and difficult task indeed.

Functional Complexity of Facilities

In the course of our work on the 1981 survey, we heard many residential program directors or their staff members say that they were seeing more children with more problems who were more difficult to care for and treat than they had seen previously. Although the question about problems, conditions, or patterns of behavior was not asked in 1966, the responses to it in 1981 do support the perceptions of those who have been providing residential group care over that period of time—especially when these data are considered in conjunction with those showing increases in proportions of children with severe emotional disturbance or disordered behavior and those reporting reductions in the average length of stay. As a colleague of ours asked after reviewing some of our findings, how have facilities been able to care for more seriously disturbed children when they are in residence for shorter periods of time? This is a very important question deserving careful attention and perhaps further study.

From our data, we suspect that one way that facilities have been able to do so is by becoming functionally more complex; that is, as the children presented for residential group care over time have brought with them a greater range and variety of problems to be dealt with in a shorter period of time, the facilities have become more complex, programmatically, in response. This hypothesis is based in part on data regarding functions that facilities reported providing in addition to their primary one. In both 1966 and 1981, facilities were asked to indicate which additional functions they performed. The responses have been summarized in Table 8. In 1981, a larger proportion of facilities of every kind reported one or more additional functions than had been the case in 1966. The magnitude of this change is such that in 1966 50 percent or more of the facilities of each kind—except those for children considered emotionally disturbed—reported only one function, their primary one. In 1981, the majority of facilities in every category reported one or more additional functions.

For 1981, Table 9 gives the percentage of facilities in each category that provided each additional function listed. The additional function designated most frequently by all facilities considered together is that of care of children considered status offenders: 40 percent of all facilities. This result is followed by care of children with drug or alcohol problems: 37 percent of all facilities. What is particularly noteworthy about these figures is that 15 years ago "substance abuse" and "status offenses" were terms not frequently used; they were not issues of piercing concern for residential group care.

Insofar as status offenses are a product of relatively recent state and federal legislation—identifying children charged with or adjudicated for noncriminal misbehaviors—their ramifications in the field of residential group care are impressive. It may be that the new terminology has served to fill a gap in the field's understanding and classification of children's problems. Should that be true, it

TABLE 8

Residential Functions Performed in Addition to the Primary One, 1966 and 1981: Percentage of Facilities

Additional functions	Total All Types		Dependent and Neglected		Pregnant Adolescent		Temporary Shelter		(Pre) Delinquent		Delinquent		Status Offender		Detention		Substance Abuse		Emotionally Disturbed		Psychiatric	
	1966	1981	1966	1981	1966	1981	1966	1981	1966	1981	1966	1981	1966	1981	1966	1981	1966	1981	1966	1981	1966	1981
One or more	44	73	45	75	31	58	44	81	48	NA	NA	68	NA	86	50	60	NA	63	51	83	26	66
None	56	27	55	25	69	42	56	19	52	NA	NA	32	NA	14	50	40	NA	37	49	17	74	34
Total	100	100	100	100	100	100	100	100	100	NA	NA	100	NA	100	100	100	NA	100	100	100	100	100
Base Numbers	2,318	3,884	955	900	201	99	54	348	414	NA	NA	829	NA	226	242	376	NA	62	307	676	145	368

TABLE 9

Residential Functions Performed in Addition to the Primary One, 1981: Percentage of Facilities, by Type of Additional Function

					Type of Facility				
Functions	Total All Types	Dependent and Neglected	Pregnant Adolescent	Temporary Shelter	Delinquent	Status Offender	Detention	Substance Abuse	Emotionally Disturbed	Psychiatric
Dependent and neglected	31	—	28	66	35	59	11	36	58	17
Pregnant adolescents	7	7	—	15	5	14	7	7	6	4
Temporary shelter	15	29	16	—	11	28	7	8	13	3
Delinquents	35	40	18	44	—	60	53	52	54	22
Substance abuse	37	29	14	34	51	47	27	—	39	42
Emotionally disturbed	36	50	18	43	45	46	21	44	—	55
Psychiatric	11	8	7	5	11	5	7	15	30	—
Boarding school	2	3	2	1	3	1	2	7	2	1
MR/DD	9	8	9	4	8	7	3	3	14	18
Physically handicapped	3	4	5	2	2	2	2	2	4	6
Chronically ill	23	1	4	1	0	—	—	2	3	7
Other	3	4	5	2	2	2	2	2	4	4
Infants	3	5	32	7	1	1	1	3	2	—
Total	3,91x	907	100	351	840	227	378	62	680	369

Note: Columns do not equal 100 percent; facilities may have more than one additional function.

could lead to new thinking about the role and function of residential group care in the lives of a significant proportion of those children placed in facilities for children considered dependent and neglected, delinquent, emotionally disturbed, or substance abusers.

The care of children with drug and alcohol problems, however, is an additional function that would appear to have a different natural history. The increased availability of illegal drugs throughout the social structure during the past 15 years has had its effect in the field of residential group care as well. The data do not distinguish between abuse of drugs and alcohol, but we believe that many of our respondents viewed them as concomitant problems.[9] We have already noted the evolution of a specialized type of care in the form of facilities that designated care of children with drug or alcohol problems as a primary function. Here we see the extent of such care in the form of facilities designating it as an additional function. Over half (51 percent) of the facilities for delinquents reported care of children with drug or alcohol problems as an additional function. Substantial proportions of facilities for status offenders (47 percent) and those for psychiatric inpatient care (42 percent) did so as well. The abuse of drugs and alcohol has obviously added a new dimension to the work of large numbers of those operating facilities for children and youth considered delinquents, status offenders, and emotionally disturbed.

The additional functions of care of children considered emotionally disturbed, delinquent, and dependent and neglected are distributed in much the same way as they were 15 years ago. Substantial proportions of facilities in 1981 that were providing care primarily for dependent and neglected children also reported caring for delinquent (40 percent) and emotionally disturbed (50 percent) children as an additional function. Similarly, a substantial proportion of those facilities designating care of delinquents as a primary function named as an additional function care of the dependent and neglected (35 percent) and care of the emotionally disturbed (45 percent). And of those designating care of the emotionally disturbed as a primary function, 58 percent reported that they were, in addition, providing care to the dependent and neglected, and 54 percent also reported care to delinquents. In 1966, this particular pattern of interrelated primary and additional functions was similar, but the percentages were substantially smaller. Put another way, in 1981 a greater proportion of facilities in each of these categories of primary function reported the other two categories as additional functions than was true 15 years ago.

What does this finding mean? We cannot be certain, but we think it means that larger proportions of facilities in each of these three categories of primary function admit children from a larger number and wider variety of referral sources than was the case 15 years ago. The tradition of specialization within the fields of child welfare, juvenile justice, and mental health is still very much in evidence. But this tradition does appear to be diminishing, as reflected in the increased numbers of facilities reporting other functions in addition to their primary one.

Conclusion

This paper has summarized only a few findings from the National Survey of Residential Group Care for Children and Youth. For the most part, we have selected information that could be compared with that from 1966.[10]

We began with comparisons of the number of children in care and of the number and type of facilities housing them. The shift in 15 years to smaller facilities is change of a magnitude not ordinarily encountered in such a relatively brief period of time. The findings suggest that recent emphases on deinstitutionalization, permanency planning, and normalization have brought forth the beginnings of a transformation in the field of residential group care.

We have emphasized that a great many facilities perform functions in addition to their primary ones and, for two reasons, have related that observation to the problems, conditions, and behavior of the children in residence. First, we believe the data reveal how difficult it is to provide residential group care, given the complexity of the problems, conditions, and behaviors of the children. Second, we think that the increase through time in the number of functions reported suggests a flexibility of adaptation to complex responsibilities by most residential group care facilities, a flexibility greater than many have believed possible.

Equally interesting, perhaps, are some of the changes in characteristics of the programs of services provided in group care that space has not allowed us to report here. Staff-to-resident ratios today are better than they were 15 years ago; substantially larger

portions of children in most types of care are attending school
in the community rather than at the facility; and family involvement
in the programs of care appears to be becoming the rule rather
than the exception. The data provide a contemporary view of residential group care quite different from the one prevailing 25 years
ago, when Erving Goffman published his book *Asylums*. The ste-
reotype of large, remote, and barren institutions no longer applies
to most facilities for children.

What about the future? It may be foolhardy to speculate about
the future of a field that has changed so much in 15 years. Still,
certain changes lend themselves to speculation about the future.
We noted that, despite the great increase in the number of smaller
facilities, a large number of children still remain in big facilities—
particularly in juvenile correction. Will the transformation of the
field continue and extend to these the benefits of smaller scale?
We do not know.

We have observed that average lengths of stay at all types of
facilities have declined markedly. At some facilities, the average
length of stay is so brief that we can hardly imagine their staffs
getting to know a child or adolescent in the time available. It seems
plausible that this change could signal more far-reaching changes
for the field in the years ahead. It may be that, in some places,
residential group care is becoming one brief point on a temporal
continuum of care or service—a point both preceded and followed
by a range of nonresidential services to children and their families.
To frame the issue more sharply, more residential group care facilities are caring for more difficult children for briefer periods of
time; the question for the near future is whether preventative and
follow-up services are to be made available and coordinated with
admission and return from group care, when necessary.[a]

Notes

1. Dore, Martha, and Guberman-Kennedy, Karen. Two Decades of Turmoil:
Child Welfare Services, 1960–1980. *Child Welfare* LX: 371–382, June 1981.

2. Pappenfort, Donnell M., and Kilpatrick, Dee Morgan (compilers). *A Census
of Children's Residential Institutions in the United States, Puerto Rico, and the Virgin*

[a]*Acknowledgments*: The authors wish to acknowledge their gratitude to Patty
Bundren, Jeanne Diamond, and Heather Richter for typing the manuscript and
accompanying tables for this paper.

Islands, 1966. Social Service Monographs, 2nd series, Number 4. 7 volumes. Chicago, Illinois: School of Social Service Administration, University of Chicago, 1970.

3. The National Survey of Residential Group Care, 1981, was made possible by a grant (No. 82-MU-AX-0036) from the National Institute of Juvenile Justice and Delinquency Prevention, U.S. Department of Justice. The authors wish to acknowledge their gratitude to Barbara Allen-Hagen, project officer, for her thoughtful guidance of our work. Due to a change in the Institute's program emphasis, however, the findings from the survey were not published. Some of the data pertaining to facilities for children considered emotionally disturbed have been published. See Young, Thomas M., Dore, Martha M., and Pappenfort, Donnell M., "Residential Group Care for Children Considered Emotionally Disturbed: 1966–1981," *Social Service Review* 62, 1:158–170, March 1988.

4. Residential group care facilities for children and youth with developmental disabilities, physical handicaps, or chronic illnesses were not included.

5. For both 1966 and 1981, the statistics are for universes, not samples. In 1966 the survey questionnaires accounted for 97.7 percent of the institutions of that era. For 1981, the percentage declined to 95.0.

6. See Young, Thomas M., and Pappenfort, Donnell M. *Secure Detention of Juveniles and Alternatives to its Use.* Washington, D.C., U.S. Government Printing Office, 1977; and Poulin, John, Levitt, John, Pappenfort, Donnell, and Young, Thomas. *Juveniles in Detention Centers and Jails.* Washington, D.C.: U.S. Government Printing Office, 1980.

7. For one such attempt, see U.S. General Accounting Office. *Residential Care: Patterns of Child Placement In Three States.* Report to the Honorable George Miller, Chairman, Select Committee on Children, Youth and Families, U.S. House of Representatives. Washington, D.C.: U.S. General Accounting Office, 1985.

8. Respondents were asked to indicate the percentage of the children and youth under care who presented severe emotional disturbance or behavior problems, moderate emotional disturbance or behavior problems, mild emotional disturbance or behavior problems, or no particular emotional disturbance or behavior problems. The estimates, therefore, rest on opinions, and the numbers thus generated should not be interpreted as necessarily resembling those that would be obtained through a national program of psychiatric evaluations.

9. The data also do not differentiate among the kinds of drugs used. We suspect—but cannot demonstrate—that youth engaged in serious abuse of the "harder" drugs are placed in the specialized facilities and that youth who are abusing "softer" drugs are placed throughout the entire spectrum of residential group care.

10. For other findings, see Young, Thomas M., Pappenfort, Donnell M., and Marlow, Christine R. *Residential Group Care, 1966 and 1981: Facilities for Children and Youth with Special Problems and Needs.* Chicago, Illinois: School of Social Service Administration, University of Chicago, November 1983.

2

Group Care in the Lives of Children in Long-Term Foster Care: The Casey Family Program Experience[a]

DAVID FANSHEL
STEPHEN J. FINCH
JOHN F. GRUNDY

THE CASEY FAMILY PROGRAM WAS ESTABLISHED in 1965 in Seattle, Washington, as a privately endowed social service agency. The aim of the program was to provide "quality planned long-term foster care for children and youth when this is the best permanent plan." The agency primarily offered foster family care and had been designed in consultation with the Child Welfare League of America with specific interest in children without family resources. As of 1988, the program has 15 divisions established in 13 western states.

In a series of research reports the authors have been examining the experiences in foster care of 585 children who had been served by The Casey Family Program from 1966 through 1984 in six divisions [Fanshel et al. 1987a; 1987b; 1988]. Only closed cases were studied, using the method of content analysis to extract data from case records describing the children. The data covered such phe-

[a]Preparation of this paper was made possible by a contract grant from The Casey Family Program, Seattle, Washington.

nomena as the living arrangements experienced by the children since birth, family and child factors making placement necessary, indexes describing the child as seen at various points while in care, and the personal and social functioning of a sample of such children in their adult years [Fanshel et al. 1987c]. We have thus had the opportunity to become engaged with information that is longitudinal in character, and this fact has made it possible to view the phenomenon of foster care from a life-course perspective.[1]

After three years of intensive involvement as researchers with The Casey Family Program, we have been most struck by (a) its relatively small scale, with the average division caring for 60 to 70 children at any one time—the Seattle Division being an exception, with over a hundred children; (b) its highly trained professional staff members who are quite stable in their jobs; (c) the relatively small caseloads; (d) the sharing of its substantial economic resources to purchase "extras" for children as needed, whether these be educational remediation, therapy, music lessons, or support through college; and (e) a strong sense of commitment to sustaining the children in its fold until they can be emancipated. The children are generally known to all staff members, and they come freely to the agency on all kinds of occasions; there is thus a sense of the agency itself becoming a stabilizing force in their lives. While the agency by design offers foster family care as a basic service, it goes beyond a conventional rendering of service through a special sense of mission to serve beleaguered children, demanding from itself a very energetic and high-quality response to the needs the children manifest.

This paper considers the role of group care in the lives of the foster children cared for by the agency. These children suffered considerable turbulence and instability before and during their out-of-home experience [Fanshel et al. 1987a]. We are interested in the mix of foster family home placements and the various times at which children were exposed to group care placements and how these facts related to their development. We also inquire about the characteristics of children who left foster family care and were then served in group care.

Foster Home Care and Group Care

Foster family care and institutional or group care can be thought of as an available repertoire of resources to be used for children requiring out-of-home care, each appropriate according to the phase of the child's placement history. Zietz [1969] has observed that the institution and foster home need not be seen as competitive services and describes the advantages of the former for certain kinds of children in terms that are consonant with the views of most other writers:

> The institutional community provides the child with opportunities to work through many problems and manifest various kinds of behavior that would not be permissible in most foster homes. Since these are children who have been damaged by emotional deprivation and rejection, they have need for warm but casual relationships with a variety of adults in whom they can find continuous acceptance. The hostile, lonely child may have need to punish the adults about him by being aggressive, destructive, or cruel. This kind of behavior can be more readily absorbed, evaluated, and treated by the institution's professional staff than by foster parents. The institution also offers the child the opportunity of working his problems through at his own pace and spares him the pain and responsibility of having to form substitute parental relationships for which he may have neither the need, the desire, nor the capacity. . . . The institution also offers the child a variety of activities that will help him to grow and to become mature and independent.

Stimulus for the Research

In analyzing close to six hundred cases, we were struck by the readiness of The Casey Family Program to place in foster boarding homes children who could not be sustained in such placements when in the care of other agencies and who had a repetition of such failures after coming to Casey. Given this readiness, the board of trustees of the program desired to strengthen its leadership function by obtaining information about the efficacy and costs of efforts to deal with interrupted foster home placements. Specifically, inquiry was made about the frequency with which group care was used, the circumstances surrounding the decision to use this type of care, and the results of such efforts. Was the child returned to foster family care after group care placement? Was the child subsequently sustained in care until becoming emancipated at the age of 18? What was the child's condition at the point of departure?

Summary of Findings

The Casey Family Program used group care placements at least once in 21.1 percent of the cases reviewed. These children were those who were likely to have been delinquent while in care, acting out sexually, or referred to a psychiatrist or psychologist because of staff concern about the child's adjustment. As the "more difficult of the difficult" [Kadushin 1967], these children who had a group care placement while in the Casey program were in a more distressed state at final exit from care than children who did not have a group care placement. There was a provocative set of associations suggesting that the use of Casey group placement might affect the pattern of outcomes.

We were able to examine associations between the children's experiences in group care placements with their subsequent adult experiences. The findings are based on a rather small number of cases and on wide and undocumented variations in the nature of the group care placements; the reader should be duly cautious. No associations were found between group care placements and such important measures as the child's subsequent job experiences as an adult, employment status, health status, drinking and drug abuse as an adult, and well-being as an adult.

Since other researchers (in particular Galdston [1979]) had previously found that boys had a different pattern of response to physical abuse than girls, we investigated whether boys and girls in the Casey program had the same patterns or not. Our results also showed this previously reported difference in patterns, and we indicate such a different pattern by specifically referring to boys.

Boys who had Casey group care placements and group care placements either before or after their Casey placements (i.e., two types of group care placements in their life experiences) had deficits in significant areas of their adult lives. Boys who had a Casey group care placement and who were discharged from Casey to another group care experience were less well-off financially and were extensively involved in criminal behavior other than armed crimes. Boys who had both a Casey group care placement and a group care placement before entry into the Casey program were not, as adults, as well educated as other Casey children and were more extensively involved in armed robbery.

Several findings suggest that the Casey program has an effective strategy for using group care placement in conjunction with foster home placement. An examination of the placement sequence of the children in the study revealed that a Casey group care placement was followed by an immediate termination of care in less than 10 percent of the group care placements. Once a child was in a Casey group care placement, roughly 25 percent of subsequent Casey placements were group care placements, and roughly 60 percent were foster home placements. That is, there was a "cooling off" of a majority of the children to the extent that one could place them in foster homes again. Part of the strategy appears to reflect perseverance on the part of the agency in keeping children in its fold even when there were rather extended sequences of interrupted foster placements. There are no major trends downward or upward in these rates as the number of Casey placements increases.

The Data Examined and Summary of Previous Findings

The 585 children in the study had first separated from both parents at a mean age of 6.8 years, and they had spent an average of 5.2 years, or 42 percent of their life spans, in out-of-home arrangements before entering the care of The Casey Family Program. Their average age at placement in the program was 12.8 years, and this was the seventh living arrangement, on average, to which they had been exposed. By the time they had left care, the children had experienced, on average, 10.2 separate living arrangements since birth. This turbulent beginning was found to be the start of a causal chain with increasingly serious consequences in the lives of children so affected [Fanshel et al. 1988].

The majority of the children (58 percent) were boys. Most (78 percent) were white, with 7 percent black, 4 percent Native American, 3 percent Hispanic, and 8 percent other. Sixty-four percent had previously been in a foster home, and many of those remaining had been in other forms of care, including 7 percent in small group homes, 17 percent in residential treatment centers, and 2 percent in institutions for delinquent children. The children had backgrounds characterized by marked instability, and many had suffered gross neglect and trauma at the hands of their families. Two-fifths were described in the records as having been exposed to previous physical abuse, and almost a fifth had experienced adverse sexual experiences, often in the form of direct molestation while living with their families. Many of the children no longer had viable families at the time they entered the care of The Casey Family Program. With respect to their mothers, 20 percent were deceased, 10 percent had had their parental rights terminated, 13 percent had surrendered their children, 15 percent had abandoned their children, 7 percent were mentally ill and hospitalized, about 20 percent were described as being alcoholic, and the whereabouts of 10 percent of the mothers were unknown. The backgrounds of the fathers were equally problematic. At the time they entered the agency's care, about a third of the children were behind their age-appropriate school grade levels. About 8 percent had a history of failed adoptions. A fourth of the children were actively showing antisocial behavior at the time of admission, and a somewhat larger group was showing marked behavioral difficulty in school. We have reported elsewhere that the more living arrangements the children had experienced before entering Casey care, the more oppositional behavior was manifested by them when studied at intake [Fanshel et al. 1987a].

We have placed under the rubric of group care the settings described in the records as "group homes," "institutions," "residential treatment institutions," "group shelters," and "correctional institutions" [Whittaker 1985]. The study first focused upon the group care experiences of the subjects while they were wards of The Casey Family Program, from admission to exit from care. When we observed that the group care experiences of these children also occurred in their pre-Casey histories and included in the study the possibility of group experience as a child's exit destination when departing from Casey care, we included in the investigation the pre-Casey group experiences and those that took place after discharge from the agency's care. We were thus able to look at the patterns of group care that had taken place over each subject's life course, ranging from no exposure to such forms of placement through having experienced group care on at least three occasions: pre-Casey, within Casey, and post-Casey. Our assumption is that policy and practice relative to the use of group care for children will be better informed if systematic information is available about the use of such living arrangements in the lives of children from birth to maturity.

Remarks on the Interpretation
of the Results Reported

There are many forces acting to shape the way a child adjusts over time, and each can contribute a piece of explained variance that is statistically significant at different stages in the child's life. This study has sought to determine the saliency of these forces in terms of predictor variables such as a child's history of being abused, age at first separation from parents, number of placements experienced, and so forth. We can use such predictors to try to understand how children adjust while in care, their mode of departure from care, their condition at the point of departure, and how their lives are being played out as adults. Some predictors overlap with each other in their ability to account for what happens to children, and some contribute uniquely to the explained variation. Much is left unexplained because human beings defy classification and insist upon following idiosyncratic paths. Despite advances in the behavioral and social sciences, our measurement procedures are far from perfect and set bounds upon what can be predicted. Group care experiences of children when treated as predictor variables thus compete with other predictors in a situation in which the collective contribution of all variables to the explained variance is modest, say 10 to 50 percent. Given these conditions, it is remarkable that some significant explained variance is accounted for by the group experiences of the children studied.

In the course of grappling with the data and the statistical analyses, our experience has been that the p-value reported with each statistical measure has been invaluable in weaving the findings into a more understandable picture. At the risk of burdening the practitioner with a research detail, we have reported the p-value of each of our findings. Our experience has been that an association significant at the .0001 level is usually undeniable empirically and obvious to us when we read the data file to verify the finding. These associations show up consistently when we run further analyses with more variables or on subsets of children. An association significant at the .01 level is almost always a stable finding. Occasionally, however, the finding does not appear consistently in further statistical analyses because it is obscured by the many other relations simultaneously influencing the association. When we report a finding significant at the .05 level, the finding is suggestive and worth noting, but it is wise to view such findings with the proverbial grain of salt; subsequent analyses with more variables or with a restricted set of cases may not confirm the association's significance, suggesting that a more complex explanation may be required.

The practitioner, policy maker, and child welfare advocate, caught up in powerful substantive issues in a dynamic field where controversy abounds, might easily lose patience with what seems to be elaborate "researchy" explanations. It is often said by those most strongly involved in the issues discussed here, "Don't bother to give me all that analytic stuff; just give me your findings. I'll take your word that you did your research piece correctly." This approach is short-sighted and incorrect because much of the question of support or withdrawal of support for social programs such as group care services rests upon an uncertain evidentiary base, in which small pieces of explained variance become the essence of the story. The complexity and fragility of the evidentiary base is no less a challenge to the researcher than that faced by the practitioner attempting to explain why Johnnie, who has had 15 placements before coming into his current service program, is at extreme risk of not being helped to become stabilized. We hope that the reader interprets our findings using the reported significance level as our means of emphasizing the clarity of some of our findings.

The Decision to Place a Child in Group Care

The data showed that 78.9 percent of the 585 subjects in the study were placed only in foster home settings while wards of The Casey Family Program; they were never placed in group care while in the agency's charge.

What factors were associated with a decision to place a Casey foster child in a group care program? There were four significant associations that together predicted 21.3 percent of the variance. Children who were delinquent while in the Casey program's care were the most likely to have a Casey group care placement ($p<.0001$). Beyond this finding, a child who was sexually acting out was more likely to have a Casey group care placement ($p<.0001$). A child who caused sufficient concern to require a psychiatric or psychological evaluation was more likely to have a Casey group care placement ($p<.01$). Children whose emotional state was characterized by moodiness or depression were more apt to have a Casey group placement ($p<.05$). The variables that were predictive of whether the child was placed in group care are those that were essentially descriptive of the child's conduct while ·in the Casey program care and associated emotional states, measured by multi-item indexes in each domain cited, and are indicative of an unquestionably "appropriate" group care placement [Janchill 1983].

Overall Effect of the Institutional Placement on the Child's Life

The two most important measures of the child's situation at exit from the Casey program are (1) the nature of the child's emancipation from the Casey program (whether the program maintained its care of the child until the child reached adulthood, whether the child was reunited with his or her family, or whether the child had to be returned to the state child care system because the Casey program was unsuccessful in its original desire to maintain the child in foster family care); and (2) the child's condition at exit from the Casey program. We seek to understand whether there is an association between the child's receiving institutional care and the child's condition on leaving the program.

Emancipation Status

A child who had a Casey group care placement was more likely to be returned to court or to be a runaway and less likely to be emancipated from care or to be returned to the biological family than a child who did not ($p<.01$). When we excluded the 118 children who were returned to their families from the total sample, we found the expected result: that a child who had a Casey group care placement was less likely to be emancipated and more likely to run away or be remanded to the court ($p<.05$).

Condition of Subjects upon Departure from Casey Care

A meausre of the condition of the children at the time they left the care of The Casey Family Program was created by combining two ratings: (a) a seven-point scale measuring the overall adjustment of the child at the time of departure, and (b) a seven-point scale characterizing the circumstances surrounding the exit from care, going from an orderly aging out to leaving in a state of acute crisis. The inter-rater reliability based upon two independent readings of 53 case records was .58.

Our earlier research reports on the factors associated with the condition of the child at exit from the Casey program [Fanshel et al. 1988]. We revised this analysis so that we could determine the associations with whether a child had a Casey group care placement. There were 11 noteworthy associations that together explained 44.4 percent of the variation in the child's condition at exit from the Casey program, compared to the inter-rater reliability of 58 percent, showing that our regression analysis has explained close to the upper bound of what can be explained, given the imprecision of this measure.

The first model of the condition of the child at exit had seven associations, as follows, in order of their apparent statistical significance.

1. A child who adapted better to Casey foster care was in better condition at exit.

2. A child who, at the time of the intake study, was seen as more hostile and negativistic at entry into the Casey program was in worse shape at exit.

3. A child who engaged in destructive juvenile delinquent behavior while in the Casey program was in worse condition at exit.

4. A child who was in conflict with his parents before entry into the Casey program was in worse shape at exit (each of 1 through 4 was significant at $p<.0001$).

5. A child who was acting out sexually while in Casey care was in worse condition at exit ($p<.01$).

6. A child who was physically abused before his entry into the Casey program was in worse condition at exit ($p<.05$).

7. A child who was more depressed while in Casey care was in slightly better condition at exit ($p<.05$).[2]

Upon including the variables describing whether a child had a Casey group care placement, we found an additional statistically significant association: that a child who had had more living arrangements before his first separation from both biological parents tended to be in worse condition at exit ($p<.05$).

The inclusion of these variables produced a much more complicated and different pattern of associations for children who had a Casey group care placement. For these children, there was no association between whether a child adjusted well to Casey foster care and the condition of the child at exit from the Casey program (the statistical significance of the difference in patterns is .0001). For children with Casey group care placements, there was no association between the extent to which a child was acting out sexually while in Casey care and the child's subsequent condition at exit ($p<.05$). This finding was in sharp contrast to the pattern for children who had had no Casey group care placements. All other associations held.

The finding is difficult to understand. If we focus only upon the children who were having a troubled experience while in Casey foster home placements, that is, the "more difficult of the difficult," there was no association between the measure of the child's adaptation to foster care and his condition at exit, nor was there an association between the extent of the child's acting out sexually and subsequent condition at exit. The net result of these relations was not strong enough to affect the outcome of the comparison of these children at exit. Based on the experience of children who had never had a Casey group care placement, we would have expected that a child who had a Casey group care placement and who was better adapted to foster care would be in better condition at exit than a child with a Casey group care placement and poor adaptation to foster care. This situation was not so.

We can think of several explanations for this pattern of associations. The first is that this finding reflects measurement difficulties with the variables characterizing the adjustment of the children to Casey foster care and characterizing sexually acting-out behavior. These variables were not perfectly measured in our study, as shown by the intraclass correlation of .63 for adaptation and .57 for sexually acting out, both measuring the agreement between pairs of case readers. A child who had a Casey group care placement was, ipso facto, poorly adjusted. The finding above then might simply be that the Casey group care placement variable is a surrogate variable for adaptation to foster care and sexually acting out for children with Casey group care placement. In other words, the same mechanism holds for both groups of children, with the Casey group care placement variable operating as a more accurate reflection of adjustment than the raters' evaluations for children in Casey group care placements. The implication of this explanation is that the association is an artifact of imperfect measurement and is of no substantive importance.

The second explanation is that this finding was caused by the regression effect. Under this explanation, only the children with the most extreme problems were placed. The regression effect explanation argues that these children then regress toward the mean so that there would be much less of an association present. In addition to the regression effect, there is also a lowering of the correlation because of the restriction of the range due to selection of the most extreme cases for a Casey group care placement.

The first two explanations are not mutually exclusive and may well be operating jointly to produce the pattern observed. Our prevailing optimism led us to consider a third explanation. If, in fact, the group care placement had the effect of "cooling out" the child and helping the child to overcome the problems that led to the placement, then the placement would have the effect of reducing or destroying the association between the child's adjustment and subsequent condition at exit.

Associations with Any Group Care

As indicated earlier, many of the children in the Casey program had had institutional or other forms of group care before entry into the Casey program, and a few had group care after exit from the Casey program. The next set of analyses summarized data considering these additional experiences with group care.

Each child was classified as to whether the child had experienced a group care placement before the first Casey placement (noted as PRE = + if yes, and 0 if no), whether the child had experienced any group care placement while in the Casey program (noted as WITHIN = + if yes, and 0 if no); and whether the child had been discharged to an institution or other group care facility from the Casey program (noted as POST = + if yes, and 0 if no). Table 1 presents the averages for each of the eight possible combinations of status on these three variables for some key measures.

Examination of Table 1 shows that the means generally decline as one goes down the table. That is, those children who had no group care placements are in the best shape with respect to any of the measures presented, and those children with group care placements before, during, and after their Casey placement are in the poorest condition. Children who had a group care placement before their entry into the Casey program were very much like children who did not have a pre-Casey group care placement but who were otherwise similar (that is, each pair of groupings above were rather like each other). There were greater differences for children who had a Casey group care placement. By far the greatest differences occurred for children who were discharged from the Casey program to a group care placement.

Multiple regression analysis was used to study objectively these associations between the pattern of group care that the child had experienced and the child's condition at exit from the Casey program. The first analysis used the child's condition at exit as the dependent variable; the independent variables were the variables indicating the child's experiences with group care and the child's sex. In the discussion of the results, we compare children with experiences of group care to the set of all children in the study who had no such group care placements.

In general, children with group care experience had deficits when compared to the group of children without group care place-

TABLE 1

Mean Subject Index Scores on Intake, Under Care,
and Exit Measures by Patterns of Group Care
Experiences over Life Course

Patterns of Group Care[a]	Intake				Under Care				Exit	
	Hostile-Negative Person		History of Juvenile Delinquency		Adaptation to Care		Acting Out/Juvenile Delinquency		Condition and Adjustment at Exit	
	Mean	SD	Mean	SD	Mean	SD	Mean	SD	Mean	SD
No PRE, No WITHIN, No POST	6.32	0.93	6.58	0.89	4.21	1.24	6.40	0.73	4.97	1.59
(n)	(165)		(165)		(167)		(167)		(165)	
PRE, No WITHIN, No POST	5.68	1.26	5.92	1.33	4.02	1.24	6.16	0.91	4.84	1.60
(n)	(195)		(195)		(195)		(195)		(191)	
No PRE, WITHIN, No POST	6.07	0.96	6.42	1.11	3.47	1.25	5.60	1.12	4.17	1.60
(n)	(26)		(26)		(26)		(26)		(26)	

	Mean	SD	Mean	SD	Mean	SD	Mean	SD	Mean	SD
PRE, WITHIN, No POST (n)	5.61 (36)	1.21	5.86 (36)	1.44	3.24 (36)	1.25	5.11 (36)	1.18	3.76 (36)	1.58
No PRE, No WITHIN, POST (n)	5.49 (39)	1.48	6.33 (39)	0.99	3.19 (39)	1.30	5.54 (39)	1.08	3.28 (39)	2.01
PRE, No WITHIN, POST (n)	5.39 (71)	1.49	5.46 (71)	1.55	2.88 (72)	1.37	5.77 (72)	1.08	2.53 (72)	1.51
No PRE, WITHIN, POST (n)	5.07 (18)	1.65	5.53 (18)	1.27	2.67 (18)	1.12	4.76 (18)	1.36	2.30 (18)	1.09
PRE, WITHIN, POST (n)	4.58 (23)	1.24	5.76 (23)	1.33	2.88 (23)	0.92	4.93 (23)	1.30	2.43 (23)	1.38
Total Mean SD (n)	5.77 (573)	1.29	6.08 (573)	1.28	3.72 (576)	1.35	5.95 (576)	1.08	4.20 (570)	1.87
F Ratio	10.4395		8.3217		15.1730		19.6763		31.0203	
F Probability	.000		.000		.000		.000		.000	

[a] PRE: Group or institutional care prior to placement in The Casey Family Program
WITHIN: Group or institutional care while client of The Casey Family Program
POST: Group or institutional care upon exit from The Casey Family Program

ments. Consequently, we have chosen to describe our findings as a sequence of decreases (that is, adverse effects). When a child is a member of two groups, the decreases for each group are to be added. Any group not mentioned in a set of comparisons below is, on average, like the group of children without any group care experiences; that is, children with group care placement experiences not discussed below had essentially the same average as children with no group care placements.

For example, this regression model explained 29 percent of the variation of the child's condition at exit, compared to our earlier model that explained 44 percent. The children who were in the best condition at exit on average were those who had no group care experiences. Children who left the Casey program to go into a group care placement had on average a very much worse condition at exit ($p<.0001$). Children who were in group care while they were in the Casey program had a much lower decrease in condition at exit but still substantial decrease in their average ($p<.0001$). Children who had both types of group care experience had both decreases and were in the worst shape. There was an indication that boys who had had group care before they entered the Casey program and who left the Casey program to go into group care also had a worse average condition at exit ($p<.05$).

The interpretation of these results must include the implicit negative findings (that is, no statistically significant difference for periods not mentioned) in our general discussion above. For example, since we did not find any association with group care placement before entry into the Casey program, children with only group care placements before entry into the Casey program on average had the same condition at exit as children with no group care experience. This fact is an important negative finding with respect to group care placement of young children.

Usually, the dependent variable in a regression analysis describes the subject at a time after the time of the independent variables, so that an observed association has the possibility of a causal interpretation. We reversed this convention in the following analyses, offer these findings as descriptive, and warn the reader not to attach a causal interpretation. For example, consider a boy who has turned out to have a decidedly bad outcome when studied as an adult: he has been involved in serious crime and is strongly addicted to drugs. Having life-course data, we can seek to understand what went on in the child's past as prelude to the disasters in his life. We can look at the role of preplacement events in the child's life at three points in time: his characteristics at intake, his experiences in care, and his condition upon leaving care. In studying the role of group care experiences of some of the subjects in comparison with children not exposed to such care, we use regression analysis to look back at the precursors of the group care experience. The reader should not be misled into thinking that we are reversing causal direction, since it would be absurd to assume that criminality in adult life caused display of oppositional behavior at the time of entry into care.

There were some small associations between the sequence of the child's experiences in group care placements and the child's experiences before entry into the Casey program. For example, with regard to the extent of hostile and negativistic personality identified at the time of the preadmission study of the child, our model using group care experience explained 11.8 percent of the variation. Children who had no group care experience were the least hostile and negativistic, on average. There was a very large decrease in the average for children who had a group care placement before entry into the Casey program ($p<.001$) and a very high decrease for children who left the Casey program for a group care placement ($p<.0001$). Children who had group care experiences during their Casey placement and who left Casey for a group care placement also had a high decrease ($p<.01$).[3]

Altogether, this model explained 9.6 percent of the variation in the extent of history of juvenile delinquency in children before their first Casey program ($p<.0001$). Children who had no history of group care experience had the least previous history of juvenile delinquency. Children who had a group care placement before their first Casey placement had a more extensive history of juvenile delinquency ($p<.0001$). Boys who were placed in a group care setting before Casey and who left Casey to go to a group care setting had still more extensive history of juvenile delinquent behavior before Casey ($p<.0001$). This relation may well reflect the fact that these boys also included a greater proportion who were physically abused ($p<.01$). Children who had a group care placement before Casey and who left Casey for a group care placement had a greater degree of mental illness before entry into the Casey program, as well.

The history-of-group-care-placements model used here explained 15.4 percent of the variation of the child's adaptation to
foster care score. Children who had no group care placements had
the best scores on average on the Index of Adaptation to Foster
Care. A child who left the Casey program to go into a group care
placement had a very large decrease in the average adaptation score
($p<.0001$). A child who was placed in group care while in the Casey
program had a large but lower decrease on average ($p<.0001$). A
child who was placed in group care before, during, and after Casey
had a relatively small increase ($p<.01$). Children who were placed
in group care programs before their entry into the Casey program
but not during their Casey placement or afterward adapted to foster
care as well as children who had had no group care experience.

In general, the history of group care placement explained 23.1
percent of the variation in the extent of delinquent behavior while
in the care of The Casey Family Program ($p<.0001$). Children who
had no history of group care placement had the least extent of
delinquent behavior, on average. A child who had a group care
placement while in the Casey program had a much greater extent
of acting-out delinquent behavior ($p<.0001$). A child who was discharged from the Casey program to a group care placement also
had a greater degree of delinquent behavior ($p<.0001$). There was
an indication that a child who had had a group care placement
before entry into the Casey program also had an associated decrease in the index score, indicating a greater extent of delinquent
behavior ($p<.05$). The implication then is that group care placements were a continuing response to such behaviors. As expected,
boys had on average more extensive delinquent behavior than otherwise similar girls ($p<.01$).

A similar set of associations held for destructive juvenile delinquent behavior while in the care of The Casey Family Program.
The percentage of variation explained was 17.2 percent, with the
greatest destructive behavior for children who had a group care
placement while in the program ($p<.0001$), slightly less for children
who were discharged from the Casey program into a group care
placement ($p<.0001$), and an indication of more destructiveness
for children who were placed in group care before admission to
the Casey program ($p<.05$). Boys also had more extensive destructive juvenile delinquent behavior on average than did otherwise
similar girls ($p<.0001$).

The placement of a child in group care while in the Casey program was associated with a greater extent of drug involvement while in the care of The Casey Family Program ($p<.0001$). No other group placement pattern was associated with drug involvement. A child who was placed in group care while in the Casey program had a greater extent of psychopathic lying ($p<.0001$), and a child who was discharged from the Casey program into a group care placement also had a greater extent of lying ($p<.0001$).

A child who had a group care placement while in the Casey program tended to be expelled from school for juvenile delinquent behavior ($p<.05$), to do more poorly in school ($p<.0001$), to be seen more often by a psychologist or psychiatrist because concern had arisen about his problems ($p<.0001$), and to show acting-out behavior ($p<.0001$).

Follow-Up Measures by Pattern of Placement

A follow-up study of 107 subjects who had been in foster home placement with The Casey Family Program in the Western Washington (Seattle) and Yakima Divisions provided an opportunity to extend the study's life-course analysis into the adult years of the former agency wards. On average, they were seen seven years after leaving the program's care. We analyzed the experiences of these former foster children by the pattern of their placements in group care programs. There were very small numbers involved, and so the results have to be interpreted cautiously. For example, only 30 of the follow-up subjects had no institutional placements ($0-0-0$), ten had institutional care while in the Casey program and were not discharged to an institutional placement ($0- + -0$ and $+ - + -0$), 48 had an institutional placement before they entered the Casey program and no subsequent institutional placements ($+ -0-0$), 11 had no institutional placement while in the Casey program but experienced subsequent discharge to an institutional placement ($0-0- +$ and $+ -0- +$), and six children had institutional placements in all three phases ($+ - + - +$). Since these variables describe the children after they became adults, we are using regression analysis in a conventional manner, and our earlier cautions do not hold for the following results.

We have previously reported the results of the follow-up study that focused upon various domains of the subjects' lives using multiple item indexes. Most of these indexes showed strong internal reliability [Fanshel et al. 1987c].

There were no associations between group care placement experiences significant at the .05 level or lower for the subsequent job experience as an adult, extent of relating to other adults, employment status, health as an adult, well-being as an adult, extent of friends as an adult, drinking as an adult, substance abuse as an adult, recalled attachment to Casey foster parents, treatment in the Casey foster home recalled in adulthood, and the degree to which the social worker was recalled to have shown a personal interest in the child.

There was one minor cloud on the results, suggesting that children in group care placements were less well-off on one minor financially related aspect: a child who was placed in group care while in the Casey program subsequently as an adult had poorer housing ($p<.001$). These former foster children, however, recalled their Casey social workers as relating better to them ($p<.001$).

Group care placement before the Casey program along with a group care placement while in the Casey program was associated with subsequent mental disturbance as an adult ($p<.0001$). That is, the subjects were more likely to have reported having a nervous breakdown, having been a patient in a mental facility, or having seen a psychiatrist for emotional problems.

There were a few associations for boys who had group care placements at two or more stages in their lives. Boys who were placed in group care while in the Casey program and who were discharged from Casey into a group care placement tended to be less well-off financially ($p<.05$) and were more involved in criminal behavior ($p<.01$), but not in serious crime such as armed robbery ($p<.001$). Boys who were placed in group care before Casey and who were discharged from Casey into group care had a greater degree of family building ($p<.01$), had a less extensive amount of education as an adult ($p<.01$), and were more involved in serious crime ($p<.0001$). These boys also felt that their social worker related less well to them ($p<.01$).

Description of the Casey Strategy of Using Institutional Placements

The present national and bipartisan philosophy of child care seems to be that children should be cared for by their biological families, that failing that option they should be in foster boarding home care with reunification as the placement goal, that adoption or some long-term stable placement is the next most desirable outcome, and that institutional placement is a "last resort" and essentially a failure of the system. The rationale is that the biological family is best and that, in the absence of this possibility, the biological family should be approximated as closely as possible. It is no doubt coincidental that the care of children by their own families usually requires little if any governmental expenditure, foster boarding home care moderate governmental expenditure, and institutional placement the greatest expenditure.

Some notable patterns emerged from an analysis of the experience of children by the number of placements in the Casey program. Figure 1 shows the percentage of children who were remanded back to court or who ran away from the Casey program by the number of Casey program placements that the child experienced. It indicates that the termination rate was relatively low, roughly 10 percent, at any given placement. The program was as likely to continue with a child if he or she had had eight previous placements or only one. Furthermore, the program was almost as likely to place a child in a foster home after eight or so previous placements as after one. This is a remarkable finding and suggests a reevaluation of the sometimes held practice assumption that a child who has failed one foster home placement should ipso facto be regarded as unsuitable for foster home placement.

The utilization of group care placement was rather high. Figure 2 plots the rate of group care placement by the number of previous Casey placements. Roughly 40 percent of subsequent placements were group care regardless of the number of previous Casey placements.

The program did not use group care placement as a means of easing a child out of the program. Figure 3 illustrates the termination rate and the retention rate of children who were placed in group care in the sequence of Casey placements. Roughly 10 per-

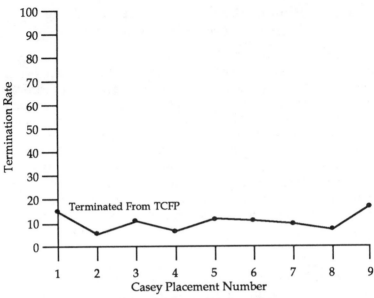

*Figure 1. Termination rate of children,
by number of Casey placements completed.*

cent of the children who were placed in group care were terminated from the group care placement, and there was little if any trend in the rate with the number of placements. Roughly 80 percent of the children in group care placement were kept in the Casey program for at least one more Casey placement, and this percentage too showed little if any trend over the number of placements. The remaining 10 percent of the children, not terminated or re-placed to another setting, who were in group care placements were emancipated or reunited with their families from the Casey group care placement.

Figure 4 shows the rate of placing a child in foster family homes subsequent to a group care placement and the rate of placing a child in a second group care placement after a group care placement. Roughly 60 percent of the children who were in a group care placement were subsequently placed in foster family care. There appeared to be a slight trend downward. Roughly 25 percent of the children in a group care placement were subsequently re-placed

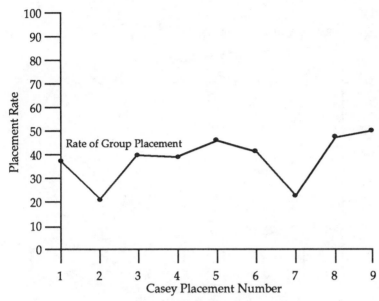

Figure 2. Rate of group care placement,
by number of Casey placements completed.

in another group care arrangement. There appeared to be a trend upward for this percentage in Figure 4.

Discussion and Conclusions

The suggestion of the regression analyses, these tables, and the cross-tabulations of institutional placements, mode of exit, and condition at exit is that children who were placed in group care were in worse condition when they were placed than children who were not, and that as adults these children were subsequently not quite as well-off in certain limited areas. In general, however, the larger picture is that these children as adults were essentially as well-adjusted and capable as the children who did not have a group care placement. In the course of time, these children appear to have made up most of the deficit in their backgrounds at the time of their Casey group care placement.

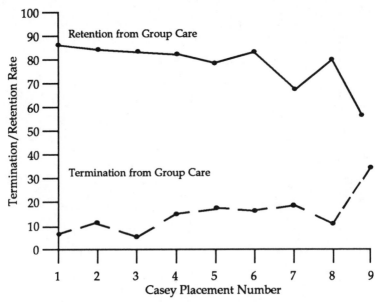

*Figure 3. Retention and termination rates
from group care.*

The Casey program was relatively successful at using an in-stitutional placement to help a child adapt to foster care and to prepare for a subsequent foster home placement in the sense that a high percentage of these children had one or more subsequent foster home placements. We have no direct information about the specific strategies that are used to accomplish these tasks. Further analyses that can contribute to practice knowledge are to consider the condition of the child with respect to behavioral tendencies before and after placement in an institutional setting, to see whether on average the placement serves to improve the child's reported adaptation, and particularly whether conduct problems are re-duced.

The approach we have emphasized here resonates well with the recommendations of the California Association of Services for Children following a recent study of ten thousand children in care:

That data be collected and presented that more ac-curately reflect the changing nature and characteristics of the children in care;

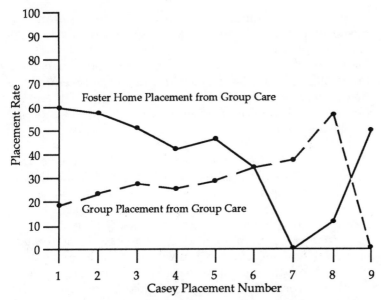

*Figure 4. Rate of placement from group care
by number of Casey placements completed.*

That such a study research new issues, such as why
children "blow out" of their placements, or why children
with similar presenting problems have varying disposi-
tions in our current service system;

That research be conducted to determine which intervention methods work—or work reasonably well—with
which types of children. [Fitzharris 1985]

Policy Implications

A scrutiny of national data suggests that more than a quarter
of the children in foster care in the United States have had such
unstable life histories that the assumptions underlying permanency
planning, as envisioned in The Adoption Assistance and Child
Welfare Act of 1980 (Public Law 96-272), are not particularly applicable. Allen and Knitzer [1983] observe that the intent of this
landmark legislation is strictly permanency oriented:

P.L. 96-272 redirects federal fiscal incentives toward the development of preventive and reunification services and adoption subsidies. It requires that any increased funds for the Title IV program (over the 56.5 million appropriated in Fiscal Year 1979) be targeted for the development of these alternative services. It prohibits the use of these funds for such services as foster care board payments or employment-related day care.

If attention is focused upon teen-aged children in foster care who have spent a good part of their lives away from their biological families, reunification or adoption by others becomes a quite remote expectation. Although the prevention of such a turbulent life experience for a child is and should be the first priority, we must have a contingency plan for the children who have fallen through our putative safety nets and have subsequently had turbulent life experiences. We estimate that between 25 percent and 30 percent of the children currently in foster care in the United States have been in three or more placements.[4] For the teen-aged group, such as the children served by The Casey Family Program, the average number of living arrangements experienced is much higher. Thus, for the Casey children, the mean number of living arrangements before entering care was seven, and reached ten by the time they left care.

If children have experienced particularly unstable life histories with many moves back and forth within their biological families and have also run the course of multiple placements with diverse agencies, it is not realistic that permanence and reunification be the primary goals for them. Rather, the prevention of full-blown deviant careers in the form of mental illness, criminality, teen-aged pregnancy, drug and alcohol abuse, suicide, and an adult life of economic dependency ought to constitute the main agenda items of the service system for these children. A panoply of services may be required to prevent the emergence of a socially crippled adult, and among these, group care facilities are unquestionably extremely important.

In the general population of children in foster care, some 300,000 in the United States at any one time, institutional care has been a declining mode of care.[5] In terms of the number of children involved, institutional placements do not begin to approach foster families as a resource for children needing care. When one considers the subset of foster children who are older and have had unstable life histories, such as those served by The Casey Family Program, however, institutional placement looms large as a needed mode of care at some time in the child's history as a recipient of out-of-home care.

Since institutional care and other forms of group care are relatively expensive compared to foster family care, it has become increasingly difficult for communities to maintain such facilities. One long-term, strategically placed observer of the child welfare scene has characterized the residential treatment institution as an "endangered species."[6] There is need for a national policy that provides a second funding stream to ensure maintenance of group care facilities by recognizing the resource needs of the foster children described in this paper.

Our review of the Casey experience shows that group care placement, when used carefully and when directed to the child's individual needs, is generally positive in its implications for these children.

Notes

1. The study population consists of closed cases of children who had been in the agency's care through 1984; the first child had entered care in 1966. Their case records were subjected to a content analysis, using a 72-page case reading schedule filled out by case readers who were seasoned clinical social workers. Previous work has described the preplacement living experiences of the subjects, their characteristics at the time of the intake study, their experiences in foster home care within the agency, their manner of exit from care, and the adjustment of a sample of these subjects as adults when seen in follow-up interviews [Fanshel et al. 1987a, 1987b, 1988; also Fanshel et al. 1987c].

2. This somewhat counterintuitive finding suggests that the depressed child is viewed with less concern, since aggression tends to be internalized rather than manifested through outwardly directed conduct problems.

3. A high score on the Index of Hostile-Negativistic Personality would indicate a low level of oppositional behavior displayed by the child at intake. A decrease in the index score associated with a group care experience signifies the child having been more oppositional in behavior at the time of entry into care.

4. A report prepared by Maximus for the Administration for Children, Youth and Families, Office of Human Development Services, U.S. Department of Health and Human Services, *Comparative Statistical Analysis of 1984 State Child Welfare Data* (dated June 6, 1986) showed that, for 22 reporting states, 21.4 percent of the children in substitute care had experienced three to five placements and 7.2 percent had

experienced six or more placements [Maximus, Inc., 6723 Whittier Avenue, McLean, Virginia 22101]. Also, a recent study of ten thousand children in care in California showed that, for the social service system, 23.8 percent of the children had three to five prior placements and 8.6 percent had six or more prior placements [Fitzharris 1985: 65].

    5. Geiser points out that, in 1910, of the 176,000 children in foster care, 65 percent were in institutions for the neglected and dependent and the emotionally disturbed child. By 1965, with 287,000 children in care, only 28 percent were in child welfare institutions [Geiser, R.L. *The Illusion of Caring: Children in Foster Care.* Boston, Massachusetts: Beacon Press, 1973, p. 167]. In a national study, Shyne and Shroeder estimated that, in the year 1977, 21 percent of some 500,000 children in foster care in the United States were in residential institutions [Shyne, A.W., and Schroeder, A.G. *National Study of Social Services To Children and Their Families, Overview.* DHEW Publication No. (OHDS) 78-30150. Washington, D.C.: U.S. Department of Health, Education, and Welfare, 1978].

    6. Comment to one of the writers by Dr. Charles P. Gershenson, whose research leadership in the United States Children's Bureau spanned some 25 years: In his view, support for residential treatment institutions is being withdrawn nationally by funding sources because of the steep climb in costs and because the outcomes of treatment efforts have not sufficiently documented the gains for children exposed to such care.

References

Allen, M., and Knitzer, J. Child Welfare: Examining the Policy Framework. In B.G. McGowan and W. Meezan (eds.) *Child Welfare: Current Dilemmas, Future Directions.* Itasca, Illinois: E.F. Peacock, 1983, p. 120.

Fanshel, D., Finch, S.J., and Grundy, J.F. *Serving Children with Unstable Life Histories in Foster Family Care.* Submitted for publication (1987a).

Fanshel, D., Finch, S.J., and Grundy, J.F. *The Experience of Children in Care with Unstable Life Histories.* Submitted for publication (1987b).

Fanshel, D., Finch, S.J., and Grundy, J.F. *The Modes of Exit and Condition Upon Departure from Foster Care of Children with Unstable Life Histories.* Submitted for publication (1988).

Fanshel, D., Alvelo, J., Grundy, J.F. and Finch, S.J. *How They Fared After Foster Care: A Follow-Up Study of Former Wards of The Casey Family Program.* Draft paper (1987c).

Fitzharris, T.L. *The Foster Children of California: Profiles of 10,000 Children in Residential Care.* Sacramento, California: Children's Services Foundation, 1985, pp. xi, xii.

Galdston, R. Disorders of Early Parenthood: Neglect, Deprivation, and Abuse of Little Children. In J.D. Noshpitz (ed.), *Basic Handbook of Child Psychiatry, Volume Two, Disturbances in Development.* New York: Basic Books, 1979, p. 588.

Janchill, Sister Mary Paul. Services for Special Populations of Children. In B.G. McGowan and W. Meezan (eds.), *Child Welfare: Current Dilemmas, Future Directions.* Itasca, Illinois: F.E. Peacock, 1983, pp. 345–375.

Kadushin, A. *Child Welfare Services*. New York: Macmillan, 1967, p. 549.

Whittaker, J.K. Group and Institutional Care: An Overview. In J. Laird and A. Hartman (eds.), *A Handbook of Child Welfare*. New York: The Free Press, 1985, pp. 617–620.

Zietz, D. *Child Welfare: Services and Perspectives*. New York: John Wiley & Sons, Second Edition, 1969, pp. 71–72.

3

Characteristics of Adolescents and Their Families in Residential Treatment Intake: An Exploratory Study

JAMES K. WHITTAKER
DAVID FINE
ANTHONY GRASSO

T HIS EXPLORATORY STUDY OF CHARACTERISTICS of adolescents and families entering residential treatment represents one agency (Boysville of Michigan) in its effort to develop a research capacity in the service of improved practice. As such, it should be viewed in the context of other ongoing research efforts at the agency. For purposes of comparison, the authors received permission to report some additional intake data from a much larger ongoing research effort by the California Association of Services for Children [Fitzharris 1985]. This data collection project provides a unique window on children, adolescents, and families entering the group care stream. A requisite for an effective, humane, and flexible group care sector is the kind of data-based management information system that made both this research effort and the California study possible. Fanshel [1982] and others support the proposition that systematic analysis of routinely gathered data is a necessary condition for the continued improvement of substitute care services.

Focus of the Present Study

This exploratory study examines intake data for all male adolescents who entered Boysville in the calendar year 1985 (n = 332). The study sought to examine characteristics of individual adolescents, their families, their service histories, and community environments to see what implications these held for developing therapeutic interventions. Subsequent analyses will explore, at a later time, the relationship of these variables to the actual processes of treatment and care within the residential setting and, ultimately, to postdischarge community outcomes.[a]

The Agency Setting and Management Information System

Boysville of Michigan is the state's largest private residential agency for troubled adolescents. Since its founding in 1948 with 15 boys, the agency has grown to where it now serves 270 boys and girls in treatment centers located at its main campus in Clinton; at a smaller campus in Saginaw; and in its group homes in Detroit, Mt. Clemens, Ecorse, Saginaw, Alpena, and Redford. The Boysville treatment program is based on a modified version of Positive Peer Culture in which the natural influences of the adolescent peer group are enlisted to bring about changes in behavior and attitude. Over the last few years, Boysville has also implemented an intensive family therapy program for all Michigan adolescents in care; specialized family foster care for up to 40 adolescents unable to return to their biological families; emergency placements and diagnostic service for 15 male adolescents in Detroit; shelter care for up to 45 children aged two to 14 in Toledo; day care and latchkey programs for up to 67 children in Toledo; and advocacy for children and families on the local, state, and national level.

[a]The authors wish to acknowledge the helpful suggestions of Brother Francis Boylan, Brother James Caley, Edward Overstreet, and the following individuals, who, with the senior author, comprise Boysville's National Research Advisory Committee: Chair Irwin Epstein, Hamilton McCubbin, Tony Tripodi, Donnell M. Pappenfort, Shirley Vining-Brown, and Dee M. Kilpatrick.

The design of the Management Information and Evaluation System at Boysville of Michigan (BOMIS) is based on the assumption that simultaneous improvement in the service technology of the organization and the accountability system will result in actual as well as measured improvement in performance. Consistent with this assumption, heavy emphasis is placed in BOMIS on providing useful information to direct-service professionals to improve their helping skills. The common value in this information system, which involves all levels of the organization, is helping Boysville's clients. With the line staff, emphasis is placed on participation in the management information system to improve skills and thereby provide more effective services to clients. Furthermore, it is believed that an information system that improves the delivery of services to clients can also provide data for assessing program effectiveness in ways required by other levels of the organization.

This system employs staff rating instruments and family client coping instruments, including several standardized measures developed by McCubbin and Thompson [1987].[b] Staff members administer these measures in a time series to clients and receive, in return, easily understandable graphic printouts on dimensions related to family and client change. The agency also gathers information on staff activity and, through the supervisory process, trains staff members on the use of interventions directly intended to effect change on these dimensions in client and family dynamics. Supervisors in this process use related information to improve the implementation of the groupwork and family systems technologies that are used at Boysville. Consequently, the program staff members routinely receive information concerning client problems and client change, middle-level managers routinely receive information from the system on staff performance, and the executive staff routinely receives information that can then be used for accountability and for influencing public policy and procuring additional funds. Staff members at all levels in the organization actively participate in the gathering and use of information because they regard it as making a valuable contribution to their efforts to serve the agency's client population more effectively.

[b]For purposes of this study, analysis was limited to data gathered through conventional intake procedures. Forthcoming analyses will examine data obtained from the youth/family coping scales.

The Research Context for the Present Study

Although a fairly sizable body of research exists for residential treatment of troubled children and adolescents, the bulk of it involves outcome analyses of data gathered through specialized research and demonstration efforts. A fairly typical study involves analysis of multiple factors associated with successful community reintegration upon discharge [Allerhand et al. 1966; Taylor and Alpert 1973; Nelson and Singer 1978]. Reviews of these outcome studies have, in the main, underscored the importance of the postdischarge environment as a prominent factor in the children's community adaptation and reintegration [Whittaker and Pecora 1984], as have the Cavior et al. [1972] study and others. The Allerhand et al. study, which involved extensive follow-up of 50 graduates of a sophisticated residential treatment agency (Bellefaire) in Ohio, summarizes the study's major finding as follows:

> Perhaps the most striking finding of the study is that none of the measurements of within-Bellefaire performance at discharge, either in casework or in cottage and school roles, were useful in themselves in predicting postdischarge adaptability and adaptation. Only when the situation to which the child returned was taken into account were performances at Bellefaire related to postdischarge adequacies. In a stressful community situation, strengths nurtured within the institution tended to break down, whereas in a supportive situation, these strengths tended to be reinforced. [p. 140]

The importance of the postplacement environment was also underscored in the later research by Taylor and Alpert, which also found that contact with biological parents while the child was in placement was positively correlated with postdischarge adjustment. These researchers conclude that neither the child's presenting symptoms nor any specific treatment variables were strongly associated with postdischarge adjustment: ". . . [it] is not possible to predict a child's postdischarge adaptation on the basis of a given set of preadmission characteristics" [p. 35]. Similar findings with respect to specific treatment variables and outcome were identified in studies conducted by Davids et al. [1978]. They conclude: ". . . treatment variables, especially conventional psychotherapy, seem to bear little relationship to subsequent adjustment . . ." Part of this lack of demonstrated effect may stem from our still primitive efforts to conceptualize and measure the key treatment variables in a complex intervention like residential treatment. Nelson et al. [1978] found that children and youth leaving residential treatment with supportive community ties to family, friends, neighbors, schools, and the like were more likely to maintain their treatment gains than those who did not. Those with support maintained over 70 percent of their gains, while those without support maintained only 50 percent. Though the sample size was small (22), this study is notable in that it measured behavior at four points in time, beginning with a pretreatment community baseline. Similar results were obtained by Lewis [1982] in a follow-up of a RE-ED program, though again, small sample size limits generalization.

The similarity of these findings should not be surprising to anyone involved in either service delivery or program evaluation in services for children and adolescents. The maintenance and generalization of treatment effects, as well as, ultimately, replication of program models remain paramount issues for those involved in residential treatment services for children. Jones et al. [1981] in their national evaluation of the Teaching Family Model of group home treatment, a model group home program that attracted much attention in the 1970s, state the concern as follows:

> TFM (Teaching Family Model) . . . has demonstrated its capability for modifying a wide range of in-program behavior . . . [but] recall that our self-report data suggested little nonmaturational change in either deviant or drug behavior across pre-, during, and postprogram phases. The message is simple, a program could be an apparent success if the criterion is modification of target behavior during the program experiences. The same program may be seen as far less successful if the criterion is the postprogram adjustment and reintegration of youth. [p. 134]

At this point, while the full meaning of the Jones findings remain open to question, at the very least they serve to temper the

enthusiasm that accompanied earlier evaluations, which reached
the conclusion that the Teaching Family Model "works better [than
comparison programs] and costs less" [Stumphauzer 1979: 119;
Kirigin et al. 1979]. Jones's analysis of national data supports no
such conclusion.

The implications of this corpus of outcome research for program administration in residential services are not entirely clear: if
more services should be targeted to the postplacement environment, for example, in providing more family-child support, what
form should such services take? How should they articulate with
in-program services? How should they vary by family type, race,
ethnicity, and presenting problem of the child? To a large extent,
much of existing outcome research is silent on these points, because
the group designs employed do not readily lend themselves to
more finely tuned analysis involving planned variations in treatment conditions. In part for this reason, as previously noted, Fanshel [1982] and others [Whittaker 1986] have argued for greater
utilization of routinely gathered data as a base for ongoing research
efforts to improve the quality of service. The occurrence of multiple,
ongoing research efforts performed on routinely gathered data has
been much less frequent than the "one-shot" outcome evaluation
in residential treatment, despite the growing sentiment for a closer
articulation of mission-oriented research and program development. The underlying implication seems to be that if the findings
of research are to be of more practical benefit to program administrators, the agency itself has to become, in the words of Reid, a
"research machine" [1978]. Indeed, one of the major impediments
to conducting continual research is the relative scarcity of integrated
management information systems in agencies that routinely, systematically, and reliably collect data on child/family/community
characteristics at intake, during the process of treatment, and at
discharge and follow-up. The logic for the research effort at Boysville has been to try to understand: (1) the salient characteristics of
children and families entering the system, (2) the nature of multiple
treatment process variables during placement, and (3) the relationship of both of these sets of factors to proximate and distal
outcomes of interest. The study reported here represents an initial
attempt to address the question of who was coming into the intake
stream.

Findings

Study Data

Table 1 presents demographic family data for the study sample. As noted, for purposes of comparison, similar data are also provided from a recent large-scale survey of residential treatment agencies in California [Fitzharris 1985]. This ambitious research endeavor is a joint project of the Children's Services Foundation and the California Association of Services for Children. The routine ongoing data-gathering effort provides valuable information on over 10,000 children (and their families) who annually are placed in voluntary group care agencies in California. Selected family intake data from the California study are summarized in Tables 2 and 3.

From the present study, 47.9 percent of the Boysville admissions were white ($n = 159$) and an equal number were black. Youths came primarily from urban population centers ($n = 253$, 76.2 percent), with fewer cases from suburban ($n = 53$, 16.0 percent) and rural ($n = 26$, 7.8 percent) areas. Mean age at intake was approximately 15.5 years. Of the 1985 admissions ($n = 332$), 39 percent ($n = 130$) resided in the main campus at Clinton, Michigan. The remainder were placed at Boysville sites throughout Michigan. For 78 percent ($n = 260$), it was their first stay at Boysville.

The Boysville sample provides some significant contrasts to the California (CSC) study. The sample was limited to males because the 1985 admissions were only 13 percent female. The CSC profile included a much larger subgroup of girls—31 percent. Racial composition also varied between studies. The California sample was more heterogeneous, containing significant percentages of Hispanics (13.9 percent) and youths of mixed ethnic background (8.8 percent). The Boysville sample, however, yielded a much higher rate of black youths (47.9 percent vs. 17.7 percent). Of interest in the future will be trends in caseload composition. The authors of the California study project increased group home resources for families of Southeast Asian refugees. The black, urban subgroup will likely continue to require services in Michigan.

TABLE 1

Sample Description—Boysville Intake, Boys Only, 1985
$(n = 332)$

	n	$\%$
Individual Characteristics		
Race		
White	159	47.9
Black	159	47.9
Other	14	4.2
Family Characteristics		
Education*		
Attended public school	202	63.1
Ever suspended or expelled	206	62.0
Emotionally impaired or		
learning disabled	81	24.4
Placed prior to Boysville[a]	251	75.6
Group homes[b]	97	38.6
Foster care	85	33.9
Juvenile detention	75	30.0
Legal involvement		
Adjudicated for status or		
criminal offense	251	75.6
Referrals to Boysville		
Department of social services	286	86.2
Juvenile court	35	10.5
Other	11	3.3
Emergency Boysville placements	79	23.8
Wardship status		
Delinquent	209	63.0
Neglected-dependent	104	31.3
Other	19	5.7
Parent's marital status		
Married	114	38.1
Divorced, separated	120	40.1
Widowed	26	8.7
Never married	39	13.0

TABLE 1 *continued*

	n	%
Family type		
Nuclear	52	15.7
Single-parent	176	53.2
Reconstituted	35	10.6
Extended	39	11.8
Adoptive	16	4.8
Foster	13	3.9
Home setting		
Urban	253	76.2
Suburban	53	16.0
Rural	26	7.8

[a]These indicators are independent measures; percentages will not equal 100 percent.

[b]Percentages for each type of placement based on total of 251 cases with a placement history

TABLE 2

Family Status—CSC Study, 1985*
(Presence and Situation of Parents)

	n	%
Parents together	1,252	16.6
Biological parent and stepparent	1,382	18.3
Unmarried couple	194	2.6
Single-parent family:		
Divorced	2,241	29.7
Separated	520	6.9
Never married	670	8.9
Death separation	453	6.0
Parents deceased	112	1.5
Parents' location unknown	360	4.7
Unknown/unspecified	366	4.8
	7,550	100.0

*From Fitzharris, T. *The Foster Children of California.* . . . Sacramento, California: Children's Services Foundation, 1985. *Reprinted with permission.*

TABLE 3

Conditions in Family History—CSC Study, 1985*
(Deficiencies in Parenting)

	n	%
Inability to control child	4,875	64.6
Inability of parent to care for self	782	10.4
Neglecting	2,259	29.9
Physical abuse	1,914	25.4
Sexual abuse	718	9.5
Psychological abuse	1,287	17.1
Substance abuse	1,456	19.3
Prostitution	118	1.6
Parents unavailable to child due to:		
Relinquishment	410	5.4
Abandonment	748	9.9
Hospitalization (mental)	334	4.4
Hospitalization (physical)	93	1.2
Psychosis	102	1.4
Incarceration	294	3.9
Suicide	59	.8
	15,449[a]	204.8[a]

[a]The total number of conditions exceed the total number of children and the percentage exceeds 100 percent because the social worker was allowed to check more than one condition in each case.

*From Fitzharris, T. *The Foster Children of California.* . . . Sacramento, California: Children's Services Foundation, 1985. *Reprinted with permission.*

Family Characteristics

The majority of youths entering Boysville came from single-parent families (n = 176, 53.2 percent). Intact homes—comprising nuclear and reconstituted families—accounted for only 26.3 percent (n = 87) of cases. A significant subset included youths from families with no biological parent present (n = 39, 11.8 percent); however, data for this group of "extended" families were not available for characterizing which relatives were heads of households. This breakdown of family type is quite consistent with the CSC data. Both studies reported a majority of cases from single-parent households. Marital status for parents in the Boysville sample generally paralleled the family type data: 40 percent (n = 121) were divorced or separated; 38.1 percent (n = 114) were married; an additional 13 percent (n = 39) had never married.

Additional family data were collected at intake to characterize boundaries between parents and children while in treatment at Boysville. Nearly 58 percent (n = 191) of parents were willing to participate in their child's treatment process. Only 4.8 percent (n = 16) of the parents were restricted from visiting the child, and in 19.6 percent (n = 65) of the families home visits were not allowed.

The California study (Table 3) provides a more detailed analysis of family problems as assessed by caseworkers at intake. Notable among these is the fact that nearly two-thirds (64.6 percent) of parents reported an "inability to control their child"—the most frequently reported problem. The implications of this and related findings on family composition have profound implications for the design of family work programs, which are discussed later in this paper.

Characteristics of the Children

Educational Background

Before Boysville admission, a majority of the youths had attended public schools (n = 202, 63.1 percent), with a significant minority in special education classes (n = 49, 15.3 percent). The average grade attained was 8.4 (S.D. = 1.38). Intake data clearly reflect a history of school problems. Fifty-two percent (n = 147) had more than 21 days of school absence in the six months before Boysville placement. Seventy-three percent (n = 206) had received formal disciplinary action, for example, suspension or expulsion, during the same six-month period. Beyond behavioral problems, 24.4 percent (n = 81) had been identified as either emotionally impaired or learning disabled.

Placement History

For the study sample, 76 percent (n = 251) had at least one previous placement before coming to Boysville. The number of previous placements ranged from one to 16 ($\bar{x}$ = 3.26; S.D. = 2.73). For students with a placement history, group homes and foster care were the primary pathways to care, with 39 percent (n = 97) having one or more of the former and 34 percent (n = 85) having at least one foster care experience. Juvenile detention occurred in 30 percent (n = 75) of these cases, while placement in private care occurred for 31 percent (n = 79) of the sample.

Legal Involvement

Approximately 76 percent (n = 251) of Boysville youths had been adjudicated for either a status or criminal offense. Adjudications were primarily truancy (23 percent), felonies toward people (15 percent), and property (43 percent) (e.g., grand theft, larceny), and misdemeanor crimes (11 percent) (ungovernable behavior, vagrancy). In general, these major presenting problems are comparable to those reported in the California study, although exact comparisons are not possible due to differing categories and ways of tabulating the data. Major presenting problems in the CSC study, as reflected in Table 4, are primarily truancy, theft, and misdemeanor crimes. These California data appear to show much lower felony rates, but this appearance may reflect allowing multiple problem codes per case. Sixty-three percent (n = 209) of the Boysville cases were identified as delinquents. The other major wardship category was neglect (n = 104, 31.3 percent).

Referrals to Boysville

The majority of referrals came from the state's Department of Social Services (86.2 percent) with an additional 35 cases (10.5 percent) referred by juvenile court. These data contrast sharply with CSC findings. In the latter study, only 37.7 percent were referred from social services. Nearly 24 percent of the 1985 Boysville admissions were considered emergency placements. This subgroup came from families (51.9 percent), group and youth homes (15.2 percent), mental hospitals (10.1 percent), and shelters (6.3 percent). No data were available on CSC emergency placements. Boysville has also contracted, through Michigan's Department of Social Services, to provide placements for youths remanded to the state's training institution. This diversion project accounted for 13 percent

TABLE 4

Presenting Problems at Time of Placement—CSC Study (1985)*

Acts by Child	n	%
Felony toward people	281	3.7
Felony toward property	649	8.6
Felony—drug dealing	89	1.2
Misdemeanor crimes	1,270	16.8
Stealing	2,007	26.6
Substance abuse	1,767	23.4
Antisocial gang affiliation	530	7.0
Aggression to people	2,237	29.6
Attacks on property	1,213	16.1
Suicidal threats/attempts	668	8.8
Self-induced injuries/accident-prone	386	5.1
Pregnancy and infant care	657	8.7
Runaway	2,717	36.0
Sexual acting out	1,136	15.0
Truancy	2,523	33.4
Subtotal	18,130[a]	240.0[a]

Physical/Psychological Condition	n	%
Withdrawal	844	11.2
Fearfulness	611	8.1
Specific phobias	77	1.0
Hyperactivity	719	9.5
Depression (severe)	847	11.2
Psychosis (chronic)	97	1.3
Psychosis (transitory)	145	1.9
Autistic behavior	86	1.1
Bizarre behavior	135	1.8
Compulsive behavior	587	7.8
Obsessive thoughts	180	2.4
Excessive lying	1,064	14.1
Passive/aggressive	836	11.1
Tenuous hold on reality	299	4.0

TABLE 4 *continued*

Physical/Psychological Condition	n	%
Impulsive behavior	2,626	34.8
Delayed social development	1,077	14.3
Enuresis-encopresis	341	4.5
Extreme dependency needs	797	10.6
Eating disorder	101	1.3
Other	670	8.9
Subtotal	12,139[a]	160.9[a]
Total	30,269[a]	400.9[a]

[a]The total number of conditions exceeds the total number of children and the percentage exceeds 100 percent because the social workers were allowed to check more than one presenting problem for each child, if appropriate.

*From Fitzharris, T. *The Foster Children of California.* . . . Sacramento, California: Children's Services Foundation, 1985. *Reprinted with Permission.*

(n = 43) of 1985 male admissions. This last group of youths may represent an important subset, since their placement is clearly less restrictive than incarceration in a closed facility.

In a related study, Whittaker et al. [1988] found that for nearly two-thirds of the youths entering from the juvenile justice service stream, Boysville represented a less restrictive placement environment. The California study yielded similar results. These and related findings dispel the identification of group care as primarily a last-resort alternative.

Relationships Between Characteristics of Children and Families

The following sections highlight significant cross-sectional findings among individual and family characteristics at intake to Boysville. These results are not intended as explanations for either problems or conditions in residential treatment today. Analyzing demographic and simple descriptive data is a necessary first step in tracking family careers in this field. Further work on longitudinal data sets and more complex measures will be required before positing putative causes for various youth and family outcomes. Analyses of this kind are presently under way.

Racial Differences

For the total Boysville sample, significant black-white differences were found on a number of characteristics. Among blacks (n = 159), 18.9 percent of the residents came from extended families without a biological parent present, as compared to only 5.1 percent (n = 8) of whites (X^2 = 28.6, $p<.001$). White residents more often came from nuclear and reconstituted family structures than blacks (20.3 percent vs. 10.7 percent and 17.1 percent vs. 5.0 percent, respectively). No differences were found in the rates of single parents (50.0 percent and 56.6 percent for whites and blacks, respectively). Black parents, however, were more likely to be widowed or unmarried than whites (11.8 percent vs. 6.3 percent and 22.9 percent vs. 4.2 percent, respectively; X^2 = 37.6, $p<.001$).

Race differences also occurred for family setting—urban, suburban, or rural. Black students came predominantly from urban areas (94.3 percent); whites were more evenly distributed among urban (57.9 percent), suburban (27.0 percent), and rural (15.1 percent; X^2 = .1, $p<.001$). Because of these differences, subanalyses were performed for whites and blacks from urban settings. The intent was to control to some degree for other factors that might be influencing white-black differences.

Among urban youths, whites had a significantly higher rate of reported abuse than their black counterparts (48.1 percent vs. 28.8 percent; X^2 = 3.96; p = 0.046). White urban youths had a significantly higher rate of parent involvement at admission (29.3 percent vs. 13.4 percent; X^2 = 8.2; p = 0.004), but no differences were found for parental willingness to participate in treatment. Black urban youths were significantly more likely to enter Boysville as an emergency placement (35.3 percent vs. 18.5 percent; X^2 = 7.08; p = 0.008). This relationship also held for the total sample. No differences were found among urban black and white residents on proportions of cases where Boysville was the first placement experience.

Interestingly, for the total sample, blacks were more likely than whites to be first placements (29.6 percent vs. 18.2 percent; X^2 = 5.00; p = 0.025). This finding may reflect the broader range of white family settings. Significant numbers of white youths with previous placements lived in suburban settings, whereas among blacks almost the entire group lived in large cities. Alternatively, racial differences on the likelihood of previous placements may be an artifact of the sample. Youths placed via the diversion program from the state's secure facility—(total, $n = 43$) were twice as likely to be black than white (26 vs. 13 cases) and nearly four times as likely to have had no previous placements (57.7 percent vs. 15.4 percent, $X^2 = 4.7$, $p = 0.03$). When diversion cases are excluded, no statistically significant race differences were found for black vs. white rates of first placement (24.1 percent vs. 18.5 percent, respectively).

Placement History Differences

For 81 cases (24 percent) Boysville represented the first placement experience. As noted earlier, the agency provides a diversion program for cases with targeted placement at the state's secure facility. Since this special subpopulation had a high rate (40 percent) of no previous placements, analyses were done with and without these cases; their exclusion did not alter the results. Therefore, placement history differences in this section were summarized for the entire sample ($n = 332$). Table 5 summarizes contrasts between youths with and without previous placements. In addition to the race differences presented above on placement history, youths without previous placements were more often sent to the main Boysville campus. Seventy-one percent of first placements went to the campus setting. Among youths with previous placement histories, only 29 percent were sent to the main campus ($X^2 = 42.4$; $p<0.001$). No differences were found between these groups on parents' marital status, religious affiliation, family setting (urban, suburban, or rural), abuse by parent, involvement with adjudications, restriction of parental visiting rights, or emergency placement at Boysville. For this last variable, 21.0 percent of youths without previous placements entered Boysville as emergencies; 24.7 percent of youths with some placement history also entered this way. Finally, for the total sample, youths without previous placements were more likely to come from single-parent households and, interestingly, had parents who were more often willing to participate in treatment (96 percent vs. 84 percent).

TABLE 5

Comparison of Youths With Prior Placements ($n = 251$) and Those
Without ($n = 81$)—Boysville Sample, 1985

	No Prior Placement ($n = 81$)	Yes Prior Placement ($n = 251$)	X^2	p
Race (% white)	38.2	53.7	5.00	0.025
Family type (% single-parent)	66.7	48.8	12.20	0.032
Home setting (% urban)	85.2	73.3	5.10	0.077
Emergency placement (% yes)	21.0	24.7	0.28	NS
Home visits restricted (% yes)	13.4	25.7	3.70	0.054
Parent willing to participate (% yes)	96.1	84.0	3.98	0.046
Prior status offenses (% yes)	22.2	39.4	7.2	0.007
Prior adjudications (% yes)	80.2	74.1	0.94	NS

Implications for Practice and Future Research

What lessons are to be learned from this brief overview of residential treatment intake?

1. *Benefits of analyzing routinely collected data:* This study and the experience of the California Association of Children's Services affirm our belief in the values of systematic analysis of routinely collected data. Shifting patterns of child and family characteristics, placement histories, and referral sources may be detected early and used as a basis for assessing risk and allocation of service resources. The combination of child/youth and family characteristics reported in the two studies suggest a level of service intensity (and resource allocation) far beyond that required when the bulk of the group care population consisted of dependent children. If there are, indeed, any more "easy cases," they are not readily apparent in the intake data reported here. As noted earlier, for youths from streams of care such as juvenile corrections, residential placement constituted a less restrictive alternative to the locked, secure institutions to which they were heading. Of similar interest is the nearly one-fourth of youths in the Boysville study who entered care directly from home. At this point, anecdotal evidence suggests that while placement clearly constitutes a more restrictive alternative for these youths, they are by no means the least troubled youths entering Boysville. For what appears to be a substantial proportion, plea bargaining and other legal means have been used to avoid previous placements.

2. *Engaging families:* A clear preference for family involvement in residential treatment is reflected in the paper by Jenson and Whittaker in this volume and elsewhere [Maluccio and Whittaker in press]. This preference is based both on values and evidence: families of children in care have too often been neglected, and family involvement is positively correlated with successful outcomes [Whittaker and Pecora 1984]. Given the urgency of this task, the family data presented here suggest a formidable challenge for clinicians, child- and youth-care workers, and adminis-

trators. The disproportionate number of single-parent families (almost all female) in both studies coupled with the range and complexity of parental difficulties reported in the California study suggest, at minimum, the need for multiple, complementary family work efforts. For example, while the nearly two-thirds of the families reporting "inability to control child" in the CSC study suggest the need for parenting skills training, evidence on the effectiveness of such training with low-income, single parents who are isolated from sources of social support is not encouraging [Dumas and Wahler 1983]. An earlier study of Boysville youths and families indicated significant differences in both the frequency and type of family involvement for black and white families, as well as for successful/unsuccessful cases—despite comparable willingness to participate in family work expressed at intake [Whittaker et al. 1987]. While we are not entirely sure what these findings mean, they suggest that family involvement for all children and adolescents entering care will continue to be a sizable and challenging task.

3. *Defining success in residential treatment:* The sizable number of youth and family problems reported at residential treatment intake suggests a reformulation of the criterion of success: What specific subsamples of youths and families, offered what combination of treatments, will produce what desirable outcomes, at what times? Experience with the Boysville data system thus far suggests to us the need for multiple indicators of success measured at multiple points in time: intake, during treatment, discharge, and postdischarge [Whittaker et al. 1988]. The intake data reported here constitute a baseline against which future gains may be measured. The great majority of these or similar indicators are provided by routinely collected data obtained from service history and treatment program forms. We are again struck with the potential for analysis in the data routinely collected by many group care agencies—without resort to complex and time-consuming standardized instruments. The collection and utilization of such data, beginning at the point of intake, provide the foundation on which future evaluation efforts should rest.

We hope that the research experience at Boysville provides a template for other group care agencies desirous of integrating systematic analysis of routinely gathered data into ongoing practice.

References

Allerhand, M.E., Weber, R., and Haug, M. *Adaptation and Adaptability: The Bellefaire Follow-Up Study*. New York: Child Welfare League of America, 1966.

Cavior, E.C., Schmidt, A., and Karacki, L. *An Evaluation of the Kennedy Youth Center Differential Treatment Program*. Washington, D.C.: U.S. Bureau of Prisons, 1972.

Davids, A., Ryan, R., and Salvatore, P. Effectiveness of residential treatment. *American Journal of Orthopsychiatry* 38: 469–475, 1978.

Dumas, J.E. and Wahler, R.G. Predictions of treatment outcome in parent training: Mother insularity and socioeconomic disadvantage. *Behavioral Assessment* 5: 301–313, 1983.

Fanshel, D. *On the Road to Permanency: An Expanded Data Base for Service to Children in Foster Care*. Washington, D.C.: Child Welfare League of America, 1982.

Fitzharris, T. *The Foster Children of California. Profiles of 10,000 Children in Residential Care*. Sacramento, California: Children's Services Foundation, 1985.

Jones, R.R., Weinrott, M.R., and Howard, J.R. *Impact of the Teaching-Family Model on Troublesome Youth: Findings from the National Evaluation*. Rockville, Maryland: NIMH (reproduced by National Technical Information Service, U.S. Department of Commerce, Springfield, Virginia 22191, PB82-224353), 1981.

Kirigin, K., Wolf, M.M., Braukman, C.J., Fixsen, D.L., and Phillips, E. Achievement place: A preliminary outcome evaluation. In J.S. Stumphauzer (ed.), *Progress in Behavior Therapy with Delinquents*, Springfield, Illinois: Charles C. Thomas, 1979.

Lewis, W.W. Ecological factors in successful residential treatment. *Behavioral Disorders* 7: 149–155, 1982.

Maluccio, A.N. and Whittaker, J.K. Helping biological families of children in out-of-home placement. In F. Cox, C. Chilman, and E. Nunnally (eds.), *Families in Trouble*, Volume 5. Beverly Hills, California: Sage Publications, in press.

McCubbin, H., and Thompson, A.I. *Family Assessment Inventories for Research and Practice*. Madison, Wisconsin: University of Wisconsin, Family Stress, Coping and Health Project, 1987.

Nelson, R.H., Singer, M.J., and Johnsen, L.O. The application of a residential treatment evaluation model. *Child Care Quarterly* 7: 164–175, 1978.

Reid, W. The social agency as research machine. *Journal of Social Service Research* 2: 11–23, 1978.

Stumphauzer, J.S. Editorial comments. In J.S. Stumphauzer (ed.), *Progress in Behavior Therapy with Delinquents*, Springfield, Illinois: Charles C. Thomas, 1979, pp. 118–119.

Taylor, D.A., and Alpert, S.W. *Continuity and Support Following Residential Treatment.* New York: Child Welfare League of America, 1973.

Whittaker, J.K. Formal and informal helping in child welfare services: Implications for management and practice. *Child Welfare* LXV(1): 17–25, 1986.

Whittaker, J.K., Overstreet, E.J., Grasso, A., Tripodi, T., and Boylan, F. Multiple indicators of success in residential youth care and treatment. *American Journal of Orthopsychiatry* 58: 143–148, 1988.

Whittaker, J.K., and Pecora, P. A research agenda for residential care. In T. Philpot (ed.), *Group Care Practice: The Challenge of the Next Decade.* Surrey, UK: Community Care-Business Press International, 1984, pp. 71–87.

Whittaker, J.K., Tripodi, T., and Grasso, A. Youth and Family Characteristics, Treatment Histories, and Service Outcomes: Some Preliminary Findings from the Boysville Research Program. Manuscript in preparation.

Part 2

Policy Issues Affecting Group Care

4

Permanency Planning and Residential Care

ELIZABETH S. COLE

RESIDENTIAL CARE FOR CHILDREN HAS ALWAYS BEEN an embattled child welfare service [Mayer et al. 1977: 38–39]. Its merits versus foster care have been argued for over a hundred years. The debate has often been bitter [Wolins and Piliavin 1967: 3]. Is it any wonder that the advent of permanency planning has been viewed by some as another attack on residential care? This thought is an inescapable conclusion when permanency planning is defined in a narrow way, such as that return to biological parents or adoption are the only permissible outcomes for child welfare services [Wooley 1982]. Permanence should not be interpreted in this skewed fashion. To demonstrate that the permanence philosophy and techniques do encompass residential care, this paper defines permanency planning and identifies the underlying principles and program elements that show how residential care is an integral part of this concept. Hindrances to implementation are also discussed.

Permanency Planning Defined

Permanency planning is a term used to define a philosophy implemented through a number of family-focused services and programs delivered to children who are either at risk of being

91

removed from their family of origin or who are in out-of-home placements. Its primary goal is to secure for each child a nurturant, caring, legally recognized family in which to grow up. When this aim is neither possible nor beneficial for a child, it seeks to reinforce ties to nurturant foster parents or caretakers.

Although this formulation reflects a hierarchy of valued parents, a helpful permanence philosophy respects the validity of each option for some children. Permanency planning impels us to view all the parenting options and see to it that each provides the best possible security and nurturance for the children who are reared in that setting. "Possible" is the key word here: it may be preferable for children to grow up in their family of birth, but that is not always possible or beneficial; it may be desirable for children to be raised by adoptive parents, but that too may not be achievable.

The philosophy of permanence has as its major value a perspective, a lens through which we view and measure options. Residential care viewed from a permanence perspective is a specialized resource necessary for those children whose problems are such that a family setting is not for a time the most suitable place to help them. Its aim is to keep children as close to normal family life as possible and to restore them to the point where they can take their place there. When this result is not possible, arrangements are made for a new family or for ties to a caring adult [Reid 1979: 99–107]. Underlying the permanence theory is a set of beliefs and assumptions about the nature of families, their helpers, and the interchanges among them. The following three major themes basic to permanence are also at the core of modern residential treatment: the primacy of the family, limited intervention into family functioning, and protection of family member rights.

A belief in the primacy of the family impels help to preserve the families into which children were born. Working with the family is no less important than working with the child. In efforts with parents, the focus should be to empower them to control their own lives and their children. This task is best done by maximizing their participation in decision making, through frequent contact and communication with their children in care, and involvement in each other's lives.

Protecting family members' rights is best done in a system that provides parents and children with good information, advocates, legal representation, hearings, and case reviews.

Key Elements of Permanency Planning in Residential Care

The new role shaped for residential facilities is to put these principles into practice through a systematic process of case planning, service delivery, and monitoring. These elements have been standard ingredients of child welfare programs for some time. Permanency planning has given them renewed emphasis and has injected some different ingredients to involve parents. Let's look more closely at how each of these elements is played out.

Case Planning

A case plan is a written contract that is mutually agreed upon by parents, children, and service providers. It includes, for *each child and family*, the *specific, time-limited* steps to be taken by family members and agency staff members. It identifies the services to be provided, activities undertaken, and resources necessary as they pertain to three goals: to keep the family together, to return children who have been separated, or to provide alternative placement. It identifies the consequences of breaching the contract.

Current case planning differs from the past in that it emphasizes the mutual contractual nature of the process. The penalties are outlined, the document is *written, mutually agreed on* by clients, *specific,* and *time-limited.* Furthermore, the issues of restoration to family, provision of new families, and involvement of present families in the program are central issues of the current case plan.

Service Delivery

The kinds of services that child welfare agencies give pursuant to permanence philosophy still fall into four broad categories: services which support families, such as counseling, home management training, parenthood education; services that supplement families, such as day care, homemakers; services that provide out-of-home placement for children; and services that provide new permanent families through adoption.

Family Involvement

Some group care leaders and experts have long recognized and supported the strengthening of families and the prevention of placement as a priority service.

> Prevention of pariah care wherever possible is the *first* and most important task of all child welfare and mental health. . . . We know of no form of pariah placement that would be an adequate substitute for a well-functioning and loving family; be it a two-parent or one-parent family, a nuclear or an extended family. [Mayer et al. 1977: 274]

Unfortunately, others have not seen a place for the residential center as a part of that preventive and strengthening activity. In fact, family-centered or home-based services have sometimes been described as antithetical to group care. A more balanced perspective on the relationship between in- and out-of-home care is offered by Small and Whittaker [1979:79]:

> Surely the goal of reform is not simply to relocate existing services so that they take place in the home, but to develop more effective ways of supporting family life by seeing troubled children and their families in a total context. In this case, the real issue is much larger than home-based vs. out-of-home intervention as competing *service strategies*. It is the challenge to organize all possible resources to provide continuity of care for children whatever their needs, while at the same time maintaining a primary focus on family and community life.

Even those who believe that residential care should and could maintain a primary focus on family admit that too often in practice this is not the case. Many group facilities are still oriented to child rescue and child care. Goals are reversed. The primary goal of helping the child and family live and cope together is overtaken by an emphasis on the child's adaptation to the institution [Finkelstein 1980: 33–41].

The renewed emphasis on family involvement requires refocusing from the child to the family. Finkelstein [1980: 35] expresses it well: "The framework suggested here is equally committed to involvement and change of every family member, regardless of which member happens to be occupying a residential bed." This philosophy needs to be conveyed to the staff by the administration through policies and programs that suffuse the institution with family involvement [Littauer 1980: 225–234; Blumenthal and Weinberg 1984; Small and Whittaker 1979].

Residential treatment centers are adding to intake intensive services to families who have come seeking out-of-home placement. The program's aim is to see if placement can be avoided. Day treatment may be offered instead of full residence. For children who should be placed, families are involved in many ways:

> Scheduling weekly visits; sharing meals; allowing overnight visits on grounds by parents and families; using family members as tutors, as volunteer coaches for sporting events, as chauffeurs for off-ground activities
>
> Seeing parents as full and equal partners in the helping process—for example, Parsons Child and Family Service in Albany, New York, calls in parents to help them deal with their child's destructive or acting-out behavior. This method is one example of keeping parents in charge while offering them help with effective child-care techniques and survival skills.
>
> Creating support groups. Parents can draw on each other's experiences, insights, and skills through group discussion. This technique extends the supportive capacity of the staff members and builds a helping network capable of continuing after the child's return home.
>
> Letting children go home frequently—weekends, during the week, holidays, and so forth

Adoption

It has been pointed out that these services to families are a long way from being in place in a great many residential programs, but, even where they are offered, parental involvement will be impossible because some parents are unwilling or unable to work with the staff members.

When preserving families or reunifying children with their families does not work, residential treatment centers have become more conscious of preparing and referring children for adoption services. Some facilities have developed their own adoption services; others have linked with an agency in the community to provide the services. A common barrier to the provision of these services is that the child-care staff may consider the child unadoptable and suitable adoptive parents impossible to find. Adoption workers, on the other hand, may be overly optimistic about what adoption can do for the child. A close working relationship between adoption and residential treatment center staffs can result in more realistic and beneficial permanent plans for children.

There are and will continue to be children for whom no type of workable family relationship is achievable during their childhood. The permanency perspective emphasizes working with these children to have them understand which adults will be there for them and provide them with attachment and guidance. As young adults they should be helped to understand the kinds of relationships that may be possible with their biological families. Although many agencies have offered help with independent-living skills in the past, these have focused mainly on the technical and economic aspects of surviving and not on the effective connections that children and adolescents need.

The Monitoring Function

Permanency planning has created dramatic changes in group care facilities in that they have taken much more seriously their role in monitoring case planning and service delivery and are using more sophisticated technology to do it. Computerized management information systems and child-tracking systems have become commonplace. Facilities have developed more rigorous review systems to monitor case planning goals and to assure parental involvement. Residential centers have become answerable to external review systems—court and citizen review boards. It is also not uncommon for children in care to have guardians ad litem and court-appointed special advocates.

If monitoring systems are not thoughtfully and efficiently designed they may, however, add unnecessarily to staff paperwork and reduce the effective helping time spent with families. Unfortunately, many people see the elimination of monitoring as the solution to a cluttered system where streamlining may be more in order.

Hindrances to Implementation

The obstacles to the implementation of permanency planning in residential care, as identified by administration and staff members, are defects in values, awareness, knowledge, skill, and resources.

Values

If belief in the primacy of the family is missing, there can be no permanency planning. Problems often begin when individuals working in the organization are unaware of their own beliefs.

Beliefs should be compared and differences identified through staff discussions.

A serious problem occurs when decisions are made regarding the abilities of families and parents without a commonly accepted standard of satisfactory parenting among staff members.

Unrealistic staff expectations about how parents should function—in general and in relation to particular children—often prevent children from returning home.

A lack of awareness of our limits as helpers often causes us to take over tasks and decisions that parents should be handling in relation to their children.

We value the peace of a routine. Active family involvement can make institutional life hectic; it requires more staff time in planning and participation.

Knowledge and Skills

We need to know more about intensive work with families.

Staff members often do not understand or appreciate different minority groups.

Staff members do not understand enough about who is adoptable, or that adoption placement need not mean a loss of contact with the original family.

Resources

There is need for a more adequately trained staff—more qualified new staff members and in-service training of higher caliber.

Aftercare is weak. Families need supportive or supplemental services after the child is returned home. These services are not in place in every community.

Very often the state or county will pay a residential treatment center only for residential care or "mattress money." This practice discourages the use of day treatment and intensive family work.

Conclusions

A few words to temper our zeal: Will permanency planning be the utopian solution some child welfare professionals have dreamed about? No. It is not a panacea for our problems. It cannot cure the societal problems—poverty, poor physical and mental health—that cause the families we serve to fracture. It will not replace the profession's needs for enough adequately trained staff armed with enough supportive services.

We should not oversell the results that permanency planning can achieve. We have always imposed on our child welfare organizations a heavier burden of expectation than any human institution can carry, and then we make them the target of our scorn and contempt when these exalted expectations fall short.

Will permanency planning make residential care unnecessary? No. There will always be children and families whose needs can best be met through services offered by residential treatment centers. Permanency planning, when it works well, can help assure that only those children who need it receive residential care, and only for as long as is necessary. It can also assist us to enhance parents' skills and knowledge and guard against the possibility that in our efforts to help a child we may unwittingly be weakening the parents' ability to raise their children and their responsibility to do so.

References

Blumenthal, Karen, and Weinberg, Anita. *Establishing Parent Involvement in Foster Care Agencies*. New York: Child Welfare League of America, 1984.

Finkelstein, Nadia E. Family-centered group care. *Child Welfare* LIX(1): 33–41, 1980.

Littauer, Celia. Working with families of children in residential treatment. *Child Welfare* LIX(4): 225–234, 1980.

Mayer, Morris F., Richman, Leon H., and Balcerzak, Edwin A. *Group Care of Children: Crossroads and Transitions*. New York: Child Welfare League of America, 1977.

Reid, Joseph. The role of the modern children's institution. In *Child Welfare Perspectives*. New York: Child Welfare League of America, 1979.

Small, Richard, and Whittaker, James. Residential group care and home based care: Towards a continuity of family services. In Sherla Maybanks and Marven Bryce (eds.), *Home Based Services for Children and Families*. Springfield, Illinois: Charles C. Thomas, 1979.

Wolins, Martin, and Piliavin, Irvin. *Institution or Foster Family: A Century of Debate*. New York: Child Welfare League of America, 1967.

Wooley, Frank C. Permanency Planning: In the Best Interest of the Child? A paper delivered at the National Conference of Social Welfare, Boston, Massachusetts, 1982.

5

Public Law 96-272: Its Impact on the Present and Future of Group Care

TIMOTHY L. FITZHARRIS

THE PASSAGE OF PUBLIC LAW 96-272, The Adoption Assistance and Child Welfare Act of 1980, culminated a major effort by advocacy groups and legislators to end overuse of foster care and foster care drift. Foster care, the reform of the mid-1930s and 1940s, had become the problem.

Foster care was reformed again in 1980 by establishing the philosophy that a child's place is with his or her family, and by requiring early reunification efforts if placement occurred. Adoption or permanent placement were favored over foster care for children for whom reunification was not possible. Stability and permanency became the watchwords of the new reform, and judicially monitored timetables were established to ensure that the new goals were met.

That the Congress was responding in 1980 to a serious problem—children languishing for years in foster care—is not in doubt. There existed no formal review system to monitor the progress of a child and no presumption that he or she would be reunited with the family or placed in a new, stable, permanent home as quickly as possible.

The great hope, then, was, and still is, that fewer children would be placed in foster care and those who were would have short stays. The viability of these public policy initiatives would be demonstrated, the reformers said, by reduced placements and reduced lengths of stay and by increased preplacement and after-care services.

Group Care in a Defensive Position

Most professionals who provide out-of-home care believe that children should remain in their own families when possible and when removed should be returned home as quickly as it is safe to do so. They also believe that when family reunification is not pos-sible, an adoption, guardianship, or other stable, permanent place-ment is in order.

During the advocacy period for P.L. 96-272 and since, how-ever, residential care providers have been placed in a defensive position. Foster care, and especially long-term group care, has somehow become the villain in this play, the thing to be avoided at all costs. Placement is criticized not only as bad for children, but as the most restrictive and expensive thing to do.

But stable, permanent homes are not available for all children, and the timely use of out-of-home care can be strategic and ther-apeutic to both child and family. Given this apparent conflict about the use of group care, it is important to review its role in the context of P.L. 96-272.

This paper discusses the effect of overselling the dangers of placement, the unsupported conclusions that still plague foster care today, and specific concerns about group care. It concludes with a list of challenges to policy makers and providers to assure that group care maintains its appropriate role in modern child welfare services.

The Effect of Overselling the Problem

In our energetic embrace of the goals and funding of P.L. 96-272, we may have done a disservice to foster family care and group care. That we wish to avoid placement, reunify children with their families quickly, or find them new stable families has been interpreted by some as meaning that foster family care and group care are inherently bad—something to be avoided at all costs.

When reforms are sought, a compelling case must be made about that which is wrong with current practice. Often, exaggerated claims or unsupported conclusions are made to effect change. This method can marshal support for the reform, but sometimes it can lead to throwing out the baby with the bath water. In some situations, overstated cases have led to avoidable undervaluing of the foster care alternative. While we want selective, timely, and judicially reviewed use of foster family and group care, we do not want them to become emasculated, under-resourced alternatives. Here are some of the unsupported conclusions that still plague foster family and group care today:

1. *Premise*: Some children should not be in foster family and group care, and some stay there too long.

Unsupported Conclusion: Foster care is bad and to be avoided at all costs.

Reality: As we become more effective with P.L. 96-272 strategies, the distillate of children remaining in need of placement will be those with multiple problems, and they will be nearly impossible to place. The selective use of foster family and group care may justify longer stays, especially if seriously emotionally disturbed and juvenile justice children begin to be placed in foster care as a substitute for institutional care.

2. *Premise*: A family is the best placement for a child; a "family-like" setting is next best.

Unsupported Conclusion: Anything not family-like is bad and to be avoided at all costs.

Reality: Some children are threatened by the closeness of a family; some children cannot be handled in nonprofessional family settings. Some biological parents are so threatened by substitute parents that they would undermine familial maintenance or reunification.

3. *Premise*: The less restrictive a placement setting is, the more natural and nurturing it is. Institutionalized settings are more restrictive than family settings.

Unsupported Conclusion: Group care is more restrictive; therefore, group care is bad and should be avoided when possible.

Reality: Usually, families—especially biological families—are better for children. But for some children, families won't work, at least initially. And for children in juvenile halls and mental hospitals, group care is less restrictive and more family-like.

4. *Premise*: Many children in foster care can go home, are adoptable, or can find stable, permanent homes if proper efforts are made.

Unsupported Conclusion: All children can either return home or be adopted.

Reality: Many children in group care today cannot or should not go home. The number of biological families available and appropriate for reunification seems to be dropping rather than increasing. And despite our best efforts, it is often impossible to find adoptive families for some children.

5. *Premise*: The goal is to avoid foster care, reunify families, or find permanent stable families.

Unsupported Conclusion: When P.L. 96-272 strategies finally become fully effective, there will be little need for foster families and group homes.

Reality: As P.L. 96-272 works effectively there will be a continuing need for residential out-of-home care, perhaps an increasing need. One hopes for more selectivity in its use, and that its duration will be planfully limited. Group care, appropriately, will be used for a more difficult child than in years past.

6. *Premise*: Prevention, reunification, and adoption strategies are more effective and cheaper in the long run than foster care.

Unsupported Conclusion: Foster Care Maintenance funds (Title IV-E) ought to be capped or used instead for prevention and family services.

Reality: If Title IV-E supports a more difficult population in the future, service requirements and lengths of stay are likely to increase, and group care costs will increase. Child welfare is not a closed system where prevention can directly save costs in placement.

7. *Premise*: Some foster parents and group home operators abuse children and/or are in the business for the money.

Unsupported Conclusion: All foster care providers are bad or are improperly motivated.

Reality: Most providers of care are service-oriented, not profit-oriented. In California, in the past ten years, service providers raised $188 million in private donations and amassed 7 million volunteer hours in support of children.

When the overselling described above is discounted, it is clear that while much more remains to be done to assure that the only children placed are those who really need placement, and to assure the high quality of care for children in foster family and group care, the role of placement in the spectrum of intervention choices is established and is crucial.

Many children are seriously abused, neglected, disturbed, and damaged. They require protection, guidance, and support to regain stability, self-respect, and self-control. Foster care provides time, caring people, and a place for these children to learn responsible behavior and to achieve healthy growth. The most frightened, hurt, and desperate of these children need quality, specialized group care. If unhelped, many will end up in psychiatric or penal institutions, or become victimizers as well as victims.[a]

The Need for Information

Surprisingly, some eight years after the passage of P.L. 96-272, and notwithstanding the law's requirement to collect data, relatively little is known about how the various provisions are working in the states. Information is lacking about the backgrounds of the families and children, what strategies work best with which families and which children, and so on.

There are also public policy questions that need answers. For example, we are pretty sure that judicial oversight is good public policy, but some argue that adversarial proceedings and legal standards of proof do not always work in the best interests of the child. Not unlike the juvenile justice diversion programs of the 1970s, we have not proven satisfactorily whether our family-oriented efforts are really preventing placements, or are "widening the net" by providing services to a population of children and families who

[a]*The Group Care Task Force Report*. Sacramento, California: California Association of Services for Children, May 1984.

would not have come within the purview of government action. Serious study of the new law's effect must be undertaken.

The Need to Put P.L. 96-272 in Context

One of the things that makes it difficult to evaluate the effect of P.L. 96-272 is that its implementation did not take place in a relatively stable environment. Almost immediately after the passage of P.L. 96-272, the states were hit with tax-cutting and expenditure limitation initiatives (e.g., Proposition 13 in California) that severely limited the resources of public service agencies. Caseloads increased and "extras" (like research, training, interdepartmental liaisons, employee orientations) were summarily eliminated. Even in departments where the new federal law was wholeheartedly embraced, compliance was extremely difficult. This problem has not disappeared. For example, the specter of Gramm-Rudman-Hollings cutbacks does not portend a bright future for Title XX and Title IV-B activities.

In addition, P.L. 96-272 implementation has been accompanied coincidentally by a significant increase in both the reports of, and the numbers of sustained petitions for, child abuse and neglect, due in part to increased public education about child abuse and the passage of mandated child abuse reporting laws. Experienced almost everywhere in the nation, this increase has had a great influence on the nature and quality of P.L. 96-272 services. There is a need, then, to sort out all that is happening if we are to give our new strategies a fair opportunity to prove themselves.

Specific Concerns About Group Care

The Lack of Clarity About Group Care's Role
Under P.L. 96-272

Perhaps because of its drafters' orientation toward preventing placement, or perhaps because of oversight, P.L. 96-272 did not specify the role of group residential care. There are definitions and procedures for case management and a requirement of "reasonable effort." There are time frames, due process provisions, and a preference for the most family-like and least restrictive setting. But there is no specification of an affirmative role for foster family care and group care; even the use of foster family and group care as viable permanent placement strategy for some children goes relatively unrecognized.

When is group care the treatment of choice? How can it be used to maintain families? When does it become the permanent placement? How do children move from foster family or group care back home, or to new homes? Should the role of group care be cut back or expanded, given the changing profile of children referred?

The Lack of Understanding About the Effect of P.L. 96-272 on Group Care

Original evaluation criteria for success under P.L. 96-272 were (1) a reduced number of children shall be placed in foster family and group care, and (2) those who were so placed shall have shorter lengths of stay. The architects of the law were so convinced of the prevention and stability features that they proposed to cap Title IV-E (Maintenance) funds when Title IV-B (Prevention/Reunification/Stability) funds reached specified levels.

But at least as regards foster family and group care, P.L. 96-272 is having a different effect. We are indeed screening out those who can stay home, be reunified quickly, or be adopted, which is a positive development for those children, but, unfortunately, many difficult children still remain in substitute care. And now it appears that the juvenile justice and mental health systems are back-filling available beds in group care with their children who need more family-like, less restrictive settings.

The consequence is that the profile of children in foster homes and group homes today is that of more damaged, difficult-to-handle youngsters with many problems. These children need treatment, more intense, closer staffing ratios, and a wider range of services. More important for the present analysis, these children will probably stay longer, and cost more, not less. Also, as other social systems use foster care resources, and as an increased number of petitions are filed, we do not expect to see a drop in the use of foster care. We predict a leveling off of the decline in its use in jurisdictions where that has happened, and a slight increase where levels have been constant. The point here is not that this result is a poor or unintended outcome of our P.L. 96-272 efforts; it should be viewed as an expected outcome of our efforts.

The Lack of Funding

We have made the point that there is not a direct funding relationship between the prevention/reunification/permanency aspects of P.L. 96-272 and the need for foster care and group care. Indeed, the opposite may be true: the more successful we are with these strategies, the more costly substitute care may become. In this context, the automatic capping of Title IV-E makes no sense. It does not win more funds for IV-B efforts, and it hurts group care.

Another funding issue has to do with the federal Deficit Reduction Law (Gramm-Rudman-Hollings). Should we actually experience five years of step-down appropriations, social services will receive the greatest cuts. Title XX and Title IV-B are not protected; Title IV-E has been given special consideration and has limited protection.

The bleak future for funding will have an unknown influence on P.L. 96-272 efforts. Clearly, we will not return to the old days and the old ways, but we may not be able to develop fully the alternative services upon which we predicated the new policies.

Getting Funds to the Services

For some states, it has been a challenge to get service dollars to where the children are. Because of budget cuts, overwhelming public agency caseloads, and other factors, most funds are allocated to administrative, emergency protective services, and case management functions, leaving little for needed programs that most directly affect the children in care.

There is a critical need to develop family maintenance, reunification, and permanency placement programs with specific goals and tasks to move the children back home or to new homes.

For example, the creation of day treatment programs can both prevent placement in foster care and provide a method of transition home from a group care setting. Aftercare services need to be developed to provide continuity in care and to assure that reunification, adoption, or other placement endures.

Administration and case management are important and must be adequately funded, but so are the service aspects, whether they are developed and operated by public agencies or contracted out to the voluntary sector. Without adequate attention to all functions, P.L. 96-272 will never reach the potential envisioned.

Recognizing the Other Case Management

Case management (assessment, planning, and service broker-age) is the central feature in P.L. 96-272. For reasons already enu-merated, public agency case management is not always rigorous; often it is crisis management instead of case management. Fre-quently, after a placement is made, the caseworker relies on the placement agency for quarterly and other required reports and assessments. Many times, it falls to the group home or the vol-untary social services agency to do ad hoc case management. This situation happens partly because of the lack of resources in public agencies and partly because the person who lives with the child daily has more accurate information than the one who makes monthly visits.

Ad hoc case management appears to be an important dynamic, especially in cases where reunification or permanency planning is needed. If this is so, voluntary agencies should play a greater (perhaps even more formal) role in case management decisions, and incentives ought to be created for voluntary agencies to move the children in the desired directions (back home, to adoption, to day treatment, to independent living). Transition services are most likely going to be developed and maintained by the voluntary sector in the future, and this change should be encouraged.

One of the important debates in the future will be whether group care ought to be simply a service that is purchased as needed or whether group care facilities ought to develop a whole contin-uum of services, taking on specific roles of moving children home, to adoption, and so on.

A List of Challenges

From the foregoing discussion, it is apparent that much needs to be done to develop the role of group care in relation to P.L. 96-

272 and to assure that its activities support, not hinder, the new public policy.

Define the Role of Group Care

Defining the role of group care in P.L. 96-272 is primary among the tasks to be completed. Is it a last resort option? Is it temporary shelter? Is it for therapy or custodial maintenance? Is it more restrictive or less restrictive? For some children, a group living arrangement is more desirable and less threatening than living with a foster family. For some children (especially abused and neglected children) a group home is more restrictive and less family-like, but for some children (especially those in juvenile detention facilities or mental hospitals), the same home is less restrictive and more family-like. We need to recognize that group homes also work in the best interests of children and in the maintenance of families in crisis. We should not make the group home serve as something it is not, but it should be held accountable for what it is.

Provide Adequate Funding

Social service funding is always inadequate, and it appears that we can expect more cutbacks before augmentations. We should demand the adequate funding of foster family and group care at the same time that we create alternatives to it. We should argue for earlier placement in foster family and group care, when indicated, at the same time that we develop strategies to shorten the stays of other children in placement.

We need to recognize that our success with P.L. 96-272 strategies will leave a distillate of children in group care who have more intense service needs and will be more expensive to serve. We will need to establish and pay for therapeutic goals for these children, not just pay for their custodial maintenance.

We need to build incentives (i.e., reimbursement rates, allowable costs, purchase-of-service contract add-ons, and blended funding) to see that the children move in the directions intended under P.L. 96-272. Much in the current system discourages movement and encourages only minimum levels of care.

Support the Supporters

As foster parents and group homes attempt to respond to an increasingly more difficult population, they will need help. Beyond funding for adequate board rates and adequate staffing levels, training, respite, professional consultation, and other services will be necessary. Recognition of the need for professional support for foster parents, for example, has led to the creation of "Foster Family Agencies" in California and therapeutic foster family care in other states.

Public agencies, which have traditionally been supported by the private sector, will have to be aggressive in supporting (backing up) the voluntary agencies in the future. This change may bring real meaning to public-voluntary partnerships.

Develop Continua of Care

In jurisdictions where ad hoc case management is the rule rather than the exception, the participation of voluntary agency social workers should be formal and integrated. In such areas, voluntary agencies should be encouraged to develop a continuum of services for children that would assure the movement of children desired under P.L. 96-272.

Develop Information

To make certain that P.L. 96-272 is good public policy, we must conduct research and do program evaluations.[b] Data collection is not an extra; it can tell us that we are on course or warn us that we have gone astray in our effort to protect children. It certainly will help to provide in-course corrections in the uncharted waters of child welfare services.

---

[b]Data collection is not just a requirement of the public sector. Voluntary agencies and their associations also need to collect data on the children they serve. See, as an example, Fitzharris, Timothy L., *The Foster Children of California: Profiles of 10,000 Children in Residential Care*. Sacramento, California: Children's Services Foundation, 1985.

Conclusion

Group care has a viable role to play in the ongoing implementation of P.L. 96-272. It is a valuable effort to clarify and strengthen that role. There is much to be done to improve group care. Today— especially given fiscal constraints and other problems—group care's future appears stronger, although different, than ever before. The remaining challenge is to develop quality programs—stabilizing, preventive, and residential—that are suited to the needs of individual children. It remains for us to provide the necessary leadership to make P.L. 96-272 work—with a viable role for foster family and group care included—as intended.

6

The New Foster Care System: A Procrustean Bed?[1]

NAN DALE

N EW YORK STATE'S REFORM OF ITS OWN foster care system has had and is likely to continue to have a major effect on the rest of the country. Less than a year after New York enacted its Child Welfare Reform Act (CWRA),[2] the federal Adoption Assistance and Child Welfare Act of 1980[3] echoed many of the same themes and prescriptions for national reform. Through an array of federal fiscal incentives and procedural mandates, the principles of prevention and permanency are now expected to become the cornerstones of each state's child welfare system. As a condition of federal funding, all states are now required to develop services preventing unnecessary placement of children in foster care and reducing the length of stay of children in foster care by encouraging their speedy return to biological or adoptive parents. Highly specific in some areas, the federal law also allows for substantial local interpretation in implementation. Many states can be expected to pattern their response on the New York CWRA model, which not only meets but exceeds the federal requirements. Thus, it is particularly important to highlight problems in New York's system. This paper seeks to do just that.

Foster care reform in New York was long overdue. The reform effort has produced some good news and some bad news. The good news is that in the years immediately following the reform movement, the number of children in foster care was indeed reduced, the length of time in care was indeed shortened, and the number of adoptions was indeed increased.[4] The bad news is that the good news may not be entirely good. Coincident with the decrease in the number of children in care has come a startling increase in the number of homeless children.[5] With the increase in the number of adoptions has come some evidence of a troubling increase in the number of disrupted adoptions.[6] Along with the shortened length of stay in foster care has come a staggering number of child abuse and neglect reports. These reports include some child fatalities resulting from abuse or neglect by biological families with a history of abuse that resulted in at least one of their children having been placed in foster care.[7] Finally, in recent years, there has been an unanticipated upturn in the number of children in care that is fast approaching (and is now expected to exceed) pre-reform levels.

The linkage between the good news and the bad news is unclear. It is not certain that the desired reforms caused the undesired developments. The coincidence, however, is profoundly disturbing and should not be dismissed without examination.

In theory, prevention and permanency are unassailable public policies. As currently implemented in New York, however, there are significant undesired costs associated with achieving these goals. Mediating between the desired good and the risked evil requires the exercise of judgment, on a case-by-case basis. To the extent that good judgment is inhibited by misdirected or overly rigid regulations, the desired goals may be lost.

Against a background description of the New York child-care system, this paper examines four fundamental problems with the implementation of the New York Act (especially as implemented by New York City regulations) and the unintended consequences to the system: first, the regulations treat all children and all foster care agencies alike; second, the regulations disregard the need to bring together the various systems that serve children in out-of-home care; third, current theories of proper child care are carved into law, stifling growth and innovation in the field; and, finally, ends rather than means are used as the measure of accountability and quality of care.

Summary of the New York State
Child Welfare System

In New York, six separate state agencies oversee care given to children who must be removed from their families. One is the State Department of Social Services (SDSS), which, among other responsibilities, licenses all facilities and sets forth the regulatory framework for foster care. The actual placement, custody, and supervision of children in care fall to the local social service districts. Of the more than 50 such districts in the state, New York City is by far the largest, accounting for approximately 60 percent of the state's children in care.[8] The city's system is run by Special Services for Children (SSC), an arm of the Human Resources Administration (HRA), a mayoral agency.

Historically, New York City has looked to the voluntary sector to provide child-care services by entering into purchase-of-service contracts with approximately 60 individual agencies. These agencies offer a range of services from the least restrictive to the most restrictive: foster family homes (FBH), agency-operated boarding homes (AOBH), group homes, group residences, and institutions (including residential treatment centers). The sixth type of facility, the diagnostic reception center, provides short-term care while a thorough assessment of the child's needs is made and transfer to an appropriate placement is accomplished.

The Child Welfare Reform Act of 1979 was promulgated by New York State in response to well-publicized criticism of its foster care system. The act established a funding structure, standards, procedures, and reporting requirements designed to prevent the unnecessary placement of children into foster care and to quicken the pace with which children were discharged from care to their own homes or into adoptive homes. It was further mandated that children be placed in the least restrictive placement possible, consistent with their needs. The CWRA also authorized SDSS to levy financial sanctions on the social service districts for failure to comply with the regulations, with the further requirement that the local district pass the sanction along to the contract agency.

In October of that year, New York City's SSC began its assessment of the agencies with which they contract: the Program Assessment System (PAS). PAS measures an agency's performance on a large number of variables, including several (considered the most important by SSC) that measure the speed with which a child is discharged from an agency's program.[9] Some of the PAS requirements are substantially different from or in conflict with state regulations.

Over time, the voluntary child-care system has become increasingly dependent on public funds. Currently, approximately 90 percent of the operating costs of the voluntary agencies are paid for from public funds (34 percent federal; 33 percent state; 33 percent local district). As public funding increased, so did public regulation. The current debate is not about the propriety of that regulation, as some have suggested—it is about the form and substance of the control. The question is not, "Should the agencies be held accountable to standards and rules?" because the answer is clearly, and fairly indisputably, "Yes." The question is, "Are the standards and rules that have been set down beneficial to children and their families, and do they accomplish what they were intended to accomplish?" The answer to this second question is the subject of this paper.

The following analysis of the four major problem areas caused by New York's regulatory system is based in part on experiences at Children's Village over the past several years. Children's Village contracts with New York City and other social service districts to provide residential treatment, group home, foster boarding home, and adoption services.

Problem 1: The Regulations Treat All Children and All Foster Care Agencies Alike

Children Are Not Fungible

The pressing need for legislation to deal with growing public concern about foster care left little time for careful lines to be drawn among different types of children and the programs that serve them. The rules and regulations that resulted apply equally to *all children in the foster care system*, regardless of reason for placement or severity of symptoms. Yet important distinctions exist. The children in foster care and the programs that serve them are not all alike. Facilities that serve highly emotionally disturbed children have been most particularly affected by laws that do not acknowledge the distinctive needs of such troubled children. The importance of these distinctions is recognized for other purposes. Indeed, agencies are reimbursed at different rates dependent upon the severity of the disturbance or handicap of the children in care.

It is not commonly understood that foster care programs in New York serve children with a remarkable range of diagnoses.[10] For example, the children in any of the programs may be autistic, have substance abuse or sexual abuse problems, may be chronic fire-setters or be suicidal, or have medical conditions such as spina bifida. Their medical, intellectual, behavioral, and emotional problems run the gamut.

Approximately 10 percent of the total foster care population are in the most restrictive level of care—residential treatment centers, or, as they are officially labeled, institutions. Children in these facilities have either already had to be removed from previous foster homes, preadoptive homes, or other less restrictive placements, or they were too disturbed to risk such placements initially. Generally, the children arrive full of rage, destructiveness, or manifest depression. They may be suicidal; they nearly always feel worthless. Their parents, too, are generally in need of intensive individual and family therapy. These children are different from others in foster care because their own needs, usually in addition to the needs of their parents, require them to be in care. Yet timetables for release of children apply to these as to all others.

The "Home Within 24 Months" Rule

All children in foster care who have a discharge objective of return to home are expected to be discharged within 24 months, or, for children under age four, 18 months. Under the state system, a case-by-case review is conducted of children in care more than 24 months, and exceptions can be granted. Under the city system, a quota system is used. Thus, for example, an agency is rated unsatisfactory if 70 percent of its children (aged 5–11) have not been discharged to home within the 24-month time limit. As a result, agencies' success rates may be the inverse of the percentage of highly disturbed children in need of long-term care who are served by the agency.

The rigidity of the time frames spurs agencies to discharge children before they are ready and rewards "quitting." An agency that gives up because a child is particularly hard to reach, and discharges the child back home, will increase its score on PAS. An agency that keeps trying, by using different approaches until something works, will be statistically punished as too laggard.

The 24-month clock starts when the child is initially placed in the system. Therefore, if a child is transferred between agencies or programs, the clock keeps ticking, and the receiving agency is responsible for meeting the original discharge date. The only concession made by the state (but not the city) to the obvious problem this rule causes is a de minimis exception: discharge may be delayed until six months after the child is transferred. An agency accepting a child as a transfer from another program where the child did poorly may reasonably predict that it may be unsuccessful in discharging the child within the remaining time allotted for treatment.

At Children's Village, 76 percent of the children discharged in 1981–1982 were returned home; the majority were returned on time, some were not. The serious problem of meeting the deadline is illustrated by looking at the common characteristics of the children who were *not* discharged within the 24-month target date.[11]

Nearly a third of the children who were not discharged on time would have had to be discharged within *their first six months* at Children's Village to be in compliance with the regulation. The average length of time in care for these children before coming to Children's Village was 5.4 years. Some of the youngsters had been in as many as seven separate institutions or foster homes; some had been repeatedly hospitalized in psychiatric facilities (nearly half from three months to three years). They were sent to Children's Village only after other placements failed to meet their needs— including preparing the family to care successfully for the child. A new judgment was made—perhaps reluctantly. The *children's needs* demanded a structured and therapeutic environment with 24-hour supervision to deal with their emotional problems. They were referred to Children's Village so that they could be controlled, treated, and reunited with their families when sufficient health had been developed in both.

Work with the entire family system, including the extended family, is essential. Usually such intense work does not take place before a child comes into care in a treatment center atmosphere. Treatment progress is often erratic, and premature return home of the child can precipitate a return to old and destructive family patterns.

The "Adoption Within 27 Months" Rule

All children with a goal of adoption are expected to be adopted within 27 months from the date the goal was set. On the surface, this aim seems a reasonable and important standard—and it is. The problem arises when the regulation is applied to all children. Again, the state allows a case-by-case review and permits exceptions to be granted; the city uses a quota system, as described above. Both systems create a mind-set that strongly suggests that workers who fail to discharge children to adoption within the specified time have failed the children and are acting contrary to the mandate of the Child Welfare Reform Act.

Among the five adoption milestones of the city's PAS that must be met, the most difficult is that of placing children in a preadoptive home within 12 months of the time they are freed for adoption. Children who are transferred to a residential treatment center after the disruption of several foster homes or preadoptive placements are included in this 12-month rule. For children freed for adoption more than a year *before* this latest placement, the treatment time allowed is reduced to three months. This rule means that children who have *repeatedly* demonstrated that they are unable to live in the community or unable to form an attachment to previous adoptive parents—children who may be acutely disturbed, violent, or antisocial—now must be patched up within three months and returned to another preadoptive placement. Would we not better serve such children by providing intensive treatment before replacement?

At Children's Village, 93 percent of the children who were not adopted on time fell into a category that allowed three months to treat and place each child.[12] Eighty percent of these children had been referred to Children's Village as a result of disrupted foster or adoptive placements.

There are good arguments for holding on to the current rules for meeting adoption milestones. Adoption of special-needs children should not be compromised. But the data suggest that the current rules must be changed to accommodate the requirements of those children for whom treatment—not automatic re-place-ment—is the first and primary need.

The New York City Mayor's Task Force report, *Redirecting Foster Care*[13] (a document that helped to mold the city regulations), made a point of the differences within the system when it declared, ". . . [i]t would be misleading to call it [this report] comprehensive . . . we have not been able to address some problems . . . most notably: . . . children who are emotionally disturbed . . . ." This point was, however, never addressed; the recommendations and much of the spirit of the task force report became translated into regulations applicable to all children, including emotionally disturbed children. Good intentions were misshapen by the overriding desire to have an easily administered accountability system. Decision making, child by child, must rely heavily on the expertise and knowledge of trained social workers, not on rules labeled "one size fits all."

Problem 2: The Regulations Ignore the Need to Bring Together the Various Systems That Serve Children in Out-of-Home Care

Unification Among Systems Is Sorely Needed

Within the foster care system, children are treated as all alike, but among the various systems that provide care to children removed from their homes, children are described as though each system cared for a different species. Neither thoughtless conglomeration nor rigid categorization is correct.

There are approximately 45,000 children in group care in New York State. The vast majority of these children (84 percent) are served by the foster care system under the State Department of Social Services (SDSS). The remaining children are found among five other state agencies: the Division for Youth (DFY), the Office of Mental Health (OMH), the Office of Mental Retardation and Developmental Disabilities (OMRDD), the State Education Department (SED), and the Department of Health (DOH).[14] These agencies overlap in purpose, clientele, and services. Referral sources often make decisions based upon available bed space or the immediately precipitating reason for the child's removal from the home.

Overlap of Clientele and Services

Each of the six agencies runs its own continuum of services, resulting in a total of 25 different types of facilities serving the needs of children. DSS, DFY, OMH, and OMRDD each operate programs ranging from less restrictive to more restrictive. Important information from the New York State Department of Social Services confirms the observation that the boundaries between these systems have become significantly blurred. The SDSS report (released in April 1984) entitled *The Changing Characteristics of Children in Social Services Funded Group Residential Programs*[15] concluded that most children in group foster care have "serious mental and behavioral problems" that meet the criteria for services provided by other state agencies. For example, the report discloses that over 18 percent of SDSS children have psychiatric problems so serious that they qualify for residential OMH programs—mostly psychiatric hospitalization.

In a previous report, *Characteristics of Children in Out-of-Home Care*,[16] the Council on Children and Families analyzed the preliminary data. They showed, for example, that SDSS institution programs were reported to have 13 percent adjudicated delinquents, as contrasted with the 30 to 40 percent found in DFY facilities. Similarly, children who displayed severe psychiatric symptoms were found in the OMH, SDSS, or DFY systems.

These state agencies are inextricably interwoven. Placement in the least restrictive setting works within the microcosm of SDSS, but becomes a contradiction in terms within the macrocosm of all child-care systems. Children who move from an institution to a group home (both under the jurisdiction of SDSS) are viewed as having moved to a less restrictive level of care. But children who move from a locked, secure psychiatric hospital setting (under OMH) to an institution (under SDSS) are not regarded as having moved to a less restricted placement—they are simply new placements in foster care. Their previous placements, regardless of how restrictive or of how long duration, are irrelevant; for practical purposes, they never happened. Once children cross the boundary into foster care, they are assumed to be like all other children in foster care.

The underlying philosophy of each agency is described in its approach to care. For example, OMH works from a medical model. The primary problem is seen to be the child's own pathology. The need for long-term care is assumed. In contrast, the foster care SDSS system works from the perspective that the primary problem is one of temporary dislocation from the parent or guardian. Short-term care is expected. The system that nets the child defines the child. Labels become firmly affixed, creating their own self-fulfilling prophecies. A disturbed child with a moderately low IQ who has been somehow channeled to an OMRDD facility will forever carry the primary diagnosis of "retarded." If this same child had been initially sent to an SDSS treatment center, he or she may well have been diagnosed as "emotionally disturbed"; the retardation, if mentioned, would have been considered as a secondary condition.

Treatment plans and discharge goals evolve within the philosophy of the setting. The type of services offered to both child and family as well as the length of service are a direct result of the type of facility. For example, in OMH, little work is expected to be done with the child's family, and access to adoption for children in this system is severely limited. The foster care system, however, promotes and regulates substantial family work in preparation for the child's return to the family. Such arbitrary distinctions do not work in the best interests of the children, their families, or the agencies that serve them.

"Streamlining," it is argued, of the kinds of children served by each of the six systems would be beneficial. Surprisingly, such specialization in care may be undesirable because children should not—and cannot—be so easily labeled. Children may act out despair and hurt in delinquent behavior on Monday . . . suicide attempts on Tuesday. Retardation or a physical handicap may be contributing to their behavior, or these may be only side issues. Furthermore, there is substantial evidence that children improve more readily when they are exposed to a more heterogeneous mixture of their peers. For example, pathologically depressed or withdrawn children will often respond more quickly when placed in a mixed group of children, including children who are more aggressive or act out more. Children's problems simply cannot be partitioned into "child-centered" vs. "family-centered," or "medical" vs. "environmental." It may well be counterproductive to encourage the system to develop agencies that handle and serve only one type of youngster.

Cooperation among all of the child-care systems must be instituted so that beds will be made available to fit the children, not the other way around. At the very least, flexibility must be added to the SDSS regulations to accommodate the actual treatment needs of the children being served, but, finally, some unification among the systems is desperately needed.

Within the foster care system, the sometimes counterfeit distinctions are evident.

Program Example

Children's Village, with the help of private funds, opened a specialized cottage for work with children who were too disturbed to remain in the regular cottages. Without this unit, every child in it would have to be (under OMH) in a psychiatric hospital setting that would increase the length of time out of the home and cost nearly six times as much. Ironically, under PAS, Children's Village will be penalized for providing this innovative program because the children are unlikely to be ready for discharge within the SDSS foster care time frames permitted. No such time limits exist in OMH.

Even more paradoxical, Children's Village is converting one cottage to a program under the direct auspices of OMH. Certain children from the campus will be transferred to this new program. Before the transfer, these children would have been required to be discharged within 24 months. From the day of transfer, they will be regarded as children in need of long-term care.

Problem 3: Current Theory Is Carved into Law

There Is No One Right Answer

New York State and City regulations enact static views of child-care and casework services. They do so by mandating methods of treatment and evaluating an agency's compliance. For example, the city's Program Assessment System (PAS), in a variation of the state's requirement, assesses family casework by counting both the number of social worker contacts with the family and the number of such visits in the family's home. The theory is that a specified number of home visits improves the quality of family work and hastens the discharge of the child back home. This theory is not supported by evidence and may be wrong. It is, however, enshrined in city and state regulations, and agencies are evaluated (and ranked) according to their success in carrying out this approach to casework. A system that recognizes only one right answer cuts off debate and stifles creativity in the field.

Program Example

Children's Village instituted a special program—Project IMPACT—for parents and their children in cases where the child had been placed in the agency's care as a result of parental abuse, or where there was substantial reason to believe that a high-risk situation existed in the home. The program consists of a minimum of fourteen 2½-hour sessions at various times—mostly nights and weekends. The sessions include individual, family, and multifamily therapy; training in parenting skills; and the creation of long-term parent and neighborhood support groups.

Parents previously thought of as hard to reach have responded extraordinarily well to this program. It is far more intensive, effective, and time-consuming than the home visits required by regulation. Nonetheless, the work and accomplishments will be rated unsatisfactory if the worker does not also make the required home visits during the same time period. In the real world, the worker cannot be expected to do both. Thus, the regulation that mandates a fixed number of home visits undermines a successful, innovative approach to the treatment of high-risk families.

The rigidity of the casework requirements also has a peculiar antifamily reverberation. Families, too, are treated as though they were all the same. If they do not respond within the mandated time periods, caseworkers are expected to move to sever parental rights so that it may be possible for the child to be adopted. The requirements leave little room for consideration of the depth of attachment to a parent or sibling, the child's feelings about adoption, and so forth. There is indeed probably a time when all the king's horses and all the king's men cannot put a family back together again, and it is fair to argue that too many social workers have failed to recognize that juncture, thereby losing opportunities for an alternative permanent home for some children. The CWRA has rightfully sought to correct our course—but overcorrections have been made. The pressure on agencies to follow a preset metronome of casework requirements may result in children permanently exiled from any family connection. Obviously, this kind of permanency is not what the CWRA is all about.

In a rigid system, ingenuity is limited to those approaches that fit within a predetermined accountability structure. By nature, these approaches are conservative and traditional. Experiments in organization, therapy, and program can only take place in an atmosphere that supports a reasonable level of risk-taking. New York's regulations have had a chilling effect on creative solutions to difficult treatment issues. Adjustments are necessary if the system and individual agencies are to be encouraged to try new and different approaches. Evaluation and accountability need not be sacrificed in the process. For example, to return to the program examples above, city or state evaluators could exempt certain cases from current casework requirements if the family were engaged in an *approved* alternative program. In exchange, the agency could be required to report on the results of the program, and government officials could disseminate information about successful programs for replication elsewhere. In such a design, agencies would be encouraged to search for new approaches, and the entire field of child welfare would benefit.

Problem 4: Ends, Not Means, Are Used as the Measure of Quality of Care

This problem is the consequence of the three problem areas already discussed. The reasoning is as follows: fungible children are served by like agencies with proven casework methods. Therefore, one can measure the quality of care and agency success by comparing the end result; that is, length of time to discharge.

A conclusion based upon false premises is a false conclusion. New York's rules and regulations prescribe the measurement of ends, not means. They rely upon statistics such as speed of discharge from care, number of home visits made, and number of children adopted. They do not measure quality of treatment. An agency can actually improve its standing by degrading the quality of care it provides—by releasing children still in need of treatment, or by prematurely placing children in adoptive homes.

Evaluation based upon ends, rather than means, has also caused a number of unintended consequences. These have been mentioned earlier, but deserve separate consideration. They include these elements:

1. There is a disincentive for agencies to accept the most difficult children, children from highly disturbed families, or children transferred from other agencies. When quality is measured by success in discharging a child back home or out of the system, very difficult-to-treat children become potential liabilities.

2. There is a disincentive for agencies to provide a continuum of services (e.g., residential treatment, group homes, and foster homes all run by one agency), because a transfer within the agency is calculated against the agency. This arrangement is bad policy because children who can move within a single agency may retain peer relations and caseworker contacts that will have to be severed when children are sent to another agency. Such a break, in itself, can set back treatment progress.

3. There is a disincentive for agencies to set up innovative programs that might enable children to remain in their current placement (rather than be transferred to a more restrictive setting) but may prolong their overall stay.

Most disturbing of all, the current method of evaluation may be responsible for the inappropriate and even dangerous discharge from foster care of many children. No attention has been paid to what happens to a child once placed out of the system—discharge alone has been the goal. Public policy has been made without consideration of critically important data. To invent rigid rules for the discharge of children without any evaluation of what happens to the children discharged is, at the very least, irresponsible.

One of the frequent reasons for the placement of children in foster care is child abuse. For children who have suffered such abuse, returning home before both the child and family are ready may place the child in serious jeopardy. In the State Department of Social Services report, *1983 Foster Care Trends in New York State*,[17] it is estimated that 60 percent to 80 percent of all of the children in foster care have been abused or neglected. According to the Mayor's Task Force Report on Child Abuse and Neglect in New York City, of November 21, 1983, the total number of reported child abuse and neglect cases has been steadily increasing.[18] The report also indicated that, in 20 percent of the families where there was a child fatality resulting from abuse or neglect, at least one child in the family had been in foster care placement before the child died. In 13 percent of the families, the child who was placed is the child who later died from abuse or neglect after being returned home.

Similarly, great damage can be inflicted on children who have no hope of returning to their biological parents when adoption is regarded as the only other acceptable end result. After years of living as foster parent and foster child, circumstances may change, and the child may become free for adoption. Happily, many foster parents then adopt the child that they have come to know and love. For a variety of reasons, some do not want to adopt although they often are willing and eager to continue to care for the children until they reach the age of majority, and frequently into adulthood. Under the new regulations, these children must now be re-placed into preadoptive homes whether they want to or not. Children are often referred to Children's Village after having been torn from the only home they have ever known—all in the name of permanency.

Permanency, the return of children to their own families or to adoptive homes, is commendable public policy. But blind adherence is not progress, it is simply lack of vision. A system that promotes such devotion by rewarding the ends (prompt discharge of children) without giving equal time to the means (the quality of care and treatment delivered) ought to be changed.

Improvement in the speed with which children are discharged out of the system may well represent the system's ultimate failure with respect to hundreds of children. Certainly, without any information about what happened to the children discharged, discharge alone represents no triumph in the provision of quality care.

Conclusion

In New York, the CWRA and the related regulations have improved and remolded the foster care system in many beneficial ways, but they have also created problems so serious that they threaten to undermine the reform. We have gone too far.

Arguments for easy-to-administer standards must fall when confronted by the actualities of troubled children, whose current problems cannot be adequately resolved and whose future potential cannot be adequately realized within the wooden inflexibilities of such standards. Although compliance thresholds have some appeal as simple, prophylactic guidelines, the facts suggest that fixed discharge standards are not in the best interests of many of the children. Irrevocable decisions may turn into everlasting regret for children who have too little control over their own destinies and whose lives are shaped by our decisions on their behalf.

The fervor of the present movement to reduce foster care is reminiscent of the policy of deinstitutionalization of adult mental patients. In that case, yesterday's solution has emerged as today's nightmare. We appear to have learned little from that experience.

H.L. Mencken is reported to have said, "For every complex problem, there is a solution which is simple, elegant, and wrong." These are complex problems—both those that underlie the need for foster care and foster care itself. It may be that the solutions will be neither simple nor elegant. It is beyond the scope of this paper to prescribe them. It is the main thesis of this paper to proclaim the need for them. Regulations ought to serve to improve the balance—not merely the legal balance between the duties of agencies and their performance under the law, but, more important, the balance between the aspirations of the agencies on behalf of the children and their families and the *quality* of the success with which they meet them.

Flexibility must be incorporated into the new laws and regulations to permit the varying needs of the system to be met without undue strain. We should not be designing a Procrustean bed for our children, requiring us to cut or stretch them in order to fit them to inflexible rules.

Notes

1. An earlier version of this article was published, under the same title, in *The Children's Village Bulletin*, Volume VII, No. 1, Winter 1983/1984.

2. The Child Welfare Reform Act of New York State.

3. The Adoption Assistance and Child Welfare Act of 1980. P.L. 96-272, 42 U.S.C. §620 et seq. and 670 et seq.

4. *Foster Care 1984*. A Report on the Implementation of the Recommendations of the Mayor's Task Force on Foster Care, pp. 1 and 2; Citizens' Committee for Children of New York, Inc. *Foster Care in New York City: Children who are experiencing a major planning problem or service delay*. September 1984.

5. Assemblyman Albert Vann's "reports to the people" summarized hearings in 1983 before his Committee on Children and Families. Vann concluded that "the problem of the homeless youth was an acute one, with no less than 15,000 such youngsters in New York City alone. Many of these young people have recently been released from foster care . . . "; *Additional sources:* As reported in Human Resources Administration. *Homeless Youth in New York City Municipal Shelter System, Demographic Profile I*. 1984, 27 percent of the homeless youth appearing in City shelters were formerly in foster care; *See also: 7,000 Homeless Children: The Crisis Continues*. The Third Report on Homeless Families with Children in Temporary Shelter by Citizens' Committee for Children of New York, Inc., October 1984; Runaway and Homeless Youth Advocacy Project. *A Review of the Status of Post-Foster Care Youth*. 1982; *Homeless Youth in New York City; Nowhere to Turn* (with Coalition for the Homeless and Runaway and Homeless Youth Advocacy Project), 1983.

6. For a discussion of the issue of adoption disruptions for special-needs children, see *Special Needs Adoption, Findings of Recent Research on the Experiences of Families Who Adopt*. Proceedings of a Research Utilization Workshop. Community Council of Greater New York in December, 1983, pp. 23, 24; Meezan, William. Toward an expanded role for adoption services. In Child Welfare, Current Dilemmas, Future Directions. Brenda McGowan and William Meezan (eds.), Itasca, Illinois: F.E. Peacock Publishers, Inc., 1983, pp. 462–463.

7. *Foster Care 1984*. A Report on the Implementation of the Recommendations of the Mayor's Task Force on Foster Care, p. 4; Mayor's Task Force on Child Abuse and Neglect. *More Can Be Done to Protect Children in New York City: An Agenda for the Eighties*. 1980; Mayor's Task Force on Child Abuse and Neglect. *Report on the Preliminary Study of Child Fatalities in New York City*. 1983.

8. See *Foster Care Trends in New York State*. New York Department of Social Services. June 1982.

9. For a review on the New York City foster care system, contract specifics, and the Program Assessment System (PAS), see Human Resources Administration/ Special Services for Children reports to Board of Estimate 1981, 1982, 1983, 1984.

10. For a general presentation of the distribution and characteristics of children in out-of-home care and a description of the services provided, see *Characteristics of Children in Out-of-Home Care*; New York State Council on Children and Families. January 1984, or *The Changing Characteristics of Children in Social Services Funded Group Residential Programs*, 1983; New York State Department of Social Services. Division of Family and Children's Services, Bureau of Resource Management. April 19, 1984.

11. The data are taken from the six months ending December 31, 1982; audited by Special Services for Children for that year's Program Assessment System.

12. The six months allowed at the time of this data analysis has now been reduced to three months in the 1983–84 version of PAS.

13. Mayor's Task Force Report on Foster Care. *Redirecting Foster Care*, 1980.

14. See note 10 above.

15. See note 10 above.

16. See note 10 above.

17. New York State Department of Social Services. *Foster Care Trends in New York State*. 1982 and 1983.

18. See note 7 above.

7

Group Care Survival: Learning from the Experience of the Hospital Field

GERALD G. HICKS

GROUP CARE IS BEING ATTACKED BY those who believe that the residential environment does not prepare children to live in families or in the community. They believe that children in group care adapt only to the structure of an institution and that this experience does not translate to community settings. Their solution, therefore, is that all institutions should be closed and children should receive care in their own homes or in a less restrictive setting than a residential treatment center. The proponents of less restrictive settings argue that all residential treatment can be avoided through family preservation programs, or, if removal from home is absolutely necessary, the most intrusive type of care should be a therapeutic foster family setting. Still others attacking residential treatment centers argue that care costing $50,000 or more per year per child cannot be afforded when it is difficult to show that this treatment is highly successful in resolving the problems that required placement. They contend that we should invest in placing children in residential treatment centers only if we can show a high probability of cure of the presenting problems.

Based on these attacks, the question is whether residential treatment will continue, and, if it continues, what it must do to survive. Residential treatment centers will survive if some rather

131

dramatic changes are made in the operation of such programs to enable the field of group care to serve children better. The focus of this paper is on how group care facilities should consider restructuring their programs and strengthening their internal operations to move beyond survival. The hospital field has undergone a significant redirection over the past ten years, and there are lessons to be learned from these changes that are applicable to group care for children. The redirections include marketing of services necessitated by the effect of external forces, extending the continuum of programs and services, strengthening the operational management of programs to permit measurement of their effectiveness, diversification of funding, and improved community understanding of programs.

Learning from the Hospital Field

Although no one would propose that the community hospital and the children's residential treatment facility are alike, there are many similarities between the two systems. Both occupy similar positions in a continuum of services. In the health industry, on one end of the continuum, there are prevention programs such as immunization, testing for water quality, and food and drug testing; then, moving along the continuum, with systems of health screening, outpatient preventive physical examinations, outpatient diagnostic and surgical services, and clinical treatment of disease; and, finally, at the most intensive end of the continuum, inpatient hospital services for only the most critically ill. Similarly, in the children's services arena, there is a broad range of services in the continuum, beginning with primary prevention programs such as licensing and accreditation, community education on child abuse and neglect, and parent education on child development. Then we move into family-based intervention programs such as parenting aides, homemaker services, foster grandparents, family counseling, and substance abuse treatment; there is also alternative family-based child care, such as foster family care, family group home care, and family therapy homes. Children's residential services in their multiple configurations are the most intensive, structured, and costly programs, placing them in the same relative position in a spectrum of services as hospitals in the health field.

Comparisons of Hospitals to Children's Residential Treatment

Comparison of children's residential services to community hospitals reveals many similarities. As noted above, both are at the most intensive end of the continuum. Both are used when less structured and restrictive programs are inappropriate. Both are needed services, critical to their respective service continua, and provide the necessary intensive intervention required at that point in the life of the individual. Both require facilities and equipment that necessitate intensive investment of capital, and both are extremely labor-intensive in their staff-to-patient ratios in order to carry out the rehabilitation of the individual. Both are community institutions and, as such, have to interpret continually to the community their need for community support.

What Hospitals Learned

Consider how hospitals operated ten years ago. Admission to the hospital was strictly a decision between the doctor and the patient. The doctor decided that you needed gall bladder surgery, for example. You entered the hospital, various tests were run, and several days later the surgery was performed. Several days later still, not counting weekends, you were discharged. If for any reason the doctor became unavailable for several days, your hospitalization was extended until his or her return. There was no interference from the insurance company who insured you or from utilization review teams. No second opinion was necessary; your personal physician always knew best. The hospital operated under the control of the physicians and surgeons who admitted patients, and the hospital costs were divided among those paying patients admitted. Hospitals were numerous and always full. The various hospitals in every community were almost identical to each other, with a full range of medical, surgical, pediatric, and diagnostic services.

Whenever new construction was needed to expand or remodel, the community was solicited for contributions to underwrite the cost, and the remaining costs were provided under federal funding, Hill-Burton grants, or included in the paying patients' bills. As citizens, most of us rather fearfully expected to spend some time in the community hospital, but thought little of leaving for treatment in a distant city or at a specialty hospital. Because hospitals were always full, elective hospitalization usually required a wait for an opening. Most individuals were not really concerned about the costs of insurance, as escalating expense was picked up by one's employer as a fringe benefit. Hospitals received little community review and were often inefficiently operated.

Current Children's Residential Services

Viewing children's group care facilities as they operate today, we see that they range from facilities that provide an intensive therapeutic milieu for treatment of severely disturbed children to facilities that have only minimal professional services for children who might more appropriately be placed in family settings.

Once admitted to any of them, children often stay for extended periods of time because they adjust well, and the social work staff members are unable to see the need for rapid movement to a family setting, or intensive work with the biological families so the children can be returned home. Lengths of care are often counted in years rather than months.

Children's group facilities, like hospitals, have always had the ability to appeal to the community for capital. When a new facility or remodeling of an old facility becomes necessary, the community is solicited for funds and usually responds with great generosity out of concern for poor, unfortunate children. Operational costs are provided by government agencies with overworked staff members willing, too often, to place a child and then give only modest input to case progress. Most government social workers are not held accountable for the money spent. High costs, therefore, are of little concern.

The general community is also usually unaware of group care problems. These "unfortunate children" are usually someone else's children, and as long as there are no major disasters or scandals at the facility, they remain unnoticed. Licensing in many areas of the country is a toothless tiger that does little to protect children. Consequently, group facilities have always had their beds full and seldom, if ever, went out of business. Licensing seldom, if ever, closes a program, and apart from loss of a license, most group care agencies are able to find a referral source no matter how questionable the program.

Hospitals Change Their Direction

It appears clear, therefore, that the position of residential group care today is in many ways similar to the community hospital as it operated ten years ago. Community hospitals have undergone significant changes in the last few years. The hospitals that once duplicated services now have empty beds and have been forced by medical planning agencies to avoid duplication of services by specializing. The hospital's exclusive not-for-profit territory has been invaded by for-profit services such as emergency treatment clinics, diagnostic laboratories, and for-profit hospitals.

In addition, external forces such as insurance companies and the government, via Medicaid and Medicare, have forced cost containment through the limitation of insurance coverages and the introduction of diagnostically related groups that control treatment and length of care. As a result of competition from other hospitals and from private organizations external to the hospital community, hospitals have moved to market their services through advertising. They have also developed within their hospital structures a continuum of services that were foreign to hospitals ten years ago. These include outpatient clinics, nursing homes, day care facilities, professional office leasing, wellness centers, and many other new enterprises to diversify their funding base. We have also seen mergers of hospitals and the formation of large corporate conglomerates to increase administrative efficiency. And, last but not least, we have observed a tremendously powerful hospital lobby geared to gain governmental and insurance company support for payment of full costs.

What the hospitals have found is that the availability of hospital beds has far outstripped the need for their service, and the amount of money available to them has, therefore, been diminished. Communities have found alternatives to their traditional hospital services. Hospitals have, in fact, gone bankrupt, have silently closed their doors, or have restructured to meet community needs.

Changes Needed in Children's Residential Services

Children's group care services can learn from the experience of hospitals. It is clear that external forces will increasingly dictate the future of group care as they have dictated the future of hospitals. Group care programs are no longer reliant on the charitable dollar for the operation of their programs. They are increasingly reliant on insurance income and governmental funding as primary funding sources. This change has moved them away from the historical isolation of private residential facilities and requires them to assume a market strategy that recognizes the need for change and the importance that must be placed on selling residential group care as a concept to the community and to governmental funding bodies. Even more dramatic needs to shift program direction will arise during the next ten years as forces for change increase in intensity and gain the political power to force changes in residential treatment. If group care facilities fail to measure and react to these forces, they, like the hospitals that have not responded to change, will be forced to close their doors.

Residential treatment agencies, like hospitals at the intensive end of a continuum of services, will be confronted with questions regarding whether their services are actually needed, with competition from rival providers, including the profit sector, and from new alternatives to residential treatment not yet thought of. External governmental demands will have a profound effect on overall direction. The only way to assure that this important service to children can continue is through critical analysis of the current position of group care within the children's continuum and willingness to change direction consistent with these new forces.

Consideration should be given to a most important fact. Residential treatment facilities that provide only a simple residential treatment program and have not broadened their service delivery system into a spectrum of programs including day treatment, intensive foster family care, independent living, and perhaps even adoption services, will find themselves isolated by the community and funding sources; their singular focus will be perceived as evidence of their unwillingness to change. Only the rare residential treatment facility that considers itself in the same class as the Mayo and Sloan-Kettering clinics of the hospital field will survive this redirection.

Residential treatment services must see themselves at the same point in the continuum of services as intensive, and therefore expensive, hospitals. The residential treatment program within agencies' expanded continuum must be a total treatment milieu. Educational and recreational resources to the children must be available on site. No longer will children be able to use community resources, because the high levels of disturbance of these children upon admission will require that intensive effort be put into redirection before they are prepared for community activities. When they are ready for community activities, they will no longer need intensive residential treatment. It follows from this fact that summer lags in services will no longer be permissible, and it will be the task of treatment facilities to assist children admitted on an intensive, short-term basis until they can move into a less restrictive and less costly system. This purpose means also that agencies must develop a continuum of services within their own structure or through compatible relationships with other organizations to provide a range of services. Such expansion permits not only a necessary continuum of programming, but a better method for measuring outcomes. The agency will be able to follow children beyond the intensive treatment phase into alternative care and produce documentation that these interventions have been successful.

Increasingly, geographic proximity will be a critical factor in decision making by community and government sources on placement of children. As movement along a continuum and work with families of children toward permanency planning are intensified, it is an inherent necessity that staff members be constantly available to children and their families. Geographic proximity, therefore, becomes necessary. Those residential treatment facilities serving children from multiple states or from very broad geographic areas within a state are in particular peril.

Residential treatment facilities must increasingly be able to show that they have been successful in their treatment of children, and that the results they observe as children move through the continuum reinforce the evidence that there was a profound change in the child as a result of the intervention. Agencies, therefore, must be forced to avoid discharging children before completion of treatment. Stated in another way, when a group care facility admits a child, it is expected that it will be able to treat the child successfully and that it has a responsibility, having intervened, to stay with the child until successful results are obtained.

External forces will demand documentation of results in previous placements of children and cost per child per placement, rather than per diem cost. That is, a $100 per day program that lasts for one year costs $36,500, but a program that costs $27,000 per placement, by keeping a child six months, may be more attractive, although the cost is actually $150 per day.

External forces will increasingly require external review of programs, beyond their own internal reviews. Accreditation by the Joint Committee on Accreditation of Hospitals (JCAH) has long been the norm for hospitals, and accreditation by the Council on Accreditation (COA) will be the norm for children's residential facilities within the next ten years. Accreditation, in fact, will give some agencies time to carry out treatment by acting as a counterbalance to the many external reviews by various government funding sources, foundations, and interest groups.

The best marketing of a sound program of residential treatment is through community understanding of the purposes of residential treatment and the success that a particular program has in providing that service. Glossy brochures and sophisticated statements about programs will increasingly be replaced with measures of children's after-placement successes or failures.

In view of this relationship with the community and the government, agencies will see the need for a public relations and community governmental relations function. Executives of residential treatment agencies must free time to represent their agencies in the community and to work with both state and local residential care associations. Like all businesses, including hospitals, children's residential agencies must realize that lobbying for financial support is as much a part of the responsibilities of the executive as is the hiring of the staff.

Funding for residential treatment over the next few years will be increasingly problematic and will require further diversification of funding sources to include not only government sources and insurances, but reliance on privately developed dollars. This requirement becomes obvious when one looks at time lags and underfunding by governmental agencies for children who are clearly their responsibility. An agency that relies completely on insurance or governmental sources for funding will significantly reduce its economic capability to provide comprehensive services. Government and insurance funds will never provide 100 percent of current costs, including money to try new service approaches. Agencies should lobby to avoid subsidizing the cost of care that government should legitimately pay, but they will need separate additional funds that can be obtained only from private fund development to try new program experiments, to develop additional practical research and evaluation capability, and to improve the quality, quantity, and stability of the professional staff. Intensive and, therefore, expensive procedures for selection and development of staff members will never be underwritten with government funds.

The complexity of programmatic structures, funding sources, and management responsibilities will increasingly force small agencies to merge with larger organizations to provide a continuum of services. Cost effectiveness will be perceived as a primary responsibility of all operations, and, in fact, if cost efficiency is lacking, the intrusion of the for-profit organizations into the field will increase. They will appear to operate efficiently, and government will prefer purchasing from them. The point here is the proprietaries' focus on costs and cost control. Historically, residential care has been program-focused, with little real attention given to enhancing management efficiency. What is needed is advanced management training for professionals in child care. To compete with business majors, child-care professionals must give as much priority to effective management as to the program.

As noted earlier, external funding sources in the community will call for external review, which will proliferate beyond current licensing to include every organization from whom a group care facility receives funds (United Ways, government agencies, insurance companies, and foundations). The support for accreditation can help, however, to offset this proliferation. If we can gain national support for an external accreditation process, foundations, governmental agencies, and United Ways may accept these studies as alternatives to their individual evaluations.

As agencies strengthen their fund development programs, they will have to bear in mind the amount of money to be set aside for operational purposes and the amount to be used for capital construction. Funds for capital construction will be particularly hard to obtain as the competition increases for all charitable dollars.

Agencies must constantly evaluate the effectiveness of their treatment methodologies and their management styles and move increasingly toward more efficient measures to control cost and to gain public acceptability. It seems an inherent part of this that children's residential services rid the field of marginal operators who hurt everyone's children and the system itself. Professionals must fight for good accreditation practices, strong licensing, and equitable external review programs, which will profoundly enhance the delivery of quality services.

Now is the time to examine these and other policy issues that we must all confront. Each agency must develop a specific long-range plan that takes into consideration the relative position of that agency within its community, the needs of services within that community, and the position that the agency can achieve and retain over ensuing years.

To do this, an agency must measure its support base within its community and how this base will be retained. It must also evaluate the support base of other similar agencies and, whenever possible, identify together how they will coordinate to cover needed services while avoiding costly duplication. Furthermore, they must together assess the service needs of their community and how their areas of expertise can respond to them, and conduct a critical analysis of current and future funding sources. Because of the heavy reliance of voluntary agencies on governmental dollars, public officials must be included in the planning. The often tedious but essential participation of public and private citizen leaders in the planning process yields strong community support. High participation will result in a high investment in the future.

Summary

In this paper, we have suggested that there is much that group care agencies can learn from the experiences of community hospitals. Both are intensive services within a continuum of services. Both are increasingly being compelled to change by external forces, and both must plan to diversify and redirect their programs in the coming years.

We have urged that voluntary group care facilities analyze the market for their services, diversify their programs, respond to their geographic community's needs, and show results from the care that they provide. A thorough look by each agency at what has happened to hospitals in its community and then the development of a long-range plan that identifies the position of the agency in the community and the community's future need for service will bring successful participation by the community in future planning, and the community's investment in the agency's future.

Part 3

Organizational and Program Approaches Considering Children's Needs

8

Parental Involvement in Children's Residential Treatment: From Preplacement to Aftercare[a]

JEFFREY M. JENSON
JAMES K. WHITTAKER

RESIDENTIAL TREATMENT PROGRAMS FOR CHILDREN AND YOUTH have historically concentrated on the child in placement with little regard for the parents' ability to assist in the treatment or community reentry process [Laird 1979; Letulle 1979]. Traditionally, when out-of-home placement became necessary, interventions in child welfare focused on the removal of the child from his or her family and subsequent placement in a residential facility. For a variety of reasons, parents received little assistance or encouragement from residential agencies to become actively involved in their child's treatment program [Whittaker 1979].

Major reforms in child welfare policy and practice in the past five years have increased parental participation in children's residential treatment services. Family involvement in out-of-home care has become an important component of permanency planning efforts for children and youth [Blumenthal and Weinberg 1984]. Legislative initiatives and empirical evidence that recognize the importance of family involvement in out-of-home placement have

[a]Reprinted with permission from *Child and Youth Services Review*, Volume 9, Copyright 1987, Pergamon Press plc.

motivated residential facilities to develop strategies that actively involve parents in the preplacement, treatment, and aftercare phases of children's residential care. This paper identifies the rationale for involving families in residential services and reviews practice innovations being used by treatment facilities to encourage family participation in children's out-of-home placement. Characteristics of families with children in placement and barriers to family participation are outlined. The final section identifies important questions and the research necessary to increase family involvement in children's residential treatment.

Rationale for Family Involvement

Philosophical and Theoretical Perspectives

The importance of the family in a child's development is a little-disputed fact. Children express a basic need to be loved and to form meaningful attachments to parents at an early age [Bowlby 1969]. The bond between child and parent has a pervasive and long-lasting influence on a young person's growth and socialization [Blumenthal and Weinberg 1984; Hess 1982].

A stable environment and a continuous relationship with family members are essential components in the normal development of a child. Separation can be a painful and damaging experience for children placed in out-of-home care. Children quickly lose their sense of identity and self-concept when communication with their biological parents is suddenly altered or terminated [Colon 1978; Laird 1979]. Similarly, studies indicate that parents frequently experience depression and feelings of guilt and failure when a child is removed from the home [Jenkins and Norman 1975]. The bond uniting parents and child does not dissolve when a child is placed in residential care. Ignoring the contributions that family members can make to a child's treatment process may intensify feelings of self-doubt, depression, and guilt for children and parents.

Legislation and Public Policy

Permanency planning, defined by Maluccio and Fein [1983] as "the process of taking prompt, decisive action to maintain children in their own homes or place them permanently with other families" (p. 195), is an important factor in increasing family involvement in treatment services. The emergence of permanency planning in child welfare in the 1970s focused attention on three major issues: (a) the unnecessary removal of children from their biological parents, (b) the lack of effort made to maintain contact between children removed from the home and biological parents, and (c) the frequent movement of children from one out-of-home placement to another [Cox and Cox 1985]. Originally conceived as a strategy most appropriate to foster family care, permanency planning expanded in the early 1980s as an effective method of working with children placed in residential facilities [Maluccio et al. 1980; Maluccio and Whittaker in press].

The problems addressed in the permanency planning movement culminated in the passage of the Adoption Assistance and Child Welfare Act of 1980 (P.L. 96-272). This act requires states to provide careful assessment and extensive casework in order to maintain children with their own families or make alternative permanent plans when parents cannot care for their child. The language and intent of P.L. 96-272 encourage residential treatment facilities to shift their focus from child-centered care to family care. Residential facilities have begun to view treatment services as temporary interventions that must incorporate elements of a child's home and community life into the treatment process in order to provide effective care [Ainsworth and Fulcher 1981; Anglin 1985; Whittaker in press]. The development of guidelines by residential agencies that define parental rights, responsibilities, and opportunities for direct involvement and the systematic participation in children's treatment and aftercare processes have been positive results of permanency planning and legislative initiatives (cf. Blumenthal and Weinberg [1984]).

Empirical Evidence

Children often respond positively to specific treatment strategies during placement in a residential program; however, follow-up studies of children placed in out-of-home care indicate that positive behavioral changes are seldom maintained following treatment [Allerhand et al. 1966; Jones et al. 1981; Taylor and Alpert

1973]. Young people often return to their former behavior patterns upon release, failing to generalize changes accomplished during treatment to their natural environments.

These findings have important implications for program development in children's residential care. Increasingly, treatment efforts have begun to focus on environmental or ecological factors that appear to be important determinants of a child's successful long-term adjustment [Lewis 1982; Whittaker and Maluccio in press]. Such factors include the availability of support from family and peer networks and the presence of supportive environments in school and the community at the time of discharge [Coates et al. 1978; Montgomery and Van Fleet 1978; Oxley 1977].

Parental involvement and family support in the treatment process for children and youth removed from their homes are among the strongest predictors of a child's ability to adapt successfully to the community following placement [Fanshel 1975; Rowe et al. 1984; Taylor and Alpert 1973]. Residential agencies must develop closer links to families and other elements of the community. The increased involvement of families in treatment processes and the development of social support networks for children in the community might enable young people to generalize gains made during treatment to their natural environments [Whittaker 1986; Whittaker and Garbarino 1983].

Characteristics of Children and Families in Placement

Studies of children placed in residential care provide details of the composition of families with children in placement. An analysis of the characteristics of 10,000 children placed in residential care in California between 1982 and 1984 revealed that 52 percent of all children in the sample came from homes with single-parent families [Fitzharris 1985]. A total of 25 percent lived with families in which both biological parents lived together or in which a biological parent resided with a stepparent. The most frequent condition in family history that led to placement was an inability to control the child in the home. This condition accounted for 65 percent of all placement factors classified as "deficiencies in parenting" by the author.

Children are beset by a number of problems at the time placement decisions and referrals are finalized. In the California sample, Fitzharris [1985] found that 83 percent of all children in out-of-home care had multiple problems at the time placement was made. This included specific acts committed by the child and physical or psychological problems present prior to placement.

Parents also experience problems prior to placement. Sociological studies report that a large percentage of children referred to treatment programs come from families marked by poverty, poor education, single parents, and residence in high-crime neighborhoods [Shaw and McKay 1969]. Working with families experiencing multiple problems poses unique challenges to treatment personnel. Wahler and his associates [Wahler et al. 1979] indicate that families living in such conditions as poverty and unemployment become trapped and socially isolated. Social isolation may have a negative impact on a family's ability to respond to treatment efforts. Because isolated families lack natural helping networks and appropriate sources of support in the community, their participation in specific treatment programs may only be superficial and provide no tangible results [Dumas and Wahler 1983; Hawkins and Fraser 1983].

These findings suggest that singular service strategies that target multiple-problem families may not be adequate to overcome the effects of environmental variables present in a family's daily life. Single interventions such as parent training may not be sufficient to meet the needs of families with children in placement that are experiencing overwhelming life circumstances or who lack basic family management skills [Doherty 1975]. Community-oriented services that seek to identify, create, and maintain support networks of children and families may be one effective method of supplementing specific interventions directed at improving parents' skills and level of functioning [Whittaker and Maluccio 1986]. Strategies that strive to increase parental self-esteem while teaching needed parenting skills may also be an effective way to involve families experiencing multiple problems in their child's residential care [Webster-Stratton 1985].

Barriers to Parental Involvement

If continued family interaction is important to a child's success during and after treatment, why have residential facilities failed to

develop effective methods of working with parents? Whittaker [1979;
1981] identifies a number of factors that explain the limited involvement of parents in children's residential care. These include
(a) lack of financial resources to provide family services to parents
of children in care; (b) location of treatment facilities in rural or
isolated areas; (c) sociocultural differences between treatment personnel and parents; (d) limited roles offered to parents of children
placed in treatment facilities; (e) parental attitudes of personal guilt
for the inappropriate behavior exhibited by their child; (f) parental
fears of continued failure in efforts to change their child's behavior;
and (g) multiple problems, such as inadequate finances, family
disorganization, and legal difficulties, facing families of children
placed in residential care.

Increasing parental involvement might require agencies to alter
existing policies that restrict family participation in children's out-
of-home treatment. Parents can provide important assistance before, during, and after placement that will help children generalize
behavioral change accomplished during treatment to situations in
their everyday life. Promising techniques for increasing parental
involvement in treatment services are being implemented by residential programs. Examples of these techniques are summarized
below and in Tables 1–3.

Increasing Parental Involvement in Treatment Services: Preplacement and Intake Strategies

Specific treatment plans for children placed in residential care
should be based on a thorough evaluation of the child and his
family situation. Information regarding family history, the parents'
methods of relating to their children, and family interactions in the
weeks preceding treatment is a valuable prerequisite to the formation of treatment plans and goals [Littauer 1980; Maluccio 1981].

Appropriate roles for parents and other family members can
be identified for those families where the youth in treatment will
return home following placement. Finkelstein [1980] suggests that
preplacement visits by family members to their child's residential
facility may create paths of cooperation between parents and treatment personnel. Littauer [1980] and others [Blumenthal and Weinberg 1984] describe residential programs that develop formal

TABLE 1

Parental Involvement in Preplacement and Intake

---

1. Preadmission orientation is conducted with all family members through visits to the institution: Residential treatment personnel arrange visits to each child's family and community [Finkelstein 1980]
2. Individual treatment plans are formulated at intake with cooperation from parents:
   a. Parents' rights, roles, and responsibilities are identified and discussed [Blumenthal and Weinberg 1984]
   b. Parents are asked to specify the child's behavior, peer relations, and family interactions in the weeks preceding placement [Littauer 1980; Maluccio 1981]
   c. Treatment plans are formalized through written agreements or contracts between child, parent, and residential staff [Blumenthal and Weinberg 1984; Littauer 1980]
3. Parents with children already in treatment welcome new parents to existing family support and therapy sessions [Mitchell 1982]

---

treatment plans and contracts prior to placement that clearly outline parental expectations in their child's care. Contracts between children, parents, and treatment personnel are also used to identify specific treatment goals and to establish routines of visiting and communication between children and parents [Krona 1980; Van Hagen 1983].

Many parents are uncertain of their ability to provide post-treatment care for their children. For these families, parental involvement might include identification and discussion of placement options following treatment. Parents unable to provide long-term care can participate in the process of determining the best permanent option for their child [Blumenthal and Weinberg 1984]. Parents might also seek help from treatment personnel in dealing with feelings of frustration and guilt [Maluccio 1981].

Preplacement and intake strategies with family members are designed to define parent and child roles and responsibilities in the treatment and reentry process (refer to Table 1). Parents can be offered a range of activities, tasks, and services in which they can participate. Written guidelines describing specific opportunities for parental involvement can be developed and discussed. Increased opportunities for involvement, specified rights and re-

TABLE 2

Parental Involvement in During-Treatment Strategies

Parental Involvement in Treatment Activities	Parent Training and Education	Parent Support Groups	Conjoint Family Therapy

1. Visitation by biological parents:
  a. Weekly cottage or center events are attended by parents [Littauer 1980; Simmons et al. 1981]
  b. Families are encouraged to spend weekends at the residential milieu with their child [Finkelstein 1980]
  c. Children return home for weekend visits on a regular basis [Astrachan and Harris 1983; Krona 1980; Van Hagen 1983; Weisfeld and Laser 1976]
2. Parents are given specific responsibilities for their
	1. Group training is provided for parents in behavioral principles, such as contingency management and contract negotiation [Doherty 1975; Krona 1980]
	2. Parents are instructed in communication, management, and coping skills [Finkelstein 1980]
	3. Problem-solving skills are modeled for parents through the use of videotapes, role playing, and assigned readings [Krona 1980; McKenzie 1981]
		1. Social events for parents are sponsored by the treatment center to reduce family anxiety and isolation [Mitchell 1982]
		2. Short-term support groups present a series of guest speakers to answer questions and discuss issues related to placement and treatment [Mitchell 1982]
		3. Long-term support groups allow parents to share personal feelings and experiences with family members of other children in placement [McKenzie
			1. Parents and children are viewed as partners in an interdependent system; children are encouraged to understand the behavior of their parents, to cope with their frustration and anger at their parents, and to develop appropriate ways of interacting with their parents [Simmons et al. 1981]
			2. Parents attend family treatment sessions hosted by professionals at the residential facility [Oxley 1977]
			3. Through extensive family therapy, par-

ents and children develop and implement behavioral contracts that outline specific treatment and reentry plans [Van Hagen 1983]

4. Group therapy that emphasizes the influence of family processes is used for children in placement; reciprocal influences of residential milieu and family processes are examined [Letulle 1979]

5. Key family members live with referred child for several weeks in residential milieu; family "co-patients" attend all therapy activities together [Catanzaro et al. 1973; Schaefer 1977]

1981; Mitchell 1982]

child's care during treatment:

a. Purchase of clothing and daily needs

b. Daily scheduling of child's activities: e.g., chore assignment, homework time, and other rules and regulations are stated by parents [Simmons et al. 1981]

3. Parents are requested to help solve a specific child behavior problem encountered in treatment [McClintock 1975]

4. Parents are contacted weekly by staff and receive weekly written reports on their child's progress [Krona 1980]

5. Children are given the responsibility of planning and carrying out activities with their parents [Simmons et al. 1981]

TABLE 3

Parental Involvement in Community Reintegration
and Aftercare

1. Parent support groups are formed during treatment to discuss community reentry and "what to expect after placement" [Mitchell 1982]
2. Aftercare family support groups are established according to the following discharge plans: a. Child returns to biological family; b. Child is placed in adoptive home or other alternative [Finkelstein 1980]
3. Aftercare teams composed of social workers, child-care workers, educators, and community service workers assist parents with their child's reentry plans and reintegration:
   a. Prerelease meetings are held to set goals for the child and parents [Harding et al. 1978]
   b. Contracts for weekly family counseling are made [Harding et al. 1978]
   c. Limitations in parenting and family management skills are outlined and specific interventions are planned [Harding et al. 1978; Van Hagen 1982]
   d. Parents help their child develop an educational plan following treatment [Van Hagen 1983]
   e. Residential treatment staff members act as resource persons by accompanying parents to meetings with school personnel, therapists, and other helping professionals for a specified period following treatment [Van Hagen 1982]
4. Liaison specialists work with children and parents to facilitate linkages between placement and home [Montgomery and Van Fleet 1978]
   a. Specialists help youths find employment and solve practical problems during reintegration [Cross-Drew 1984]

sponsibilities for parents, and defined ways of helping may lead to greater parental participation in treatment services for children.

Family Involvement During Residential Treatment

Increasing parental involvement in children's residential care during placement requires shifting the focus of treatment from child-based to family-based services. This shift requires treatment personnel to view the family, not just the child, as the central unit of service [Maluccio and Whittaker in press].

Recent innovations and strategies used by residential treatment facilities to promote parental involvement suggest that family-focused care is becoming increasingly important in the rehabilitation of disturbed or troubled children. Whittaker [1979] identifies four methods of involving parents in their children's treatment: (a) parental involvement in daily treatment activities; (b) parent training and educational groups; (c) parent support groups; and (d) conjoint family therapy. (Refer to Table 2.)

Parental Involvement in Treatment Activities

Parental involvement in the daily routine of children's residential treatment can take many forms. One important strategy is parental visitation. The importance of visits by parents of children placed in out-of-home care is well documented [Fanshel 1975; Finkelstein 1974]. The results of research conducted by Fanshel and Shinn [1978] and Aldgate [1980] suggest that frequency of parental visitation during placement is positively associated with a child's successful return to his or her biological family. Although conducted in the context of foster care, these findings have direct implications for residential treatment.

Residential facilities promote family visitation in different ways. Encouraging parents to provide care for their children on weekends is one popular strategy [Krona 1980; Van Hagen 1983; Weisfeld and Laser 1976]. Astrachan and Harris [1983] describe a program in Ohio that has reversed the concept of traditional weekend visits home. In this residential program, children live with their biological parents five days a week and reside at the treatment center on weekends. The "weekend-only" program has been successful in increasing the time children spend with their families. It allows children to continue enrollment in local schools and maintain relationships with their families while receiving support and consultation from treatment therapists and child-care workers. The program has also been used for youths in transition from seven-day residential treatment to complete discharge. This strategy may be especially applicable to families with patterns of acting out that occur primarily on weekends, for example, alcoholism, drug abuse, or other types of excessive behaviors [Astrachan and Harris 1983].

A second strategy to increase parental involvement is providing parents with specific responsibilities for their child's care during treatment. Parents may be given child-care responsibilities, such as purchasing their children's clothing, or they may be asked to help establish study periods and other rules for their child [Simmons et al. 1981]. McClintock [1975] describes a program in which parents are requested to perform an active role in solving their child's behavior problems during treatment. Krona [1980] emphasizes the importance of weekly staff-parent meetings and suggests that written progress reports be sent to parents on a regular basis. Special cottage or center events and activities have also been suggested as methods of increasing parental involvement [Littauer 1980].

Parents can be involved in virtually all areas of agency programming. Increased efforts to involve families in the daily activities of residential facilities may improve a parent's ability to assume greater responsibility for the care of their child.

Parent Training and Education

We have previously noted that parents of children placed in residential care experience multiple problems when their child is removed from the home. Many parents lack the family management skills necessary to supervise and monitor their children. Some parents fail to provide consistent expectations and responses to their children's behavior. Training parents to identify behaviors they want to change in their child and teaching them such management skills as modeling and contingent positive reinforcement might be effective ways to work with families of children in residential care.

Interventions with nonresidential populations that teach family management skills demonstrate significant reductions in observed and parent-reported problem behaviors exhibited by troubled youths [Moreland et al. 1982; Webster-Stratton 1985]. Unfortunately, these interventions have seldom been applied to families of children in residential environments. Doherty [1975] describes a parent training program that teaches mothers of institutionalized adolescents specific ways of controlling their children's antisocial behaviors. Mothers receive training in behavioral principles, such as contingency management and contract negotiation, and meet weekly with other parents to discuss progress and to modify specific behavioral steps being applied. An evaluation of the program revealed that 12 of the 18 participating families experienced a decrease in children's problem behaviors during treatment [Doherty 1975]. Families that did not reduce the occurrence of their child's problem behaviors lacked cooperation from a male figure, as well as structure and organization in the home.

Parent education groups for families of children in treatment focus on skill-building and problem-solving techniques. Finkelstein [1980] describes one treatment center's approach to teaching communication, management, and coping skills to parents by grouping families and children together according to discharge plans. Other authors report that videotapes, role playing, and assigned readings to parents have proved effective in improving a family's problem-solving skills [Krona 1980; McKenzie 1981].

Maintaining family participation in ongoing interventions, such as parent training and educational groups, is difficult. Problems of attrition [McMahon et al. 1981] and the overwhelming life circumstances and social isolation confronting families with children in care [Wahler et al. 1979; Whittaker 1979] pose tremendous challenges to the implementation of parent training strategies.

Parent Support Groups

Evidence suggests that individuals generally seek and receive assistance from parents, friends, or relatives prior to seeking the advice of professional helpers [Collins and Pancoast 1976; Gottlieb 1981]. Support groups that assist parents in coping with feelings of guilt and isolation and that encourage mutual support with other parents might be an effective way of promoting family involvement in residential placements. Parent groups that provide empathy, encouragement, and practical solutions to problems might be less threatening than skills training classes conducted by social work or mental health professionals.

McKenzie [1981] describes several support groups for parents of children placed in a residential treatment center in California. These groups include a new parents' orientation group, an educational group that teaches child development and parenting techniques, and a support group that increases personal growth through mutual problem-solving strategies. Issues discussed in the ten-week support group include termination, assertiveness, and marital relationships. The group also seeks to build a supportive network for isolated families in the community.

The Walker Home and School in Massachusetts has encouraged parental involvement by forming long-term support groups that allow members to share personal experiences and to discuss their children's upcoming reentry plan [Mitchell 1982]. Transportation and attendance problems experienced by inner-city parents resulted in the formation of a separate support group for parents living in the Boston area. The home also operates short-term support groups to provide initial orientation to parents and to help families locate resources that might be beneficial to their children following release from care.

The structure of support groups for parents of children in out-of-home care requires careful consideration of the types of families being served, the content and purpose of the groups, and the duration and intensity of treatment being provided [Anglin 1985]. Support groups hold promise as effective interventions in residential treatment facilities and could be implemented at all stages of the treatment process.

Conjoint Family Therapy

Conjoint family therapy includes all family members in a therapeutic encounter. This approach to rehabilitation is based on the notion that the difficulty experienced by the child in placement also affects the functioning of other family members [Whittaker 1979]. Successful treatment of the child in placement will ultimately require changes in the family's overall functioning. In this context, parents and children are viewed as partners in an interdependent system.

Therapeutic sessions hosted by professionals at residential centers is a common approach used to encourage parents to interact with their child and treatment personnel. Van Hagen [1983] describes therapy sessions directed at developing and implementing behavioral contracts between the child in placement and other family members. The reciprocal influences of residential treatment and family processes have also been examined through family therapy methods. Letulle [1979] suggests that recognizing disruptive patterns of residential behavior in a child may clarify previously unknown or vaguely perceived family processes that occur naturally in the child's home environment. Such processes can be discussed and challenged in family therapy sessions to help family members understand and identify the points of conflict. Some programs have adopted models of structural family therapy specifically for use in a residential program [Bro. J. Caley, personal communication, October 1985; W. Seelig, personal communication, October 1985]. Other programs have invited family members to reside with their child for limited time periods at the treatment facility [Catanzaro et al. 1973; Schaefer 1977].

Residential facilities must reexamine existing incentives for parental participation in daily treatment activities, in training and support groups, and in family therapy sessions. Promising approaches have been reported. Efforts are needed to expand these innovations to a greater number of troubled children and families.

Community Reintegration and Aftercare

Evaluations of treatment effectiveness have demonstrated that the degree of support in a child's posttreatment environment is an important predictor in determining successful long-term adjustment [Allerhand et al. 1966; Nelson et al. 1978; Taylor and Alpert 1973]. These studies suggest that children leaving residential care with supportive ties to family, peers, neighbors, and schools are more likely to maintain treatment gains following release from treatment. Yet residential facilities have done little to encourage the establishment of aftercare services for troubled children [Jenson et al. 1986]. Until recently, parents of children in care received no assistance in the coordination of aftercare services for their child.

Our review suggests that aftercare components are becoming more prevalent in the treatment programs of residential facilities (refer to Table 3 for examples of parental involvement). Parent groups are being organized by treatment personnel to discuss issues of community reentry [Mitchell 1982]. Aftercare teams of social workers, child-care workers, educators, and community service workers are being assembled to build support networks for children and families during community reentry [Harding et al. 1978]. Van Hagen [1983] and others [Montgomery and Van Fleet 1978] describe attempts to build links between placement, home, and the school to which a child returns at discharge. A "resource developer" was hired to help clients find employment in a study of adolescents placed in residential care in California [Cross-Drew 1984]. An evaluation of the program revealed significantly higher rates of posttreatment employment for youths placed in the experimental condition. Cahill and Meier [1984] describe an innovative reunification-aftercare program to reach families of young maltreated children returning from residential placement.

These examples demonstrate the increasing recognition of aftercare as an effective method of working with children and families. Further research is necessary to develop coordination between residential facilities and community-based agencies concerned with improving the posttreatment support networks of children and families. Schools, community centers, youth service agencies, and residential facilities need to define and expand their roles in aftercare services. Aftercare interventions that encourage interaction between residential treatment centers and community resources might help troubled children maintain the positive changes they are able to make during out-of-home placement.

Discussion

This review of family involvement in children's residential care suggests that treatment facilities have increased their efforts to include biological parents in children's out-of-home placements. Strategies that enhance links between treatment centers and family and community support systems have been developed. Parent training and support groups have been implemented and evaluated. Opportunities for parental involvement in treatment activities have been defined and offered to parents. Finally, efforts have increased to include parents in the community reintegration and aftercare planning process for their child's return home.

Yet the effectiveness of parental interventions in children's residential treatment remains unclear. Outcome research in residential treatment suggests that family support is critical to a child's posttreatment adjustment [Allerhand et al. 1966; Taylor and Alpert 1973]. Specific factors, such as frequency of parental visits [Borgman 1985] and family management skills [Oxley 1977], have been identified as important determinants in a child's success following residential care; however, few evaluations of family-based interventions have been conducted in residential programs. Studies that assess individual components of family intervention, for example, parent support groups, parent training classes, and family therapy, might identify more effective ways of involving parents in children's out-of-home care. Research is also needed to identify the effects that frequency and duration of family involvement have on children's adaptation following treatment. These results might provide agencies and policymakers with information regarding the costs and benefits of providing structured parental involvement in treatment settings.

Residential facilities must improve their relationships and strengthen linkages to communities and neighborhoods. The emerging practice innovations that involve parents in children's treatment programs are encouraging. Efficient implementation of these interventions is needed to produce effective programs and positive changes for troubled children and their parents. Organizational and structural changes might be necessary to ensure adequate implementation. Staff training might be required to sensitize treatment personnel to the roles parents can perform in children's out-of-home care. New positions might be necessary to develop resources and make appropriate referrals for families once a child is returned to the community. Funding sources for family work during posttreatment services must be further developed.

Case management systems might be an effective way of involving families and coordinating the treatment and community reentry stages of children's residential care. Case management systems place responsibility for service planning and delivery on a person or a team who works with the child and family. Case managers develop appropriate service plans, assure access to services, monitor service delivery, and advocate for client needs [Weil and Karls 1985]. Investigators at the University of Washington are currently testing the effects of a case management system on the antisocial behavior of institutionalized adolescents in the Seattle area [Haggerty et al. 1987]. Residents are assigned case managers three months before their release from treatment. Reentry plans are made, and school and home visits are conducted to ease the transition to community life. Case managers continue intensive work with clients and families for six months following treatment. During this period they act as mediators in crisis situations, encourage clients to join prosocial activities, and locate community services for clients and families.

Studies that examine the characteristics of the families of children placed in residential care are also needed to inform intervention efforts. Whittaker is presently examining the family characteristics of delinquent adolescents placed in a large group care program [Whittaker et al. 1987]. Preliminary results of the investigation will be used to develop an empirical basis for selecting appropriate interventions for working with families of children in placement.

Effective technologies and methods of involving parents used in other service fields, such as special-needs adoption and prevention, might also be considered for application in residential treatment environments. The development of family-based services has achieved significant attention in foster care [Maluccio and Whittaker in press] and developmental disabilities [Schilling and Schinke 1984]. The extensive use of parent groups in working with families of children suffering from developmental disabilities may prove to be of valuable assistance to the development of such groups in children's treatment services.

The involvement of biological parents in children's residential care is the most critical component in the evolution of family-based group care services. Residential settings must be viewed as a support system for those families who wish to maintain their child in the home, not as substitute placements for families who have failed. Innovative strategies in the preplacement, during-treatment, and aftercare phases of a child's out-of-home care must be attempted, evaluated, and disseminated to practitioners and policymakers.

References

Ainsworth, F., and Fulcher. *Group Care for Children: Concepts and Issues.* London: Tavistock, 1981.

Aldgate, J. Identification of factors influencing children's length of stay in care. In J. Triseliotis (ed.), *New Developments in Foster Care and Adoption.* Boston: Routledge & Kegan Paul, 1980, pp. 22–40.

Allerhand, M.E., Weber, R.E., and Haug, M. *Adaptation and Adaptability: The Bellefaire Followup Study.* New York: Child Welfare League of America, 1966.

Anglin, J.P. Developing education and support groups for parents of children in residential care. *Residential Group Care and Treatment* 3(2): 15–27, 1985.

Astrachan, M., and Harris, D.M. Weekend only: An alternate model in residential treatment centers. *Child Welfare* LXII: 253–261, 1983.

Blumenthal, K., and Weinberg, A. Involving parents: A rationale. In K. Blumenthal and A. Weinberg (eds.), *Establishing Parental Involvement in Foster Care Agencies.* New York: Child Welfare League of America, 1984, pp. 1–16.

Borgman, R. The influence of family visiting upon boys' behavior in a juvenile correctional institution. *Child Welfare* LXIV: 629–638, 1985.

Bowlby, J. *Attachment and Loss.* New York: Basic Books, 1969.

Cahill, B., and Meier, J. *Secondary Prevention of Child Assault: Provision of Specialized Foster-Adoptive Placements and Reunification-Aftercare to Prevent Drift and Recidivism.* Unpublished paper, 1984. Childhelp, U.S.A., 14700 Manzanita Boulevard, Beaumont, CA 92223.

Catanzaro, R.J., Psani, V.D., Fox, R., and Kennedy, E.R. Familization therapy: An alternative to traditional mental care. *Diseases of the Nervous System* 34: 212–218, 1973.

Coates, R.B., Miller, A.D., and Ohlin, L.E. *Diversity in a Youth Correctional System: Handling Delinquents in Massachusetts.* Cambridge, Massachusetts: Ballinger, 1978.

Collins, A., and Pancoast, D.C. *Natural Helping Networks.* Washington, D.C.: National Association of Social Workers, 1976.

Colon, F. Family ties and child placement. *Family Process* 17: 289–312, 1978.

Cox, M.J., and Cox, R.D. The foster care system: An introduction. In M.J. Cox and R.D. Cox (eds.), *Foster Care: Current Issues, Policies, and Practices.* Norwood, New Jersey: Ablex Publishing, 1985, pp. x–xii.

Cross-Drew, C. *Project Jericho Evaluation Report.* Sacramento: California Department of the Youth Authority, 1984.

Doherty, G. Basic life-skills and parent effectiveness training with the mothers of acting-out adolescents. *Journal of Clinical Child Psychology* 31: 3–6, 1975.

Dumas, J.E., and Wahler, R.G. Predictors of treatment outcome in parent training: Mother insularity and socioeconomic disadvantage. *Behavioral Assessment* 5: 301–313, 1983.

Fanshel, D. Parental visiting of children in foster care: Key to discharge? *Social Service Review* 49: 493–514, 1975.

Fanshel, D., and Shinn, E.G. *Children in Foster Care: A Longitudinal Investigation.* New York: Columbia University Press, 1978.

Finkelstein, N.E. Family participation in residential treatment. *Child Welfare* LIII: 570–575, 1974.

Finkelstein, N.E. Family-centered group care. *Child Welfare* LIX: 33–41, 1980.

Fitzharris, T.L. *The Foster Children of California: Profiles of 10,000 Children in Residential Care.* Sacramento, California: Children's Services Foundation, 1985.

Gottlieb, B.H. *Social Workers and Social Support.* Beverly Hills, California: Sage, 1981.

Haggerty, K.P., Wells, E.A., Catalono, R.F., Jenson, A.M., and Hawkins, J.D. *Project ADAPT: A Community Transition Program for Juvenile Delinquents.* Unpublished manuscript, 1987. University of Washington, Center for Social Welfare Research, Seattle.

Harding, E.H., Bellew, J., and Penwell, L.W. Project aftercare: Followup to residential treatment. *Behavioral Disorders* 4: 13–22, 1978.

Hawkins, J.D., and Fraser, M. Social support networks in delinquency prevention and treatment. In J.D. Whittaker and J. Garbarino (eds.), *Social Support Networks*. New York: Aldine, 1983, pp. 333–356.

Hess, P. Parent-child attachment: Crucial to permanency planning. *Social Casework* 63: 46–53, 1982.

Jenkins, S., and Norman, E. *Beyond Placement: Mothers View Foster Care*. New York: Columbia University Press, 1975.

Jenson, J.M., Hawkins, J.D., and Catalano, R.L. Social support in aftercare services for troubled youth. *Children and Youth Services Review* 8: 41–65, 1986.

Jones, R.R., Weinrott, M.R., and Howard, J.R. *Impact of the Teaching-Family Model on Troublesome Youth: Findings from the National Evaluation*. Rockville, Maryland: National Institute of Mental Health, 1981.

Krona, D.A. Parents as treatment partners in residential care. *Child Welfare* LIX: 91–96, 1980.

Laird, J. An ecological approach to child welfare: Issues of family identity and continuity. In C.B. Germain (ed.), *Social Work Practice: People and Environments*. New York: Columbia University Press, 1979, pp. 174–212.

Letulle, L.J. Family therapy in residential treatment for children. *Social Work* 24: 49–51, 1979.

Lewis, W.W. Ecological factors in successful residential treatment. *Behavioral Disorders* 7: 149–155, 1982.

Littauer, C. Working with families of children in residential treatment. *Child Welfare* LIX: 225–234, 1980.

Maluccio, A.N. The emerging focus on parents of children in placement. In P.A. Sinanoglu and A.N. Maluccio (eds.), *Parents of Children in Placement: Perspectives and Programs*. New York: Child Welfare League of America, 1981, pp. 5–14.

Maluccio, A.N., and Fein, E. Permanency planning: A redefinition. *Child Welfare* LXII: 195–201, 1983.

Maluccio, A.N., Fein, E., Hamilton, J., Klein, J., and Ward, D. Beyond permanency planning. *Child Welfare* LIX: 515–530, 1980.

Maluccio, A.N., and Whittaker, J.K. Foster family-based treatment: Implications for parental involvement. In R.P. Hawkins and J. Breiling (eds.), *Issues in Implementing Foster Family Based Treatment*. Rockville, Maryland: National Institute of Mental Health, in press.

McClintock, D.R. Involving parents in solving a group problem in residential treatment: A case report. *Child Care Quarterly* 4: 44–47, 1975.

McKenzie, C.A. Shifting the focus to the family in residential treatment. *Social Work Papers* 16: 12–23, 1981.

McMahon, R.J., Forehand, R., Griest, D.L., and Wells, K.C. Who drops out of treatment during parent behavior training. *Behavioral Counseling Quarterly* 1: 79–85, 1981.

Mitchell, C.A. Planning with parents: The use of groups in residential treatment. *Social Work with Groups* 5(4): 32–45, 1982.

Montgomery, P.A., and Van Fleet, D.S. Evaluation of behavioral and academic changes through the Re-Ed process. *Behavioral Disorders* 3: 136–146, 1978.

Moreland, J.R., Schwebel, A.I., Beck, S., and Wells, R. A review of the behavior therapy parent training literature, 1975–1981. *Behavior Modification* 6: 250–276, 1982.

Nelson, R.H., Singer, M.J., and Johnsen, L.O. The application of a residential treatment evaluation model. *Child Care Quarterly* 7: 164–175, 1978.

Oxley, G.B. A modified form of residential treatment. *Social Work* 22: 493–498, 1977.

Rowe, J., Cain, H., Hundleby, M., and Keanne, A. *Long-Term Foster Care*. London: Batsford Academic and Educational, 1984.

Schaefer, C.E. The need for "psychological parents" by children in residential treatment. *Child Care Quarterly* 6: 288–299, 1977.

Schilling, R.F., and Schinke, S.P. Coping and social support for parents of handicapped children. *Children and Youth Services Review* 6: 195–206, 1984.

Shaw, C.R., and McKay, H.D. *Juvenile Delinquency and Urban Areas*. Chicago: University of Chicago Press, 1969.

Simmons, G., Gumpert, J., and Rothman, B. Natural parents as partners in child care placement. In P.A. Sinanoglu and A.N. Maluccio (eds.), *Parents of Children in Placement: Perspectives and Programs*. New York: Child Welfare League of America, 1981, pp. 375–388.

Taylor, D.A., and Alpert, S.W. *Continuity and Support Following Residential Treatment*. New York: Child Welfare League of America, 1973.

Van Hagen, J. Aftercare as a distinct and necessary treatment phase: Results of the St. Vincent's aftercare study. *Residential Group Care and Treatment* 1(2): 19–29, 1982.

Van Hagen, J. One residential center's model for working with families. *Child Welfare* LXII: 233–241, 1983.

Wahler, R.G., Afton, A.D., and Fox, J.J. The multiple entrapped parent: Some new problems in parent training. *Education and Treatment of Children* 2: 279–286, 1979.

Webster-Stratton, C. Predictors of treatment outcome in parent training for conduct disordered children. *Behavior Therapy* 16: 223–243, 1985.

Weil, M., and Karls, J.M. Historical origins and recent developments. In M. Weil and J.M. Karls (eds.), *Case Management in Human Service Practice*. San Francisco: Jossey-Bass, 1985, pp. 1–29.

Weisfeld, D., and Laser, M.S. Residential treatment and weekend visits home. *Social Work* 21: 398–400, 1976.

Whittaker, J.K. *Caring for Troubled Children*. San Francisco: Jossey-Bass, 1979.

Whittaker, J.K. Family involvement in residential treatment: A support system for parents. In A.N. Maluccio and P.A. Sinanoglu (eds.), *The Challenge of Partnership: Working with Parents of Children in Foster Care*. New York: Child Welfare League of America, 1981, pp. 67–88.

Whittaker, J.K. Formal and informal helping in child welfare services: Implications for management and practice. *Child Welfare* LXX: 17–25, 1986.

Whittaker, J.K. Family support and group child care: Rethinking resources. In R. Small and G. Carmen (eds.), *Permanency Planning: The Reformation of Group Child Care*. Washington, D.C.: Child Welfare League of America, in press.

Whittaker, J.K., Fine, D., and Grasso, A. *Youth and Family Characteristics in Residential Treatment Intake: An Exploratory Study*. Unpublished manuscript, 1987. University of Washington, School of Social Work, Seattle.

Whittaker, J.K., and Garbarino, J. *Social Support Networks*. New York: Aldine, 1983.

Whittaker, J.K., and Maluccio, A.N. Position paper on out-of-home care: Prepared for the resolutions committee, biennial meeting of the Child Welfare League of America, November 1986. Unpublished manuscript, 1986. University of Washington, School of Social Work, Seattle.

Whittaker, J.K., and Maluccio, A.N. Changing paradigms in substitute services for children and youth: Retrospect and prospect. In R.P. Hawkins and J. Breiling (eds.), *Issues in Implementing Foster Family-Based Treatment*. Rockville, Maryland: National Institute of Mental Health, in press.

9

Transforming the Child-Care Institution into a Family-Oriented Care System

JACK K. DANIELS
OWEN TUCKER, JR.

N O MODEL FOR CHANGE CAN BE DIVORCED FROM the leadership necessary to guide an agency as it labors to give birth to new vision and new direction. The authors of this paper are actively engaged in helping a group care facility implement a family-oriented continuum of care. One is the administrator of the church-related child-care agency in which he grew up as a resident; a Methodist minister with 25 years' experience in the field, he is a national leader in the child-care movement. The other is director of family treatment and education at the same agency; a Presbyterian minister with experience in group care, he is a nationally certified supervisor in marriage and family therapy and a consultant in family life programming.

This is a "how-to" paper. It outlines the importance of a family model to group care, traces the development of the new model as it emerged in the life of one agency, then describes the model and how it is being implemented. In the process, it also delineates how a church-related agency views its mission and implements its philosophy of care.

As one of the oldest and largest church-related children's homes serving Texas and New Mexico, the agency referred to in this paper is steeped in the traditions of child care. Its services include a group

167

:ampus caring for over 200 children who remain in residence 12 to 18 months; a working ranch setting serving 50 prede-uent boys; a foster care division serving some 115 children in ter homes; and the Children's Guidance Center, which furnishes comprehensive mental health care to the programs of the home. The home's main campus consists of 18 separate home units and various support facilities located on 130 acres of wooded, rolling hills.

This paper urges the importance of an agency always remaining flexible, open to new ideas, and constantly seeking ways to improve concepts and practices. Openness is crucial to an agency in keeping pace with the changing needs of clients, but it must be balanced with an avoidance of fads and change merely for the sake of change. In pursuit of this goal of balanced transformation, our attention now turns to the importance of the family model.

Importance of the Family Model

The family has always been the fundamental human community. It socializes its members for citizenship and, when it works right, nurtures and supports them from conception to death. The formative influence of the family is seen in the development of children's sense of identity, the learned ways they have of coping with daily life and the surrounding environment, their ability to relate to others in need-satisfying ways, their view of the world, their understanding of human values, and the way they relate to God. Thus, the family has pervasive power in creating human personality, proclaiming faith perspectives, and shaping human society. Families are, therefore, the central unit for helping all persons.

Group Care and the Family

The field of child care has not, however, always placed a premium on the importance of the family. Alan Keith-Lucas and Clifford Sanford [ca. 1977] remind us of the three stages in the development of children's homes. First came the orphanage, which was concerned to save children from degradation and poverty. In most cases, family ties were completely severed, and the institution became the child's guardian, replacing the family. The child grew up in the orphanage, often going to school and church on campus.

Next came the child-centered stage in which children were viewed as victims of broken homes and family disintegration. Developments in the fields of psychology and education led to children being regarded as having emotional problems, and some institutions responded by changing into residential treatment centers and psychiatric facilities. Most agencies moved toward smaller, more home-like living units, a more open campus, and the use of social workers. Agencies in this stage often sought to rescue these "victims" from their problem-plagued families, though many tried to return the child to the family as soon as possible.

Third is the family-oriented stage. Agencies in this stage function as a resource for those families who need a period of separation while they work out their problems. Placement is part of a purposeful plan to give the family this opportunity. Reconciliation within the family is the primary goal, but adoption, foster care, or long-term group care may also be appropriate. What is essential is that the family be actively involved in the development of the plan, where appropriate. This type of agency goes beyond the increased work with families in stage two to develop a consistent process of co-planning with the family, which results in a continuum of experiences through which both the child and the family may move.

In this third stage, the children's home views the family as the client and orders its program accordingly, allowing the agency to make a valuable contribution by enabling it to enter preventive services in a rational and organized manner. In doing so, it will not only be serving today's children; it will also be encouraging a pattern of family living that will prevent the breakdown of the family in the next generation.

The Changing American Family

Prevention programming is crucial in a day when the pattern and makeup of the American family are changing. The concept of the stepfamily is here to stay, and researchers tell us it takes four to seven years for a new stepfamily to become stable. There is a decided increase in family abuse—not a new phenomenon, but discovered to be a major problem in our society. At least one million teenagers run away every year, and half of them are "pushouts," who are unwanted by their families. New technologies are changing our mode of production and making many workers redundant, creating financial havoc for families. Alcohol abuse and substance abuse have risen dramatically. These are only a few of the areas of concern; many more could be listed.

The campus admissions statistics of our own agency reflect these family dynamics and social forces. A recent analysis of these statistics yielded the following picture of the population we serve: severe conflict with parents, 29.9 percent; attachment loss due to family disruptions such as divorce, desertion, or illness of parent, 19 percent; attachment loss due to family financial problems, 19 percent; abuse, neglect, and incest, 6.9 percent; and inadequate parenting skills, 5.2 percent. Thus, fully 80 percent of all admissions were family-related problems. And it seems likely that family problems were at least a factor in the other 20 percent.

What can a child-care agency do to address these problems and help the condition of the American family? What is already being done that we can become a part of? These and other questions were among the factors that prompted us to search for a new vision and new directions. As a church-related child-care agency, our central commitment is to participate in the Holy Spirit's transforming work in persons, families, communities, nations, and the world. We do this task believing God creates us for relationships through which we give and receive mutual care and love, and believing God is at work in all families to redeem, transform, sustain, and nurture them toward healing and wholeness.

Stated in another way, a church-related agency does not view itself simply as an agent of change; it is also a channel through which the power of Christ and the values of life in Christ are brought to bear upon human relationships. We operate from a sense of mission, as well as a philosophy of care. It was this sense of mission, along with our awareness of the trends developing in child care, that prompted us to ask the questions we were asking.

A New Direction

The idea of a family-oriented care system took several years to emerge. Because of the loss of some federal funding, cutbacks had been made in one of the agency's programs, and we were faced with empty buildings and no program to put in these facilities. For three budget years, agency staff members were invited to suggest proposals for the use of the Settoon buildings. The first two years the proposals had to be rejected either because they were not in the vanguard of child care, they could be accomplished in some other way, or the money could be better spent. The third year the idea of a family treatment and education center emerged.

This idea made great sense. It was on the leading edge of child care. It would allow the agency to combine several goals in one program: to have a process of family treatment for the benefit of families who had children in care, to enter prevention programs in an organized way, and to extend the expertise of other professionals involved in helping troubled families. One of the major presentations to the board was a proposal to design a program that would work and that would be in accord with sound financial principles. The board, as it usually does, questioned the proposal thoroughly, but once it had been approved, supported its establishment by challenging the administration to find the best way to accomplish it.

The Administrator's Role

The role of the administrator in facilitating change is threefold. First, the administrator must be willing to take the risks change entails. He or she must encourage innovation and challenge the staff to question methods and policies to ensure that the agency performs its mission to the best of its ability.

Second, the administrator must make sure he or she and the staff members are aware of changes in society and in professional practice. They must know what new programs are being developed and what new needs are not being met.

Third, the administrator, by action and example, can make change and innovation as much a part of the agency's daily operation as they need to be in creating new programs. Through department and staff meetings, new ideas can be presented and discussed. Recognition of those who innovate is a vital method for helping these new ideas to become part of the agency's organizational climate. Grass-roots innovation is encouraged, as well as those ideas that might come from an administrative think tank.

The Church-Related Agency

In a church-related agency, the help given children and families represents a blending of two foundations. First is as a ministry of the church. Ministry is a part of its identity, defines its purpose, and provides its motivation. As a ministry of the church, the agency is motivated to serve God by helping those in need. The church has always been a family-oriented agency, and, historically, the clergy were the first family counselors.

This identity also makes a difference in the way families seeking placement view the agency. Typically they see the agency as an extension of the pastoral care ministry of the church, which produces an initial trust of the agency in most cases. This church-related perspective will not be foreign to many readers, since many agencies have had and continue to have religious roots, and many child-care workers have religious values that they seek to incorporate into their professional lives.

The second foundation is professionalism. Our agency formalized this commitment in 1963 when we affiliated with the Child Welfare League of America (CWLA). The commitment to a high quality of services inherent in any profession is appropriate to the agency's commitment to honor Christ by the way it serves children and families. Initial trust in an agency's quality of care is confirmed or impaired by its degree of professionalism. To be both faithful to its mission and effective in its programs and services, the agency must blend these two foundations into a practical continuum of care. The development of a family-oriented care system is viewed by our administration as the key concept where ministry and professionalism come together.

Implementing the New Direction

The first step toward meeting the board's challenge was the development of a new mission statement and new organizational goals. This purpose was accomplished through campuswide meetings and discussions involving the entire staff at every level. The new mission statement asserts:

As an agency of the United Methodist Church, Methodist Home offers a multiple-service, Christian child-care ministry to children and their families in Texas and New Mexico. The program facilitates normal growth and development with the goal of enabling children and their families to enhance their wholeness and freedom in order to achieve and to become more productive individuals of greater dignity and worth.

New organizational goals allowed us to put this mission statement into operation. First, the following agency objectives were adopted: a staff that is supportive of and dedicated to Christian values; an atmosphere of caring that allows children and families to feel that the agency has their best interests at heart; a spirit of unity, purpose, responsibility, and accountability in the agency's professional functioning; and an attitude of acceptance and affirmation that allows children and their families to build on existing strengths. These self-imposed expectations developed by the staff form the parameters of our vision and are promoted in employment practices, policies, and publications.

This mission was further implemented in terms of four central tasks expected of the child-care staff: first, to provide a supportive living environment in which a child can reflect upon socially acceptable actions, thoughts, and feelings with a new objectivity; second, to set and maintain constructive limits for self-expression so that the child learns how individuality can be channeled positively; third, to demonstrate constructive alternatives for handling feelings and provide opportunities for trying out new ways of behaving that are more socially acceptable; and fourth, to relate to the child with love and compassion so that skillful redirection can be accomplished with the influence of spiritual values.

In addition, eight objectives were identified as guidelines for work with families: first, to assure parents that the child is in good hands; second, to reassure parents of their own continuing involvement in the life of their child; third, to define clearly the functions, rights, and duties of the parents during placement; fourth, to expect parents to support the child's placement and treatment; fifth, to help parents to change their own attitude toward the child; sixth, to help parents with problems not directly related to the child; seventh, to help parents resume full-time parenthood; and eighth, to provide care and guidance to the family after the child has left the agency.

Relationships: The Key

The decision to place a child away from home is never easy; however, when both the family and the child agree that temporary separation is best for all concerned, and when both the family and the agency accept the responsibility to work on relationship goals during placement, this difficult decision can be the first step toward a brighter future. The most important tool in this process is relationships. Years of experience have taught that the most successful placements of children in care are those in which families remain vitally involved and invested in significant relationships with their children.

Consequently, during the time of placement, the agency seeks to build genuine relationships of trust and mutual respect, not only with the child, but also with the family. When this process happens, both the child and the family become personally motivated to accept the help offered and are enabled to grow and change. It is this context of relationships, grounded in Christian values of compassion and caring, that enables the family to accept the professional insights, concern, and objectivity they need to define the problems that confront them and to take positive steps toward resolving them.

Having set the stage with a new mission statement and operational guidelines, we next turned to designing the family program. Department directors were asked their views on the value of a family program and how their department might use such a program. From these comments, an initial design was created, and the program was put into the 1984–85 budget. A director, who arrived on campus in October, was hired, and the Settoon Family Treatment and Education Center officially got under way in January 1985.

The New Model

Implementing a new program in an agency is seldom easy. When that program signals a major new direction for an agency steeped in tradition, the task does not just multiply, it takes a quantum jump. Most of us get set in our ways long before we realize it. Organizational systems become trapped in security blankets of trusted procedures and mythical beliefs that a given policy or procedure was etched in stone by the founders. In this way, systems seek to ensure stability and organizational maintenance. The opening of the Family Center brought into sharp focus the reality of the new direction. Hence, implementation of the program had to come to grips with three basic issues.

The first issue was expressed in a comment by a campus staff person who said, "Child-care agencies have worked with families for a long time, so what's different today?" What's different is primarily a matter of degree and emphasis. Seasoned child-care workers have known for some time that when children are separated from their parents and placed in group care, the positive changes that take place in them will be lost or significantly modified if they return to an unchanged family. Consequently, group care agencies and their consultants began some time ago to pilot family-oriented approaches that would increase their degree of involvement with the family. This increased involvement is causing agencies to shift their emphasis and redefine their philosophy of care. Increasingly the family unit, not the individual child, is the primary focus of agency care. There is a significant difference between working with families and seeing the family as the primary unit of care.

The second issue was also expressed by a campus staff person who said to the new director, "I think the main thing they are paying you for is to find ways to overcome resistance." For the local agency, often the issue is not that of individual child versus family. Rather, the real issue is how to make the program shift, given the reality that agencies, like families, tend to resist change. Since such changes can have wide-ranging effects, this resistance is essentially good. It serves a useful protective function, guarding the agency against fads. Given time and kindness, however, most people will eventually make the shift. Those who do not eventually leave the agency and are replaced with people who have the "right stuff." What is emerging from the experience of agencies like ours that are making the shift is simply this fact: the results in the lives of children and families are worth the cost.

The third issue was raised by the size of our organization: how to get the whole campus community moving in the desired direction and working in concert. That, after all, is a part of what is meant by a continuum-of-care concept. The resolution of this issue is precisely why there must be a deep commitment from the top.

But that commitment cannot be just to the new direction; it must equally be a commitment to the staff members being asked to make changes—which means offering the training needed to move in the new direction and supporting those who are willing to innovate.

With these issues in mind, we began building upon and expanding the initial design. The resulting model is a blend of many ideas gathered over time and drawn from a number of sources. It was developed with a group care agency in mind, but it is quite adaptable to other agencies. In fact, it has already been adopted by another agency and is working effectively in that setting. Obviously, the first steps are having a staff person trained in working with family systems and the availability of facilities that lend themselves to therapy and training.

Description of the Model

The model is built on the foundation of two generic concepts: treatment and education. Treatment incorporates several components. First is family therapy with families who have a child in placement. Its objective is to see if the problems that initially caused the child's placement can be resolved so that the child can return home successfully. If this objective appears impossible, the second objective is to help the family clarify the issue of placement and accept whatever decision is made in the healthiest way possible.

The second component of treatment is short-term intervention in problem situations, which are described later. These interventions have two goals: to offer caseworkers a backup support system whenever they have a difficult family to work with, and to salvage placements with troubled and troublesome families. Third-party interventions augment the campus program and offer families an additional option for resolving problems.

Education also incorporates several components. First is staff development. For the caseworkers the emphasis is on understanding family dynamics and how to work with family systems; the objective is to enhance their skill as family caregivers. For the therapy staff, the emphasis is on skill development in family therapy and short-term interventions; the objective is to develop approaches that are effective in working with a variety of family problems.

The second component is training community professionals who work with families. This component also enhances agency outreach because it focuses on community professionals drawn from agencies or institutions that are a part of the child-care or mental health network, and from the clergy. Many of these professionals are referral sources for the agency and persons to whom we refer families needing additional services or long-term aftercare. The training facilitates networking among professionals and between campus and community. Since participants pay a fee, it is also cost-effective. These training seminars have two objectives: practical skill development in working with families, and pastoral care of church professionals.

The third component is family life education. These programs have three objectives: family enrichment through prevention programs, building better relationships between staff members and the families being served, and enhancing the staff's understanding of work with families. Family life education programs are a good way to bond families and staff members together through experiences of mutual growth.

Models, however, are only as good as their feasibility and relevancy. Agency programs are only as good as the degree of investment by staff members and family participants. With this brief description of the model, we turn now to how it is being implemented.

Stage One

Implementation of the model has been a gradual process, taking place in stages. The first stage was to establish the Family Center as a viable treatment program on the main campus. The center is a fully equipped treatment and training facility. One of its distinctive features is a family wing to house families in treatment for a short-term stay, allowing work with families in an atmosphere that approximates a home setting. It also enables prescribing innovative treatment interventions. This feature was necessary since most of the families travel some distance for treatment sessions. The campus caseworker, who is the primary referral source and always viewed as the case manager, is involved in all family sessions either as a participant in the therapy room or as an observer behind the mirror. In this way, the work of the center and that of the case-worker are closely tied together in a mutual effort.

The main campus is a basic care facility. On a continuum-of-care scale, it lies between foster home placement and a residential treatment facility. The children come mostly from troubled family situations, but not all of them are necessarily emotionally disturbed. In most cases, however, the families do need some type of treatment and training to restore them to effective functioning. Given the kinds of family problems that bring children to our attention, and the extent to which the family is intricately involved in both the problem and its lasting solution, it makes good sense to have family treatment available as one of the services offered by the agency, as the following statistics show.

The case statistics for the first two years of operation indicate we saw 65 families. Within these 65 families were 54 adolescents and 14 latency-age children who were campus residents, 54 children who were family siblings, and 108 adults, for a total of 230 people served. The average length of treatment is six to 12 two-hour sessions held every two weeks or once a month. In the third year, the case statistics more than doubled. Current projections indicate that close to 100 families will be seen in the next 12 months.

The families represent the following types of situations: blended families, 35 percent; single-parent families, 30 percent; adoptive families, 10 percent; biological families, 15 percent; sibling process (used when parents or other significant adults are not available), 7 percent; and foster families, 3 percent. Measuring effectiveness is viewed in terms of the family's successful completion of agreed-upon goals. An informal survey was made following the first two years of operation and the results charted on a continuum from "highly effective" to "highly ineffective." Fully 76 percent of the families seen placed above the midpoint on the continuum, and 24 percent placed somewhere below the midpoint. We were not "highly ineffective' with any family, but were "highly effective" with 12 percent. These results are due, in no small measure, to the competency of the staff members who make up the therapy teams.

After the second year of operation, we began to focus on developing the short-term intervention component of treatment. Building on the initial design and two years of experience, eight specific intervention points were identified: first, when a child is having difficulty due to inadequate family support, such as lack of visiting; second, when a family is in crisis and in need of supportive care; third, when inappropriate interactions between the child and the family jeopardize continued placement, such as encouraging defiance of rules; fourth, using the family's presence at the six-month plan of service to work on preestablished goals to strengthen the child's placement and enhance family strengths; fifth, when parental rights have been terminated, or no significant family members are available, using a family-type sibling process to facilitate family roots and identity; sixth, when the child is acting out on the home unit, since research indicates disruptive behavior tends to be reduced by bringing parents in to assist the campus staff with the problem [Morgan 1987]; seventh, crisis intervention with families threatening premature removal of the child; and eighth, at the time of discharge planning to facilitate the reintegration of the child into the family setting.

These potential intervention points are discussed informally with the caseworkers in the routine of daily contacts. All interventions are now being used—some handled by the campus caseworkers and some by the center's staff—and account, in part, for the increase in the number of families seen during the third year. In short, the center is receiving a steady flow of referrals, and campus staff members report they are becoming more involved with families in their casework. An excellent working relationship exists between the center's staff and the campus caseworkers, and between the caseworkers and family members, due, in large measure, to the openness of the campus staff members and their commitment to quality care.

Stage Two

The second stage in implementing the model involved two of the three education components. First was the development of training seminars for the clergy, which was mandated by the board in its approval of the center's design. They have two objectives: practical skill development for parish ministry, and the care of church professionals. In the first year of operation, a monthly series of seminars was begun, emphasizing an in-depth, small-group experience lasting from one to three days, depending on its focus. Over the past three years these seminars have drawn participants from 31 of the 48 Methodist districts we serve, plus five other denominations. Participants receive CEU credits from the agency.

The next year, seminars were added in and for local Methodist districts, led by the center's director. These seminars have averaged 20 to 25 participants. Formal and informal evaluations of both programs are highly favorable. They are enabling us to build a network of referral and support for the agency and also providing a group of professionals to whom persons needing a local contact can be referred.

One of the most successful programs offered by the center is "Family Updates." These monthly one-day or two-day seminars deal with the broad area of working with families and include campus staff members, the clergy, and other professionals drawn from the child-care and mental health fields. Formal evaluations consistently show high ratings. All participants receive CEU credits from the local community college, and social workers receive CEU credits from the state accrediting agency. Two graduate schools have also approved both seminar programs as independent study coursework. This program has allowed us to link many areas of staff development and community outreach into one program. It has also allowed for cross-fertilization and the enhancement of a sense of unity and purpose campuswide.

Stage Three

The third stage in implementing the model involved the admissions process. Most agencies do a good job of gathering information about the child, such as developmental history, behavior patterns, social history, school performance, and psychological assessment. Often they rely heavily on the family to provide much of this information. A family model, however, also involves developing an understanding of how the family functions.

If an agency is to see the family as the focus of care, it must be able to answer the question: what stresses this system, putting it at risk for dysfunctional parenting and the development of emotional/behavioral disturbances in its children? To answer that question involves a shift in the way the agency goes about the intake process. It means gathering additional kinds of information, and gathering it in a different way. This information is highly valuable in working with a family even in a more child-centered agency, but it is essential in agencies seeking to develop services tailored to the needs of families.

The center's director began meeting with the admissions staff members to become familiar with their intake procedures and to suggest ways that the process could be made more inclusive of families and family assessment. This occasion was the first time the family model had significantly engaged "how it has always been done on campus." Although the admissions staff members were well trained in the child-centered approach, most were quite open to the evolving new family-oriented direction. Nevertheless, some distinct philosophical differences emerged, and the administrator intervened. First, he asked the director to keep him informed by way of reports. Second, he visited the unit and, during an admissions care presentation, took the opportunity to explain elements of the new concept. The director and the admissions staff also spent a goodly amount of time working on their relationship and on their differences.

It is to their credit that the admissions staff had the maturity and openness to explore new directions in the midst of confusion and philosophical differences, and new developments began to emerge. First, we began emphasizing the family being present and actively involved in the intake process, and making clear that the agency regards itself as a partner in parenting, not a rescuer of children from parental failures. Second, we improved our methods for gathering a history of the family itself, not just a history of the child. Third, we began developing methods for assessing family structure and family functioning. Fourth, we began placing emphasis on clearly identifying the reason the family was not living together, in an effort to avoid any suggestion of "what's wrong with the child."

Attention was then drawn to the process of transfer from the admissions unit to campus residency. Since this event can be a difficult time for both child and family, involving both grief and separation anxiety, families tend to resist attending the transfer conference. Nevertheless, it is vital that the family go through the experience together. The transfer conference is a crisis point and, depending on how it is handled, can either further distance the family from the child or begin the process of eventual healing. Hence, it is worth "hanging tough" on the issue of family attendance.

The admissions staff and campus staff members worked together to redesign the transfer conference. The result was a process that: (1) allows for the fullest possible utilization of the information gathered by the intake process; (2) involves the family as fully as possible; and (3) maximizes the child's sense of security and belonging. The following objectives were identified: determining the beginning level of family involvement (i.e., letters, phone calls, weekend visits, and so on); building relationships between the family and campus staff; highlighting family strengths; and firming up placement goals.

Next we sought to identify specific points at which short-term interventions would be helpful in problem placements. Again, building on the initial design created by the department directors, six intervention points were identified: first, when a youngster is viewed as appropriate for placement, but is considered at risk because of an ambivalent family; second, when it has been determined that a family will continue to give destructive messages to a child after placement; third, when the issue of placement needs clarification for whatever reason (e.g., initial length of stay); fourth, when a family is invested in the child's return home and starting a family process early would facilitate that eventuality; fifth, when a family is currently in a crisis that is hindering the intake process; sixth, when the intake staff, for whatever reason, is having difficulty with a family or feels unsure about placement.

It is now routine for the center's staff to join with the admissions staff to assess a difficult placement, and most often the placement is strengthened. The admissions staff has used the Family Updates to strengthen their skills in working with families, and one member of their staff is receiving training in family therapy at the center. Recently the admissions unit was reorganized to integrate it more fully with the campus group care divisions, and we are awaiting completion of this change.

Stage Four

The fourth stage in implementing the model involved the development of family life education programs for families who have children in placement. The agency had already begun several programs before the center was developed. First, the Boy's Ranch had offered single parents a weekend experience in parenting that was highly successful. The results were described as (1) strengthening the family units involved; (2) facilitating mutual understanding between the agency and the family; and (3) creating a stronger bond between the agency and the family. Second, the agency's External Affairs department had long been involved in a program called Positive Parenting. This effective program uses agency staff members to conduct miniseminars in and for local Methodist churches. Thus, a tradition of education programming had already been established.

At present, one of the casework supervisors on campus has been working with his staff to research several target populations that might benefit from such prevention programs. Within the next few months, a program will be implemented as as pilot project. Learning from this experience, we then plan to identify other groups and design programs germane to their needs.

Future Plans

The center's director has recently completed a three-year research project, developing a model for the continuing education of parish clergy in family pastoral care. The next step will be a market survey among Methodist district superintendents and a randomly selected group of parish clergy. If this project gets off the ground, it will be an innovative program in the training of the clergy, and a major step in extending the family model beyond the parameters of the agency. It will also tie the church and the child-care agency more closely together in a joint ministry to families.

Conclusion

This paper has attempted to face realistically how a church-related child-care agency makes the transformation from a child-centered focus to a family-oriented continuum of care. In so doing, it recognizes that the healthy agency always takes a balanced, evolutionary approach to change. It has also kept in mind that those of us in church-related child care are essentially a pilgrim people, with no fixed point of reference save the needs of children that launched us, and the goals of responsible ministry and professionalism that serve as our markers along the way.

Paradoxically, the model presented here is not new. Various elements of the model are already being used by many child-care agencies across the nation. In this regard, we are rediscovering our roots. Carl Carstens, the first director of CWLA, said in a speech delivered in 1927:

> If family ties are to be conserved and family responsibilities insisted upon, systematic attention is needed in dealing with the families of children for whom we are caring. . . . The agency which receives children into care has the obligation of undertaking systematic social work with the family if there is any semblance of family life or family spirit left. . . . When the child comes into care, the family comes with it. . . . By such means reconstructive and recreative work with families becomes possible, the child does not remain away from his home any longer than is necessary, and there is ample opportunity for his adjustment and follow-up.

So the idea of a family care system is not new: we are only coming back to where we started, yet know the place for the first time. What is new is that it is being tried, and it is enhancing the work of church-related group care agencies, both in programs of out-of-home placement and in prevention of family breakdown. It will also help the church realize that child care is a vital force in carrying out its mission.

References

Keith-Lucas, Alan, and Sanford, Clifford (eds.). *Group Child Care as a Family Service.* Chapel Hill, North Carolina: University of North Carolina Press, ca. 1977.

Morgan, Rebecca A. *The Effects of Family Visitation on the Moods and Behaviors of Children in Residential Care.* Unpublished master's thesis, May 1987. The University of Texas at Arlington.

10

Programming to Meet Children's Needs: The Integration of a Comprehensive Service System for High-Risk Adolescents[a]

DAVID C. DROPPA
CHRISTINE H. DONNORUMMO
JUDITH S. MICHAEL

T HE CONCEPT OF INTEGRATED SERVICES FOR children and adolescents with social, emotional, and behavioral problems is of relatively recent origin. During the 1800s and early 1900s, the typical service for children was a single service: an orphanage, school, or child guidance clinic. A few programs developed more complexity during the 1950s and 1960s, but it was not until the late 1970s and early 1980s that more comprehensive service systems for troubled children were designed.

This paper describes the development, composition, and operation of an integrated, comprehensive service system to meet the needs of high-risk children. Of interest to administrators and clinicians will be the matrix of services represented, barriers to successful integration and corresponding strategies, and program

[a]The authors wish to acknowledge the contribution of Nancy Johnson, M.Ed., in the development of this paper.

features that contribute to successful treatment of a high-risk adolescent population.

History and Nature of Parent Organization

Three Rivers Youth (TRY), is a not-for-profit agency located in Pittsburgh (Allegheny County), Pennsylvania. It was organized in 1970 through the consolidation of two residential programs: the Termon Avenue Home for Children, an institution founded in 1880 by the Women's Methodist Association, and the Girls' Service Club, a home for adolescent girls founded in 1914 by the Junior League of Pittsburgh. The mission of the new agency was to provide a network of group homes for adolescents. The target population was high-risk adolescents 13 to 18 years of age, with histories of early childhood abuse and deprivation, lack of supervision and guidance, multiple placement failures, and severe educational and vocational deficits. Their behavior was characterized by juvenile offenses, status offenses, aggression, withdrawal, school failure, drug and alcohol abuse, pregnancy, poorly developed peer relationships, and lack of respect for authority. The agency has also been careful not to screen out children who also present severe behavior problems, with the result that increasing proportions of caseloads comprise adolescents with conduct disorder and borderline diagnostic characteristics.

From 1970 through 1982, TRY developed a network of eight community-based group homes: residential treatment programs for adolescents located in neighborhood residences, each with a team of professional houseparents, a full-time supervisor, and a social worker. The group home program served a racially integrated population, and care was taken to maintain, whenever possible, a mix of houseparents in each unit along age, sex, and race dimensions. The houseparent team was modeled after the extended family concept, successful in most communities. In general, individual child-care staff members, rather than houseparent couples, were used. The agency was able to purchase each of its residences, contributing to the stability of each unit within its neighborhood. Each group home used health, educational, recreational, social, and religious resources available in the community.

In the beginning, the agency adopted a psychodynamic approach to treatment, relying primarily on individual and group intervention. Based on experience with the high-risk population and work with families in the first eight years, and with the aid of consultants, the agency developed a family systems treatment approach, which required intensive retraining of the staff. Later, this approach was supplemented with a behavior management system designed by the staff. The latter features a developmentally based level system emphasizing the adolescent's sense of responsibility and involving the adolescent and peer group in strategic clinical thinking. A strong educational diagnostic-prescriptive program, with educational advocacy for each youth, is an important aspect of the residential program. Qualities stressed in working with adolescents and families include persistence, caring, and willingness to confront unproductive attitudes and behaviors. The adolescent is involved in setting goals and giving and accepting feedback. Empowerment and involvement of the adolescent in decision making with adults are facilitated through a Youth Advisory Board.

During the early 1980s, the agency began to consider the development of a multicomponent treatment system. Interest grew as experience demonstrated that multiple problems needed multiple answers, including greater accessibility of adolescents to relevant programs. A pilot project that highlighted the potential of this approach was a summer program specializing in employment training for youths who saw no hope of obtaining or keeping a summer job. All of the youths in the residential program were successfully employed that summer, as well as a number of high-risk youths living in their own homes and referred by two city high schools. Interest quickly developed in the idea of a year-round job training program for those who were not able to graduate from high school before having to leave the residential program.

The administrative team also thought about other types of programs that would enable the agency the better to meet the complex needs of high-risk adolescents, and to engage more successfully the few who were not being sufficiently helped by a single-stream residential service. In 1981, TRY participated in a study, which was conducted by the Child Welfare League of America, that indicated it would be strategically sound for the agency to move toward more diversification. The findings were based on local and national trends not only in terms of needs but also in terms of funding and availability of services.

In 1982, TRY was successful in obtaining funding as part of the Act Together national demonstration to implement model programs for high-risk adolescents. An integrated service system was designed, based on past experience and assessment of the unmet needs of the adolescents that the agency had been serving. Act Together, a private Washington-based corporation, used funding from the federal Departments of Labor and Justice, combined with foundation matching funds. The fiscal design for TRY's demonstration involved phasing out Act Together funds as other funding sources increased over the span of the 18-month project. Under the Act Together demonstration, TRY accomplished the diversification of its services, with increased emphasis on programs to serve adolescents who live in their own homes, and on more consistent family outreach. As the network of services developed, the agency turned its attention to integrating the services, with continuity of treatment planning across a broad spectrum of problems and changing needs of troubled adolescents.

The TRY Comprehensive Service System

The current mix of services includes five residential and four nonresidential programs. Figure 1 shows how these programs interface. Five *residential* programs are available to adolescents referred by counties or states placing the adolescent under a court order of dependency or delinquency:

a. Two group homes for adolescents who need more supervision and treatment than is available at home or in other residential care

b. Two residential Teen Parent programs serve adolescent girls who have children and need assistance in becoming effective in independently caring for both themselves and their babies

c. A staff-secure residential Intensive Treatment Unit, for adolescents who need behavioral control and stabilization: This unit includes an in-house school program and

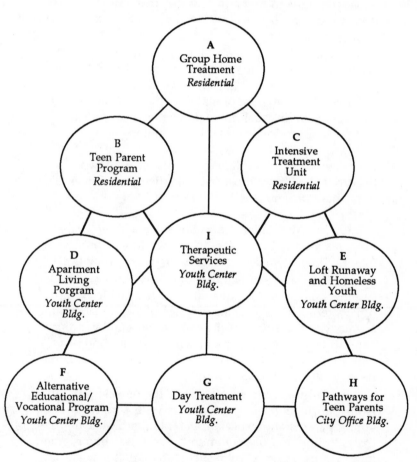

Figure 1. Three Rivers Youth, Intergrated Service System.

can be used for assessment, residential treatment back-up, or the first phase in a program of progressively less structured placement for adolescents with especially difficult social or behavioral problems

d. A small Apartment Living Program assists older adolescent girls in preparing for independent living: The program emphasizes acquisition of budgeting and money management skills

e. The Loft, a program for runaway and homeless youths—for adolescents who are at immediate risk of running away from home as well as for those who have already run: The program provides temporary shelter, crisis counseling, individual and family therapy, information and referral services, and a 24-hour hotline

Four *nonresidential* programs are available to the youths in residential care as well as to those living in their own homes. The age range for these programs is 13 to 21.

f. The Alternative Educational/Vocational Program prepares youths for success in the world of work, while helping them to make up necessary school credits.

g. The Day Treatment Program serves the youths returning home from residential care: It provides a structured afternoon and evening program of individual, group, and activity therapy, as well as educational and vocational support to the young person, while working intensively with the family; it also serves as an alternative to residential placement for some youths.

h. Pathways for Teen Parents, the newest program, is an information, support, and referral service to help young parents and expectant parents, both male and female, to find and use community services: The program links young parents with shelter, job training, health, counseling, and other services.

i. An adolescent partial hospitalization program, called Therapeutic Services, is available to youths or young adults in need of a highly structured and intensive day or afternoon/evening program: This program is a central service in the integrated treatment system; youths from each program have access to it as needed.

The programs are geographically distributed over a two-county area. A variety of locations, from central to city to suburban communities, in community-based settings, supports personalization of service to individual clients instead of institutionalizing services on one campus.

The integrated program design has led to achievement of the agency's initial goals. Despite the severe problems of the adolescents referred, it is rare that a child cannot be successfully treated using the integrated system approach. Varied sources of referral now exist, and adolescents can gain access to the system from a variety of points. The residential program receives referrals from a five-state area. Referral sources to most of the nonresidential programs are equally diverse, representing a broad cross-section of community agencies, police, schools, churches, and families. The agency also has a high level of fiscal diversity, with funding from state and federal grants, county and state per diems, third-party insurers, private and corporate foundations, United Way, and private contributions. To enable comprehensive service delivery, slots are maintained in some programs for internal referrals, reducing the likelihood of adolescents and young adults falling between the cracks, as often occurs in interagency referrals.

The idea of a continuum of care is attractive to most referral agencies and funding sources. There appear to be two reasons for this preference: first, the desire to achieve fiscal economy when the client receives the appropriate level of service and can move to less intensive and less costly programs over time, and, second, to comply with the philosophical and regulatory move toward less restrictive placement in accord with permanency planning regulations. At TRY, each program is marketed and funded as a single service, and contracts are negotiated between TRY and the county, state, or federal funding source, with separate program or unit costs for each type of service. A degree of economy is also achieved with an integrated model because administrative and central supportive services are not duplicated. Issues regarding authorization for transfer of a client from one service to another are managed by involving the placing agency or referral agency in the planning process. There is some pressure from regulatory and legal bodies that do not sufficiently understand a continuum-of-services perspective to become involved in questioning or subverting such transfers, sometimes to the detriment of continuity of treatment. Although the continuum-of-care model is well accepted in the health care field, it is relatively novel in social services. It is important that it be thoroughly communicated and understood at legal, regulatory, and governmental levels.

Examples of Integrated Programming for Adolescents

Because the TRY system offers a continuum of services, from more restrictive (such as the Intensive Treatment Unit, where adolescents are placed by the courts) to voluntary (such as the Loft and Therapeutic Services programs, to which youths are frequently self-referred), adolescents can move through the system with services targeted to their changing treatment needs. For example, Yolanda, a 16-year-old delinquent and assaultive teen parent with a history of running from home and placement, was referred to TRY when a second pregnancy was confirmed. After an intake assessment, she was admitted to the Intensive Treatment Unit. When Yolanda completed the program, she was transferred to the residential Teen Parent Program, where she delivered her second child, whom she placed for adoption. When her first child joined her in the Teen Parent Program, Yolanda began to work on parenting goals. Because completion of high school during her remaining time in placement was extremely unlikely, Yolanda was enrolled in the educational/vocational component and concurrently attended Therapeutic Services. This combination of services (residential, educational/vocational, and partial hospitalization) resulted in Yolanda's gaining parenting skills, receiving her high school equivalency diploma, and completing clerical training on a nonprofit job site, while achieving social and emotional goals in the partial hospitalization program. Upon her move to independent living, Yolanda participated in a reduced level of services in the Therapeutic Services program, and the risk of reinstitutionalization was dramatically reduced. At one-year follow-up, Yolanda, now 19, was employed, living independently with her child, and was not regarded as a risk for inpatient services.

Roger, a young man with a history of unsuccessful residential placements, initially entered the Day Treatment program, but four months later his mother was hospitalized and he required group home placement, where continuity of his treatment goals could be maintained. Roger was admitted to TRY's boys group home. When the home situation stabilized, Roger was able to move back, again with Day Treatment/Therapeutic Services support. During several crises at home, Roger received emergency shelter services through the Loft Program for Runaway and Homeless Youth. Now living independently and employed, Roger continues to attend Therapeutic Services two days a week.

Multicomponent Integrated Planning

Although it is easier to talk about integrated programming as moving the child through a multicomponent system, it is more accurate to conceptualize integration as a process of fitting the programs to the child's needs. The starting place for program decisions—whether at time of referral, after admission, at the time of initial treatment planning, at treatment review, or when planning strategies to prevent a crisis—is the identification of the youth's needs, deciding what resources are appropriate, and in what sequence. Through a case management process, program resources are targeted to produce an effect when needed. Frequently the youth is helped to change because of the relevance and timing of the intervention, as well as the fact that staff members from several components—some in which the youth may no longer be active— are cooperating in support of intervention, and communicating this fact, as well as providing encouragement to the young person and to his or her family. To put in place a comprehensive, multicomponent system may appear to be the major achievement, but this step is only the beginning. Upon analysis, what seemed like three years of growing pains (after the comprehensive system was in place) actually comprised two phases: first, building structures to facilitate the integrated programming; and second, for staff members at all levels to learn the processes for working with each other within the structures. The growing pains and solutions in each of these phases, referred to as integrative structures and integrative processes, respectively, are the focus of the next two sections of this paper.

Development of the Integrative Structures

Once the multicomponent system was in place, it quickly became evident that the matrix of new programs was not working effectively together to provide integrated services. As a client moved from one program to another, the receiving program frequently acted as though it were starting fresh, failing to use the knowledge base of the referring program, while the referring program covered hurt feelings with a seeming attitude of mistrust that "their" client would receive proper care.

Assumptions that sibling rivalry, mistrust, and pride would not exist within an agency with common goals were sadly without foundation. Early in the development of the system, an agencywide conference was held with 15 key managers and therapists to further the ability of programs to work together. The integration of the Therapeutic Services program with other components was used as a case study. Information from this conference was taken into administrative and other meetings, where the following series of strategies was carried out.

First, it was decided to hold a weekly meeting with managers from each unit to increase communication, coordination, and planning. This meeting eventually evolved into a biweekly management meeting that included all managers, consulting therapists, and administrative staff members.

Second, a meeting was held with all agency staff members and, after a "getting-to-know-one-another" exercise, the 40 participants were divided into six subgroups to brainstorm ways of increasing coordination of effort. Each group recorded its suggestions, which were then discussed by the entire group. The administrative team later developed strategies for implementation. Ideas from this meeting led to modifications in the orientation of new staff members, a revitalization of interest in, and implementation of, a youth newsletter, and a monthly meeting of program staff members to increase communication and program planning at the line staff level.

Third, it was recognized that when new programs were installed, they had to be "marketed" internally, not only to supervisors and therapists, but to line staff members, whose perceptions would be most keenly recognized by the youths themselves.

Fourth, a weekly Clinical Case Conference was established, with representatives of each unit in the agency attending. The conference, chaired by the director of training, was an arena for clinical strategy planning regarding clients whose treatment programs were increasingly affected by more than one component. Initially used for crisis consultation, the conference soon became valued for preventive planning, particularly useful before a client made the transition from one unit to another.

Fifth, training in management and systemic dynamics was set up for key staff members from each component.

Sixth, the Youth Advisory Board, which had included two youths from each residential unit, was expanded to include youths from nonresidential components as well. Meeting monthly with the executive director and an agency therapist, the Youth Advisory Board has proved to be a potent integrating force at the client level.

As the system increased in complexity, case management emerged as a problem. When two or more units were providing services to one client at the same time, the flow of information among units was sometimes spotty or nonexistent, and processes for making coordinated decisions were unclear, tending to cause polarization, conflict, and fault-finding. John, a client in the educational/vocational program, talked one of his teachers into driving him back to the group home after school, since she lived nearby. On one hand, she began to believe John's stories that he was not being treated fairly in the group home; the group home staff, on the other hand, were alarmed by what they perceived as an inappropriate relationship between teacher and student. Although feelings intensified on the part of the staff in both programs, the procedures for communication and conflict resolution were unclear. These issues reached a crisis point after John ran away from the group home and enlisted his mother's support in approaching his juvenile court judge to request a transfer to another agency. A clinical case conference was immediately scheduled with line staff members from the group home and educational components attending, including the houseparents and teacher. The conference explored the intense feelings of the staff members in both units and then moved to assist them to take responsibility for understanding and better managing the clinical issues for the young man and his family. Next, the management team, working as a unit with leadership from the executive director and consulting psychologist, put into effect a new case management process.

The Case Management System

It was decided that, for clients receiving more than one service simultaneously, the therapist in each program would be assigned as a case manager. From among these therapists, a primary case manager would be designated, with authority to coordinate treatment planning. Written policies and procedures spelled out lines of communication, procedures for written and verbal communication, authority of the case manager, and mechanisms for resolving conflict. Although some limited problems in communication and coordination inevitably remain, this case management system has brought about a much higher level of interunit cooperation.

Coordination of Intake Process

More recently, the management team began to address the need for a systematic process of treatment planning at the point of initial intake. Decisions regarding which program would serve a client and in what sequence appeared somewhat haphazard, at times related more to the point of entry for a new client rather than to treatment needs. Out of the management team, two specialized committees were developed. The first committee worked for approximately one year to standardize and streamline all client forms, so that, regardless of program unit, uniform and complete information would be available for each client. A second committee began work on an integrated treatment planning system, to ensure more standardized goal setting across program lines. Currently being implemented is the appointment of an intake coordinator who will oversee intake functions across all programs in the agency, so that, regardless of the point of entry, questions can be asked about level and sequencing of treatment for the client and family.

Integrative Processes/Staff Management

Once the major integrative structures were in place, we erroneously believed that effective integration would flow naturally. It was soon discovered that more subtle, pervasive, and perplexing barriers to integration persisted in the ways that program staff members were working with each other within the structures. Sometimes it seemed as if staff members were unaware of what the structures could do, were unable to use their authority, and would not trust each other to work together in behalf of mutually shared clients. Despite these hindrances, integration has appeared to fall into place across the entire agency during the past year. We note a more sophisticated use of integrative processes as staff members at all levels have become more available as resources for each other. It has been interesting to explore why this is so.

First, staff members are encouraged to be open about frustrations and opinions that might otherwise go underground. In an agency system, feelings of pain and anger are frequently projected upward toward the administration or downward, either to line staff or, ultimately, to the clients. The staff began instead to use existing structures (team meetings, unit meetings, and management meetings) to acknowledge lack of understanding about other programs, disagreement about decisions, and to express feelings of being discounted or "dumped on." At a special clinical case conference for staff problems, attended by almost every Youth Center staff member, the management and line staff expressed intense feelings about frustrations in working effectively together and then focused on having too few staff members to do the work necessary with such difficult youths. The executive director, who does not usually attend clinical case conferences, came in and, at an appropriate point, expressed her frustration at being unable to develop the fiscal resources quickly enough to add staffing that was needed to do the job in a more ideal manner. Once these feelings were expressed, the conference was able to focus on ways that staff members could work together more effectively, even with current staffing constraints. Perhaps as a result of this kind of openness, staff members at all levels began to trust each other's intent. Communication of the staff's experiences, including frustrations, fear, and pain, has created more understanding among all sectors in the agency. The consulting psychologist and director of training facilitated much of this teamwork and also provided training for working with an increasingly difficult population.

Second, the significance of intrastaff authority and empowerment has begun to be realized more deeply. The mandate to work with the toughest, most failure-battered youths clearly originates from the agency's board of directors and executive director. The agency mission and philosophy are communicated to all levels of staff in various agency, team, clinical, and training meetings. The executive mandate has built-in teeth: the referral file of any youth not recommended for acceptance following review at the program level is referred to the executive director for final review. The executive's question is always the same: "What would it take to work with this child?" It is clear that the final decision rests at the executive level, although acceptance of the mandate at lower levels reduces the incidence of disagreement at the top level. Likewise, a recommendation to discharge a child because of behavior problems requires executive review and approval. Review and intervention steps built into the system make this recommendation an extreme rarity.

Encouraging and enabling managers at all levels to use their authority in the service of integration has paid off. The residential program supervisor directed that for a particularly perplexing clinical case conference, line staff members from two residential units must attend, no matter what it took. The richness of perceptions brought to the conference by line staff members resulted in especially productive strategy planning.

The counterpart to effective use of authority has been the empowerment of the program staff, which has been especially rewarding as it occurred at the line level. Program staff members began to assume ownership of the Program Staff Meeting, as well as using the meeting to talk to their counterparts in other units. At one meeting, houseparents from the Intensive Treatment Unit stated that, due to crises in that unit, they could not always attend this monthly meeting. With encouragement from line staff from other units, the houseparents began to talk about the intense emotional stress of their work with severely disturbed adolescents and received in turn expressions of understanding and respect from other staff members.

More recently, a relief houseparent in the Teen Parent Program initiated a process of inviting residents from other units, four at a time, to dinner at her program. Reporting the positive results of this innovation at the next monthly program staff meeting led to interest in each unit learning enough about one other unit to give a report about that unit in a subsequent meeting. The staff of the Youth Center proposed a New Year's party at their program site, to include youths from all the residential units. The party was such a success that two youths who had run away from their group home called and asked to be picked up to attend the event, and, before the evening was out, staff members from several units were exploring with these two girls the issues that had led to their running away and were developing combined intervention strategies to continue to work with the two girls.

Empowerment appears to have freed the creative energy of staff members to build structures they need to work better with clients they share. An example is the use of the Intensive Treatment Unit (ITU) as a consulting resource. The ITU initially held two spaces as backup for group home residents who needed a short-term stay, benefiting from the unit's special structure and supervision. Over time, staff members together designed a consulting structure as a resource to the other group homes. Using this structure, the resident, houseparent staff, consulting therapists, and supervisors from both units meet to discuss current issues and needs of the resident. In a short time the ITU consultation process developed so successfully that not only do residents rarely require backup in the ITU, but spaces are no longer held.

At the Youth Center, runaways admitted to the Loft shelter needed a group treatment experience with young people who were managing to live at home and relate to their parents with varying degrees of success. At the same time, the census in the Therapeutic Services program was increasing, and staff members in that unit were frustrated because they could not provide more diverse groups for their clients. The Loft staff volunteered to design and facilitate groups for youths from both programs and, as a result, runaways temporarily sheltered at the Loft now regularly attend Therapeutic Services groups a minimum of two days per week.

Conclusion

As new programs are added to a continuum of services, more opportunities occur for the creation of integrative structures and the development of staff processes. When both structures and processes are initiated at the program staff level, the entire system is freed to develop in sophistication, complexity, and effectiveness. The planning, design, and implementation of integrated programming and supportive structures are facilitated by staff members becoming more available as resources for one another, by management and administrative staff members consistently setting the example for integrative work, and by staff members becoming more open and empowered. These efforts are reflected at the service level: in the course of one year, 70 percent of TRY's youths are involved in programming with more than one component.

Lest it appear that integrative processes in a multicomponent service system are primarily a line staff responsibility, it is important to note that without clear, solid, and consistent working together and role modeling at management and administrative levels, effective integration would not continue for long. Priorities must be chosen, clarified, and maintained by strong leadership. From clear decision-making processes, sound procedures, mutual program understanding, and strong staff commitment, a successful integrated system emerges. The advantage of a comprehensive service system over a single-component system is the greater number of treatment resources to which there is easier access, albeit the integration of a comprehensive service system is hard, challenging work, requiring many meetings and continuing individual and team self-analysis. The effort is worth it, the possibilities exciting, and, most important, the development of the adolescents is supported by an effective blend of services, offered when they are ready to use these. The rewards for providing integrated programming for children go hand in hand with the effort.

11

The Partnership of Child-Care Institutions and Child-Placing Agencies

JAKE TERPSTRA

Residential care can be a powerful rehabilitative tool for children and their families. Because a number of parties are involved in the process, it is particularly important that they work in coordination to respond to the needs of the child and the family.

Children in substitute care generally feel highly vulnerable, particularly those in child-care institutions. The size and complexity of group care programs, as well as the control these have over children, contribute to this feeling of vulnerability. There is an additional factor that causes the children and sometimes the institution staff to feel vulnerable: the distance, both literal and figurative, that often exists between the agency that placed the child and the institution that cares for the child. These negatives, however, can be minimized with careful planning and cooperation. This paper considers the issue and suggests ways to eliminate or reduce the distancing factors.

Many of the causes of lack of cooperation between the two organizations have to do with money. For example, cooperative effort requires regular and frequent contact, including travel, telephone calls, and correspondence, all of which require staff time as well as direct expenditures. High caseloads often are an obstacle to cooperation. Hiring well-qualified staff members and providing training contribute to understanding and appreciation of cooperation; these practices also are costly. These reasons are all significant, and at times critical, but they are mentioned here only to call attention to their importance, not to focus upon the need for resource development. The emphasis here is upon "doing the best you can with what you have," regardless of the relative adequacy or inadequacy of resources; it assumes a basic adequacy of resources.

Some factors may also be attitudinal. Agencies that place children into child-care institutions are under public auspices. Attitudes about which is of "better quality" or "more realistic" can hinder effective communication. Institution staff members also can develop "rescue fantasies" and fail to appreciate the critical linkage function of the placement agency.

Terms and Functions

Early in this century, family foster care began to replace institutional care to the point where the term foster care became practically synonomous with family foster care. Eventually, however, it was recognized that institutional care is also needed. In reality, it is widespread and comprises an ever-increasing array of group care services, which include staffed group homes. The term foster care, however, tended to remain with family care.

Simultaneously, the preponderance of family care and the application of the term foster care to family care tended to contribute to the idea that children in family care are within the child welfare system while children in child-care institutions are in another system. Although the care provided by institutions may be more intense, both are very much a part of the same out-of-home care or foster care system.

While this distortion is not universal, it is sufficiently prevalent to have delayed residential child-care participation in recent child welfare concepts, policies, and practices. Concepts of permanency planning have been more readily applied by child-placing agencies to children in family foster homes. This development has been slower and less consistent in residential group care, as though the concepts were fundamentally different from or alien to those settings. Child-placing agency staff members have tended to feel that once they have placed children in a child-care institution everything will be taken care of, and the case planning and case management responsibilities are fewer than those for children they have placed into family homes. Some institutions that care for children, such as medical and psychiatric hospitals, are not regarded as substitutes for care by the child's family and therefore are not considered foster care. Some residential care of children with severe developmental disabilities who need long-term alternatives to family living is not regarded as foster care. Nevertheless, the normal range of group care programs in the child welfare system do provide substitute or foster care for children who are temporarily unable to live with their families.

The terms "placement" and "care" are sometimes used interchangeably, contributing to role confusion. Once the child has been placed, the child is not in placement but is in care. Careful use of these terms helps to clarify the roles and responsibilities of child-placing agencies and child-care services. Only child placement agencies provide placement services, and only child-care providers have children in care. Their roles are different. Some child welfare agencies provide both child placement and child-care services, each with discrete functions and responsibilities.

Child-Placing Agency Functions

Child placement is the process of placing a child with someone other than the parents for full-time care. Placement consists of all the activities needed to move a child into adoptive or foster care, or from one foster care provider to another. The movement of a child from one component of a group care program, such as seven-day residential care to five-day treatment or to an independent-living group home within the same agency, is not placement, but case management. A fundamental component of child placement is the decision to place a child with a family or other provider of care and selection of the particular provider. This care may be temporary, or it may be intended to be permanent, as with adoption. The decisions involved in placement follow decisions for the child to be separated from his or her family and often are made by the same agency. The child-placing agency then has the responsibility to supervise the substitute care of the child and to continue case planning and case management. Juvenile courts sometimes place children into child-care institutions having placement authority; juvenile courts then, in effect, are child-placing agencies.

Sometimes child-placing agencies contract with others to carry out certain components of the placement process. For example, they may arrange to have adoption of foster home assessment studies performed by someone else. They also may obtain counseling services from someone else. The child-placing agency is responsible for all aspects of the placement process, and the subcontracting party is accountable to the agency for carrying out these particular activities properly.

There are limits to the amount of contracting out that a child-placing agency can do and still remain a bona fide agency. State licensing rules may set limits on these actions. The components that cannot be delegated are the decision to place the child and the concomitant selection (also a decision issue) of the particular provider of care. Being the essence of child placement, they are the central functions of the entire process.

A state license to operate a child placement agency, as well as a legislative mandate for public agencies, authorizes the agency to place children but not to place a particular child. This apparent contradiction is explained by the fact that, although the law and the license authorize the child-placing agency to engage in activities that are normally parental rights and responsibilities, such authorization does not give the agency control over any individual—control must be delegated individually for each child and can be given only by parents, a court, or someone to whom parents' rights have been transferred by a court of law.

When a child-placing agency decides to place a child, the question that immediately confronts the agency is, "What kind of care should the child receive?" The answer, of course, hinges upon an array of considerations:

> The strengths and needs of the child and the family
> The feelings of the parents toward the child, and vice versa
> The estimated length of time needed for rehabilitation of the family and the child

The support the family and others can provide while the child is in care

The child's special needs—physical, emotional, educational, learning, behavioral

The level of care needed to manage the child's behavior

The extent to which the child currently is able to relate positively to adults and peers

Cost variations among different types of care

There is a growing body of literature to help guide this process (see the bibliography), but, to complicate matters further, the choice of options has increased considerably in the last ten years. For example, specialized family foster care and day treatment are relatively new resources that have program intensity somewhere between family foster homes and group care programs. In-home preventive services and day care as alternatives to foster care are also used, though the potential for both is apparently far greater than actual use. All these resources increase the variety of options available to children, but their selective use requires extensive knowledge and skill.

Once a general category of service has been selected, the search for the best particular child-care provider begins. In actual practice, this selection often is based upon past experiences with certain providers. If a particular family home or group care program has done a good job with other children and has cooperated with the agency, the staff tends to use the same resource again. Absent other criteria, this manner of choice offers at least some assurance that the care provider will be beneficial. It does not, however, provide a careful analysis of either the needs of the child or the resources to deal with those needs.

Careful selection includes an analysis of the needs of the child and the child's family. The analysis may include psychological testing and psychiatric assessment; it is especially important that the assessments be done by the best-trained staff. Emergency shelter care staff members and emergency foster family home parents should be among the most sensitive and highly trained. Like the staff members of a hospital emergency room, they should be excellent diagnosticians and initiators of a further assessment and treatment process. The child-care resources being considered also must be carefully assessed. Generally, assessments of children are more carefully and thoroughly done than are assessments of the child-care provider, particularly if the provider is a group care program. A thorough understanding of the program into which the child is to be placed is as important as the understanding of the child, since placement is the matching process that brings them together. Understanding may be facilitated by visits and discussions with staff members of these facilities, as well as attendance and participation in case presentations.

In general, the placement agency needs to know the answer to two major questions in selecting a child-care institution: can it cope with the child's presenting problems, and is it equipped to deal with and resolve the underlying problems of the child and the family. Determining the answers to these questions requires the cooperative efforts of both agencies. Firsthand current knowledge of the child-care program is essential and includes evaluation of the specifics of the program relative to the needs of a particular child. Referrals (placements) based upon literature and telephone conversations alone are always inadequate.

All the components of effective work with children and families by both organizations point to the need to place children within a distance that makes frequent visiting relatively convenient. Placing a child more than a few hours' travel time from his or her family and community is to reduce sharply one of the most potentially valuable treatment components.

Making a placement includes three essential elements: criteria, judgment, and process. Selection/placement criteria alone are not a sufficient basis for selection. Professional judgment also is needed because there are many variables in each case, and because programs always are in a state of change. Placement into a particular program requires a certain amount of negotiation to plan individualized care for the child as well as to decide the division of agency responsibilities, such as who will work with the child's family, how the agencies will cooperate, and who is expected to provide aftercare. The details of this process may be taken for granted by seasoned child-placing agency staff members who repeatedly use the same resources, but new staff members generally are unaware of the need for them, and of their complexity.

The question occasionally arises regarding which organization has primary responsibility for being sure that a given child is admitted into the right program. The question cannot be given an either-or answer: each is fully responsible. Neither agency can assume that the other knows more key information and thereby abdicate a portion of the decision. Each agency must be sufficiently thorough in understanding all aspects of the match to be convinced that the child's and family's needs will be addressed in a knowledgeable way. If a child is inappropriately placed, each agency should consider itself 100 percent responsible for the error or, conversely, should consider positive outcomes the results of their original matching decision.

When child-care institution staff members deny admission of a child because they believe their program is not suited to the child's needs, they have a commensurate responsibility to make suggestions to the child-placing agency regarding programs they consider suitable.

Planning Toward Permanence

The referral-intake process sets the stage for virtually all the activities that follow. These include an assessment of the child and family made by the child-placing agency, as well as the agency's overall goals and plans for them. Agreements must be made on which aspects of the needs each agency will work on, from intake through aftercare. For example, arrangements should be made for group care program staff members to attend case reviews of the child-placing agency, and child-placing agency staff members to attend staffings of the group care program. The expected participation of the family is clarified at the outset, preferably before the child leaves the home, certainly before the child-care institution makes a decision to admit the child.

The content of the work with the family once a child is in care should be focused on eight different areas: (1) assisting the parents to understand the program and how it is attempting to help their child; (2) assuring and assisting the parents in their own continuing role in the life of their child; (3) defining the functions, the rights, and the duties of the parents during care; (4) supporting the child's care and treatment; (5) helping parents to change their own attitude toward their child; (6) helping the parents with problems that are not directly related to the child; (7) helping parents to resume full-time parenthood; and (8) aftercare. Parental involvement is critical to the process of helping the child and family. Parental involvement processes that include parents as co-clients, co-managers, co-therapists, and co-educators can enable the child and family to manage the rehabilitation process.

One aspect of parent participation is the financial contribution they will make toward the care of their child. Normally, this amount is decided by the child-placing agency staff. Many families whose children need substitute care have multiple problems, including financial, and are not in a position to contribute significantly. Expectations of family contributions must take into consideration that rehabilitation of the family is a fundamental goal. Therefore, contributions must not increase the family's financial burden so that it reduces the family potential for rehabilitation. Neither should families be relieved of all responsibility in this respect. Regardless of the family's financial status, therefore, it is essential that they contribute something regularly. For example, they may be expected to furnish only certain items of clothing. The symbolic value of this clothing, both to them and to their child, will help to clarify and keep in focus the parent-child relationship.

It is assumed that the parents also have been involved throughout the planning process if they are willing and able. The same is true for the child. Without their general acceptance of the plan, treatment is limited. This situation does not mean that treatment cannot be beneficial, but invariably it is more difficult. There also is the practical consideration of the child's basic loyalty and sense of belonging (often buried under the debris of conflict and anger). The parent-child relationship, regardless of what it is, will continue long after agency involvement is finished. Whatever the agency does to improve that relationship has lifetime value to the family. The question of which of the two agencies is to be actively involved with the family will vary from case to case. The key issue, however, is that there be such involvement, where possible, and that the agencies cooperatively work out a plan for carrying it out. Confirming such agreements in writing is essential.

A related question is the extent of the parental role each agency has. Each of them takes a part of that role. When parents' rights have not been removed, general good practice suggests that parents be encouraged to carry out as much parental responsibility as is feasible, with agency effort directed toward supplementing that role rather than replacing it.

Preplacement Visits

Many child-care institutions require preplacement visits. This practice generally increases the possibility of successful subsequent treatment. There is every reason to include parents in such visits, as well as in the actual placement. If the child, parents, and child-placing agency worker are able to participate in the visit, a clear message is conveyed to all the parties that each is a party to the plan and has a vested interest in its success.

A word of caution about preplacement visits may be in order, however; they must be carried out in such a way that the child is not on trial. The child-care institution intake decision is to be made before the visit takes place. Many children coming into foster care already have received as many rejections as most of us have experienced in a lifetime; they do not need another major rejection from the system that is designed to help them. They generally perceive residential care to be a last resort; the plan to admit a child should not be reversed as a result of a preplacement visit. There are two exceptions to this principle. If new information emerges during the visit or if the child's reaction to the visit is extremely negative, admission may be contraindicated and should be reconsidered. Occasionally, child-placing agencies are unwilling or unable to provide full information about a child, including negatives such as fire-setting, assaultive behavior, or certain illnesses. Obtaining such information may make it necessary for the institution staff members to reconsider their decision to admit the child.

Delineation of Roles and Divisions of Tasks

When the decision for admission has been made, the specifics of who does what are incorporated into the case plan. This process often comes into focus most clearly regarding contacts to be made with the family, and the coordination of continued planning, including aftercare, which may be carried out by the child-placing agency or included in the purchase-of-service agreement. A key thread running through this process is the child-placing agency worker's contact with the child while in care. That worker, in some respects, is a cooperative colleague of the group care program staff, while at the same time being responsible for supervising the care that the child receives. He or she is the person who holds the institution accountable for doing what it said it would do. Good practice requires that the placing agency staff social worker visit children in child-care institutions at least quarterly.

Before the placement, the agency worker may have been the child's caseworker as well as case manager. When a child is placed, the casework role transfers to the group care program social work staff, but the case management responsibility does not transfer. There are multiple reasons for the transfer of casework: the placing agency staff member generally cannot be available when needs arise unexpectedly, and, perhaps most significantly, he or she is not a part of the group care staff team. Discussion of the transfer can be held during the preplacement visit when both social workers are with the child and, when possible, also with the parents.

What then becomes the placing agency social worker's function with the child? It shifts into a combination of roles: agency representative, advocate, friendly visitor, and, in some respects, parent substitute. The agency worker must be willing to relinquish the casework therapist role and work with the group care staff in staying abreast of developments in the case, while also assuming responsibility for providing general case direction. In all but very unusual circumstances, the worker upholds the group care program to the child and to the child's family.

The placing agency worker role may include casework with the child's parents when it is needed, but the circumstances under which this work is to occur should be clearly understood by both agencies. This function also may be purchased from the child-care institution. As care of the child proceeds toward the child's leaving the institution, the placing agency worker's involvement increases somewhat. Often many important decisions must be made at that time, and involvement with the child's family increases. If the plan calls for resumption of the casework role by the placing agency caseworker, that process is started while the child is still in care. That relationship can be used supportively to help the child through the transition from residential care to living at home, or wherever the child goes next.

There may be additional players in the process. For example, there may be a court or a third-party payer, either of which may hold one or both agencies accountable in certain ways. Generally, this fact does not change the relationship that the child-placing agency and the residential care program have with each other, although it may make the picture more complex. As stated previously, the juvenile court may, in fact, be the child-placing agency.

In most instances the case direction is set at intake, if not before, and all activities of both agencies are directed toward the established goals. Occasionally it is necessary to make mid-course corrections. Perhaps the most drastic correction, although infrequent, is the shift away from the child's return home. When the initial case plan is made, it must be built upon a certain amount of optimism about positives in the parent-child relationship even though the potential may appear bleak at that time. With rare exceptions, the initial case direction must be toward family restoration. When the efforts of both agencies have been directed toward helping the family to regain stability and to return the child, and the parents then are still unable or unwilling to respond in a positive manner, it may be necessary to plan in another direction. A definite direction should be established within the first three months. Adjustments in the direction can be made at a time when circumstances change, but, for effective treatment, goals and directions must be clear. In all but extreme circumstances, agencies do not have the moral right to plan toward anything other than family restoration until strong efforts to work toward it have proven futile.

The tentativeness of the initial case plan must be removed rather quickly. Although this decision is the primary responsibility of the child-placing agency, it cannot adequately make this decision in a vacuum without the observations and recommendations of the residential group care staff, including those staff members who provide direct child care. There are six general categories or possible options for children who are determined to be ready to leave residential group care—movement to return to parents or relatives, adoption, family foster care, day treatment, less restrictive group care, or independent living. Each option requires the cooperative effort of both agencies. The movement of a child from one program component of a residential group care program to another must be communicated by the group care staff and understood and supported by the placing agency staff as a part of the child's treatment.

Whichever direction is chosen, it is essential that all involved parties be oriented to the plan. The original agreement should have designated which agency will do the necessary work in the child's community. If return home is the plan, it will include any needed work with the family during the child's care, plus aftercare when the child returns home.

If the goal is adoption, the placing agency staff must be involved in specific planning as soon as possible. This organization could be the agency that placed the child. If the group care program is part of a multi-service agency, the child-placing component could carry out the adoption.

If the child cannot return home, live with relatives, or be adopted, family foster care may be the next option. Placement into family foster care does not necessarily preclude subsequent adoption. A key ingredient here is the intent to establish a relationship that lasts indefinitely. If the child, even a teenager, does not have his or her own family, a psychological family still may develop, even without legal ties—one of the circumstances where the concept of permanency planning comes into focus; that is, "the process of helping a child to live in a family which offers the hope of establishing lifetime family relationships." This concept presumes that when the child becomes emancipated, the family will continue in a supportive relationship in which family elements will exist indefinitely.

The remaining option following foster care is emancipation or independent living. This option may be arranged by the placing agency, the institution, or by another organization that operates primarily for that purpose. Some states have developed licensing requirements for child-placing agencies that operate independent-living programs.

Regardless of which agency assumes the primary responsibility for helping the child to live independently, preparation for it should begin early in the child's care. Even where treatment for emotional problems occurs, the preparation can be woven into it as part of the child's reality; it provides opportunity for having and working toward specific goals. There are many facets to an independent-living program, but a factor of special import to the child is the connections or relationships that are established with others. Whoever places or cares for the child can contribute by helping the child to find, identify, or develop relationships that can be supportive later. Often the most meaningful and enduring relationships are relatives, especially siblings. Volunteers, including foster grandparents, also can be helpful and supportive.

Some independent-living programs are operated by organizations as their sole service; others are components of child welfare agencies. Children who enter independent-living programs may be a mix of those who were in foster care and those who were not, but who need help in their emancipation process. Although organizations that operate independent-living programs exclusively may be used to good advantage, components of their service must also be incorporated into basic foster care programs. Preparation for independent living must become an integral part of child-care services for older children, rather than begin at exit as an add-on or auxiliary service. And in a sense, learning responsibility all through childhood is groundwork for eventual emancipation.

The child-care staff of the group care programs can be especially helpful to anyone who will care for the child subsequent to leaving. They know the most about the child's day-to-day behavior and responses. Their direct communication with the person who will next be responsible for the care of the child, including the child's parents, can help to make the transition smoother.

Before services to children following care were recognized as an essential component of foster care service, no provision was made for them in case planning, and, therefore, they also were not included in purchase-of-service agreements. A child-placing agency that places a child in residential care should plan aftercare as a basic component of its services or arrange to purchase it from the child-care institution at the time the child is placed.

In spite of quality service and planning, there are times when it is necessary for a child who had been in foster care to need an additional period of care again. Unless there are compelling reasons to the contrary, it is in the child's best interests to return to the same child-care provider. The enhanced stability and feeling of acceptance this return provides to the child are obvious. It also makes it possible for the foster home or group care program to build upon what was accomplished before. Readmission requires the cooperation of both agencies almost as much as the initial placement.

A somewhat similar, if far less weighty, issue is the desire of some children to return for visits, sometimes to visit staff members or children who may still be there or simply to visit the premises. Warm welcomes are always in order and may provide an opportunity to put a positive cap on a period of trouble in the child's life. Closure of this kind can have much value for the individual.

Conclusions

Residential group child care often is not well understood by child-placing agency staff members. This lack has many negative implications for providers and users of services, increasing nonselective use of services, thereby reducing success. To the extent that this result is true, everyone loses. While this loss may never be thoroughly remedied, significant progress would be made if agency staff members who place children at least understand the institutions they use. The resulting reduction of distance between child-placing agencies and child-care institutions would sharply increase the effectiveness of each. Development of a partnership is a realistic goal that can be accomplished through careful cooperative effort between organizations, case by case, and step by step with each case.

With new types of services for children and their families increasing rapidly, the need for skill in selectively using those services increases proportionately. Because the selection process is carried out by both the child-placing agency and the agency providng child-care services, each must know the range of available services in order to be able to make wise placement-intake decisions that best serve the needs of children and their families. Cooperative effort of both agencies is essential, with specifics of this cooperation varying with the type of program involved. Much work needs to be done to clarify specific tasks and to delineate responsibility for carrying them out.

With the current increasing volume of need for service, coupled with increasing severity of problems, the need for service quality also increases. If increased service quality, quantity, and selective use of services, plus cooperative partnership of involved agencies can be achieved, children will be better served, with more efficient and economical use of resources.

There are no indications that human problems and needs will diminish in the foreseeable future. Careful, cooperative, and selective use of resources, based upon sound need assessments, will improve existing services in the short run. They also will reveal patterns of need to help guide the field of child welfare in expanding the most effective services and developing new kinds of services.

Bibliography

Blumenthal, Karen, and Weinberg, Anita. *Establishing Parental Involvement in Foster Care Agencies.* New York: Child Welfare League of America, 1984.

Dukette, Rita. *Structured Assessment: A Decision Making Guide For Child Welfare.* School of Social Work, Loyola University, with assistance of Region V Department of Health, Education, and Welfare, Washington, D.C., April 1978.

Keith-Lucas, Alan, and Sanford, Clifford (eds.). *Group Child Care as a Family Service.* Chapel Hill, North Carolina: University of North Carolina Press, ca. 1977.

Kreuger, Mark. *Careless to Caring for Troubled Youth.* New York: Child Welfare League of America, 1983.

Maidman, Frank. *Child Welfare: A Sourcebook of Knowledge and Practice.* New York: Child Welfare League of America, 1984.

Maluccio, Anthony N., and Simanoglu, Paula A. *The Challenge of Partnership: Working with Parents of Children in Foster Care.* New York: Child Welfare League of America, 1981.

Mayer, Morris F., Richman, L.H., and Balcerzak, E.A. *Group Care of Children: Crossroads and Transitions.* New York: Child Welfare League of America, 1977.

Michigan Department of Social Services. *Placement Guide: Children and Youth Services Manual.* Lansing, MI, 1982.

Paul, Sister Mary. *Criteria for Foster Placement and Alternatives to Foster Care.* Albany, New York: New York State Board of Social Welfare, 1975.

Residential Child Care Guidebook. Interstate Consortium on Residential Child Care, DHS, Trenton, N.J., September 1980.

Shostack, Albert L. *Group Homes for Teenagers: A Practical Guide.* New York: Human Sciences Press, Inc., 1987.

Taylor, Robert B. *The Kid Business.* Boston: Houghton Mifflin Co., 1981.

Whittaker, James K. *Caring for Troubled Children.* San Francisco, Washington, London: Jossey-Bass, 1979.

12

Applying the Residential CYCIS Behavior Assessment Component in Child-Care and Treatment Agencies

MYRTLE ASTRACHAN

T HIS PAPER DESCRIBES A METHODOLOGY THAT CAN BE applied to residential and day treatment programs for purposes of accountability, decision making, and treatment planning. Boards of trustees and funding sources are demanding objective evidence that treatment organizations actually do perform the tasks with which they are charged. Third-party payers also press for standards that contain objective criteria for specifying length of treatment and a rationale for continuation of treatment.

Residential treatment and group care programs require each child to have services from a number of staff members from different departments. Techniques for equating the information from each source and relating facts and impressions to an overall treatment plan consist mainly of staff conferences, verbal reports, and documentations in the record of staff observations. When care and treatment continue over time, anecdotal reports are subject to selective forgetting and other distortions of memory. Treatment planning and decision making in clinical programs are often a matter of professional consensus, with the case conference a major arena for the discussion. Decision making of this kind is subject to many psychological influences that can operate against valid analysis of significant data about the child. Although some of this difficulty is unavoidable in decision making by a group, it is greatly accentuated when there is no source of clearly documented, easily retrievable, clinical data that have a common language and are systematically collected.

The Beech Brook Child Assessment and Treatment Tracking System addresses these difficulties. (The CYCIS Program at Beech Brook was developed and implemented with funds from the TRW and Cleveland Foundations.)

Residential CYCIS

Under the sponsorship of the Child Welfare League of America, the American Public Welfare Association, and the National Council of Family and Juvenile Court Judges, a model computerized case management system was developed and termed CYCIS (Child and Youth Centered Information System).[1] In March 1982, tests in Summit County, Ohio, marked the successful conclusion of the CYCIS national prototype project. It was recognized by some of the participants in the project that the technology of CYCIS could be adapted to produce a smaller, microprocessor-based version that would be appropriate and helpful to residential treatment centers; it was identified as "Residential CYCIS."[2]

Like the original CYCIS, Residential CYCIS uses menus to guide the user through the various processing steps, tables to support simplified information storage and retrieval, and an event structure to provide the user with virtually unlimited flexibility in defining the activities the treatment center wishes to study. Residential CYCIS also adds the Beech Brook Child Assessment and Treatment Tracking System to the program management component of the original CYCIS. This addition provides a capacity for examining specific evaluation data from the various staff members serving a child and family and for integrating the data into useful information to assist in a therapeutic treatment process. It also produces reports that show the areas in which a child can function competently, the areas that need improvement, the types of behavior that change over time, and progress made in identified behavior goals. These reports are available on line or in printed form.

As a result of these capabilities, Residential CYCIS can provide monitoring of the treatment process and assistance for clinical personnel in decision making. The part of Residential CYCIS that is specific for the monitoring of treatment and case planning is known as the Beech Brook Child Assessment and Treatment Tracking System. It was initially developed at Beech Brook in 1982[3] and has been continually in use for the past five years, both in manual and computerized versions. It was originally computerized for the IBM PC-XT microcomputer, using the THEOS[4] operating system, the TAILORBASE[5] application development software package, and a BASIC language compiler. It was subsequently modified to run under both the THEOS-8 and THEOS-16 operating systems. A UNIX-based[6] version is under consideration. The Child Assessment and Treatment Tracking System is available presently both as a module of Residential CYCIS and as a stand-alone system compatible with over 40 different microcomputers.

Beech Brook Child Assessment and Treatment Tracking System

The Beech Brook Child Assessment and Treatment Tracking System uses 56 categories that are rated once a month, by multiple raters, on a scale from one to five. The behavior being rated is a sample of behavior for the one week of the month that precedes the ratings. These categories were adapted from the Devereux Elementary School Behavior Rating Scale and then expanded to pertain to both nonacademic as well as classroom settings. The categories, designed to include significant symptoms and important developmental characteristics related to emotional disturbances in children, are defined so that the higher the score, the more adequate is the behavior. A score of four defines a behavior that is frequent; a score of five defines a behavior that occurs every day. The scoring is based on the assumption that consistency of behavior is more important in tracking clinical progress than frequency of behavior.

Ratings are made independently, but concurrently, by assigned representatives from any three components of the program. The raters are always staff members who work directly with the child. Beech Brook is presently using raters from the school, therapeutic activity, and cottage programs. A group home program could use ratings from different shifts. If the department ratings for cottage life are eliminated or are adapted to children's behavior during transportation, the entire tracking system can be applied to a day treatment program. In addition to the ratings made by the staff, a rating is also made by at least one member of the family. Family ratings can be entered for as many as four family members and totaled as separate ratings or as a combined score. A self-rating is made by the child during a supervised period with the child's therapist or child-care worker.

Ratings are made once a month. If ratings are made more often, the paperwork required becomes more complex, and the information gathered reflects data more readily retrievable through logs and incident reports. Monthly ratings have been found in the Beech Brook experience to reflect best the longitudinal course of treatment. The raters are directed to record the experience of the week just before the rating, rather than to describe the entire month. This method reduces memory error. Families are directed to record scores based on information of a recent weekend or week-long holiday. If a child does not have home visits, ratings by parents are eliminated.

The categories that are rated apply to anxiety reactions, developmental difficulties, conduct disorders, oppositional disorders, attention deficit problems, and a wide range of problems characteristic of elementary school-age children.

Examples of some categories that are currently being tracked are hyperactivity, bowel soiling, talk about feelings, runaway, logical speech, completion of work, feeling anxious, blaming others, and so on. Substitute categories could be changed to adapt the tracking system to an adolescent population or one that was different from that of Beech Brook. The computer program is sufficiently flexible to allow for the omission of data from any department. A complete list of all the categories and their definitions, with a sample rating form, is included with this paper.

After the monthly data are entered into the computer for all the raters, it is possible to track children in a variety of ways:

Track each *category* to monitor the appearance, disappearance, or changes in the intensity of a behavior or reaction.

Track each *department* to study differences in the occurrence of child responses according to the area of program.

Track *parent* ratings in comparison with staff ratings or child self-evaluations.

Track the *child's* self-evaluations in relation to parent and/or staff evaluations.

Track differences among ratings of different family members.

Track different staff members for supervision.

A variety of ways of combining the data have been developed and applied clinically. They are also posted on a blackboard in cumulative form at the case reviews and are explained to the parents and reviewed by the staff members present.

The following scores have been found to be useful.

Staff Composite Score

This score is an average of all staff member ratings for all 56 categories. It is useful as a single, composite measure to describe the overall adjustment level of each child in the program, each month, during the total stay. With this score it is possible to examine for such phenomena as initial honeymoon, predischarge regression, seasonal variations, effects of holidays, overall progress or lack of improvement, readiness for discharge, or justification for continuing stay. Categories such as hyperactivity, pays attention, temper tantrums, crying, and so forth, can be examined, particularly with respect to psychotropic medication. Data on categories such as bowel soiling or wetting often are found to be useful when staff members change in a program and are then found to be giving erroneous historical information at case reviews.

Target Composite Score

This score is an average of staff ratings for a subset of selected categories pertinent to each child; this score is more sensitive to clinical change than the staff composite score. The target categories are identified in the client treatment or client rehabilitation plan. The changes that are found in the target composite score are appropriate to document progress in achieving aspects of the treatment plan. Improvement in the target score is a condition for planned discharge. Unless there is positive change in the target subset, the treatment program cannot be said to have met its treatment obligation, regardless of whatever other positive changes may have occurred incidental to placement.

Parent Score or Family Average Score

This score is an average of ratings made by family members for all 56 categories. It is useful to indicate changes in the child as experienced and reported by the family; it is also used in comparing the perceptions of the child in staff ratings and in family ratings.

Family—Staff Score

This score expresses the difference between the family score and the staff composite score. When the staff score is higher than the family score, the result will have a minus sign. When the family score is greater than the staff score, the result will have a plus sign. The assumption is that in successful treatment the ratings of the staff and the family will become closer. If a conspicuous difference is found, the finding needs to be understood clinically. Ratings by the family that persist in being markedly lower than staff ratings over a period of time are one criterion for residential treatment rather than a day program. Family ratings that are consistently higher than staff ratings should initiate thinking in favor of day treatment. Often the identification to the parents of the discrepancy between their score and that of the staff results in a flow of new material from the parents.

Child Evaluation

This score is the average of the child's self-rating; this score is usually higher than any staff or family score. It is important to check the printed matrix for the categories about which the child is concerned; it is not unusual for the areas in which the child gives low self-ratings to be different from the categories that the staff or parents identify as problematic. This result leads to important clinical planning. The child evaluation score is viewed as related to insight. It is also related to the extent to which the child is open to sharing his or her concerns.

OK Score

This score gives the number of categories in which the staff describes the child as doing sufficiently well to earn category scores of four or more. The data suggest that children need an OK score of at least 40 to indicate readiness for discharge.

Some children, however, never have an OK score of less than 56 (100 percent of the categories). These children either are improperly placed in residential treatment or are excessively defended in the program. Such excessive defenses require special strategies.

Developmentally handicapped children often have an OK score of less than 15. It is rare that they reach the criterion of 40, indicating readiness for discharge. The persistence of low OK scores with developmentally delayed children is evidence of their continuing need for service, although not necessarily in out-of-home care.

Not-OK Score

This score gives the number of categories in which the child is doing poorly to such an extreme degree that any staff rater has given a rating of one to the category. It is rare that children are ready for discharge with elevated Not-OK scores. The appearance of ratings of one for behavior in school, as rated by the teacher, indicates that a child is lacking in some area required for public school attendance in a regular class. If such ratings still appear at the point of discharge planning, they initiate discussion of the need for specialized school placement. A Not-OK score by a family member needs to be examined by the family therapist to see if it is also an area of concern to the staff.

OK—Not-OK Score

This score is the difference between the OK and Not-OK scores; it has a minus sign when the value for Not-OK is greater than for OK. The score is useful as an indicator of the effort it takes to care for a child; it can be used to compare workloads of different employees.

Number of Goals

This score is the total of the categories in which a majority of staff members give a rating of two or below. If the child is in day treatment, a parent rating is substituted for the cottage ratings. This total is very sensitive to clinical change in the child. It is anticipated that a child who is ready for discharge will have a zero goal score for at least two months.

The categories in which staff members (or staff members and parents, for day treatment children) agree that the child is functioning poorly are called goals because these categories become the areas to be addressed by the staff during the following month.

A monthly printout gives the staff a copy of all the raw-score ratings in matrix form; it also reports all the scores described above. The monthly printout displays the categories that were identified as goals and also specifies whether each goal is one that has never been identified before for that child ("new goal"), a repetition of a goal identified in the past month ("same goal"), or a return of a goal formerly identified in the past but not in the preceding month ("return goal"). The appearance of a large number of return goals should stimulate concern among the clinicians as to the reason for such a regression. One possibility would then be to determine, in the case management section of the Residential CYCIS technology, or in the clinical record if the Child Assessment and Treatment Tracking System is being used as a stand-alone methodology, whether any event might be related to a significant change in tracking status.

The names of the raters are included in the printout. It is possible to use the ratings as a basis for supervision, but this use is not encouraged in the early phase of implementation. It is also possible to examine the work of different aspects of the program (child care, therapeutic activity, school) from the perspective of departmental effectiveness rather than child performance, but this examination is not encouraged in the early phases. The focus of the implementation of a Child Assessment and Treatment Tracking System should be on coordinating staff efforts with increased understanding of the child, rather than on using it as a supervisory tool to monitor staff performance. This method will produce much better staff participation and enthusiasm. Additional uses can be developed later, once the staff is familiar with the system.

In addition to the monthly printouts, complete reports of the scores and the patterning of goals for the entire period of treatment are part of the semiannual care review, treatment conferences, or interdisciplinary patient monitoring meetings. Figure 1 and the ensuing analysis constitute an example of one such complete report.

The Child Assessment and Treatment Tracking System Summary for this child is an example of a nine-year-old child who has shown marked progress. Beginning in December 1984, the summary charts 12 ratings until February 1986. Because of holidays or the child's illness, occasional rating periods may be missed. Problems at admission resulted in target categories being identified as blames others, anxious, clinging, crying, disrupting others, wetting, fighting, teasing, sexual interaction, self-endangering, temper tantrums, attention, truth, feeling healthy, and stealing.

An analysis of the Child Assessment and Treatment Tracking System Summary shows that the Staff Average Score has an upward trend into a range that is consistent with planning for discharge. The Parent Average Score is initially much lower than the Staff Score. The Parent Average shows much fluctuation, but near the end of treatment it is coming close to the Staff Score. The child's self-rating shows a greatly improved sense of self-satisfaction, with a change from 4.25 to 4.89. The Target Average Score has also increased from 4.04 to a score of 4.72 out of a possible maximum of 5. An analysis of a matrix printout (not included) would indicate that all the targets identified at admission are in an acceptable range at the last rating period except for blames others, anxious, and clinging.

Consistent with the impression of progress is the increase in the OK score from 26 to 46, and a decrease in the Not-OK score from 7 to 0. Also, goals developed by the computer system have decreased from 13 to 0.

This summary is discussed at case reviews. The data may also be presented graphically in three-point average smoothed-line trends, or the data may be averaged for each score for the last three months of treatment and any other treatment period. When the earliest placement data are used, the first month is usually excluded. Scores from the summary have been included in the agency criteria for admission, criteria for continuation of stay, and criteria for discharge in conjunction with length-of-stay norms.

NAME _____ Child # _____

	12/84	1/85	2/85	4/85	5/85	7/85	9/85	10/85	11/85	12/85	1/86	2/86
Staff Average	4.01	3.75	4.09	3.82	3.87	3.88	3.76	4.21	4.17	3.99	4.13	4.38
Parent Average	3.41	3.50	4.16	4.20	4.56	4.20	3.71	—	4.25	4.30	4.16	—
Child Average	4.25	4.36	4.53	4.29	4.44	4.34	—	4.46	4.88	4.34	4.87	4.89
Parent/Staff Average	-.60	-.25	+.07	+.40	+.69	+.32	-0.05	—	+0.08	+0.31	+0.03	—
Target Average	4.04	3.99	4.44	3.96	4.19	3.96	3.96	4.52	4.56	4.33	4.52	4.72
OK Score	26	27	37	26	32	29	24	36	38	30	36	46
Not-OK Score	7	8	1	4	5	9	7	0	1	4	2	0
OK—Not-OK Score	19	19	36	22	27	20	17	36	37	26	34	46
Goals	13	7	3	3	6	1	2	0	2	0	2	0

Figure 1. Child Assessment Treatment Tracking
System Summary.

Serious effort has been made to conform the tracking system to clinical needs. It is designed to be rapidly scored, easy to understand, and not so lengthy as to be burdensome. Staff members do not avoid the task. Although some research advantage might accrue by having behaviorally anchored steps for the rating levels, this method is not consistent with the way in which staff members think in their everyday work. Any bias that staff members may have in their ratings is likely to be the same bias that influences their work and affects the treatment progress. There are other treatment tracking systems that include many more than the 56 categories used in the Beech Brook system. Among these are COBRS of George Thomas, in Georgia, and GLAS at Green Chimneys, in New York. The Beech Brook System was planned to be no longer than could be readily grasped in the holistic way in which many clinicians think about their patients. If the introduction of the Child Assessment and Treatment Tracking System changes treatment planning and/or delivery, it will be because the tracking identifies new ways of understanding the children, not because the computerization requires data to be available in any particular way to a data-processing center.

Conclusion

The Child Assessment and Treatment Tracking System provides for tracking of children throughout the entire length of stay in a group care program with multiple staff members. It can be applied to residential treatment, day treatment, or foster and adoptive home programs.

It can assist clinicians and administrators in decision making about treatment planning by increasing the accuracy of information concerning clients who are in care over a period of time. Because the recording is systematic, the effect of memory distortion in anecdotal reports given at case reviews can be reduced. Anecdotal reports can be made more specific and pertinent to clinical problems when the attention of staff members has been focused on the categories identified for study in the computer system. Decisions regarding treatment choice and treatment duration can be subject to review in terms of objective criteria involving the computerized reports.

The computerized tracking system makes it possible to include multiple sources of information in developing an understanding of the child's status. The Child Assessment and Treatment Tracking System includes child self-evaluation and information from parents, as well as scores from a variety of staff members. The system can coordinate this information in multiple ways that can assist case planning, staff supervision, and the evaluation or comparison of attitudes of family members. Because of the comparison between adjustment as rated by the staff and as rated by family members, criteria can be developed for choosing between day treatment and residential treatment. The involvement of children and parents in the tracking system is consistent with the involvement of the family in treatment and a recognition of the importance of reports by the consumer about services received.

The Child Assessment and Treatment Tracking System can be used to set standards and objectives for accountability. Agencies can develop impact objectives that include anticipated percentages of clients who will show positive change in the tracking system scores or combinations of scores. The tracking system also can be an appropriate and efficient way to provide the objective information regarding treatment progress that is needed by agency boards, funding sources, and third-party payers to justify program continuation.

The Child Assessment and Treatment Tracking System provides for a continuing sensitivity to the changing clinical needs of each child. Both positive and negative phases of treatment can be identified rapidly, and timely adjustments made. At all times, however, the plans for responding to the computer information should be determined by clinicians, according to the individual needs of children. There is no reason to lose the empathy and dedication that have been landmarks of quality care just because a machine with perfect memory joins the treatment team.

Beech Brook Child Assessment Treatment Tracking System Symptoms and Definitions (I)

1. **Blames Others**
   Says: "It's other child's or staff's fault." "He made me do it." Complains of unfairness.
2. **Anxious-Worried**
   Looks sad or frightened; talks about fears. (Score here for nightmares and night fears.)
3. **Clinging**
   Underfoot, hanging on to adults.
4. **Crying**
   Show of tears, sobbing.
5. **Destructive to Property**
   Breaks, tears, throws things; kicks, scratches things; fire-setting.
6. **Disrupts Others**
   Interrupts conversations or work of others; distracts them.
7. **Bowel Soiling**
   Not using bathroom for feces.
8. **Wetting**
   Not using bathroom for urination. Wetting clothes during day or night bedwetting.
9. **Evasive**
   When questioned by an adult, child looks away, doesn't answer, changes the topic in order to not respond. Likely to say "I don't know."
10. **Assaults Children**
    Initiates attacks with a rock, bat, or weapon with intent to hurt. Use of weapon is involved.
11. **Hurts Other Children**
    Pinches, bites, spits, kicks, pulls hair or other acts that hurt other children.
12. **Assaults Adults**
    Punches, attacks with intent to hurt. Initiates attack on adult *with or without weapon*.
13. **Fights with Children**
    Physical (not verbal) engaging in mutual fighting. May not be clear who started fight.
14. **Hyperactive**
    Runs indoors; jumps on furniture; doesn't sit at table for entire meal.
15. **Impulsive**
    Child is impatient, can't wait, wants immediate gratification when he or she wants it.

16. **Indecisive**
    Child has trouble making choices and making up his or her mind.
17. **Self-Comforting Act**
    Self-stimulating actions like rocking, twirling, tics, rubbing motions, thumb sucking.
18. **Lacks Confidence, Inadequate**
    Talks of failure, says: "can't do it," "don't know how," calls self "dumb."
19. **Self-Blame**
    Calls self "bad"; says he or she is to blame for problems of parents or other children.
20. **Messy**
    For example: tracks mud, spills milk, shower overflow, throws food, spits on floor, etc.
21. **Sexual Interactions**
    Genital activity involving others, usually involving some genital exposure. Private personal masturbation is not included.
22. **Self-Endangering**
    Child does things that are dangerous to self, such as: going on roof of buildings, hanging out car windows, swimming in restricted areas, playing with matches or fire (unregulated).
23. **Scapegoat**
    Child is subject of other children's exploitation, things are taken, is "picked on" by others.
24. **Smoking**
    Smoking or possession of cigarettes with intent to smoke.
25. **Stealing**
    Child takes money from stores, staff members, children, or family members. Or child takes things from stores or enters premises illegally to take things.
26. **Swearing**
    Child uses vulgar and/or profane language. (Intention to provoke is not important, as that is covered under next category.)
27. **Teasing-Provocativeness**
    Child says or does things that will arouse an excited or angry response from staff or children. For example: name calling, insults.
28. **Temper Tantrums**
    Yelling, screaming, throwing self around; lasts long enough that it may require physical holding to restrain safely.
29. **Withdrawn, Loner**
    Avoids contacts with others; spends much time alone.
30. **AWOL**
    Child leaves home or program without permission.

31. **Self-Hurting Act**
    Biting, striking or cutting self, hair pulling, deep skin scratches, picks at sores, other self-impairing acts, pica.

Beech Brook Child Assessment Tracking System
Developmental Characteristics and Definitions (II)

1. **Shares Things**
   Child is willing to share toys when asked appropriately but is not required to give them away.
2. **Says What (S)He Feels**
   Child can put feelings into words: I am angry, I feel sad, I feel worried, rather than act out.
3. **Helps Others**
   Gives assistance, either voluntarily or when requested, to adults or children.
4. **Can Play Alone**
   Is able to occupy self without adult involvement in a nondestructive way.
5. **Can Play with Others**
   Can play with other children a reasonable length of time without fights.
6. **Completes Tasks**
   Finishes chores, school work or game without repeated reminders by adult.
7. **Takes Care of Self**
   Does things such as brushing teeth, bathing, combing hair, dressing, with minimum supervision.
8. **Takes Care of Possessions**
   Takes toys indoors after play; picks up toys and clothing; does not break toys and throw them around. Child may need reminder but has idea of taking care of things.
9. **Expresses Appreciation**
   Expresses some appreciation when given something. Says "thank you." Some indication that child recognizes being given something or being helped.
10. **Non-Demand Asking**
    Is able to request rather than to demand what he or she wants; is not whining, says "please."
11. **Takes Turns**
    Offers to take turns or is able to do this upon suggestion in order to resolve conflict with another person.
12. **Accepts Responsibility**
    Can admit failure, error, or achievement without evasion. Does what child is supposed to do without continuous supervision.
13. **Strives for Success**
    Seems to want to do something well and gain praise.

14. **Tries Hard**
Able to put forth effort.
15. **Pays Attention**
Is able to look at you when spoken to and to hear what is said.
16. **Calm**
Unexcited due to emotional comfort—not sadness or withdrawal.
17. **Respects Rights of Others**
Does not go in other people's rooms or take their toys, food, clothes.
18. **Feels Healthy**
Is free from complaints of pains and aches.
19. **Tells Truth**
Does not lie, exaggerate or fantasize.
20. **Logical Communication**
Speech makes sense; no bizarre talk, or irrevelant noises. (Exaggerated fantasies of self-importance should be scored under No. 19.)
21. **Acts Appropriately Serious for Age**
Able to be serious when appropriate rather than be silly or clown irrelevantly.
22. **Uses Staff or Parents Appropriately**
Asks for help for own needs, not to tattle or get others in trouble.
23. **Shows Initiative**
Has good ideas that child develops on his or her own without adult suggestions. Volunteers.
24. **Follows Rules**
Obeys; understands need for rules without challenging external authority ("can't make me").
25. **Speech Fluency**
Easy flow of ideas verbally. Adequate vocabulary for age.

Child Assessment Treatment Tracking Rating Scale

Name _____ Date _____ Program _____ Rater _____

Revised 10/82	Never (5)	Rarely (4)	Moderately (3)	Often (2)	Daily (1)
1. Blames Others					
2. Anxious-Worried					
3. Clinging					
4. Crying					
5. Destructive to Property					
6. Disrupts Others					
7. Bowel Soiling					
8. Wetting					
9. Evasive					
10. Assaults Children					
11. Hurts Other Children					
12. Assaults Adults					
13. Fights with Children					
14. Hyperactive					
15. Impulsive					
16. Indecisive					
17. Self-Comforting Act					
18. Lacks Confidence, Inadequate					
19. Self-Blame					
20. Messy					
21. Sexual Interactions					
22. Self-Endangering					
23. Scapegoat					
24. Smoking					
25. Stealing					
26. Swearing					
27. Teasing-Provocativeness					

28. Temper Tantrums					
29. Withdrawn, Loner					
30. AWOL					
31. Self-Hurting Act					

10/15/82

Name _____ Date _____ Program _____ Rater _____

Revised 10/82	Never (5)	Rarely (4)	Moderately (3)	Often (2)	Daily (1)
1. Shares Things					
2. Says What (S)He Feels					
3. Helps Others					
4. Can Play Alone					
5. Can Play with Others					
6. Completes Tasks					
7. Takes Care of Self					
8. Takes Care of Possessions					
9. Expresses Appreciation					
10. Non-Demand Asking					
11. Takes Turns					
12. Accepts Responsibility					
13. Strives for Success					
14. Tries Hard					
15. Pays Attention					
16. Calm					
17. Respects Rights of Others					
18. Feels Healthy					
19. Tells Truth					
20. Logical Communication					
21. Acts Appropriately Serious for Age					
22. Uses Staff or Parent Appropriately					
23. Shows Initiative					
24. Follows Rules					
25. Speech Fluency					

10/15/82

Notes

1. CYCIS is a product of Child and Youth Systems, Technology and Management Support (systems).

2. Residential CYCIS is a product of Walter R. McDonald & Associates, Inc.

3. Beech Brook is a psychiatric treatment center located in Cleveland, Ohio.

4. THEOS is a product of THEOS Software Corporation.

5. TAILORBASE is a product of Tailored Business Systems.

6. UNIX is a product of Bell Laboratories.

Bibliography

CYCIS: Child & Youth Centered Information System. CYCIS-Data Project, 1346 Connecticut Ave. N.W., Washington, D.C., November 1980.

Friedman, R. The use of the computer in the treatment of children. *Child Welfare* LIX (3): March 1980, 152–159.

McCathren, R. Summary of Residential CYCIS Capabilities. Flyer distributed by CYSTEMS, 1985.

Millman, H., and Schaeffer C. Behavioral change: Program evaluation and staff feedback: *Child Welfare* LIV (10): December 1975, 692–702.

13

*Preventing and Managing Child Abuse in
Group Care: Report and Recommendations
of a Survey on Practice*

JOAN DiLEONARDI
EARL KELLY

As RECOGNITION OF CHILD ABUSE HAS increased in this country, reporting rates have risen dramatically. Paralleling this increase, but somewhat slower, rates of reported physical and sexual abuse have increased in institutions designed for the care and protection of vulnerable children—those removed from their parents for abuse or neglect and those too emotionally disturbed to be able to live in a family setting. Those who have chosen the care and nurturing of such children as the focus of their working lives react strongly to reports of abuse in facilities designed to help those children recover from the effects of earlier lack of care. The general public reacts even more strongly. Anyone working in the field can think of children they know, who, having been abused by earlier caretakers, do their utmost to provoke abuse from those who seek to help them by winning their trust. It is understandable that the children would do so. In their eyes, the fact that we have not yet hit them or called them names or reacted to sexually provocative behavior may not mean that we are deserving of their trust; it may only mean that they have not found the action that would provoke

239

the familiar, dreaded response that yet has the comfort of the known and predictable.

The purpose of the survey reported here was to get a picture of what was happening nationally in child-caring agencies that, as members of the Child Welfare League of America (CWLA), have a commitment to a high level of professionalism and concern. Our interest was, of course, in what was happening to the children. It was also in what the effect of greater awareness and monitoring has been on the provider agencies. That is why the study focuses on preventing abuse, the first step, and management, where prevention has not been adequate, of abuse in institutions. Highly publicized charges of abuse may at times result in media scapegoating of the institution far beyond what would seem reasonable. An out-of-control situation may do damage to the victim, other children, family members, and the institution itself far beyond that of the original incident.

In the course of discussion with the group care agencies, it became clear that a number of directors and their agencies were experiencing nightmarish problems regarding alleged and substantiated incidents of sexual and physical abuse of children in care. Multimillion dollar litigation, loss of public confidence, loss of funding, confrontational protective service investigations, demoralized staff—all of these issues can occur and are happening in group care agencies.

Conversely, a refusal on the part of the institution to recognize when even mild abuse is taking place, by denial or by blaming allegations on the child's emotional disturbance, may do far greater damage to the child involved than earlier events that led to the child's placement. Children in group care were placed with agencies with a promise of safety, nurture, and assistance in working out problems of the past and fears of the future. The whole message to them has been, "This is a caring place. We will protect you from further harm and help you grow. Trust us." If we violate that promise and trust, we have failed. We must then see what we can do to ensure that this harm does not happen again. Many agencies who responded to the survey were frank and open. Many shared with us the reasons why they felt that they had had no incidents. Many who had allegations of physical or sexual abuse told us what they had changed as a result. Many sent us ideas and copies of material; many of these ideas are conveyed in this paper.

The Sample

All agencies in the current CWLA membership list that provide residential or group home programming were sent a questionnaire and cover letter in the summer of 1986. From this initial mailing of 166 letters, 100 completed questionnaires were received. A second mailing was sent in the fall to those agencies that had not responded. From these, an additional 45 questionnaires were received, and several letters explaining why they had not participated, for an unusually high 88 percent total response rate.

Two of the states that responded included figures on allegations and founded or indicated cases on children in placement statewide. These are used for comparison with the responses of the agencies.

The surveys were divided into three sections. The first sought brief general information about the agencies; the second asked for their experience with allegations of physical abuse; and the third about their experience with allegations of sexual abuse.

The Agencies

The responding agencies represented all sections of the country and all CWLA regions. Among them they provided care for just under 10,000 children. During the past two years they reported a total of 346 allegations of physical abuse and 136 allegations of sexual abuse, or a total reporting rate of 48.2 allegations per thousand children in care. Is this high, low, or average? Since national figures are not readily available, comparisons were made with reporting rates for the general population in the two states for which data were available, as noted above. Refer to Table 1.

This result gives some indication that in both populations of children in substitute care, the rate of reported allegations was substantially higher than in the general population, but the percentage of those allegations substantiated upon investigation was lower. It seems a positive indication that agencies are, on the whole, doing their job. They are dealing with children who, because of their past history and current problems, are more likely to be provocative and more likely to be abused. They are usually, as they

TABLE 1

Reporting Rates of Physical and Sexual Abuse

Two-State Group Average	Reporting Rate	% Founded
General population	20.7	43.0
Substitute care	106.0	28.5
Study sample	48.2	23.2

must, following legal mandates, reporting those allegations and having them investigated by the legal authorities.

Number of Allegations

A major question was how many allegations of physical and/ or sexual abuse the agency had had in the past two years. Fifty-three (39 percent) reported no allegations, surprising considering the volatile populations served. Thirty-four (25 percent) had allegations of physical abuse only; 16 (12 percent) had allegations of sexual abuse only, and 33 (24 percent) had allegations of both.

Generally the larger agencies had more allegations, but agencies with more allegations did not necessarily have more substantiated cases. The agencies fall roughly into the following categories:

The proactive that are on the alert for abuse and have procedures to detect it and deal with it; some of them have reports, some do not, but their responses indicate awareness and concern

The positive reactive that have had reports and modified and strengthened procedures as a result

The negative reactive that have made few or no changes after the incidents, either because they were not substantiated or because they fired staff members, with no follow-up

The 25 percent that had allegations but did only internal investigation, a practice that is against the law in most states

Physical Abuse

Agencies were asked to give a brief description of the most serious incident alleged. In the allegations of physical abuse, they divided roughly into striking the child (38 percent); use of excessive force in subduing a child (20 percent); use of extreme force, such as breaking a child's arm (15 percent); and a variety of other charges such as leaving a unit unsupervised, allowing children to hurt each other, pushing, and so forth.

When asked to check those listed items that might have been contributing factors, inadequate training and inadequate supervision of staff members were cited most frequently. Refer to Table 2.

Since one of the study questions was whether agencies had a plan in place for dealing with alleged incidents, they were asked who was first informed of the incident and whether that was by plan. Although the titles of those persons varied from child-care supervisor to executive director, 87 percent of the agencies said that this report was according to plan.

They were then asked who, outside their own agency staff, had been informed of the incident and whether those persons had been helpful. Table 3 shows the responses for physical abuse.

Although very few agencies had media involvement, none thought it helpful. In fact, all felt it was destructive to child, staff, and agency. Perhaps the major surprise in the responses was the

TABLE 2

Factors Contributing to Alleged Abuse

	% Yes
Inadequate screening of staff	21
Inadequate staff training	36
Inadequate coverage because of vacations, illness, and the like	16
Inadequate supervision	29
Unsafe setting or environment	7
Other	38

Note: The "other" category included a number of items such as not getting requested references, being on a camping trip, and other individual responses.

TABLE 3

Involvement and Helpfulness of Those Outside the Agency Staff
in Allegations of Physical Abuse

Agency/Person	% Involved	% Helpful
Licensing agency	51	43
Protective services	75	61
Police	19	13
Courts	3	3
Board of directors	15	9
Newspapers	3	0
Funding sources	18	16
Other children	44	33
Parents	58	34
Other	20	11

Note: Although licensing agency, protective services, and funding sources are listed separately, in many cases they are the same agency or under the same direction.

small percentage of cases in which the agency board was involved in any way. This fact is probably related to the small percentage regarded as serious incidents.

When asked to describe the aftermath of the allegation, 30 percent of the agencies reported terminating the staff member(s) involved; 5 percent reported resignations; and 14 percent reported suspensions. Five percent reported that other disciplinary action was taken, and 13 percent increased training for all staff members.

They were also asked if, in hindsight, there was anything they would have handled differently. More than half (58 percent) said yes. Many of the suggestions dealt with staff selection, training, coverage, program design, and documentation of personnel actions, and are discussed later.

Sexual Abuse

In response to the questions about sexual abuse, 49 of the agencies surveyed reported a total of 136 allegations, of which 34 (25 percent) were substantiated upon investigation. This number was a much lower substantiation rate for sexual abuse than in the two-state general population rate of 42 percent substantiated. Again, this finding seems an indication that the agencies are becoming alert and aware of the need to investigate. Fifty-four percent of the incidents were heterosexual in nature, 36 percent were homosexual. A higher proportion of the sexual abuse incidents (42.5 percent vs. 23 percent) were regarded as very serious. The descriptions of the incidents included rape or intercourse with children (25 percent), sexual fondling (46 percent), and verbal sexual harassment. Unlike physical abuse, in which the perpetrator was a child-care worker or house parent in 93 percent of the incidents, this personnel category was responsible in 63 percent of the incidents, with foster parents, administrators, or other professionals responsible for the rest. This finding would indicate that enhanced screening procedures should not be concentrated only on child-care workers.

Again, in contrast to the physical abuse situations, only 12 percent of the respondents felt that inadequate training was a contributing factor, a drop from 36 percent in the other category. A higher proportion (34 percent) felt that inadequate supervision was more problematic in sexual abuse. Most agencies felt that reporting had been handled according to plan. The pattern of involvement of others in the sexual abuse allegations was also somewhat different. Refer to Table 4.

The percentage of cases in which the police were involved increased from 19 percent for physical abuse to 64 percent for sexual abuse. Media involvement was much greater for sexual abuse, with 22 percent reporting radio and television or newspaper involvement, compared to no radio or television and 3 percent newspaper involvement for allegations of physical abuse. This question evoked comment that the media were not only unhelpful but often harmful, including comments that the publicity was harmful not only to the agency but also to the children involved.

Many of the comments about the sexual abuse allegations were directed at the necessity to be sensitive to the needs of staff members who had been accused. Most suspended the accused staff members during the investigations but were concerned about lasting damage to the reputation of those who were accused but cleared of the charges. Formal procedures were seen as necessary in screening, selecting, and training staff members, but so was a clear stance, making sure that all staff members know that abuse will not be

TABLE 4

Involvement and Helpfulness of Outside Agencies

	% Involved	% Helpful
Licensing agency	69	32
Protective services	77	55
Police	64	51
Courts	31	25
Board of directors	43	32
Newspapers	13	4
Radio/television	9	0
Funding sources	22	18
Other children	49	30
Parents	20	42
Other	20	11

tolerated and that all allegations will be reported and investigated. The agencies were also concerned about handling issues of false charges not only with the child involved, but also with other children in the unit.

Strategies for Abuse Prevention

What follows in this report is the presentation of several key areas that emerge as major themes of agency experience, especially with respect to the child-care staff. Observations from the questionnaire as to how agency practice could be improved are described for each critical area. These agencies are highly sensitive to the necessity of having written policies and procedures proscribing institutional abuse. Their four major areas of concern discussed are staff members, behavior management, supervision, and reporting procedures.

Staff Selection

How to hire the best possible candidates for positions on staff is certainly axiomatic in terms of being able to provide quality child-care programming. Here is a summary of staff selection ideas obtained from the questionnaires.

The best prevention lies in screening, and screening begins with verifying personal and employment background references, including academic background. Some states require a police check and a Child Abuse Registry check. A background check occurs following some sort of written certification that the applicant has not been convicted of child abuse. It is also extremely important to study past employment references. An illustration throws light on this: It was learned that an employee fired for "cause" from one child-care facility had subsequently worked at two other group care facilities; the employment termination had been related to physical abuse of children.

Some agencies discuss the desirability of psychological testing such as the MMPI (short form); the California Psychological Inventory has been cited as an instrument that would have applicability in this area. A number of agencies are now using some type of staff selection instrument.

Determine drug abuse specifically on employment questionnaire; ask if the prospective employee is on psychotropic medication.

Use a trial-day concept, an extended observation period for staff candidates. Require prospective candidates to write descriptions of their experience, and examine their perception of events. Seek perceptions of regular staff members about the prospective employee, and especially the children's reactions to the applicant.

Check for emotional imbalance through such strategies as a role-playing method of hiring that would require staff candidates to face simulated anger and hostility from children.

Have starting salaries that will attract competent staff. Pay salaries that attract the best qualified.

Keep in mind a possible abuser profile. Abuse may be an impulsive act, yet behind such behavior often lies clearly unresolved identity conflict or emotional immaturity.

Have several people interview prospective staff members, as a hiring committee to compare impressions and judgments.

Utilize a probationary period in agency personnel practices so that employment can terminate without cause up to six months after hire. Then have in place suspension and dismissal provisions. This policy enables the agency to suspend an employee until an investigation is completed.

Hire those people who demonstrate high self-esteem. Don't hire just to fill a vacancy. Discuss childhood experiences; did the candidate experience abuse as a child? Multiple interviewers will help in this assessment.

Have a nepotism policy, and don't deviate from it. Nepotism tends to build in protectionism and the potential of concealing any abusive situations that could occur within the system.

From these responses, here are three key prevention variables to be considered regarding staff selection: (1) carefully document previous employment history of prospective job applicant; (2) a staff selection device should be considered, though there is no apparent agreement on what particular type of device would be recommended; and (3) include language within agency personnel practices allowing immediate suspension and dismissal of an employee who may be the subject of an abuse allegation.

Management of Behavior in a Group Care Setting

Children are often referred to residential treatment and group care facilities because of behavior problems at home, school, and elsewhere. A principal role of line staff in any child-care facility is the management of aggressive and disruptive behavior by children in residence. But staff members are not automatons who, robot-like, carry out treatment programs. The survey findings point up two primary observations regarding allegations of physically abusive behavior that can occur between staff members and children in group care settings. These observations are classified from the standpoint of the staff and the children.

> *Staff members who impulsively become physically aggressive with children in care are out of control.* According to tabulated information from the questionnaires, this problem may be the largest area of abuse complaints, such as: a staff member who slapped a child who called him or her names, or a staff member who lost his or her temper and slapped a child in the face.

> *Out-of-control children who are being restrained by the staff* provide the second largest area of abuse reports. The problem involves physical restraint of a child. Often, but not exclusively, a physical confrontation may occur in relation to restricting a child to quarters, or time-out arrangements.

A ten-year-old boy in school was out of control, name-calling, hitting staff; a staff member applied restraint, breaking the boy's arm in two places.

Recommendations for Out-of-Control Staff Members

Have written policies that carefully outline how staff members are to handle out-of-control behavior in children. Reduce the amount of discretion child-care workers can exercise through careful definition of disciplinary options available to them in direct care of children.

Give children alternatives and avoid head-on power struggles between child-care workers and children. Putting stress on control of client behavior at all costs leads to the potential for excessive physical confrontations between the staff and the children.

Develop the capability to increase the child-to-staff ratio quickly if required. Third-party intervention is a valuable method to develop some distance between the staff and the children. A neutral third party can be successful in intervening. Always have supervisory backup available and use the supervisor as third-party negotiator.

The abuse complaint may have been one in a series of abuse-like issues followed by a serious incident. A staff person may demonstrate inclinations toward abuse by such encounters with clients. These incidents should require careful review; supervisors must be trained to be alert to development of such patterns.

Inexperienced staff members may be targets for child abuse by manipulative children. Children often become uncertain and fearful of a new staff member's capacity to protect them, and this fear may lead to their setting up physical confrontations with the staff member, leading to a complaint by the child. New staff members should work closely with the senior staff before working a regular unit assignment.

Keep the staff fresh. Avoid overtime duty assignments. Have available trained substitutes who may come in quickly on relief. An illustration of excessive workload is a residential program where staff members work a routine of two weeks on before time off is provided.

Staff versus children. Allowing this atmosphere to develop implies accusations cast back and forth at each other. In some agencies, polygraph testing has been employed to determine "who is right" in an abuse allegation. Some respondents felt that when a child gives a report in the presence of the staff member who is the subject of the allegation and in front of parents and others, this practice leads to a healthy airing of the issues.

Recommendations for Out-of-Control Children

Here we are referring to instances in which the child must be physically restrained, and instances when time-out or seclusion may be used if offered by the agency.

The agency defines at the outset in written policies when a child should be restrained. Identify specific behaviors that will necessitate either control-room placement, or placement in quarters, or other reasonable disciplinary alternatives. At the time of admission, these policies are to be distributed not only to the parents, but to the regulatory agency worker, probation officer, or others; this precaution should obviate any surprises when restraint is used by an agency.

Training in crisis intervention techniques refers to life-space interviewing, a method of intervention in a crisis situation to defuse a volatile situation. Teach ways and means to cool down an emotionally charged situation through distancing, processing the event, and negotiation.

Training in physical restraint techniques is being marketed, such as that of the Mandt System, CPI, and other methods of teaching passive restraint. The goal is to inform the staff members thoroughly that they are trained in order to minimize the possibility of anyone becoming injured. One idea is to train senior staff members who in turn would be certified to instruct others. In this way, someone is always available on staff to provide training.

Avoid placing new staff members in the position of being responsible for managing out-of-control children. They feel their responsibility keenly and can be easily frightened, especially of acting-out children. To compensate for their insecurity, they, in turn, become too aggressive with the children. Three key prevention variables were suggested for management of behavior: (1) teach crisis intervention skills; (2) teach passive restraint procedures, with certification if possible; and (3) when a child is in a psychological crisis, the staff member should not be isolated with the child in a one-on-one situation—backup should be in close proximity.

Effective Supervision

Council on Accreditation standards specify that supervision must be a continuing and integral part of an agency's operations. What, however, is supervision of good quality for child-care workers? How does quality supervision relate to abuse prevention?

Staff members, especially child-care workers, need an opportunity to express negative feelings about children. The supervisor must be prepared to work on the negative ambivalence expressed by child-care workers. In agencies where token economy systems are used, supervisors should ensure that child-care staff members have an opportunity to ventilate their negative feelings toward children because when the emphasis is entirely on the children's level of compliance with a system, the workers need support and recognition of their contributions. Otherwise an emphasis on a rigid ideology may seem to be of more importance than the development of trusting relationships with the children.

Watch for overidentification or projected rage toward children by the child-care worker. The extremes would be noticeable; that is, the child who can do no right or the child who can do no wrong. The child who is specially liked or the child who is intensely disliked by a child-care worker should be noted by the supervisor. The potential abuser may show excessive fondness for children, seeing them as special, which may be a symptom of distorted affection. Or the potential abuser may have a real aversion to a particular child, representing an unconscious fear that needs to be discussed. Countertransference feelings of staff members must be expressed in the supervisory process to provide some psychological relief.

The supervisor must know the code regarding child abuse and child protective service reporting guidelines. In some states, mandated training is required for all staff members.

There must never be unplanned visits of children to staff members' homes—no special one-on-one activities unless they are carefully reasoned team decisions and are fully discussed by all concerned, with the explicit understanding that such visits may place both child and worker at risk.

Supervisors should be very careful to review all incident reports and to examine carefully all staff roles and responsibilities related to any abuse-like incidents.

It is important to deal with the concept of psychological entrapment of staff members by children, especially manifested by those children who have been previously abused. As part of the psychological defense system, the child who has been sexually abused can be seductive to staff members; the child who has been physically abused can provoke rage and aggression from staff members. The child sets up staff members to treat him or her in the same way others have done, to reinforce his or her negative self-image; the negative self-image is a better identity than none at all.

It is important for supervisors in every agency to maintain a low threshold culture for reporting abuse. There must be a positive abuse-free culture in every agency: incidents of aggression or serious acting-out behavior must be discussed in team meetings at supervisory levels in order to develop a culture where all staff members are sensitized to their approach with children. Staff members must be aware of the necessity to report every incident that might be abusive rather than making that determination individually.

Here again there are three key prevention variables: (1) team meeting materials and progress notes on each child should be carefully documented; (2) individual supervision should be available to each child-care worker and each professional staff member; and (3) special staff-child relationships should be avoided.

Reporting Procedures

Each group care facility should have in operation an incident reporting system that is a special place within each child's master file. Reports should be filed here on any incidents of physical or sexual abuse or any unusual management issue that requires documentation on the part of staff members involved. An incident that occurs in the living unit between a child and a staff member requires a formal written report whether it is accidental or not accidental.

A report should be completed immediately by all those who were involved in the situation. These reports should be separate from logs or other communications and should note time recorded, date, and all pertinent information as to who, what, why, when, and where.

A written report prepared by the staff and reviewed by the director should be made available to Child Protective Services (CPS); it should be signed and dated, and a copy should be placed in a separate section in the client's file. The keynote of the relationship with CPS should be cooperation, not confrontation.

Deal openly and honestly with the parents and parties directly involved in an abuse complaint. As soon as the facts are ascertained, the parents of the child should be told exactly what is known by the agency. The call should preferably be made by the person having the closest relationship with them, such as their therapist.

Some respondents to the questionnaire indicated that any abuse should be documented by photographs.

The key prevention variables around reporting are (1) a critical incident reporting system should be in place; and (2) reports of the injury that occurred should be documented in writing by the parties involved in the incident.

Summary

This survey of CWLA agencies providing residential treatment indicates that most agencies are taking measures to prevent child abuse and to minimize the damage to children, staff members, and the agency when it does occur. The agencies reported at a higher rate than the general public but had a lower rate of substantiated abuse. Many made recommendations for prevention of abuse, centering on the key areas of staff selection and training, behavior management, and reporting.

Perhaps the most important general recommendation is that agencies should develop a low threshold culture for child abuse; that is, recognition on the part of board members, administrators, supervisors, and line staff that the children being served are susceptible to abuse and may provoke it. It also means that small incidents that may be precursors to actual abuse, such as repeated favoritism or scapegoating of a child by a worker, are discussed and dealt with in supervisory sessions and staff meetings. It means that abuse prevention is a primary consideration in hiring, training, and supervising staff members, and that staff members receive positive reinforcement for doing well at a difficult job. Institutions that develop a low threshold for abuse will find that they more readily gain the trust and respect of the children, the parents, and the community.

14

The Young Child in Group Care

SUSAN S. STEPLETON

IN CONSIDERING GROUP CARE OF ANY KIND FOR very young children, one must acknowledge that it is a radical intervention that can be deemed appropriate only if no other modality can meet the child's needs and only if the residential setting can guarantee that the specific developmental requirements of young children can be satisfied.

The Case Against Institutionalizing Young Children: What It Means

The literature documenting the negative experience of institutionalization on young children began with Rene Spitz in the late 1940s and has continued to be produced [Segal and Yahraes 1978; Bowlby 1968; Oswin 1979; Gaddini 1984]. It is clear that the primary developmental and emotional needs of children in these studies were not met. A distortion of the fact arises, however, in assuming two things: first, that the institutionalization experience was the only negative factor operating in the lives of the children studied, and second, that the extremely insensitive institutionalization experience involved represents the only possible kind of group care that can be provided.

J. Langmeier and Z. Matějček point out, "Some extreme conclusions have been drawn . . . e.g., a bad family is better than the
best institution since it offers the opportunity of having that unique
emotional tie to the mother." They assert that, for many abused
and neglected children, the needed emotional tie is completely
unavailable from the biological mother (or anyone else in the home
setting), and that for children who have no attachment experiences,
that tie can, in fact, be provided for some period of time only in a
group care setting.

The Need for Early, Intensive Intervention

It is the vehement and adamant position of this paper that
removal of young children from the biological family, or from any
family setting, should be undertaken only in the most extreme
cases. Early attachment experience may well be the single most
important factor operating in healthy physical and emotional development of children, however, and if the natural opportunity for
that to occur (mother-child bonding) is unavailable or must be
interrupted, then an alternate attachment process must be a part
of whatever intervention is necessary to meet all of the child's
needs.

When obvious and significant physical, emotional, and developmental problems are identified in early infancy, the very best
opportunities for remediation also occur during those early years.
Intensive, early intervention may well completely overcome problems that, if identified later, would be overwhelming. In other
cases, a progressive decline may be halted so that problems at least
remain at a manageable level.

The early intervention argument is greatly strengthened by
recent discoveries about the abilities and needs of infants. Aaronson [1978] summarized today's radically different view of the
involvement of newborns in the world around them, noting that
they are far from helpless and that they respond to and interact
with the world around them from the first days of life after birth.
Pawl [1984] spells out the need for early intervention in detail,
arguing that mental health services should be routinely available
in the infant/child health system from birth on and should be par-

ticularly aggressive if the parent-child relationship is not developing well.

Much the same position is taken by Martin [1984]: "Inasmuch as character disorders such as borderline personality disorder are felt to be linked to parenting styles and infant behaviors in the first four years of the child's life, it seems clear that psychological intervention in infancy should have high priority." And, in the same vein, "Any individual at-risk infant may need speech therapy, physical therapy, cognitive therapy, occupational therapy, psychotherapy and other therapeutic modalities."

Call [1984], dealing with the same subject, explores two areas in some depth. First, he notes typical infant behavior and the faulty interpretations made of it by potentially abusive and neglectful parents. His list includes thumbsucking, interpreted as unacceptable immaturity; biting, interpreted as hostile aggression; turning away from the bottle or spoon, interpreted as disobedience; and excited movement of arms, or scratching, interpreted as hostile aggression.

Call then draws out implications of the failure of attachment between parent and child. When healthy attachment does not occur, he describes the resulting failure to thrive:

> The criteria for diagnosis include the absence of normally present attachment capacities in the newborn, such as sucking rhythms, rooting behavior, visual and auditory orienting responses to the mother, anticipatory approach behavior at feeding, temporally organized vocal and gaze reciprocity with the mother, reciprocally organized play and games. The dominant expression in the infant is one of apathy.

> The associated symptoms include inferior weight gain, poor muscle tone, a vacuous visual expression, a weak cry, excessive sleep, mild or moderate automatic instability, and a feeding disturbance without specific organic cause as an explanation of the disorder.

He notes, "The disorder is extremely incapacitating. The course is usually downhill. Spontaneous recovery cannot be expected without intervention."

It is an encouraging sign that the literature reflecting insights about the seriousness of early abuse and neglect and the need for intervention is growing. The evidence that early maltreatment requires early and intensive, multidisciplinary intervention is becoming incontrovertible [Egeland et al. 1983; Allen and Wasserman 1985; Allen and Oliver 1982].

Residential Treatment for Young Children

What then does a group care program look like that has been developed to provide early, intensive intervention while responding to the primary, essential need of very young children for a strong attachment to their own parents or to alternative caregivers?

The Salvation Army Hope Center[a] came into being in 1977 as an emergency shelter for children between the ages of birth and 12 years who had to be removed from home because of severe abuse or neglect. Over time, it became clear that the children displayed extremely serious problems that were receiving no attention from the program, and the program was changed to concentrate on the age group—birth to six years—when greatest developmental results were possible and for which services were most severely limited.

Furthermore, a comprehensive treatment program was developed that could address both the presenting problems of the children that were likely to interfere with successful family placement and the extension of treatment to the families of the children. Intake criteria changed to include children whose abuse and neglect experiences had led to emotional, psychological, behavioral, or developmental problems; medical/developmental problems such as non-organic failure-to-thrive; serious lack of attachment; overt sexual acting out; emotional disturbances; serious developmental delays; and multiple failed foster placements. The degree of problem(s) must be so severe that family placement is not feasible and the intervention required is more intensive than can be provided in an outpatient setting.

Do such children exist in the birth to six years age group? Indeed they do: children admitted to the center for treatment have included:

[a]Formerly The Salvation Army Residence for Children

Three-year-old twins who had been removed from their mother for the second time and who had "failed" four foster family placements in three weeks because of extreme behavioral problems, constant tantrums, extremely aggressive behavior toward adults and other children, and extreme destructiveness

A child of four and a half who had experienced four different foster family placements in the previous eight months, resulting from progressively worsening symptoms of rejection, including bedwetting, hoarding of food, chronic sleep disturbance, and physical aggression toward younger children in the home

A sexually abused girl of four and a half whose foster family sought treatment after four months in placement due to the child's continuing self-destructive behavior: pulling out her hair and eyebrows, scratching her face, and chewing on the inside of her mouth, causing ulcerated sores

A six-month-old preemie (26 weeks' gestation) of a 15-year-old mother, experiencing serious feeding problems and other medical complications requiring constant monitoring, and active, directed stimulation to encourage the development of muscle tone and coordination

A boy of three and a half admitted with a diagnosis of atypical pervasive development disorder and mild mental retardation, where the foster home failed due to his extremely aggressive behavior, serious sleep disorders, speech impairment, and almost total lack of social skills

Nine youngsters admitted over a period of 12 months, with an average age of just under four years, who had already had stays in inpatient psychiatric hospitals and who often arrived under heavy medication

Once more it should be reiterated that group care for children from birth to six years of age is a radical intervention, even for children whose situations are as acute as those described above. Not only must all the elements in any residential treatment program be present, but maximum attention must be given to assuring that the early bonding process is achieved and that health and developmental emphases germane to the age group are in place.

The bases on which the center program is built are the consistent, nurturing relationships between child-care workers and individual children, therapeutic/developmental approaches aimed at normalizing the child's interaction with the world around, and very active therapeutic/educational work aimed at reunification of the biological family.

Relationships

Because it is a given that many of the children at Hope Center have serious attachment problems, and because all children aged birth to six years are moving rapidly through the most critical period of learning about and developing practice in relationships, the concern that children be bonded to some particular child-care worker is paramount. Overcoming the alienation and desertion that many of the older children (four- to six-year-olds) feel is extremely complex and requires endless patience, as with preadolescents and adolescents in group care. The situation, however, is even more difficult with children who have never been attached to anyone. Many youngsters come to the center as failure-to-thrive babies and must be taught painstakingly to allow touch, to make eye contact, to register affect. Because early cries of distress have gone unanswered, many have missed "hooking into the world" entirely and do not understand the most primitive kinds of parent-child nonverbal communication, on which all other communication builds.

Developing the child's ability to attach requires not only a primary worker to go through the lengthy process with each child, it also requires a consensus by the entire staff—relief child-care workers, social workers, consultants in all areas, cooks, secretaries, volunteers—that a warm, nurturing, highly verbal environment is to be maintained for all children at all times. Two forms of communication are vital.

Therapeutic communication views language as the single most important and powerful tool that can be used with the children and imparted to them for their use (Refer to Figure 1). All talking to children (except in loud games or emergencies) is in a quiet, slow, calm tone of voice, emphasizing simple words. Adults try, wherever possible, to talk to children on their own level, stooping or sitting on the floor, so that eye contact is easy. Body gestures—open arms, smiles, hugging, responding to child's touch—are integral components of communication, facilitating it in an important way, particularly for preverbal or nonverbal children.

When verbal direction is not adequate to handle a situation, a mutually agreed-upon system of *behavior management* comes into play. It consists of eight separate and distinct techniques that capitalize on the fact that, given their young age, children still actively want a relationship and approval from the adults around them (Figure 1).

Therapeutic/Developmental Input

Once a warm, consistent, positive, nurturing environment is created, the more formal components of the program can be brought into play: play therapy, group therapy, therapeutic preschool, and infant stimulation.

Play therapy and group therapy take on new meaning when the client group is preschoolers, many of whom have serious speech delays. Play therapy becomes an extremely potent way to help children identify the bad things that have happened to them and move toward understanding and acceptance, as well as learning how to relate to people and how to communicate. Some children are seen in play therapy as often as three times a week. The behaviors that are managed appropriately by child-care workers in the group living situation are allowed to emerge and be dealt with in these sessions.

Pat, who never kicks a child-care worker, frequently kicked the play therapist who forced him to confront his feelings about an inadequate mother who had deserted him several times. Because he had learned that Superman was adopted, he learned he could signal the therapist that he wanted to talk about his family worries by pretending to be Superman.

Sherrie, a three-year-old twin returning to the center after a disastrous attempt at family reunification and several unsuccessful foster family placements, wet herself 20 times a day and could not allow herself to be held and cuddled. The child-care workers accepted the behavior with little fuss and encouraged Sherrie in all of the acceptable things she did. The play therapist helped her transfer her "messing up" of herself to the play therapy room. Although there were a few things over which she was not allowed

Therapeutic Communication		Behavior Management	
Why It's Said	Example	Technique	Objective
To communicate security and well-being	"I'm bathing you with this nice warm water—feel it on your tummy and between your toes."	Ignoring	To reduce undesirable behaviors by not giving the child reinforcement
To express thoughts and feelings in a nonviolent way	"I think you threw all of your books on the floor because you're sad that your mom didn't come to visit."	Switching the activity	To move to an activity that would be more therapeutic; e.g., a rowdy group could be moved to gross motor activities to discharge energy
To attract positive attention	"I like the way you asked for applesauce."	Reinforcing desired behavior	To increase the frequency of desired behavior
To instill self-confidence	"I'll bet you had fun making that picture!" (Not "What is that?")	Redirection	To offer the child help in seeing the options available to him or her to behave appropriately

To create positive expectations	"When you finish making your bed, it will be your turn to get out the blocks."	Natural consequences — To help a child become aware of the real results of behavior and to assist in making more appropriate choices
		Shaping — To help a child systematically make small gains in a step-by-step approach to meeting a major behavioral goal
		Modeling — To show children visually what appropriate behavior looks like
		Time-out — To help a child regain control of his or her own behavior (for very young children, time-out is for very short periods of time and does not involve confinement in a time-out room)

Figure 1. Examples of Therapeutic Communication and Behavior Management.

to have control (e.g., the therapist's keys), many other things were explained to her as totally under her power during therapy (e.g., the light switch in the room). After weeks of tearing the room apart, and especially being extremely violent with one doll, Sherrie began to take care of the doll. Her wetting fell off dramatically. Finally, she could let herself be taken care of, after she had cared for the doll.

Group therapy at the center has little to do with the management of group living, as in some residential programs. Instead, groups generally are made up of children who share particular treatment goals or diagnoses. Sessions are short, and there is always at least one co-therapist, who may be a child-care worker or a graduate student.

One group consists of four children who are three to five years old, all of whom have siblings and have a very difficult time sharing. The goal of the group is to increase the children's empathy for each other. So that they would not have to share too much initially, there were three therapists, meaning that each child got a great deal of attention. Group sessions focused on sharing toys, sharing people, expressing feelings when sharing did not happen, and working out strategies for sharing. Not only have the children increased their ability to share and take turns in the group, but the behaviors are carrying over into their living areas. Other groups have dealt with grief and desertion and with aggressive behavior.

As is well documented, children who have suffered severe abuse and neglect to the point of deprivation often exhibit severe developmental delays. At the center this delay may mean children who are four years old and have no language, or three-year-olds who can barely walk. It may mean 18-month-old children who make no sounds, do not make eye contact, and cannot yet sit alone. To remediate these delays and encourage normal development, all children at the center are involved in either infant stimulation programs or therapeutic preschool. Both are highly structured daily activities designed to focus on the child's greatest deficits and capitalize on strengths that exist.

Particularly during the hours between 9:00 and 12:00, the staff is augmented by volunteers, graduate students, foster grandparents, and others so that children can be worked with either individually or in very small groups. Language is used in these activity settings, as described above, even with the very youngest babies.

Many children have speech therapy to deal with the most severe delays. Activities are all geared to allow the child to experience success while challenging and reinforcing forward movement in development.

Medical/Safety Concerns

Because of the age group and the fact that many children are not yet toilet-trained, the staff-child ratio must be very high. In addition to coping with all of the other pressures of residential child-care workers, child-care staff members must also practice rigorous hygiene and sanitation measures to prevent the spread of disease. All physical and environmental matters become a backdrop, but an essential one, for the therapeutic nurturing that is the main thrust of the program.

Since children between birth and six years require active and high-quality medical care to keep up with well-baby issues, and because the center's children typically are the product of difficult, unwanted pregnancies where there was little or no prenatal care, medical input is an integral part of the treatment planning and daily activity. A physically safe environment must be maintained at all times—electrical outlets covered, breakable objects out of sight, car restraints always used. Food service staff members must be prepared to handle special diets for infants and failure-to-thrive youngsters.

Available Treatment of Choice

All that has come before in this paper probably is of less importance than this last topic, which underlines the necessity that residential care for infants and preschoolers should not and cannot be provided in isolation. A continuum of care, with three principal outpatient services, must be available to ensure that family reunification is always the goal for children and that no child is in residential care who can be treated successfully in a less restrictive setting.

Family Therapy

All caretakers of children who are in treatment at Hope Center—biological, foster, and adoptive parents, and significant others who constitute the child's family—are offered participation in the family program. For many families, participation is written into a juvenile court service plan. The primary goal of the family program is to give the child and biological family every possible chance of reuniting or, in fact, of becoming a functional family for the first time. Failing that, the program facilitates the move toward alternative permanent placement for children. Services provided by the family therapist and the social service, health, preschool, and child-care staff members give support to the family unit through individual family sessions, involvement in a parent support group, and highly individualized and intensive parenting skills training. Aftercare continues active support for the family after the child reenters the home and continues on a decreasing frequency as long as necessary.

Day Treatment

Some children with problems as severe as those described earlier do have family situations with enough strengths to allow them to avoid placement and remain at home if intensive services can be provided. In other cases, children in placement are ready to return home or move into foster care, but only if intensive services are made continually available. For these children, the center provides day treatment, a full-day therapeutic program consisting of behavioral, educational/developmental, health, and psychotherapeutic interventions to remediate developmental delays, and assess and remediate medical problems, and reduce the negative emotional/behavioral effects of abuse and neglect.

One parent or other primary caretaker of every child in day treatment must agree to participate in whatever range of needed family interventions are identified through a family assessment. Daily transportation is provided for all children, and many families ride to the center in the van on the days that they are scheduled for therapy. A mothers' group is held weekly to provide parenting training and mutual support, and to socialize the mothers, many of whom are extremely isolated.

Therapeutic Foster Care

Specialized foster care services are designed to provide continuity for young children no longer in need of the intensive residential program but whose needs still require a skilled and consistent level of care and intervention. Therapeutic foster care services are provided by foster families who are licensed by the center. This concept of foster care represents the merger of the knowledge and skills of the center with the nurturance, stability, and support of the foster family into an effective treatment team. It is predicated on three elements: the emotional nurturance and physical care of the child, a comprehensive understanding of the needs and problems of the child, and the techniques to deal effectively with them.

The objectives of the program are realized through its two principal components: skill-based training, in which foster families participate in an intensive 26-hour preservice training curriculum designed and delivered by Hope Center staff members; and support services, through which the staff continues to be completely available to foster family and child after placement, as determined through the development of an individualized support plan.

Continuum of Care

These three major outpatient services augment the residential treatment program to form a continuum of care, the primary objective of which is to provide children and families with treatment in the least restrictive environment. The continuum is viewed as extremely dynamic, with movement among its components occurring as often as necessary for children to receive the most appropriate intervention at any given time, all aimed at returning them as quickly as possible to family care.

The full continuum has been in place only a little more than a year, but there already are many examples where children have used the full range of services.

A two-year-old girl with severe developmental delays and neurological problems was placed in residential treatment after severe neglect and physical abuse by her single father, who tried to participate in the family program, but finally recognized his inability to parent the child. She was placed in a therapeutic foster home while continuing placement in the day treatment program. She has now "graduated" to a regular day care center, although she and the foster family continue to receive active support services. Termination of parental rights is expected to occur soon, and the child's progress is such that the outlook for a permanent adoptive placement is good.

A five-week-old boy with serious head injuries from suspected abuse was placed at Hope Center until he stabilized medically, and in order that the ability of his very young parents to parent him and his older brother could be assessed. The child was out of danger medically long before his parents were ready to provide a safe home for him, even though they are receiving family therapy, marriage counseling, and parenting education from the center's staff. The child was placed in a therapeutic foster home. Twice a week he and his brother (in a regular foster home) are transported by the center staff or volunteers to family sessions with the parents. The children are in a protected home environment, but are in close, regular, guided contact with the parents, so that eventual reunification of the whole family is a realistic goal.

A hyperactive, behavior-disordered two-year-old boy placed in a regular foster home was about to be removed and placed elsewhere because the family, with whom he had a strong attachment, could not manage his behavior. The placement was saved by admitting him into day treatment, and support for the foster family is making it much easier for them to provide a good environment for the child, and to deal with his visiting the biological mother, to whom he will probably return.

A set of three siblings, all of whom had been in the center for a period of time, were returned to their mother against the recommendation of the center. Because one of them was moved into day treatment, it was possible to monitor the situation closely. After a period of deterioration, when the children were in an extremely dangerous situation, the center staff was in a position to move in very quickly to protect the children. After attempts at foster placement, the children, who had been severely neglected and abused in the interim, were returned to the center program, where they all are making rapid progress. Therapeutic foster care will be a realistic option for them.

It must be added, however, that for very practical, systemic reasons the continuum does not always work easily. Often funding and/ or capacity make movement along the spectrum somewhat sluggish. This problem calls for a discussion of advocacy for adequate funding of services; it cannot be undertaken here, but must be acknowledged.

Conclusion

Group care may be the temporary treatment of choice for a small group of very young abused and neglected infants and preschoolers. It is clear that early, intensive intervention can have a dramatic effect on the myriad problems faced by very young children who have been severely abused and neglected. Although residential treatment of very young children may be the treatment of choice, it *must* facilitate the process of bonding/attachment; it *must* provide every opportunity for biological parents to attain or regain the ability to parent; and it should occur *only* in the context of a dynamic continuum of service, allowing rapid movement to meet changing needs.

When all of these considerations are met, group care can, in fact, greatly enhance the ability of young children to overcome the damage done to them.

References

Aaronson, May. Infant nurturance and early learning: Myths and realities. *Child Welfare* LVII (3): 165–173, 1978.

Allen, R.E., and Oliver, J.M. The effects of child maltreatment on language development. *Child Abuse and Neglect* 6: 299–305, 1982.

Allen, R., and Wasserman, G. Origins of language development. *Child Abuse and Neglect* 9: 335–340, 1985.

Bowlby, J. Effects on behavior of disruption of an affectional bond. In J.M. Thodey and A.S. Parkes (eds.), *Genetic and Environmental Influences on Behavior*. Edinburgh: Oliver Boyd, 1968.

Call, Justin D. Child abuse and neglect in infancy: Sources of hostility within the parent-infant dyad and disorders of attachment in infancy. *Child Abuse and Neglect* 8: 185–202, 1984.

Egeland, B., Srieufe, L., and Erichson, M. The developmental consequence of different patterns of maltreatment. *Child Abuse and Neglect* 7: 459–469, 1983.

Gaddini, Renata. On the origins of the battered child syndrome: Abuse as acting out of preverbal events. *Child Abuse and Neglect* 8: 41–45, 1984.

Langmeier, J., and Matějčekz. Psychological aspects of collective care in Czechoslovakia. In Henry P. David (ed.), *Child Mental Health in International Perspective: Report of the Joint Commission on Mental Health of Children*. New York: Harper and Row, 1972.

Martin, Harold P. Intervention with infants at risk for abuse or neglect. *Child Abuse and Neglect* 8: 255–260, 1984.

Oswin, Maureen. The neglect of children in long-stay hospitals. *Child Abuse and Neglect* 3: 89–92, 1979.

Pawl, Jeree H. Strategies of intervention. *Child Abuse and Neglect* 8: 261–270, 1984.

Segal, Julius, and Yahraes, Herberg. *A Child's Journey*. New York: McGraw-Hill, 1978.

15

The Healing Process: Day Treatment For Emotionally Disturbed Children

LORRAINE SIEGEL

D AY TREATMENT HOLDS A UNIQUE POSITION ON THE continuum
of care. It falls between the least restrictive environment of outpatient services rendered within a child guidance center or by a
private practitioner and the most restrictive environments of a traditional mental health hospital or residential treatment center.

This special position offers day treatment programs more opportunities for flexibility, both within individual programs and between programs, than the more traditional mental health services.
"Day treatment within this context may provide either short or
long-term transitional care between resources, or it may be the
primary initial treatment choice" [Zimet and Farley 1985: 732].

Although day treatment programs can differ, most have many
similarities. They recognize, appreciate, and make use of the interplay of family, child, and environment. Since the normal "work
day" for children takes place in school, the day is usually organized
around school experiences, where interactions with peers and adults
are used as the basis of therapeutic interventions. Most programs
use specific behavior management techniques to help children who
have loss-of-control problems. Individual and/or group therapy for
children and their parents or caretakers are usually available. Cooperation and communication among all staff members are central
to success in day treatment programs.

While most day treatment programs have these elements in common, there may be a hierarchical difference between those programs sponsored by schools and those sponsored by mental health institutions. In the former, academic and physical needs may take priority; in the latter, emotional and social learning is usually the priority. The State Department of Education, and the Office of Mental Health in New York State have recently organized an effort to assure that day treatment programs have a special status integrating the best of both mental health and educational approaches.

Several trends influenced the growth of day treatment. First, there was an increased awareness of the damage to children and families caused by separation. Greater knowledge about mental illness was producing a change in a philosophy that put all the responsibility for the child's pathology on the parents; parental inclusion, rather than exclusion, was being viewed as crucial in the treatment of children with mental illnesses. Second, there was the general movement away from institutionalization of the mentally ill and toward meeting their needs within a community context. Third, in the case of children, state education laws were mandating local community school districts to provide appropriate education for children with handicapping conditions. For those children handicapped by emotional problems and/or mental illness, education could only be provided appropriately when emotional needs were also met.

> Day treatment attempts to provide a total comprehensive treatment program which will touch upon all aspects of a child's life. More specifically, its objectives are to relieve anxiety, promote the development of adaptive skills, improve interpersonal relationships, increase motivation to learn and improve academic skills, increase self-knowledge, develop self-control and enhance self-esteem. [Zimet and Farley 1985: 732]

> The day treatment approach allows the child to maintain his relationship with his family, thus minimizing the severe separation trauma many children endure with full residential placement . . . it fills a gap in service between out-patient therapy and residential treatment; provides an

opportunity for the parents and child to grow together and increases the probability that the child can be maintained in the family following discharge. [Zimet and Farley 1985: 734]

The Nannahagen School Day Treatment Program

The Nannahagen School Day Treatment Program, founded in 1970, is a collaboration of a voluntary not-for-profit child-care agency, a school district that serves emotionally disturbed children, and the County Department of Community Mental Health. As such, the three groups serve as funding sources. The program is subject to the requirements and regulations of the State Education Department and the State Office of Mental Health. The program serves approximately forty children and their families per year.

All children in the program must be approved by their local Committee for Special Education (CSE) and must be classified as emotionally disturbed. Approximately 75 percent of the children are also organically impaired and/or learning disabled. Diagnostically, they span a broad range from psychosis to adjustment reactions. About 20 percent of the children are psychotic. About 50 percent are diagnosed as attention deficit disordered or hyperactive, and about 30 percent have impulse or character disorders. Two of the youngsters have been diagnosed as having Tourette syndrome.

All the children come from diverse social, cultural, and economic backgrounds as well. The population is 50 percent black and 50 percent white; approximately 10 percent Jewish, 40 percent Catholic, and 50 percent Protestant. Twenty percent of the children come from welfare families and 20 percent from upper-middle-class and professional families; the remainder are from working-class families. As compared to the general population, a larger percentage of program children come from single-parent or blended families; only 20 percent of the population come from intact families. Three of the children are in foster or adoptive situations. Over 90 percent of the children, previous to admission, were in special education and/or some form of psychiatric treatment, including psychiatric hospitalization.

For a large number of the children, admission to the Nanna-hagen Program represents a last chance to remain at home with their families. The largest number of children, about 85 percent, discharged from the program return to their community schools; of the remaining 15 percent, some children are discharged to res-idential programs, to hospitals, or to other specialized programs. Some of the children will require a special setting such as the Nannahagen Program for their entire school career. Since day treat-ment can be viewed as the midpoint of a continuum of care for children, some children come to Nannahagen for the first time from both less and more restrictive settings and are discharged to these settings. For some children, Nannahagen serves as a stabilizing force between hospitalizations. Because of the program's availa-bility to these children and their families, hospitalizations usually become less frequent and of shorter duration. The program offers a full range of psychiatric, social work, psychology, and special education services; individual, family, and group psychotherapy services are provided. Aftercare and intensive treatment for fam-ilies can be provided by a child guidance program at the same location.

Each ingredient of the program has its own identity, but the special value of day treatment is the planned integration of all these services. To achieve this integration, close communication among all staff members is carefully structured into the program. A close liaison is maintained between the program and the community, especially the school district from which the child comes. Some children come from multiproblem families who are involved with multiple agencies in the community. In these cases, Nannahagen maintains contact with all of the agencies and carries out a coor-dinating function to decrease the number of persons and agencies to whom the families must relate.

Case Illustrations

The case of Oliver is discussed here to demonstrate the many services along the continuum of care for disturbed children that were utilized by one family. Within this case context, the flexible position of day treatment along the continuum is shown.

Oliver was originally referred from his community school at age 6.6. Although he had an IQ in the superior range, he was not learning because of what were judged to be emotional problems. In school, he exhibited extremely impulsive and aggressive behavior and had a very short attention span. He threatened peers and adults verbally and was physically abusive to other children. Although we did not know it at the time he was accepted, Oliver was setting fires at home, making it necessary for his mother to move twice. At the time of admission, Ms. A. enthusiastically agreed to participate in Oliver's treatment, a precondition of a child's acceptance into the program.

Oliver, a very attractive olive-skinned youngster born out of wedlock, was the only child of Ms. A., a slim, pretty red-haired woman who supported herself and Oliver on welfare and occasional waitressing. She had been in several foster family and institutional placements as a child and teenager. Out-of-home placement had been suggested to Ms. A. for Oliver both by the mental health agency where Oliver was seen for outpatient treatment and by the school. When she refused to consider this option, the referral for day treatment was made.

Oliver's progress in the Nannahagen Program was uneven. There were periods when he functioned adequately academically and socially, and other periods of regression. Ms. A.'s involvement in his treatment was also uneven and ranged from weekly kept appointments to periods when months passed without her being seen. After 2½ years of maintaining Oliver in the program, he began to deteriorate sharply. In spite of all efforts, we could not avoid a psychotic episode, and Oliver was hospitalized. When the hospitalization took place, it was understood that the program was prepared to readmit him at the appropriate time. Oliver made gains in the hospital, and in less than three months was stabilized sufficiently to return to Nannahagen. During the time he was in the hospital, staff members maintained contact with the hospital staff, visited Oliver regularly, kept in contact with Ms. A., and acted as liaison between the school district and the hospital.

Following Oliver's return from the hospital, he and his mother made progress. She became more involved in treatment and was able to make some environmental changes in Oliver's behalf. Oliver used his good intelligence to make academic gains and, with improved impulse control, was able to make social gains as well. This process continued for about two years. Considering Oliver's fragility, however, there was no suggestion that he return to the community school. About two years after his hospitalization, Oliver again began to regress, and again we could not prevent the onset of another psychotic episode. The hospitalization this time was characterized by many stormy, violent periods, and few gains appeared to be made for a long time. Ms. A. did not make a connection with the treatment staff at the hospital and seemed to be using this period of time to disengage from our staff as well as from Oliver. When discharge plans could be made, our staff participated actively with the hospital staff in their formulation. It was agreed among all the professionals that residential treatment would be the most appropriate plan. Given Oliver's history and pathology, however, as well as Ms. A.'s continued resistance to this plan, he was not an easy child to place. Nannahagen agreed to readmit Oliver while continuing to work toward residential placement. Later, Oliver was placed, with his mother's cooperation. That was 2½ years ago. Oliver is now ready to return to the community, where his local school district has an appropriate class placement, and Nannahagen's Child Guidance Center will provide treatment for Oliver and his mother.

Viewed in terms of having prevented out-of-home placement, this case may appear to have been unsuccessful. The availability of day treatment, however, prevented placement for almost five years, laid the groundwork for a more successful placement when it did occur, and provided an ongoing stable relationship with a treatment agency. "Typical" day treatment cases do not exist. What can be said, though, is that while Oliver represents the case of a psychotic child from a chaotic, multigenerationally disturbed family who may require lifelong intervention from mental health agencies, the case of Gary is at the opposite end of the spectrum.

Gary, a blond, pudgy, ten-year-old from an intact family, was referred by his local school district because of its inability to intervene effectively in a deteriorating school situation. Until about a year before the referral, Gary had been functioning satisfactorily. At that time, absences from school increased at an alarming rate; interest and perfor- mance in academic areas were rapidly declining, and Gary was isolating himself from peers. While the parents, an educated middle-class couple, were concerned, they tended to minimize the situation and were resistant to any referral for treatment; they said it was a phase that would pass and pointed to Gary's older brother, who was a super- achiever. The parents finally accepted placement for Gary in the Nannahagen Program, rationalizing that it was a special school that would put their son back on track.

To some extent, they proved to be correct. After 1½ years, Gary's pattern of absences had been reversed, he was expressing interest in using his ability academically, and he had become reinvolved with his former group of friends in the community. Everyone agreed that he should be discharged from the program back to a mainstream community school class. Gary's discharge from the pro- gram took place two years ago, and from all reports he continues to function well in the community.

Although day treatment programs generally serve a popula- tion of children with severe disturbances and a long history of problems, the case of Gary illustrates the use of day treatment as a crisis intervention. Gary's problem behavior at the time he was placed in day treatment revealed no significant underlying pa- thology. Without the intensive intervention of day treatment, how- ever, his difficulties would most likely have been prolonged and may have resulted in longer-term negative effects. This situation is frequently the case in the histories of many children referred at an older age for residential and day treatment.

Principal Functions of Day Treatment

Day treatment has been described as providing a network of services under one roof. Their purpose is to prevent "negative side effects of removal from home and community: stigma, regression, dependency, and separation from family, friends, school and other community support systems [Ross and Schreiber 1975].

The services offered at the Nannahagen Program to achieve these ends and to return children to less restrictive settings include continuing evaluation and assessment, case management, individual and group psychotherapy for the children, family therapy, individual and group parent counseling and psychotherapy, psychopharmacology and crisis intervention, behavior management, and special education.

Maintaining a close liaison with all of the agencies and institutions in the community that impinge on the life of the children and their families is crucial. This relationship not only prevents duplication of services but reduces chaos, helps in the setting of priorities, and enables the services provided to be most effective. The case of Victor is an illustration of these benefits.

> When Victor, the third from the youngest in a single-parent welfare family of ten, was admitted, we discovered that the family was involved with the Department of Social Services, Child Protective Services, two mental health agencies, and three private social agencies. In a meeting called by Nannahagen, we were able to coordinate and integrate all of the services needed by this family. The Department of Social Services continued to perform income maintenance, and Child Protective Services continued to perform home monitoring. Of the six other agencies, one that offered day care service for Ms. D.'s grandchildren continued to provide it. All other services were then taken over, with the agreement and cooperation of the other agencies, by the Nannahagen Program and its affiliated child guidance center. This change has eliminated

duplication of services, reduced chaos in this family, and, most significantly, made it possible for Ms. D. and those of her children in need of treatment to make a real investment in it.

Parent Involvement

The Nannahagen experience supports the literature that stresses parental involvement as a prime ingredient in day treatment: the parent is viewed and treated as a partner. Linnahan [1977] says, "The key to the healing of a severely disturbed adolescent in his community is intense work with his family. Long after he leaves the [day treatment] center, they will still be intimately involved in his support and in the direction of his growth." Critchley and Berlin [1981] comment, "We have come to the conviction that parental participation in the milieu and educational aspects of our program and in family, couple or individual psychotherapy, depending on the severity of parental disability, is critical to the improvement or recovery of the disturbed child . . . parents are despairing about helping their child. Parental involvement in every aspect of the program and in family or individual therapy begins to reduce this helplessness and to promote feelings of competence, effectiveness and finally playfulness and spontaneity in all family members."

Although social workers at Nannahagen carry the task of long-term work with parents, the teachers regularly keep the parents informed of their child's progress academically and socially. A minimum of two full-scale team meetings with parents are held annually. Crises are dealt with by the full team with the participation of the parents. There are also several meetings with the staff members and parents throughout the course of the year. The purpose of these meetings is to provide parents with an educational and social experience. Parents are encouraged to communicate to staff members any development in the home environment.

Treatment with parents can be on an individual, group, couple, or family basis. Monthly contact with parents is mandatory, but many families are engaged weekly or twice weekly in different modalities. For instance, Oliver's mother was seen individually on a weekly basis to help her with the severe management problems that he presented. She was seen every other week with Oliver, where the focus was on the relationship and on establishing better communication. She also participated in a weekly parent group, where she was able to share feelings and gain support. Groups for parents with disturbed children have been highly effective. Many of the parents feel shame about having children with these problems, and for some it has resulted in isolation. Through the sharing of mutual experiences, the group method relieves guilt and helps parents mobilize themselves to be more effective with their children. It also provides a network for some of the more isolated families.

The family of Gary, whose case was described earlier, resisted his placement in day treatment and minimized his problems. In addition, they did not see that they had any part either in the problems or in their solution. Although they would not commit themselves to participation in a group, or come in as a couple, they accepted family treatment, saying that as long as Gary had to be in Nannahagen, they would try to help. As they listened to Gary and his brother in these sessions, and, in turn, were themselves listened to by the worker, they did become involved, achieved insights about themselves as parents and about their relationship with their children, and were able to make some positive changes.

Some parents for various reasons do not honor the mandatory agreement on monthly contact. Since Nannahagen admits children from all of Westchester County, and public transportation is poor, parents without a car have a real problem. Some families are themselves seriously disturbed, with such grave conditions as physical or sexual abuse of children, depression, schizophrenia, multiple divorce, chronic unemployment, and criminal behaviors. Our program admits children from a broad range of cultural and ethnic backgrounds. In some of these cultures, the need for mental health services has negative connotations. This attitude sometimes results in a parent's unwillingness to participate in the program. To overcome nonparticipation, in-home outreach services are offered; contact in the home fulfills the parental obligation to participate. Beyond this service, however, the in-home contact makes parents feel nurtured, and the reality of the home provides an illustration of many concrete problems on which the family can begin to work. Some families feel more secure on their own home territory and are able to be more open with the worker, particularly in situations where cultural and ethnic considerations are interfering with involvement of parents in treatment.

The following are two examples of reaching out to families in very different situations.

The first concerns a black family living on welfare, with a long and largely negative experience of social workers and social agencies. When the youngster, eight years old, the oldest of four siblings and the only child not the biological child of the father, came into day treatment, the father was enraged at his own lack of control, and the mother was extremely depressed and passive. In-agency contacts with the family took place in long luncheon meetings to provide nurture to the parents as much as to the children. It was clearly recognized that forming an alliance with this family would be very difficult. Finally, in-home weekly treatment sessions were initiated, and, over an extended period of time, the worker came to be trusted, and productive work was done, primarily with the mother. She became an advocate for herself and her children and was able to set and carry out realistic goals for herself and her family, especially in education and housing. The child who was in day treatment has now been successfully reintegrated into his community school.

The second situation is that of a lower-middle-class family where the mother is a chronic schizophrenic with a history of many hospitalizations. The child in day treatment is severely disturbed and also very reactive to the mother. The goal with this family has been to help the mother to remain stabilized. Therefore, we have taken on the responsibility for prescribing and monitoring the mother's medication; maintaining a minimum of weekly in-person contacts with her; keeping a regular contact with the father; communicating with the agency providing as-needed homemaker service—and with the homemaker, when necessary. There are periods of time when the worker has been in daily telephone contact with the mother, serving a supportive and organizing function for her. The youngster has been in day treatment for almost two years. The mother has remained stable in that she has been able to hold a two-hour-a-day job, has not been hospitalized, and has used homemaker services only minimally. The youngster has also made good progress socially, emotionally, and academically.

These two examples highlight the positive results that can take place even with the most difficult families when parents are treated as an integral part of their youngster's treatment. When children are in day treatment, the daily effect of the child's behavior acts as a constant reminder that there is a need for change. Although many parents may assert that it is the child who must change, there is usually a gradual acceptance of the necessity that changes must occur within the family as well. Day treatment offers child and family the opportunity to work on the improvement of family and individual functioning together. Through the mutual ongoing investment in change, families grow. All of the problems that bring youngsters into day treatment do not go away, but the ability of children and parents to cope with the problems that do remain improves significantly. Nannahagen looks forward to increased parents' participation by including them in policy making; as aides in the milieu; and through the formation of a parent organization, for fund raising and expanded social and educational programs.

Conclusion

That day treatment programs are proliferating is not surprising, in view of their capacity to minimize separation trauma and to maximize a concentration of unduplicated treatment modalities in the family as a whole. They provide an extremely important service in the direction of the less restrictive side of the continuum of care.

References

Critchley, B.L., and Berlin, Irving M. Parent participation in milieu treatment of young psychotic children. *American Journal of Orthopsychiatry* 51 (1): January 1981.

Linnihan, Patricia C. Adolescent day treatment: A community alternative to institutionalization of the emotionally disturbed adolescent. *American Journal of Orthopsychiatry* 47 (4): October 1977.

Ross, Andrew L., and Schreiber, Lawrence J. Bellefaire's day treatment program: An interdisciplinary approach to the emotionally disturbed child. *Child Welfare* LIV: March 1975.

Zimet, Sarah G., and Farley, Gordon K. Review article, day treatment for children in the United States. *Journal of the American Academy of Child Psychiatry* 24 (6): 732–738, 1985.

16

Independent Living: A Continuum of Services for Adolescents

MARY JO COOKE
MARGARET DiCORI
ROBERT L. GASS
DOROTHY SEWARD

OLDER ADOLESCENTS POSE DIFFICULT DILEMMAS FOR every agency responsible for placing children in substitute care. In general, this population has difficulty adapting to the more traditional forms of foster care. In addition, many of these teens have little or no family contact and, consequently, need to develop skills to live independently.

This paper discusses an independent-living program for older adolescents that is an alternative to traditional types of placement. It opens a continuum of services for adolescents who function on different levels and reflects the collaboration of a public and a voluntary agency.

Program Development

In 1981 the Massachusetts Department of Social Services and The New England Home for Little Wanderers were engaged in separate planning of independent-living programs for adolescents between the ages of 16 and 18. The Department of Social Services (DSS) was a new state agency, officially born in July 1980, with one of its mandates to ensure permanency planning for all children in the state's child welfare system. By 1982, the DSS was becoming more and more troubled by the lack of foster homes for older adolescents and the need for transitional programming for young people coming out of group care and having consistent difficulty adjusting to substitute care.

The New England Home for Little Wanderers, a multi-service child welfare agency offering residential care since 1865, was becoming more and more concerned about the number of young people graduating from either its residential or group home programs who could not return home, and for whom continued group care or substitute care programming was inappropriate.

In this instance, a public and a voluntary agency identified a common need. Through its Norwood Area office, which serves 12 suburban towns up to 20 miles southwest of Boston, the public agency solicited proposals for an independent-living program, and the voluntary agency was awarded the program in the spring of 1982. Both agencies then joined in planning the new program, which was called the Norwood "Cluster" because it would represent a variety of services clustered around a staffed apartment. It would be a flexible, client-driven program that would adapt to meet the clients' changing needs. The program was designed at that point to serve female teens only, since this group was the population identified by both agencies.

The development of the Cluster program was based on a number of factors and theories. First, there was a belief in community-based care, that is, the ability to provide services to children in the community in which they reside. This situation enables a continuity-of-care model where teens are able to connect with community services while in a program and remain involved with these services when they leave the program. A community-based model also allows and encourages family involvement in the teens' lives and enables the program to involve families in the support of the adolescents and in treatment.

Another factor influencing the way the program evolved was a needs assessment conducted in the DSS office, which revealed that requests for foster homes for teenagers far exceeded the number of available homes. These were requests for teenagers who were unable to return home and for whom other permanent plans (i.e., adoption, guardianship) were not appropriate. The initial model of the program therefore contained a foster home care component, the difficulty (practical impossibility) of recruiting foster homes for adolescents, although a variety of recruitment techniques were used, eventually made this component unrealistic.

It soon became clear that another type of program, less restrictive than typical group care, had to be developed. Based on the ages of the teens needing placement (16–18 years), when the developmental task is separation, independence, and preparation for ultimately living on their own, it was decided that an independent-living program would best meet their needs.

One theory that was very useful in the development of the Cluster program was highlighted in the article, "Reactive Depression in Youths Experiencing Emancipation," by James L. Anderson and Brian Simonitch, which appeared in the June 1981 issue of *Child Welfare*. This article reviewed experiences in the Independent-Living Subsidy Program in Oregon and identified certain stages that most youths go through before they become independent: anxiety, elation, fear and loneliness, and quiet confidence.

The initial model of the Cluster program contained three components: (1) a specialized foster care component that was set up to have five foster homes—one, an intensive treatment home, and four specialized foster homes; (2) a supervised apartment that is now called Experiential Living or Staffed Apartment; and (3) a co-op apartment now called Supervised Independent Living. This model was designed to meet the needs of adolescents on a continuum from more to less restriction. It was the intention of both agencies, at that time, that adolescents would enter the program at either the foster home or staffed apartment components and move toward supervised independent living.

After the first year, the foster care component was dropped, as mentioned earlier. Two components were added, however: Alternative Living (serving clients in their own homes or foster homes), and Aftercare (supportive time-limited individual or group counseling). These additions enable Cluster to serve more clients and increase the flexibility of the program in meeting clients' needs.

It became clear in the first year that for the program to meet clients "where they are," adolescents could enter the system at any point; that is, staffed apartment, supervised independent living, or alternative living. They could also move throughout the system; older adolescents need a chance to test things out, and a program that always can hold on to a client in some part of its program was crucial to each client's success. The only exception to this movement was that no clients could return to the staffed apartment once they had successfully completed their stay there. This behavior was seen as regressive, since the staffed apartment is the most restrictive part of the program.

Once the new program design had been in use for two years, both agencies decided to add a staffed apartment for males, which opened in July 1985.

Program Design

The experiential living or staffed apartment component of the program is a semi-independent living residence. Age range here is 16 to 19 years. The staffed apartment can serve a maximum of ten clients at a time. Length of stay is one to 1½ years. Child-care staff members monitor the clients evenings and weekends, and social work staff members supervise during weekdays. The program currently runs separate components for males and females. Though the residents are monitored 24 hours, the focus is on semi-independent living. Clients are required to sign a contract upon entry in which they agree to obey house rules, follow through with program requirements, and work on individual goals.

Residents are expected to be involved in a day program, such as school and work, full-time employment, job training, or a job search program. They are expected to attend a weekly skill training group and house meeting and also to agree to a budget and savings plan geared to full- or part-time work.

One example of how the program increases client responsibility is the curfew policy. The house curfew is 10:00 P.M. during the week and 1:00 A.M., Friday and Saturday. At three months clients may be eligible to apply for extended curfew through their social worker. These curfew times are midnight on week nights and 2:00 A.M. on weekends. To obtain extended curfew, clients must be following through regularly with all aspects of the program. To apply for extended curfew, clients must prepare a written case and submit it to their social worker. The client and social worker present the case to a board, consisting of two staff members and two residents. The board makes its recommendation to the director. At six months, a client may apply for self-imposed curfew. The goal is for clients to be able to set their own curfews based on their own values and daily routine, as they will need to do when they are living independently.

Skills meetings are weekly 90-minute sessions for teaching the seven independent-living skill areas of the program: cooking, health care, career development, drug and alcohol information, household maintenance, and tenant issues. This group format serves as both a formal medium for group teaching and a forum where clients may again learn about appropriate group behavior. The format includes discussions led by social workers, child-care staff members, and individuals from the community. There are participatory meetings that may include values clarification exercises, meal preparation, and games. Video equipment has been used to do mock interviews, and movies on alcoholism, suicide, and homosexuality have been presented for discussion.

Skills meetings are mandatory for those clients living in the staffed apartment and supervised independent-living components. They are optional for clients in the other two components. Clients who attend skills meetings range in age from 15 to 20.

Clients in the supervised independent-living component are subsidized in apartments or rooming houses. From six to ten clients (age range is 17 to 20) may be served at one time. The length of stay varies depending on the educational plan and may range from six months to one year.

Clients work with the staff to find affordable housing, negotiate with landlords, and arrange for moving. They sign a contract agreeing to abide by program rules and to follow through with program requirements. The rules include no overnight guests and no alcohol or drug use in the apartment. Clients are also expected to abide by the landlord's rules or lease and to have respect for their neighbors and roommates. The program requirements include a day program of school and work or working full-time. Clients must budget and save a portion of their earnings. The subsidy money from the program is held by the social worker in a checkbook. Checks for rent, food, and utilities are written together by the social worker and client. Clients are reimbursed for groceries on a receipt system and present receipts and a menu to their worker.

Clients are expected to attend the skills meetings and meet with their worker at least weekly, but may meet with their worker more often, as necessary, and especially when they first move into a new living situation. The focus of this component is to prepare clients for the time when they will be self-supporting.

The alternative living component of the program provides out-reach services to clients who are living in foster homes, with friends, or in conflictual family situations. This component can serve four to six clients at a time with an age range of 15 to 18 and for a length of time from six months to one year. The role of the outreach component may be to assess a client's ability and readiness to enter the staffed apartment or independent-living phase of the program. The worker and client may work toward finding an apartment and preparing for the move. The focus of this outreach may also be to help clients stabilize in their current living situation. The worker may help the client to obtain health care, job training, or GED preparation. Clients are encouraged to attend the skills meetings and meet with their outreach worker weekly.

The aftercare component is a support for clients who have successfully completed the staffed apartment and/or independent-living components. Aftercare is not limited to numbers or age range of clients and lasts for six months. It gives clients the opportunity to be with others who have lived through the unique experience of the Cluster program and gain support in living independently. If there are several clients in aftercare, a group is held monthly. Clients may meet with the outreach worker on a contractual basis and are also asked to provide feedback as to their experiences in the program.

The Curriculum

The development of a formal curriculum has proved invaluable in helping clients develop the necessary skills for independent living. Research and assessment have yielded the important sub-jects: education, job preparation and maintenance, health and hy-giene, food and nutrition, budgeting and money management, leisure time, and household maintenance; they are taught in several ways. In the staffed apartment, child-care workers talk about daily living skills and work with the clients daily on what they need to be doing to attain their goals. They have chores that they are taught and then supervised on. Clients meet with child-care staff members individually on many things. Group skills meetings address other curriculum areas.

The content can be basic, from a staff member demonstrating how to use a cookbook and prepare a meal, to having the client read and answer a worksheet on apartment hunting.

In the supervised independent-living component and the alternative component, all clients are urged to come to the skills meetings. They also receive individual instruction on specific skills from their caseworker.

Currently, quite a bit of curriculum information is published and available to programs. Some materials are in workbook formats with student and teacher manuals, and some are topic-specific. Using a mixture of both has been most helpful.

As child-care staff members are hired, we look at the life experiences they can build upon to teach daily living skills. Child-care staff members are supervised weekly, both individually and in a group by the social work staff. In the past, one staff member was in charge of a specific curriculum area and responsible for all the clients learning that information. At present, each child-care worker is assigned to one or two clients and responsible for teaching the entire curriculum. They take on the roles of primary teachers for the clients.

In the alternative and supervised independent-living components, the caseworker is responsible for making sure each client has mastered all phases of the curriculum.

Collaboration

Public and voluntary agency collaboration was initiated at the beginning of the program with the joint hiring of the director of the Cluster program. The referral process demonstrates the continuing collaboration between the agencies. In Norwood DSS, all potential placement cases, including Cluster candidates, are presented to an in-office decision-making panel, which decides whether placement is appropriate, the type of placement, permanent plan, and tasks to be completed to achieve a permanent plan. This procedure allows DSS to assess clinically whether an adolescent is appropriate for Cluster and encourages a referral to alternative living for an adolescent who is not currently appropriate for Cluster but whose permanent plan is independent living; this early referral enables Cluster to eventually move a client into a staffed apartment or supervised independent living.

Once the panel approves, a referral is sent to Cluster, whose staff interviews the potential candidate with the DSS social worker. The clients are then responsible for contacting Cluster to express an interest in the program. The director of Cluster and supervisor of Norwood DSS discuss each referral, reviewing the pros and cons and specific needs of each referral. After treatment plans are discussed for each referral, these two principals usually have no difficulty in agreeing on appropriate candidates for Cluster.

In addition to the referral process, the director and supervisor meet regularly to discuss referrals, the program, and the adolescents who are currently being served by Cluster. Also, both work together to resolve issues of mutual concern. For example, the Special Education Department of a local school system contacted the director to discuss special education needs of clients served by the Cluster program. Both the director and supervisor arranged to meet together with the school people. Collaboration continues with the front-line staff. DSS social workers have ongoing contact with the Cluster staff; they work together with the client in joint meetings and in joint problem solving. From the perspective of DSS, there is a feeling of ownership of Cluster and a strong desire to have a successful program. From the Cluster side, there is a strong feeling of support and availability of DSS staff.

Clients Served

The Cluster program has served 79 clients from its inception in July of 1982 to the present writing. Thirty-nine clients were admitted to the staffed apartment component, 28 into independent living, 32 in the alternative component, and 16 in outreach. Figure 1 depicts the flexibility of the program, showing the number of clients who have used one or more components. Figures 2 and 3

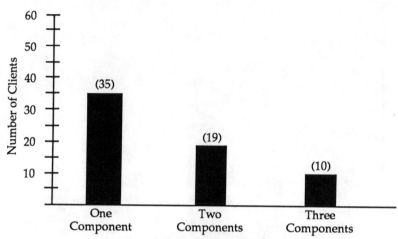

Figure 1. *Flexibility of the program.*

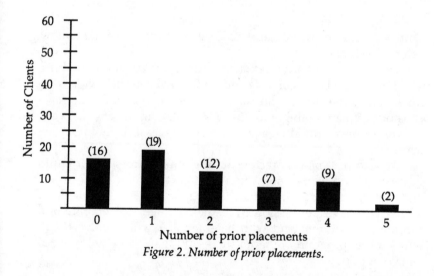

Figure 2. *Number of prior placements.*

reflect the number of placements and where clients have come from before entering Cluster. About half of the clients come from families that abuse alcohol and drugs. The clients themselves often have a history of substance abuse, and a large number have been identified as having been physically and/or sexually abused. An emerging

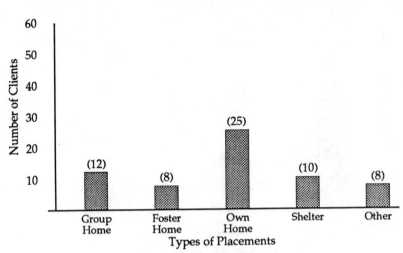

Figure 3. Types of previous placements.

trend is the number of clients who have been adopted and are now facing placement.

The clients who are most successful in this program are those who have some inner controls and minimal violent behavior, who are able to accept limits and rules to some degree, and who have a history of maintaining a job or jobs or staying in school. Teens who need long-term intensive treatment are least likely to be successful.

Beyond personal characteristics are other factors important to success: (1) the teen's motivation is vital (there are ways to test this); and (2) family support for the program is also a key element. Teens who have permission from their families to separate and become independent and who have families who involve themselves in the program are more successful than those without parental support.

Perhaps the most important observation to be drawn from the Cluster experience is that independent living for all children is a process, not a program. It does not begin at a specific age: preparation for eventual emancipation is part of growing up. Neither is there a specific age at which it can be said that independent living is established. Since Cluster clients have had more difficult backgrounds and fewer supports than is true for the general population, special efforts are called for in helping them, and in extending the program's continuum role to influence earlier preparation and, if necessary, to extend beyond their teen years.

Results

Success in Cluster is measured by how its clients are able to function every day in the community. Can they do their own banking, shopping, cooking; can they relate to employers; can they reach out for help in times of crisis? It is significant that when adolescents who leave Cluster have later difficulties, they often contact Cluster for assistance even after several years have passed.

In objective terms, some clients enter college, obtain satisfactory employment, maintain their own apartments, often with their own children. Others do not do so well. It must be remembered, too, in relation to any future formal outcome research, that a delineation of clients who can best use the Cluster program is made at intake, enabling the program to use its resources in behalf of the most appropriate clients.

Summary

The five-year history of the Cluster program has yielded certain observations that deserve reemphasis.

1. Independent living is a process, not a place. It is crucial that any independent-living program have the programmatic and administrative flexibility to meet clients "where they are." Older adolescents need the chance to test things out, and a program that always can hold on to a client in some part of its continuum is vital to each client's progress.

2. Skill development and support are essential to independent living.

3. Independent living as a "curriculum" must be in mind long before a client reaches the age of 16. Residential treatment and foster care programs must start working on this goal in the early adolescence of their clients.

4. Public and voluntary agencies should review their planning efforts for older adolescents. Independent living is clearly one area that the public and private sectors have identified as a need. Mutual planning and collaborative efforts work and should be encouraged.

5. There needs to be more public discussion about age 18 as the arbitrary cutoff for services and the measure for success. In our culture, it is extremely rare for an 18-year-old to be expected to be financially independent and, given the history of the clients who are considered as appropriate for independent-living programs, this measurement of success is even more unrealistic.

6. Formal protocols of what constitutes success for graduates of independent-living programs need to be developed. At this point in its experience, the Cluster program has concluded that clients' ability to hold a job, their development of appropriate interpersonal skills in dealing with the external world, and their ability to seek help when crises arise must be part of any formal measurement of success.

17

The Sage Hill Program for Competency Promotion

RODERICK DURKIN
MICHAEL FORSTER
THOMAS E. LINTON

Sage Hill Camp, Inc., operates two summer camps: one is the ghost town of Montezuma on a patented mining claim, 11,000 feet high on the Continental Divide in the Colorado Rockies; another is the 100-acre "Old Ramsdell farm," in a secluded section of Vermont's Green Mountains near the town of Jamaica. The coeducational summer camps for troubled teenagers and their families are run in conjunction with a year-round program. The brief but salient residential experience in the relatively closed system of a summer camp away from the distracting and often pernicious influences of a community is used to develop a positive peer group and to break down barriers between youths and adults. These relationships, in turn, are prerequisite to a year-round community program that sustains and augments the positive changes engendered in the camp and helps youngsters with any legal, medical, drug, school, and family problems.

Sage Hill targets that large segment of the population of teenagers who don't need long-term residential care but who do require support to remain in and benefit from community living in their own homes, foster homes, or group care facilities.

This paper details the fundamentals of the Sage Hill program. After outlining our theoretical orientation, we briefly consider, in turn, the characteristics, structural components, and psychotherapeutic strategies of the summer camp program; the year-round follow-up program; staff recruitment and preparation; and program evaluation. In conclusion we suggest some implications of the Sage Hill experience for child and youth care work, and summarize the major features of a reproducible model based on that experience.

Theoretical Bearings: Competency Promotion

Sage Hill is theoretically grounded in the idea of promoting competency in individual youth and family systems. Like most theoretical constructions, the concept of competency is complex. Here we remark briefly on three key dimensions of the phenomenon of human competency.

Intrinsic Motivation

In several essays [1959; 1961; 1963], Robert W. White argued for the existence of an intrinsic biopsychological human motivation for competence. This competence, or "effectance," White conceptualized as effective interaction with the environment. The urge for competence is not reducible to the classical drives based on tissue needs. Drives are not affected by environmental feedback, but competency is; drives seek end-states of tension relief, while competency moves the organism to curious, explorative, and manipulative action in complex interaction with its environment.

> There is a competency motivation as well as competence in its more familiar sense of achieved capacity. The behavior that leads to the building up of effective grasping, handling, and letting go of objects, to take one example, is not random behavior produced by general overflow of energy. It is directed, selective, and persistent, and it is continued not because it serves primary drives, which indeed it cannot serve until it is almost perfected, but because it satisfies an intrinsic need to deal with the environment. [White 1959: 318]

Others have made similar points regarding an essential human need for competence. Allport [1961], who discussed an urge for "self-related striving," said:

> It would be wrong to say that a need for competence is the simple and sovereign motive of life. It does, however, come as close as any need (closer than sexual) to summing up the whole biologic story of development. We survive through competence, and we become self-actualized through competence.

The task of the helping person, then, is not to instill the desire for competence, but to find ways for clients to realize their intrinsic motivation for competence in personally satisfying, prosocial ways.

Extrinsic Learning

Intrinsic motivation is not sufficient for the effective emergence of competence, however; of equal importance is the quality of the environment itself. The individual's development of a specific range of competencies is the product of an ongoing interaction of person and environment. There are two noteworthy aspects of this interactive process: (1) experiential learning; and (2) social learning.

Organisms learn through a questing, explorative, manipulative engagement with the things (other organisms, objects, and processes) occupying the life-space in which they find themselves. Learning is thus a dialectical process of actively experiencing the world, and, through this process, of changing one's self. "Dealing with the environment means carrying on a continuing transaction which gradually changes one's relation to the environment" [White 1959: 322]. Maximal learning will occur in environments rich in stimuli provided by persons, objects, and activities.

For human beings, the process of learning for competence has a large social or ecological component. A wide array of social factors, mediated by both individuals and institutions, heavily influence the outcome of the competency-building process: appraisal, comparison, reward and punishment interactions, social roles, and models at the micro level, as well as macro social structures insofar as they shape available forms of opportunity, power, and recognition. Bandura [1969] has discussed the major conditions for effective social learning or relearning: new behavior should not entail serious negative consequences; the benefits of new behavior should be immediately apparent to the learner; moral or value sanctions against the new behavior cannot be feared by the learner; authority figures must not oppose the acquisition of new learning; models of new behavior should be present consistently, as well as other regular means of reinforcement.

Development

A general typology of competencies includes *intrapsychic, interpersonal,* and *environmental* competencies. *Intrapsychic* competencies include understanding our emotions and how they affect us (affective education), such as judging ourselves realistically, controlling our impulses, and making our needs known. Our *interpersonal* relations require us to be competent in perception, forbearance, flexibility, and appropriate assertiveness; that is, those skills necessary to get along with others. Regarding the *environment,* we need to be able, for example, to recognize dangers and opportunities, work productively, and use available resources to meet our needs effectively

Yet competencies necessarily emerge in a developmental context. Especially when dealing with children, careful consideration must be given to the nature, pace, and sequencing of normal development along various competency dimensions—physical, cognitive, psychoemotional, social, linguistic. Developmental schema have something to offer to the understanding of competency development. The point here is only that all considerations of competency learning assume some sort of developmental context.

The primary assumption of a competency approach to child care is that troubled children have experienced poor and/or misdirected competency development. There is much they have not learned, and much, usually, that must be relearned. It appears likely that much of the socially inappropriate behaviors that earn for them labels such as "delinquent," "disturbed," and "troubled," are mischanneled efforts to achieve mastery of dysfunctional environments. The essential purpose of the competency-promoting milieu, therefore, is to replace vicious circles of defeat, failure, alienation, and negative behavior with health-producing circles of engagement with a stimulus- and opportunity-rich learning and success-oriented culture. Whereas a lack of socially acceptable competencies undermines the child's self-esteem and acceptance by the community alike, the ability to do socially valued things well provides enhanced self-regard and increases the likelihood of acceptance by peers, parents, and others.

The Sage Hill Summer Camp

Treatment Goals

The primary treatment goal of the Sage Hill Program is to promote, through a group approach, the normal growth and development (i.e., the competence) of the individual, and to treat pathology only as it interferes with the pursuit of competence. This goal is based on the assumption that a valid approach to treating illness is to promote health—an assumption especially relevant to the treatment of adolescents, where the distinction between true pathology and adjustment reactions is unclear. The flux of adolescence offers rare and unique opportunities for resocialization, a teaching of behaviors missed earlier.

The promotion of competence in no way precludes addressing issues of psychopathology, nor is their existence disregarded. A psychological understanding of the individual's personality (motivations, defenses, strengths, and so on) is necessary to aid the development of competence. In the Sage Hill Program, however, psychopathology is addressed in the context of its interference with the pursuit of competence and is thus more amenable to treatment. Murphy's law—if something can go wrong, it will go wrong—is true psychologically. Sooner or later one's psychological problems (excessive dependency, aggression, poor interpersonal perception, impulsiveness, and the like) will emerge; at the point at which they emerge to block competency acquisition, they are dealt with in specific context.

Camp Characteristics

Advantages

The summer camp was specifically chosen as a means to promote various competencies and to develop the positive peer group and staff-child relationships necessary to sustain an effective year-round community program. Summer camps are oriented to the 24-hours-a-day, seven-days-a-week needs of children rather than to the nine-to-five convenience of adults. Camps are fun, adventurous, enjoyment-oriented, and free from the stigma of "total institutions" such as detention centers and residential treatment programs. The activities are not evaluative and are thus less threatening than, say, school. It is hard to fail at a camp. Summer camps fill a natural break in the rhythm of children's lives, which, without positive and structured activities, can be a bad time. A summer camp "vacation" break is less likely to windup isolating children from their communities.

The setting—the rugged high country of Colorado or the gentle rolling hills of southern Vermont—complements and assists the work, which is close to nature and in harmony with it. Though not trying to make life unnecssarily hard in order to "build character," we choose to live simply and without the luxuries and frills of urban life.

Furthermore, the relatively closed setting of a camp forces people to live with the consequences of their actions because feedback is immediate. This fact in combination with the controlled nature of the milieu both promotes the development of interpersonal competence and permits sufficient flexibility to make necessary programmatic mid-course corrections.

From a programmatic perspective, promoting competence provides a common denominator to which individual staff members can relate. The goals and means to promote competence are more clearly defined and generally acceptable than are those for treating psychopathology.

Finally, the promotion of competence in the context of the opportunity-rich camp milieu is less likely to evoke an adversary relationship between adults and young people than is a psychopathology focus. Because competence has a great positive instrumental value, campers tend to be receptive to its development.

Size

Each Sage Hill camp is small, never accepting more than 20 children. Larger numbers are not compatible with the individualized goals of the program. Experience suggests that about 20 percent of new campers each year, plus or minus 10 percent, depending on the difficulties of the new campers and the cohesiveness of the camp group, is optimal. If more new campers are accepted, they may overwhelm the existing group, while a smaller number diminishes the group incentive continually to reaffirm existing norms and solidarity.

The vast majority of children are black, Chicano, Hispanic, and Native Americans, and virtually all come from low-income families living in the Denver and New York metropolitan areas— where the staff members also live during the year. The children are referred from a wide variety of children's services, including mental health centers, group homes, the juvenile court, psychiatric aftercare, foster care and special education programs, grass-roots community action programs, Boys' Clubs, and so on. In some cases, individual social workers, teachers, probation officers, psychologists, community leaders, and relatives refer children as well; every effort is made to sustain the involvement of the referring adult with the child, and in most cases these individuals become part of the service network that staff members rely upon during the year-round program.

Admissions

The promotion of competence as a treatment goal permits the camp to accept a wide range of youngsters. Adolescents diagnosed as retarded, schizophrenic, neurotic, juvenile character disorders, and inadequate personalities have been accepted into the program. The reliability, much less validity, of these diagnostic categories is questionable, as are their usefulness for treatment purposes. Whatever the individual child's difficulties, there are always clearly identifiable areas in which he or she can become more competent. The question vis-à-vis the program is: Can the program help this particular child? This decision is determined on the basis of candid face-to-face discussion followed by a trial visit and, finally, negotiating a mutual agreement to participate in the program.

Coeducational

Each camp is coeducational, allowing the youngsters to get to know one another as real persons rather than as the hyped sexual stereotypes promoted by the media and exploited by advertising.

The mistaking of these stereotypes for reality all too often contributes to the pseudomaturity so commonly found in troubled teenagers. Another rationale underlying the coed camp is that developing adolescents often encounter difficulties in their heterosexual relationships because they are inappropriately seeking to satisfy unmet infantile needs. The controlled setting of the camp and its guided group interaction reveal these difficulties and can help youngsters to acquire interpersonal competence in developing new relationships.

Structural Components

The Sage Hill camp purposely attempts to create and use a cohesive, salient group to support the individual pursuit of competence. The group helps provide the motivation to individuals to "want to do what they need to do." Three major facets of the program involve the individual in the group: the work program, the evening meeting, and the junior counselor program.

Work Program

Campers and staff members working together have built and maintained the entire facilities of the two camps.

In Colorado, a two-story house straddles a ravine with Morgan Creek rushing underneath, with a deck cantilevered out over a waterfall. To build this house, 8,000 pounds of concrete for the footings had to be carried in buckets by hand into the ravine. This work was done without a single complaint. In Vermont, a two-story, 24 by 32 foot precut log house with a full cement block basement was built. Other work projects have included clearing land, making roads, and building cabins and outbuildings. One of the most popular and instructive projects is for campers to select a tent site and build an eight- by ten-foot wooden platform for their own tent. This task entails selecting a site, bringing materials there, building a foundation, sawing the lumber, and nailing it together—a highly personal, satisfying, and instructive project in carpentry and cooperation. It is simple, assuring success, and the results of poor workmanship are of little consequence.

Work projects provide experiential learning in which the individual is placed in a position to learn for himself (with help when requested) what the program is trying to teach. The several functions of work projects in the program are as follows:

> Youngsters are directly involved in the program and given a sense of ownership and a vested interest in the smooth functioning of the camp. This attitude is particularly important when a new group is being assembled.

> Campers earn one-third of their camp fee irrespective of what their parents (or others) pay, which helps them to value the program further and avoids the ambivalence toward gift giving. It also provides a basis from which to negotiate a balance between work done by the campers in return for the activities provided by the camp.

> The projects provide a superordinate goal that helps break down barriers between staff members and campers and provides nonverbal cooperative tasks to bring both groups together.

> The work provides an intrinsically satisfying way to promote interpersonal competence, good work habits, and technical skills. Work is tailored to the skills and ability of the individual, thus minimizing the risks of failure. It is a truly positive experience, a by-product of which is self-esteem enhancement. For many, the building of personal, useful, and enduring projects in which something is learned is a rare experience.

> Personal difficulties of the individual—impulsiveness, inability to get along with others—invariably appear in the course of working. The individual can be helped on the spot with positive and beneficial results.

> Building camp facilities, in addition to being a valuable experience, cuts the cost of development by about 60 percent. Work that needs to be done is one of a camp's greatest assets. Almost invariably former campers returning even years later will go to projects they worked on and recall the project in detail and sometimes show it with great pride to their wives, children, or companions.

Evening Program

Each night after dinner, when everyone is usually relaxed, there is a camp meeting, patterned after the New England town meeting. The meeting reflects efforts to democratize the program and to gain the maximum involvement of the campers. Campers have a nontoken voice in decisions on camp affairs, and the chairing of the meeting is rotated among the campers. Agenda topics might include planning activities, deciding on work projects, rule setting and policy making, interviewing new staff members and campers, deciding on salaries—virtually anything of significance to the life of the camp. Group decisions are binding in all but matters of life and limb. Though the practice of allowing children such significant influence in the administration of programs may strike many as both radical and unwise, it is our experience that the dangers of faulty group decisions made in this way are usually more apparent than real.

The meetings are as a rule quite lively and engaging. Typically, at the beginning of summer, or with a new group, meetings are painfully brief and superficial, but as the group process engages each individual, the meetings become longer and much more salient for the individual and for the group as a whole.

The evening meetings are decidedly not therapy groups—which in any case may not be suitable for groups that live together, because personal feelings and information discussed in the therapy context may be misused as ammunition in conflicts within the living group.

The meetings and general democratic character of the program serve the following specific functions:

Promoting competence in such areas as problem solving, consequential thinking, discussion, compromise, interpersonal perception, and self-examination

Gaining the active involvement of campers in the program—in such a management-by-consensus system, the extra time invested in hearing everyone out is more than compensated for by time saved in gaining acceptance of a decision

Breaking down barriers between staff members and campers

Monitoring the program closely and supplying rapid and ongoing feedback for programmatic mid-course corrections

Junior Counselor Program

Junior counselors are recruited from the ranks of returning campers, thus assuring the involvement of older teenagers who may outgrow the program as campers but can still benefit from the program and/or are under pressure to get paying jobs. They are chosen because of their previous success as campers and demonstrated commitment to the program and its goals.

Junior counselors make a number of important contributions. They serve as excellent teachers and role models for younger campers. They provide program continuity over the years. They typically bring an enthusiasm, commitment, and adolescent passion that is rarely equaled by the adult staff. They are familiar with the country, projects, and facilities as well as the goals and rationale of the program. The junior counselor program offers a prestigious achievement toward which campers can work.

On the basis of the staff's knowledge of them, junior counselors can be given responsibilities commensurate with their demonstrated skills and abilities. Those who are good leaders and have proved their ability to work well with others can accept more group-work responsibilities. Those who are good mechanics, carpenters, or masons can work at what they know best, thus precluding a bad experience for them and saving the camp from disruption due to an inadequate employee. This familiarity is in favorable contrast to new adult staff members, who, even with the best interviews and references, are essentially an unknown quantity and who must learn about the program while on the job.

Some junior counselors have gone on to successful careers in the social services. One of the advantages of this program is that it can spread new-career training over the adolescent years, an approach likely to be more effective than a crash program for adults. Furthermore, training can be tailored to the unique interests, skills, and personality of the junior counselor. Yet even when these counselors do not go on professionally, the training is of great help in developing widely applicable personal competencies. The junior counselor becomes more competent in assertiveness, leadership, work, and interpersonal skills.

In sum, the junior counselor program is extremely valuable to the camp and the adolescent alike. The camp benefits in terms of the continuity, teaching effectiveness, and role modeling of the young counselors. The young people themselves benefit from training, competency acquisition, personal growth, and a paying job.

Psychotherapeutic Strategies

A number of psychotherapeutic strategies are used in the promotion of competence and the treatment of interfering pathology. For example, the trial visit enhances chances of a good client-program match and thus reduces the chance of a mutually negative experience. This procedure also sets the stage to involve the youngsters. They see firsthand what the program is like and work in it. Using techniques from reality therapy [Glasser 1965], the youngsters negotiate a commitment to do their share of the work and to participate in the meetings. They are then held accountable to this negotiated agreement and excuses are not accepted—individuals are held responsible for their actions.

A behavior modification perspective is reflected in structuring the program. It is assumed that one can change behavior directly and thus work from the outside in. This approach is not incompatible with working from the inside out, as in insight-oriented therapy. The short-term effectiveness of punishment, which does little more than suppress behavior, is avoided, and a definite effort is made to reinforce desired behaviors positively. For example, youngsters are paid for their work daily in order to reward positive behavior promptly. The behavioral approach of breaking down complex behavior into teachable discrete skills is also commonly used.

Some of the techniques of client-centered therapy [Rogers 1965] are used to help clarify emotions interfering with activities or interpersonal behavior. Life-space interviews, as described by Redl [1959], or marginal interviews as described by Bettelheim [1950], are also used. The interviews promote interpersonal competence and are particularly useful in that they take place as the behavior occurs rather than after the fact, when one can only deal with recollections of events.

In general, the guided group interaction approach of the program provides many opportunities to teach better, more effective interpersonal skills per se, particularly with persons of the opposite sex. For example, in the case of a fight, the youngsters may be asked to reverse roles and describe the fight from the other's point of view. This method helps them to see their own provocations, the cues they miss, and the opportunities to engage. In this way, many aspects of interpersonal competence can be taught without having to first explore and understand infantile or psychopathological origins.

The Year-Round Follow-Up Program

A major goal of the camp is to develop a positive peer group. The treatment goal of competency promotion in the closed, stimuli- and opportunity-rich milieu of the summer camp facilitates the formation of a cohesive peer group. Many teenagers' problems have a major etiological component of social influence and peer pressure, as in school failures, drug problems, running away, and delinquency. The camp seeks specifically to develop a set of group-anchored values to support achieving personal competence and to insulate campers from negative teenage counterculture values when back in the community.

During the year, the camp-formed group is kept together through a schedule of regular meetings and a variety of activities chosen to enhance group cohesiveness. Activities such as parties, ball games, birthday celebrations, skiing and camping trips, or going on whale watches, are chosen in light of their relevance for group development. From this perspective, it is better for ten youngsters to bowl on two lanes than to sit in relative isolation at a movie. In such ways the group, carefully cultivated in the summer camp, is maintained during and over the adolescent years to support and enhance the changes engendered in camp.

The summer camp workers also staff the year-round community-based program. In large measure the year-round program is effective exactly because of the relationships between adults and children developed during the summer residential experience. A genuine community has been formed over the summer; staff members and youngsters are known to one another. As a result, staff members are trusted and thus are better able to advocate for campers and their families with regard to their legal, medical, psychiatric, drug, family, welfare, immigration, school, and other problems. Often caseworkers, probation officers, and other professionals have not been sought out to help precisely because they are not known and trusted.

Clearly, given the multiple problems faced by youths and their families, workers must be skilled in outreach, networking, and intervention with relevant collateral individuals and agencies such as schools, courts, and medical and psychiatric resources. In most cases the program has managed to sustain the involvement of professionals who have referred children to the program; over the years this involvement has helped enormously in developing a genuinely useful network of individual and programmatic resources available to year-round workers striving to provide and integrate relevant follow-up services for these needy yet frequently hard-to-reach young people.

This outreach-networking component of the program is theoretically grounded in Sage Hill's ecological perspective on competency development. Because teens' problems are viewed ecologically—as part of a complex skein of social relationships—the program's efforts to promote competency simultaneously seek to help children become more acceptable to their community, and the community to become more accepting of them. During the summer residential experience, this perspective implies involvement of parents and/or parent surrogates: parents are always welcome at the camp and are represented on the parents' board, and one week each summer is set aside for family camping. In the year-round program, staff members employ a systems approach in their engagements with families. As with the individual, the goal of family work is to promote the competence of the family *qua* social system. Specifically, it seeks to help families cope more effectively with teenagers' problems rather than exacerbating them. In this regard, Sage Hill staff members act as models and guides, sometimes as explicit teachers, and as information and referral workers.

By promoting intrapsychic, interpersonal, and environmental competencies among individuals and systems, the Sage Hill Program seeks to reduce strains within the family or residential group. The program's ability to provide long-term support over the adolescent years is the key to its effectiveness in helping to stabilize the family, foster home, or group home setting. This support improves the chances of permanency in a child's living situation and helps to aviod unnecessary residential care.

Staff Recruitment and Training

Staff members are recruited primarily from graduate programs in the social and health sciences. The Sage Hill Program is affiliated with varied graduate programs and has been able to recruit talented, sensitive, hard-working, competent, and, most important, caring staff. Working in the camp has been used to meet residency internship and field work requirements.

While the backgrounds of staff members may be medicine, psychology, education, or social work, all staff members function as child-care workers. The role is similar to that of the educateur, or social pedagogue, which proved highly successful in European children's programs [Linton 1971]. Like the educateur, the Sage Hill workers are action-oriented generalists who help to integrate the youngsters' experiences, both in the summer residential and the year-round community programs. They are at once leader, teacher, mentor, confidante, and companion. They will know the family, the friends, the employers, the communities of youth in care; if necessary they will use any and all of these factors to help the individual achieve competency-enhancing objectives. The professional role is viewed as a flexible one, with a premium on concern for and commitment to the group of children in care.

Workers are provided an extensive in-service training in the knowledge and skill necessary to function as effective educateurs. Training topics include learning theory, behavior modification, and modeling; systems theory and the role of ecological factors in the process of competency development; competency acquisition in the context of human growth and development; group dynamics; networking and advocacy; therapeutic recreation; and life-space interviewing and other psychotherapeutic techniques and interventions. Applied skills in specific work-related areas (e.g., carpentry), as well as in high-interest leisure activities (indoor and outdoor games, arts and crafts) are also heavily emphasized. In most instances, experienced staff members well versed in Sage Hill philosophy and practice conduct training; where appropriate, professional trainers and consultants are hired to train in specific knowledge and skill areas.

At the same time, the importance of flexibility and creativity are stressed in the overall preparation of workers. In any interaction between a child-care worker and a youngster (or youngster's eco-system) the worker's options are conditioned by the uniqueness of the situation and the people involved. The ability to respond in a selective yet creative manner is essential to promoting normal growth and development in troubled children. Indeed, effective and positive child-care work sometimes requires that workers "put their principles aside and do what is right" [Fletcher 1966].

Implications and Conclusion

The experience of the Sage Hill Program suggests the following implications for programs seeking to help troubled adolescents succeed in community settings:

Combining a brief and positive residential experience with a supportive community-based program can reduce the need for costly, long-term institutional placement.

Empowering teenagers to govern responsibly their own affairs affectively binds them to the program and teaches a range of important competencies.

A competency orientation is an extremely fruitful approach to treating troubled adolescents.

Promoting competency can more fully potentiate the richness of the residential program and the community milieu alike by recognizing situations, interactions, relationships, and problems as opportunities for learning/competency acquisition.

With its developmentally grounded theory, relatively clear-cut identification of central child-care knowledge and skill areas, and recognition of the effective child-care worker as a skilled, engaged, and pivotal generalist, the competency promotion perspective serves as an ideal theoretical basis for professional child-care work.

References

Allport, G. *Pattern and Growth in Personality*. New York: Holt, Rinehart and Winston, 1961.

Bandura, A. *Principles of Behavior Modification*. New York: Holt, Rinehart and Winston, 1969.

Bettelheim, B. *Love Is Not Enough*. Glencoe, Illinois: The Free Press, 1950.

Fletcher, J. *Situation Ethics*. Philadelphia, Pennsylvania: Westminster Press, 1966.

Glasser, W. *Reality Therapy: A New Approach to Psychiatry*. New York: Harper and Row, 1965.

Linton, T. The educateur model: A theoretical monograph. *The Journal of Special Education* 5 (2): 155–190, 1971.

Redl, F. Strategy and techniques of the life-space interview. *American Journal of Orthopsychiatry* 29: 1–18, 1959.

Rogers, C. *Client-Centered Therapy: Its Current Practice, Implications and Theory*. Boston, Massachusetts: Houghton-Mifflin, 1965.

White, R. Motivation reconsidered: The concept of competence. *Psychological Review* 66: 297–333, 1959.

———. Competence and psychosexual stages of development. In M.R. Jones (ed.), *Nebraska Symposium on Motivation*. Lincoln, Nebraska: University of Nebraska Press, 1961.

———. *Ego and Reality in Psychoanalytic Theory*. New York: International Universities Press, 1963.

18

The W-A-Y Program:
Work Appreciation for Youth

NAN DALE

Aɴ ᴇxᴄɪᴛɪɴɢ ɴᴇᴡ ᴘʀᴏɢʀᴀᴍ ᴛᴏ ᴛᴇᴀᴄʜ ᴡᴏʀᴋ ᴇᴛʜɪᴄs to troubled youngsters has been developed at The Children's Village. Now in its fourth year, the W-A-Y (Work Appreciation for Youth) program has already received national attention. It has five stages through which the children progress, the last of which—the Work Scholarship—helps the participating children to accumulate a substantial fund to be used for their higher education or job training. The most unusual features of the W-A-Y program are the young age of the children involved in the early, developmental stages, the general design of the program, and the Work Scholarship aspect of W-A-Y that continues after its participants leave The Children's Village, staying with them through high school.

This paper describes the five stages of the W-A-Y Program[a] with particular emphasis on the final stage, the Work Scholarship. Stages One to Three take place on the campus of the Village's residential treatment center. Work ethics are taught first in the cottage, then in the "neighborhood," and then in a centralized work program. Stage Four of the program involves youngsters

[a]More in-depth program material about the program, including a brief videotape, is available from The Children's Village.

working at regular jobs in the local community. Finally, the Work Scholarship phase of the program is a separate demonstration project that is testing a new approach to encouraging its participants to stay in school, work part-time, and save for their future education or job training. Work scholarship recipients, all of whom have participated in earlier stages of W-A-Y, earn a unique kind of financial incentive that allows them to accumulate a sizable nest egg for post-high school job training or college. Boys are selected for Work Scholarships while still in residential treatment, but participation continues after leaving—for up to five years. A great deal of data from the project is being carefully compiled and preserved so that our findings will enable us to assess whether such a program can make a long-term difference in the lives of a selected group of high-risk youths.

Background

The Children's Village serves an exceptionally needy population. The residential treatment program operates from a sprawling 150-acre campus just north of New York City, in Westchester County. This program accepts only boys between the ages of 5 and 14 (at intake) who have moderate to severe levels of emotional and behavioral problems. Approximately 75 percent of the boys return home after an average of 18 months, during which time both the children and their families receive intensive clinical services in addition to the milieu treatment provided to the youngsters. Those boys who cannot return home are transferred, when ready, to one of the group homes or foster homes operated by The Children's Village, or, whenever possible, placed for adoption.

Many of the boys in care, who are placed both by the courts and by families and guardians, have been subject to abuse and neglect, and all have demonstrated a chronic inability to function in school and/or home. Many have been involved with the criminal justice system. The numerous critical treatment needs of the children create competing demands on the agency's time and resources. Only a fraction of the worthwhile approaches that might assist the boys can be tried.

The agency's decision to devote considerable resources to teaching work ethics was based on three premises: first, the typical backgrounds, behaviors, and attitudes of The Children's Village boys leave them at high risk for adult unemployment; second, the young age of the children and the fact that they live at the Village for a year or more provides an unusual opportunity for gradual, natural learning of new values; and, third, the Village staff believes there is a correlation between long-term mental health and employability.

The Children's Village boys fit the profile of those who end up unemployed—and unemployable. Most have already demonstrated antisocial or bizarre behavior; nearly all are far behind in school; many come from families with a long history of unemployment. Resignation, apathy, and aimlessness are frequent responses of these youngsters to their life circumstances, perceived by them to be less painful alternatives to striving or caring. Feeling themselves unworthy, they in turn reject societal norms as worthless and evince little interest in preparing for the future.

Life at The Children's Village is structured to reverse these attitudes both by treating the underlying despair and by helping the boys develop competency in a wide range of endeavors—from academics to social skills, art, music, sports, and so on. The agency is in an unusually strong position—stronger than schools that see youngsters for only a portion of the day—to shape values and attitudes about complex issues, including work. Unlike most youth employment programs, The Children's Village has a chance to reach youngsters before they have experienced work-related failures and to instill new values slowly and sequentially. The environment can be controlled to ensure reinforcement of early lessons and gradual introduction to the real world of work. By beginning in the child's cottage (his temporary home), there is a possibility of imbuing feelings of work as a natural way of life.

Finally, and perhaps most fundamentally, The Children's Village has come to view work as a key to future emotional stability. Mental health gains developed in these high-risk boys while at the Village—the primary goal of residential treatment—will quickly disintegrate if they cannot hold jobs later in life.

Program Goals and Obectives

The goal of the W-A-Y program is for children to develop, use, and respect the skills, principles, and standards necessary for getting and keeping a job, and making appropriate choices in daily activities.

The program is carefully linked with other Village programming and builds directly on lessons taught first in the cottage program. The boy's involvement in the work program is an integral part of his treatment. As with the other services offered at The Children's Village—clinical, educational, medical, recreational, pastoral—the W-A-Y program operates for the purpose of helping youngsters to grow and develop, to begin to take control of their lives and go on to be productive members of society.

The broader goal of the program, and that of treatment center programming in general, is for each boy to learn that he is responsible for his own actions and decisions, that his actions have consequences (good and bad), and that he has choices and possibilities. The following are the program's objectives:

> To provide each child with practice in demonstrating control over his life
>
> To nuture in each child a positive attitude about work
>
> To teach each child the mechanics of getting a job
>
> To teach each child the mechanics of keeping a job
>
> To provide each child with practice in working independently
>
> To provide each child with practice in cooperating with others
>
> To provide each child with practice in planning for future constructive use of money

W-A-Y consists of five sequential stages. The first four stages require increasingly greater independence and maturity. The goals of the program guide all of the components, and the objectives are the same throughout. Only the type of supervision, job, and setting change as boys move through the program's developmental stages. Work Scholarships are then available to those boys who have demonstrated, at earlier stages, a higher level of motivation, including the motivation to graduate from high school and go to college or to pursue job training.

The Program's Five Stages

When a boy arrives at the Village, he makes a beginning by fitting into a daily cottage routine with 12 to 15 other children. His cottage is part of a larger "neighborhood unit" of four to six cottages. It is within the confines of his cottage home that he first experiences an environment designed to create a sense of regularity, security, health, and safety. The cottage staff uses the events of day-to-day living to teach competence, pride, and respect for self and for others. It is natural, therefore, for children to begin to learn about work ethics in this, their home environment.

Stage One of the W-A-Y program consists of *non-salaried, on-going chores and community service*. In this first stage of the program, children begin learning about the self-satisfaction that comes with completing a task or benefiting others and begin to develop self-motivation. These are fundamental values upon which the remainder of the program rests. The messages given in the cottage are that everyone helps out at home without getting paid for it and that helping others voluntarily has its own rewards. Children at this stage are given close supervision by their cottage staff so that they can complete their work successfully.

Some of the boys at the Village have never done even the simplest household chores before admission; others have done chores at home or in a previous placement but frequently they have been paid to do even routine tasks such as making their beds. Too often, they expect some kind of concrete reward for doing their chores—money or treats. We give praise. Sometimes we give points as part of a larger behavior modification program. We say, "Nice job, thanks for helping." In addition to normal household chores (e.g., dishes, sweeping), some of the boys also do volunteer work in the local community (e.g., visiting and entertaining nursing-home residents). This portion is an aspect of W-A-Y that has been difficult to put into practice. Philosophically, community service is an important part of the program, one we expect to develop more fully in the future.

Stage Two of the program is for children who are ready to go beyond the limits of a household environment, into the neighborhood of clustered cottages. It consists of *unit-based, beginning salaried job experiences*. Now children must apply for jobs and they are paid (approximately 50 cents to a dollar per hour) for working in what is equivalent to their neighborhood. As in other W-A-Y components, jobs vary in difficulty, so there can be opportunities for boys of varying ability and stages of readiness to work. At this juncture, there is still close on-the-job supervision. A youngster may pursue a job, flounder, try again, and fail or succeed, all within arm's reach of his home base. Job opportunities are similar to those found in any neighborhood, such as raking leaves, shoveling snow, and washing cars. In this stage, unit staff members begin to introduce procedures (applications, job evaluations, and so on) and to prepare their boys for more demanding activities organized at work sites located around the campus.

Boys who want to pursue a *salaried campus job* advance to Stage Three of the program. Wages ($1.00 to $1.50 an hour) reflect the reality that youngsters are still learning how to work. All boys who have done well at level two are encouraged, but not required, to apply for a campus job at the Boy's Personnel Office. This stage of the program (and those beyond) are not appropriate for every boy in residence. Some are too young, too disturbed, or not yet developmentally ready to participate. Conversely, some youngsters who do poorly in other Village programs seem to thrive in W-A-Y work sites. Among other factors, there is less competition and less need for well-developed socialization skills required in the work environment than in other areas of Village life. At present, approximately half of our population (150 boys) participate in Stage Three.

At this stage, procedures are formalized—boys must get references from Stage Two jobs, fill out applications, and be interviewed. In addition, their individual and group counseling is expanded, and they are exposed to more real-life work situations. Here, workers are fired, promoted, and earn salary raises; they learn to give notice to change jobs, to deal with job dissatisfaction, to handle themselves on the job. For example, a boy who has walked off a job (a Stage Two or Three job) will find he cannot get a good reference for another one. He may then have to go back, apologize to his previous boss, and work at the old job again before he makes responsible plans to leave it and seek another one he likes better.

In Stage Three, boys are counseled to negotiate totally new situations and personalities, work with minimal supervision, and solve work-related problems appropriately. Work site supervisors and a W-A-Y counselor provide support and structure to help youngsters learn how to resolve problems that arise on the job. Counseling takes place on the job when a problem arises, as well as on a one-to-one basis outside the work situation. Work takes place in any of about a dozen work sites around the campus—at the Village store, in the greenhouse, in the woodworking shop, at the boys' newspaper, and so on. Each work site provides a variety of job opportunities; some even require additional credentials. For example, before a boy may apply for one of the higher level (and higher paid) jobs, that of being a computer assistant teacher, he must attend computer school. For this attendance, he has to pay (from his salary at a lower-level job) for 12 hours of computer instruction. The computer program is part of The Children's Village recreation program.

Cottage staff members are expected to reinforce the work ethics being taught at this level. That task is not always easy in a treatment center milieu. Boys who act out in the cottage, for example, may not be held back from going to work by their cottage workers. The message we want to convey is that people go to work regardless of home conditions; if you are sick, you call; if you must miss work, you make appropriate arrangements. For cottage staff members searching for suitable sanctions for misbehavior, the temptation is great to forbid a youngster to go to work when he likes his job and truly wants to go. Considerable staff training across all programs is necessary to ensure that the work ethics taught in W-A-Y are not compromised by staff members or other departments seeking to teach important, but conflicting, values.

Stage Four of the program is designed for those boys who do well in Stage Three and are old enough to *hold a part-time job in the local community while still in residence* at The Children's Village. This stage also includes residents in our group homes, who are older and already situated in a community setting. To be eligible for a job in the community, youngsters must be developmentally ready, have shown mastery of skills and attitudes promoted in earlier stages of the program, and receive approval from their treatment team.

For the most part, youngsters find their own jobs, with leads from staff members and, if needed, more aggressive support. Again, unlike most youth employment programs, jobs are not handed out to participants; youngsters are expected to compete for jobs. Earlier stages of the program will have taught the mechanics of looking for work, prepared the boy to deal with disappointments, and helped him develop perseverance. Additional help is available, but it is offered judiciously. For example, a W-A-Y counselor will accompany a youngster as he goes job hunting but will stand outside the door while the boy goes inside to inquire about an opening. Some positions (especially jobs obtained through summer youth employment programs) are acquired more easily. But all boys arrange their own interviews and follow-up. Once a youngster has a job, counseling continues (with the boy, not the employer) from either a W-A-Y counselor or child-care or social work staff members.

Youngsters who do well in Stages Three and Four are told that they may apply for a Work Scholarship.

Stage Five, the *Work Scholarship,* is a privately funded demonstration project available only to boys who have been successful at earlier stages of the program. Those selected for a Work Scholarship receive services and support for up to five years after they leave The Children's Village, an earned financial incentive, six months of formalized classroom training focused on developing work ethics, and individual long-term counseling. Those who wish to apply must fill out an application and be interviewed. Selection is based on an objective ranking taken from interview scores and ratings submitted by selected members of each applicant's treatment team. The number of boys selected is limited by the amount of private funds available. Thus far, generous donations have made it possible for us to select 15 to 18 boys each of the four years of the program, bringing the total number of current participants to 60. From its inception, the Work Scholarship program has been guided by an advisory committee comprising experts in the field of youth employment and research.

To be considered for the program, a boy must take the initiative of applying on his own. Often the boys selected for this program still have many unsolved emotional and behavioral problems, but they seem to possess a certain grit that sets them apart from others. They communicate a determination to succeed and a willingness to try although the odds are unfavorable.

The Children's Village then enters into a contract with each scholarship recipient. Parent(s) too, if available, must sign the contract. It states that the youngster agrees to stay in school, work part-time for part of the year and save a percentage of his earnings for his own college education or job training. In exchange for working and putting aside part of his earnings, savings are matched (doubled and even tripled in later years) by private donors. How much each boy saves and the ratio of the match is controlled by the youngster's level of participation and his job and school success.

Funds, both those that are donated and personal savings (and all earned interest), become available after the youngster graduates from high school, to be used only for job training or further education. The advisory committee is consulted on this as on all other elements of the program. Students who leave school before graduation of course receive their own earned money (but not until the year they would have graduated had they stayed in school), but they forfeit all of the matching funds.

In addition to the matching funds incentive, youngsters receive counseling and preemployment training during the first six months of the program and ongoing informal counseling for the four or five years of their participation. The program includes both group and individual counseling, with each Work Scholarship Counselor having a caseload of approximately 20 boys.

Counseling begins while the boys are living on the campus of the treatment center. Once discharged, however, most of them return home (some transfer to a group home or are adopted) and are therefore spread out among the five boroughs of New York City and surrounding counties. The counselor continues to follow up with the youngster, and if possible, the parent(s), in their home community.

At this point, the counselor's primary role is to help the boys focus on their future, stay in school, work, and save. The counselor may, for example, arrange tutoring; help a youngster who is suspended from school to reenter; encourage a boy who is fired to find another job; counsel another to save his money and see the potential of the matching funds rather than spend it on clothes; or work with family members to persuade them to support the boy's efforts.

Nearly all of the youngsters come from impoverished homes and, if they work, they are often under pressure to contribute money to the very real needs of the family. Similarly, some of the boys feel an obligation (or are pressured) to drop out of school to help support or care for younger siblings, or a parent. Thus, the counselor is expected to work with all members of the family to balance the immediate needs of the family with the youngster's need for family support of his aspirations for a better life. Because the program requires such an extended postponement of gratification—five years of saving toward an uncertain future goal—the work of the counselor both with the youngster and his family is a critical component of the program.

The majority of boys selected for Work Scholarship are 13 years old. This fact allows them to remain in the program throughout their high school years. As important, these youngsters will have had five years of rehearsing the habit of working, saving, and planning for their future. And they will have done so knowing that they will have some concrete resources to help them convert their dreams into reality.

For boys under the age of 16 who either cannot find a job or who are doing poorly in school, volunteer work or being tutored may substitute (temporarily) for working during the school year. Hours spent doing volunteer work are matched with donor dollars toward the post high-school fund.

Although these boys have been selected on the basis of their demonstrated higher potential to succeed, they are still emotionally disturbed boys. Their troubled backgrounds and underlying emotional and behavioral problems continually reemerge and threaten the progress that they have made or are making. The possibility of the growing nest egg appears to be a less powerful component of the program than the ongoing counseling. Two case examples demonstrate this point.

Sample Cases of Scholarship Recipients

Case G.

G. came to The Children's Village after years of serious depression and aggressive behavior. No one at home seemed to care about him or for him. He began running away, sleeping on the streets, and talking of suicide. He was bounced from relative to relative until he was finally placed in foster care. For the next eight years he was in and out of foster homes. His behavior became more and more difficult to manage. Three years ago he was sent to The Children's Village.

While at The Children's Village, he gained emotional stability and a renewed interest in life. He was enthusiastic and proud to receive a Work Scholarship and was an excellent worker while on campus. His mother continued to be only vaguely interested in his welfare but, under court order, he was discharged to her despite reservations on the part of the treatment team, and G.'s own reluctance.

Getting along at home has proven extremely difficult for G. His old symptoms of depression and anger surface frequently as a result of the general lack of interest shown by his family in what he is trying to achieve. The family is not connected to the larger community, and G. describes himself as being quite alone with his problems and his aspirations.

G. has worked off and on during the school year, sometimes saving and sometimes not. With the help of the W-A-Y counselor, he got a summer job last year and mananged to meet his savings requirements. Academically, he is barely holding on, but he has not dropped out of school. He still expresses a desire to succeed and to use the W-A-Y scholarship to his advantage, but he also frequently withdraws and loses contact with the scholarship counselor.

Case W.

W. was sent to The Children's Village because his behavior in school was uncontrollable as a result of the severe disorganization and violence in his home. Since that time, his psychotic father has been removed to a mental hospital, and his mother has willingly participated in family therapy with W. during his placement here.

W. excelled while at The Children's Village and was awarded both a W-A-Y Work Scholarship and a Children's

Village scholarship to parochial school upon his discharge back home.

He got off to a great start after his discharge. Though too young to find a paying job, last summer W. was determined to take advantage of the scholarship program. With his sincere, articulate presentation, he won a volunteer junior counselor position with a YMCA. What began as a trial position turned into a highly successful, 270-hour volunteer experience.

In the fall, with a recommendation from his school and volunteer sponsor, W. obtained a paid job cleaning up in a factory warehouse. Some of his old problems began to return, however, and he was fired after a couple of months. He was able to discuss his problems with his counselor and to accept responsibility. Recently he has begun to work again.

Aside from showing occasional immature behavior, W. has performed very well in private school most of the year. His grades have been acceptable though not near his ability level. Recently, however, he began acting out at home and at school. The W-A-Y counselor is working with him and his mother to try to prevent more serious problems from developing.

Although the family lives in one of the most impoverished, dangerous, and dilapidated neighborhoods in the city, they are coping. Mother and son are intent on W.'s getting his education, and both see the Work Scholarship program as a real opportunity for him.

The W-A-Y scholarship project is designed to shed light on the value of an earned incentive and follow-up counseling for working, saving, and completing high school. Through a five-year study associated with the program, participants are being compared with those of a group termed Outreach, and given less intensive treatment.

Comparison (Outreach) boys are held to the same eligibility and selection criteria as scholarship boys except that their plans call for a projected discharge date six months after they are designated as part of the comparison group. Boys in the comparison group do not receive ongoing in-person counseling or any matching funds. Also, because they are scheduled to leave The Children's Village so soon, they are unable to participate in the Work Scholarship six-month counseling and formal training period.

Comparison group boys do receive some outreach services after they are discharged—a quarterly news bulletin, *The Grapevine*, containing helpful information about community resources and getting and keeping jobs, and access to the W-A-Y counselor by telephone. The counselor may give advice on how and where to find a job, may refer the caller to a particular job placement resource, or may just listen and provide counseling related to personal, school, or work problems. Equally important, both groups—the treatment group (the recipients of Work Scholarships) and the comparison (Outreach) group—receive a letter informing them that they have been selected because their treatment team considers them to have excellent potential to do well in the future, in school and work.

Over the next five to ten years, the research study will periodically compare school and work status and measure attitudinal adjustment for boys in both groups. Given the differences in the services offered to the two groups, it will be possible to learn whether a scholarship incentive, reinforced by ongoing in-person counseling and other supports, constitutes a better investment in the future of these boys than a much more limited intervention with no tangible rewards for continued work and progress in school.

Conclusion

A Work Appreciation for Youth Program has been developed at The Children's Village. Known as W-A-Y, the program addresses the question of how best to provide at-risk youths with the kinds of experience that will help them to develop a sense of control over their lives. The approach the program takes is developmental, long-term, and preventive.

W-A-Y rewards productivity and effort and teaches concrete skills that are transferable to the real world. Every stage of the program builds upon what was learned in the preceding stage. Every stage has the potential to teach the same material—cooperation, decision making, and the concept that actions have consequences—but under different, increasingly more challenging circumstances.

Evaluating the program is a continual process. The extent to which W-A-Y imparts work ethics and in what measure participants feel responsible and capable to compete for jobs are yet to be determined fully. In the interim, as the program is being refined and modified, The Children's Village will continue to search for the best possible program model to help troubled boys develop a core set of positive values about work, achievement, and their futures.

19

Considering Constitution: The Role of Neuropsychology in Program Development for Group Care

RICHARD G. DOIRON
EDMOND R. STOLKNER
STEPHEN L. BUKA

THE FIELD OF GROUP CARE HAS ESTABLISHED ITSELF as a major treatment force for children who are unable, by virtue of biological, psychological, social, or environmental handicaps, to adapt and develop within their families and communities. As the field prepares itself to serve the coming generations of special-needs children more effectively, it will be especially important to understand the constitutional makeup of the child. Knowing how constitution affects and is affected by psychological, social, and environmental factors could be a major asset to professionals who wish to develop treatment programs whose effects are the most resistant to decay over time.

Neuropsychology, and pediatric neuropsychology in particular, is especially well suited to provide such an understanding through the study of brain-behavior relationships in the developing child. This field, with its grounding in both the physical and the psychological aspects of brain functioning, can provide a large picture of the behavioral equation. It can tell us a great deal about

329

how constitution, as measured by neuropsychological techniques, interacts with psychosocial and environmental factors to produce particular behaviors or responses to life situations.

This paper has three goals: (1) to present a theoretical model in which the child's competence in adapting to stress is influenced by constitutional as well as environmental factors; (2) to show what the field of pediatric neuropsychology can contribute to understanding of the child's constitution; and (3) to enhance understanding of the individual needs of children, and the development of programs for groups of children who have similar constitutional characteristics and life histories.

Role of Constitutional Factors in Child Development and Behavior

As successive efforts are made to integrate a range of contributing disciplines, the evolving field of group care has experienced dramatic shifts in theoretical orientation and methods of practice. In the recent past, "the theory base for residential treatment consisted of a patchwork of theoretical remnants borrowed from child guidance practice, traditional psychotherapy, social group work and special education" [Whittaker 1978]. Whittaker goes on to note that although the composition of this theoretical patchwork is changing (to include recent attention to elements of social learning theory, family therapy techniques, and community-based practices), we still lack a unified theory for residential treatment.

Since the turn of the century, theoretical movements dealing with the causes of human behavior have influenced current theories for group care. The psychoanalytic period viewed individual behavior as a product of the intrapsychic battle of persons within themselves. Therapeutic efforts focused on these intrapsychic and dynamic forces within the personality and on alternative means of resolving psychic conflicts. During the learning-theory period, attention was focused on the reinforcing and punitive features of the environment and their influence on current behavioral patterns. Therapies addressed both the individual and the environment through manipulation of reinforcing properties of the environment. The recent family systems period has expanded on elements contained in both of these earlier models, describing human behavior as a dynamic process influenced by environmental factors. According to this orientation, human behavior is developed and shaped by the influences of social systems involving the individual, such as the family, peer group, and community groups. Treatment follows from consideration and modification of these social dynamics.

Although this brief sketch clearly fails to do justice to the richness of thought of these three periods, it does highlight some important features of past theoretical orientations that influence contemporary group care practices both directly and indirectly. In particular, each of these perspectives focuses on the relative plasticity of the individual, whose behaviors result from the forces of various influences, both internal (intrapsychic) and external (environmental). In the polarized nature vs. nurture debate, these three views all emphasize various features of nurture—environmental factors that influence the individual from birth onward. This emphasis is quite attractive; it conveys a sense of optimism that once-deleterious environmental influences can be modified to effect desired changes in behavior.

A diverse body of recent research suggests, however, that the nature side of the debate deserves reconsideration. The extreme behavioral form represented by schizophrenia provides an instructive example. Working with the offspring of schizophrenic parents, Schulsinger et al. [1984] and Silverton et al. [1985] demonstrated that the combination of schizophrenic parentage and adverse perinatal events placed individuals at much greater risk for the development of schizophrenia than either condition alone. These findings suggest that, for schizophrenia, it is the combination or interaction of biological (schizophrenic genotype) and environmental factors (perinatal events) that has the greatest influence on subsequent development. This position has been supported by many investigations of behavioral development, ranging from the extreme behavioral form represented by schizophrenia and criminality [Hare 1986] to studies of parental attachment [Cicchetti 1984]. In the nature vs. nurture debate, both sides win.

Given this information, it is our view that the psychologically and sociologically motivated theories of human behavior reviewed above must be enlarged into a "biopsychosocial" model of behavior in which an individual's unique biological constitution interacts with the psychosocial environment, both by bringing forth certain influences from this environment and by affecting the ways in which these environmental influences are received. By the term "constitutional factors" is meant "factors, usually present at or soon after birth, whose behavioral consequences appear gradually during the child's development" [Wilson and Herrnstein 1986]. These factors may be genetically determined (such as gender) or partly heritable (such as temperament). This view should provide no less reason for optimism concerning therapeutic efforts to effect behavioral change. It merely emphasizes the need to consider individual constitutional factors as an essential part of the behavioral equation, around which the vital influences of the psychosocial environment flow.

Neuropsychology as a Measure of Constitution

Neuropsychological assessment is especially well suited to provide a picture of certain constitutional factors, such as how a child's brain is organized to think and respond to his or her environment. This specialized form of testing uses a variety of tests of brain functioning. Structured test batteries have been developed that effectively differentiate children with structural/known brain disease, from those who suffer from minimal brain dysfunction (learning-disabled and/or conduct-disordered), and from children with no history of cerebral dysfunction or adjustment problems [Reitan and Boll 1973].

The pediatric neuropsychologist uses a number of perspectives in analyzing the specialized tests administered to children. These include the child's level of test scores, his or her pattern of performance, the adequacy of motor and sensory-perceptual functions on the two sides of the body, and the presence of specific deficits that occur almost exclusively in individuals who have sustained brain injury [Reitan and Davison 1974].

Through this specialized form of assessment, the clinical neuropsychologist is able to provide not only valuable diagnostic information about a child's clinical condition and how neurological factors are influencing it, but also a picture of the child's general level of functioning and particular areas of cognitive strengths and weaknesses. Through such testing, the child's ability to process information, engage in problem solving, think abstractly, transfer learning from one context to another, modulate and direct emotions, correctly perceive social situations, and adapt to the situational demands of the environment is assessed.

The particular neuropsychological tests that form these test batteries, and the analytical perspectives that are used in evaluating these test findings, provide a good understanding of certain temperamental characteristics of the child. Of those described by Thomas et al. [1968], activity level, adaptability, intensity of reaction, threshold of responsiveness, quality of mood, distractibility, and ability to persist at activities and tasks are all easily observed during the approximately five hours of neuropsychological testing done with each child.

The test battery used in our study was the Halstead-Reitan Neuropsychological Test Battery—Intermediate Level [Reitan 1969; Reitan and Davison 1974], supplemented by the Reitan-Klove Sensory-Perceptual Examination and the Halstead-Wepman Aphasia Screening Test [Reitan 1969; Reitan and Davison 1974]. This test battery assesses such functions as abstract thinking, tactile perception, nonverbal auditory perception and sustained attention, auditory acuity, lateralized fine motor functions, visual-motor coordination, perception of bilateral sensory stimulation, tactile discrimination, tactile recognition of numbers, and speech and language problems.

In addition, each child was administered the Wechsler Intelligence Scale for Children—Revised Version [Wechsler 1974]. This general measure of intellectual ability includes measures of verbal abilities, social knowledge and judgment, immediate memory, concentration, verbal concept formation, auditory attention, auditory memory, motor persistence, visual-motor coordination, visual recognition, organizational abilities, sequential thinking and concept formation, nonverbal reasoning, and overall problem-solving abilities.

In our estimation, neuropsychological test data as a measure of constitution provide a picture of the efforts of children to adapt to environmental demands by learning ways to meet their needs. Their task is to manage the stresses that arise not only from within but also from without, coming from people and situations in the environment. Children's ability to make use of their endowed characteristics and what has been learned in order to respond successfully to environmental demands will determine whether they can become well-adjusted and productive members of society, who can live in a harmonious relationship with others. An important advantage of this perspective is that it views children and their interactions with their environment in a nonjudgmental way. It also permits a more discriminating analysis of where stress points are and what might be done the better to anticipate, manage, and eliminate these stressors, to the extent possible. It looks at the fit between children's constitutions and their environment with the assumption that the better the fit, the less stress and the fewer stress-induced behavioral problems will develop.

Use of Neuropsychology Test Findings in Program Development in Group Care

The study group consisted of ten boys meeting the DSM-III criteria for conduct disorder (four undersocialized aggressive, three socialized nonaggressive, one socialized aggressive, one undersocialized nonaggressive, one diagnosis deferred), who were in a behavioral unit of our residential treatment program at the time of the study. The study produced extensive neuropsychological test and intelligence test data, as well as measures of personal and social functioning and history and developmental information. This information yielded important points of similarity in the constitutional makeup of these youngsters and also permitted assessment of how they interacted with their residential environment and their world in general. The researchers were able to understand better which aspects of the residential treatment program were especially well suited to their needs and abilities, and which factors in both residential living and in their environments tended to cause stress for them.

The average age of this conduct-disordered group of boys was 12 years 6 months, with a range of 10–14 years. A review of their case records revealed that the majority of them were born of mothers who had medical problems and were obese. The youngsters experienced birth difficulties and delays in development, particularly in language development. In eight of the cases, the children came from homes where the mothers were the primary caregivers and the fathers were no longer in the home. In the remaining two cases, a nuclear family constellation existed, but the fathers were seen as ineffective, uninvolved, and/or alcoholic. The clinical records also indicated common histories of parental substance abuse, as well as physical and sexual abuse of the children. Family disruption was the norm with this group, and financial deprivation was present in all but one case. As infants, these youngsters were described as having short attention spans, prone to hyperactivity, variable in their moods, difficult to satisfy, poor at developing rhythmicity, and poor at learning basic adaptive skills. In addition, they were seen as highly reactive to their environments, unable to deal adequately with stimulation, and poor at communicating their needs through verbal means. As young children, they were regarded as difficult to manage, and as they matured they were viewed as developing conduct and antisocial problems. In summary, the records indicated a relatively homogeneous group of children who had common environmental backgrounds, and developmental histories that were suggestive of similar constitutional features.

Although educational and behavioral information was also obtained as part of this study, the emphasis here is on the neuropsychological test data, including intellectual test results.

Figure 1 presents mean scale scores for WISC-R IQ values. As shown, these youngsters have a Full Scale IQ at the lower limit of the average range. Verbal intelligence is in the borderline range, and performance or nonverbal abilities are in the low-average range. An analysis of their verbal subtest scores indicates that, with the exception of the Similarities subtest, a measure of the ability to see how verbal concepts are related (this subtest also measures emotional sensitivity and intuitive abilities), all other verbal measures are well below average. On performance (nonverbal) measures, their abilities are, for the most part, in the low to mid-average range, (fifteenth to fiftieth percentile) with the exception of tests that measure visual motor control and planning ability (Picture Completion, Picture Arrangement, Block Design, and Object Assembly). Social perception is an area of relative strength, with the group average being at approximately the fifty-fifth percentile of a normal population. In summary, this test profiles youngsters who are socially sensitive and perceptive and are able to solve problems of a nonverbal (visual-spatial, visual-motor) nature, but who lack basic language and communication skills and have poor ability to control and plan their behaviors. It might be said that their ability to be sensitized and affected by their environment outstrips their

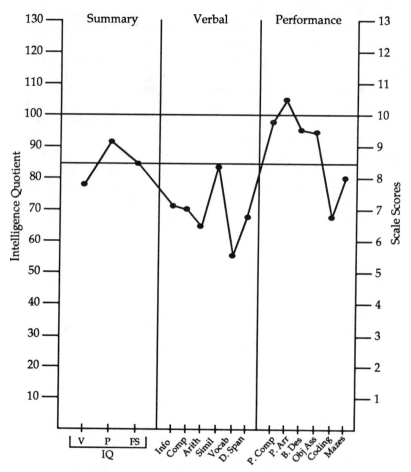

Figure 1. Wechsler intelligence scale for children—Revised
(average scores for ten boys in residential treatment).

ability to understand, communicate, and control their thoughts and feelings. These children are, therefore, particularly at risk of being unable to deal adequately with the stressors in their environment.

A review of Figure 2 reveals that this group has a limited capacity to think conceptually and to reason from cause to effect, when compared with normal children. When asked to follow a visual sequence of numbers, these youngsters did reasonably well, but their performance became much poorer when they were re-

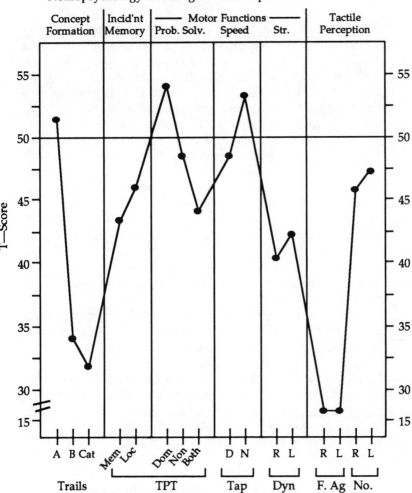

Figure 2. Halstead-Reitan neuropsychological test battery (average scores for ten boys in residential treatment).

quired to follow two sequences concurrently, one of numbers and one of letters. The complexity of the task as well as the language component caused by the introduction of letters apparently over-taxed them. A similar finding occurred on the Category Test, a measure of complex problem-solving ability that requires that a concept or principle be deduced from a set of objects that are pictured on groups of slides. These ideas may include concepts of sameness, number or quantity, shape, or size. Individuals are never told what particular concept is being sought; rather, they must develop their own hypothesis, test it out, and adjust subsequent responses on the basis of the success or lack of success they have had with previous responses. This group of conduct-disordered boys showed a clear inability to engage in deductive reasoning or to develop internal rules to organize their problem solving.

The group did somewhat better on those measures, such as the Trail Making Test, where environmental cues are more obvious; however, it is in psychomotor and motor functions that this population shows its particular strength. The youngsters were especially able to place six wooden geometric forms in a board located directly in front of them while blindfolded (Tactual Performance Test). They were required to do this test with their dominant hand, then their nondominant hand, and finally with both hands working together. Upon completion of the test they were required to draw a picture of the board and correctly locate the respective shapes in proper relationship to each other. This latter measure tests memory and spatial visualization.

Psychomotor and motor functions are closely correlated with mechanical abilities. It is not surprising, therefore, that youngsters with this type of test profile prefer to interact physically with their environments, since their physical skills are their primary areas of strength. They are frequently described as enjoying hands-on activities, liking physical work, and prone to using physical means as stress reducers and ways of releasing anger.

Tactile-perception was particularly poor on a test of finger agnosia in which the person, while blindfolded, must accurately report which of his or her fingers is being touched. The group did somewhat better on the fingertip number writing test, which involves, as its name indicates, the ability to determine which number is being written on the tips of one's fingers. Since the group did better on the fingertip number writing test than on being able to determine which fingers were being touched, it might be said that more concentration is required on the fingertip number writing test, thereby focusing attention better.

Neuropsychological testing, therefore, supports intellectual test data that reflect problems in higher-level conceptual abilities and the ability to develop internal rules of organization of thoughts, feelings, and behaviors. Since abstract reasoning and higher-level conceptual thinking are the most demanding of all mental activities, it is not surprising that individuals who have sustained brain injury usually show the most impairment on tests of this type. Our group showed similar patterns of impairment. They were able to interact physically with their environments but were prone to misunderstand the demands of the environment. They were poor at developing internal organizational plans to govern their behaviors.

Rather, they are likely to depend more on the external structure of their world or the structure provided for them by a highly defined job. It is not surprising that they have fared as badly as they have in dealing with the social environmental complexities of today's large middle and junior high schools. These are youngsters who are at risk of withdrawal and avoidance or of physically aggressive responses to what they perceive as threatening. They are physically active, poorly regulated, highly reactive, and poor adapters. Their mood, quite possibly because of their difficulties, is often negative and depressed, and they frequently have given up on environments, such as school, where their social perceptions tell them that they are not measuring up and have little chance of doing so. At that point they are at risk of not only avoidance and aggressive outbursts against the environment, but also of problems of substance use in search of biochemical solution to a problem that seems to have no other.

We can now discuss how we used the information we learned about these youngsters to develop a better treatment program for them. Information provided by neuropsychological assessment has been useful to the treatment team in Belfast Cottage (the residence of our sample of ten conduct-disordered, preadolescent boys). It has validated existing treatment modalities and enabled team members to adapt individual treatment plans and the treatment environment to address children's constitutional deficits more effectively. Child-care workers were receptive to changes in treatment methods suggested by data concerning constitutional strengths and weaknesses provided by neuropsychological assessment. These changes led to the evolution of Belfast Cottage from a family-type environment dependent on the worker's personal styles and competence to a program based on a supportive milieu that provides structure, well-defined limits and roles, immediate feedback, stability, and the opportunity for constructive physical activity. The level of structure and direction provided by the staff increased in response to the residents' needs for structure and adult direction. Expectations and consequences are regularly made clear to the residents, both orally and in writing.

The Belfast program is a unique example of how the fields of neuropsychology and child care can join forces to plan for the treatment of disturbed children. The authors of this paper include a neuropsychologist, a clinical researcher, and a senior child-care worker (responsible for program development and implementation as a pivotal member of the treatment team). This mix of clinical and experiential knowledge has enabled us to be involved in all levels of residential care: theory, clinical perspective, programming, and implementation—an unusual research design in that a clinical and practical experience were combined to gather data and ideas of both a clinical and a practical nature. The information gained through the study was presented to the child-care workers who were responsible for the final program design and implementation.

Data collected at the Sweetser Neuropsychology Clinic has helped the Belfast Cottage workers to understand the constitutional basis for behavior better; that is, to adapt to children's needs instead of punishing them for not changing to fit adult expectations. In proactively planning for the treatment of this group, the Belfast team has used this perspective to look beyond the behavior itself. Specific constitutional deficits have been found to be common to a significant number of this sample, and programming has been adjusted to meet their needs. Constitutional weaknesses commonly found in this sample, the resultant behaviors, and the subsequent changes in the Belfast program in response to those weaknesses are described in the following section.

Constitutional Weaknesses: Implications for Group Care

Low Adaptability

The boys in this sample do not handle change or transition well. They are easily confused, frightened, and frustrated. Frustration frequently turns to anger, which is then externalized and manifested as acting-out behavior. A very highly structured environment with a minimum of transitions was the Belfast program's response to these children's needs. The need for a high degree of structure with this population was recognized experientially by child-care workers and teachers long before this study. The neuropsychological data served to validate current practice, however, and led to a program that is philosophically based upon this population's inability to handle change and unstructured time. Virtually every moment of every day is programmed, and the children have a minimum amount of free time. What little unstructured time the day does contain is highly supervised and, therefore, subtly structured. Any unavoidable changes in program are treated as times when there is a need for extra support of children rather than extra consequences for behavioral difficulties. As children progress in their program, they are exposed to less adult-imposed structure in order to encourage them to be more flexible and adaptable.

High Social Awareness—Low Verbal Skills

Visual awareness of social expectations in the absence of the necessary accompanying verbal and language skills causes major social-interactional difficulties for these boys. Because they are able to "read" social situations they become adept at presenting themselves as more "with it" than they actually are. This behavior frequently leads to increased, unrealistic expectations of such children because they appear to be quite capable of understanding and performing tasks that are beyond their actual abilities; this problem may become exacerbated as the children build unrealistic expectations for themselves and are constantly frustrated by their inability to meet these expectations. Frustration and failure often lead to anger, to acting out, and/or to refusal to try new ventures that might become yet another arena for failure.

Information obtained from neuropsychological testing was instrumental in bringing about significant change in the attitudes and expectations of staff members as they were educated about this population's awareness-ability discrepancies. As staff members have lowered their expectations of these boys, realistically they have become able to help them lower their self-expectations of near-perfect behavior and performance. Learning has become a more enjoyable and less frustrating experience.

Inability to Perceive the Long-Term Consequences of Behavior

Inappropriate or unsuccessful behaviors are repeated constantly because these children have difficulty understanding cause-and-effect relationships. They are genuinely surprised when their negative behaviors lead to a negative consequence. They appear to believe that once their inappropriate behavior has stopped, any consequence for that behavior should also come to a stop. Experience has demonstrated that it is difficult to expect these boys to learn through the use of long-term or extended consequences. Any consequence that does not follow the offending behavior immediately or shortly thereafter is perceived as a punishment by a vindictive staff member rather than as a logical consequence for the behavior itself.

Programming for these boys relies heavily on immediate and logical consequences administered in an emotionally neutral manner. For example, a boy constantly arguing with others during an activity would be warned of the inappropriateness of his behavior. If the behavior continued, he would be required to take a time-out from the game. If the behavior still continued, he would be removed from the game. The negative behavior is confronted immediately, the consequence is applicable to the offense, and it is not punitive. The typewritten expectations for each time period (meal time, shower time, bed time, and so on) and the consequences for failure to meet these expectations are posted in each boy's room and in a common area. In this manner, the boys may better own their behavior instead of perceiving a consequence as arbitrary or unfair.

Inability to Work Toward Long-Term Reward

Efforts to use a ladder-type level system where each step upward was achieved by behavioral consistency over an extended period have repeatedly resulted in a roller-coaster effect. The inconsistency and repeated failures of the children could not be addressed by fine-tuning the ladder system; the entire system had to be replaced. The present program is designed with many and varied rewards for positive or appropriate behavior on an hour-by-hour basis. These reinforcers are both primary (staff attention, food treats) and secondary (points to be spent like money at a "motivation store").

Each boy is rated eight times throughout the day on four target behaviors tailored to his individual behavioral needs. A common target might be, "I will listen without interrupting." The boy is given immediate feedback, both positive and negative, as his card is marked by a staff member. The previous motivation system rated the target behavior three times daily on a scale of one to five, a rating system that was both too vague and too infrequent to do more than monitor the daily behavior of the child. The new system with its positive emphasis (the child either does or does not receive a point depending upon whether or not the target is achieved during a time period) appears to encourage documentable behavior change that the boy himself can appreciate.

Central Processing Problems

Problems with attention and auditory and language processing are common with this group. Instructing these children can be particularly frustrating and irritating because their distractability may make it appear that they are intentionally behaving in a rude or oppositional manner. This area is one in which data collected through a neuropsychological assessment have been particularly helpful in programming. Cognizant of these deficits, staff members strive to make instructions brief, clear, and concise; directions are simple and are given one step at a time. Whenever possible, a staff person will work with the child as a model; most of the boys in Belfast Cottage are visual rather than verbal learners. Staff members repeat instructions and often have the child repeat them back to determine whether the child has heard them.

Inadequate Language Structure

Physical acting out often is the response of children disturbed by strong emotional issues, but lacking the language skills necessary to vent or express their feelings. The boys in our population simply cannot draw up the words necessary to make themselves understood. Situations that require an explanation on their part often elicit denial or avoidance. Understanding the characteristic language deficits enables the child-care worker to help the children acquire the words needed to communicate their thoughts and feelings.

Low Ability to Learn Incidentally

The boys in this sample tend to be concrete thinkers; they are not able to understand abstract concepts. Experience has demonstrated, and neuropsychological data have validated, that these children respond positively to education that is direct and contextual. Whenever possible, staff members try to make learning experiential and applied rather than conceptual. The boys generally do not learn incidentally; the staff must continually grasp the moment and make each incident a learning situation as it arises. This task essentially is done through reenacting incidents with the children involved; a staff member will model the appropriate behavior, then the child will demonstrate the modeled behavior.

Neuropsychological data have helped the Belfast staff to understand this population's learning styles better, and to use the children's strengths instead of always trying to remediate their weaknesses. While there has not yet been a formal evaluation of this program's relative success or failure, clinical observation suggests that the consistency, structure, and well-defined limits have diminished undesirable behaviors earlier in treatment. As the system has focused less on negative behaviors and has become more reward-based, the group's attitude has become observably more positive, and boys have tended to leave this success-oriented program feeling more positive about themselves. Postdischarge maintenance of these behavioral and attitudinal changes requires greatly increased family, school, and community supports based on understanding of these children's strengths and weaknesses. Without these continuing supports, the prognosis is particularly poor because of this population's constitutional deficits.

Our research and programming design involved a representative from the potential program implementers as well as a clinician and was a practical approach to a common organizational problem. It is more often the case that the clinical staff does research and consults to the line staff who may or may not be involved in program design but who are totally responsible for program implementation. The Belfast program was designed entirely by line staff members who were open and receptive to suggestions based on clinical data about constitutional deficits. This receptiveness to change was fostered by the child-care workers' feelings of ownership: this was their program from start to finish.

None of these necessary program changes would have been possible without administrative understanding and support. We were given nearly total freedom to make whatever program changes we deemed necessary, at our own pace, as long as those changes did not require adjustments in staffing or run counter to agency policy.

Conclusions

Pediatric neuropsychology has been described as a valuable means for assessing cognitive functioning, an important constitutional feature of the child that requires consideration when making treatment decisions. This paper has argued that efforts to derive a unified theory for residential treatment must consider the vital role of constitutional factors, in concert with psychological and social influences, in contributing to the conditions that result in group care placement. The successful application of neuropsychological assessment techniques with one group of children in a residential treatment facility serves as an example of the potential benefits of this approach. We have discussed the integration of a rather new and technical specialty field within an ongoing treatment program.

As a theory, there are ample grounds for agreement among professionals concerned primarily with biological and constitutional features of the child and those more attentive to psychological and social features. The burden of responsibility lies with the group care practitioners, who may be unfamiliar with some of the recent developments in the study of the relationship between constitutional factors and related methods of assessment. We urge them to invite the "constitutional specialists" into their programs, to apply their tools, and to use their results for innovative program development. In addition to neuropsychological data, genetic, biochemical, physiological, early developmental, and medical information can be invaluable for indicating which constitutional features of the child deserve consideration in program decisions. Often, much of this information is available but underutilized when developing treatment plans.

The specialists, for their part, must also make particular efforts to achieve this interaction. To be effective, assessment of constitutional features must not be considered in isolation from the child's social and psychological features, the treatment population, and the treatment setting. Assessment techniques may need to be modified for use with a particular population, emphasizing, for example, information that may be collected within the setting of the residential program, or, as in the case of neuropsychology, altering methods initially designed for work with more neurologically impaired populations. Information must be gathered and conveyed with the intent of clearly communicating the findings to the treatment staff members who will be making the ultimate programming decisions. There is reason to believe that these efforts can contribute to the development of a more unified theory of group care that, in turn, will help us to achieve our ultimate goal: the better to serve children in need.

References

Cicchetti, D. The emergence of developmental psychopathology. *Child Development* 55: 1–7, 1984.

Hare, R.D. Twenty years of experience with the Cleckley psychopath. In W.H. Reid, D. Dorr, J.I. Walker, and J.W. Bonner (eds.), *Unmasking the Psychopath: Antisocial Personality and Related Syndromes.* New York: Norton & Co, 1986.

Reitan, R.M. *Manual for Administration of Neuropsychological Test Batteries for Adults and Children.* Indianapolis, Indiana: Reitan, 1969.

———— and Boll, T.J. Neuropsychological correlates of minimal brain dysfunction. *Annals of the New York Academy of Sciences* 205: 65–88, 1973.

———— and Davison, L.A. *Clinical Neuropsychology: Current Status and Applications.* Washington: V.H. Winston & Sons, 1974.

Schulsinger, F., Parnas J., Petersen, E.T., Schulsinger H., Teasdale, T.W., Mednick, S.A., Moller, L., and Silverton, L. Cerebral ventricular size in the offspring of schizophrenic mothers: A preliminary study. *Archives of General Psychiatry* 41: 602–606, 1984.

Silverton, L., Finello, K., Mednick, S.A., and Schulsinger, F. Low birthweight and ventricular enlargement in a high-risk sample. *Journal of Abnormal Psychology* 94: 402–407, 1985.

Thomas, A., Chess, S., and Birch, H.G. *Temperament and Behavior Disorders in Children.* New York: University Press, 1968.

Wechsler, D.I. WISC-R manual. *Wechsler Intelligence Scale for Children—Revised.* New York: Psychological Corporation, 1974.

Whittaker, J.K. The changing characteristic of residential child care: an ecological perspective. In *Social Service Review.* Chicago, Illinois: The University of Chicago, 1978.

Wilson, J.G., and Herrnstein, R.J. *Crime and Human Nature.* New York: Simon and Schuster, 1986.

Part 4

Improving Group Care Through Research

20

Integrating Research and Agency-Based Practice: Approaches, Problems, and Possibilities[a]

KATHLEEN WELLS
JAMES K. WHITTAKER

It is a source of uneasiness to some that axioms of one decade so quickly fade out and then, still later, return as new revelations. A healthy orientation to evidence, it seems, should protect us from inability to see in one year what had been so visible ten years earlier and becomes equally visible ten years later. Evidence orientation, plus a sense of history, might foster a little more conservatism about granting the status of an axiom and about snatching it away again.

—Elizabeth Herzog,
"Research, Demonstrations and Common Sense,"
Child Welfare XLI (1962)

EㅤLIZABETH HERZOG'S CAUTION OF OVER a quarter century ago rings loud and clear today as a principal reason for linking research

[a]Preparation of this chapter was supported in part by Cleveland Foundation Grant No. 85-593-32R to the Bellefaire/Jewish Children's Bureau. The points of view stated in this paper do not necessarily represent the opinion, position, or policy of the foundation, however, and this should not be inferred.

351

and practice in group child care. A healthy orientation to evidence and a sense of history are probably two of the most promising guides to increasing quality of service in group child care. If not these, what will guide service is very likely current funding priorities, the latest treatment fads, or the conventional wisdom of practice. Evidence suggests that each of these factors alone, or together, is insufficient to inform practice and may lead to negative consequences for group child-care practice and the children in care (and their families).

The difficulties in establishing and maintaining such linkages are not insignificant, however, and were the subject of extended discussions at both the 1976 and 1986 Child Welfare League Conferences on Group Care. These difficulties receive considerable attention, as well, in the present volume.

The problems of integrating research and group child-care practice tend to be expressed as stereotypic attitudes about research:

> Research has little of substance to offer, because the clinical gains children achieve in residence are evident.

> Past research has had little effect on practice; more investigations are therefore useless.

> Research, even if it can be useful, is not critical to improving practice and as such is a luxury only wealthy agencies can afford.

Purposes and Assumptions

We suggest that, however entrenched such attitudes appear, they are not intractable and, indeed, point to important issues that deserve consideration. This paper seeks to illuminate these attitudinal and other barriers to integrating research and practice; to propose solutions to them; and, building upon both, to construct a framework for research program development in group child-care agencies.[b]

[b]An earlier version of this paper was presented by the authors at the 1986 Child Welfare League of America Conference on Group Care in Houston, and the first half is based upon a paper by Wells, Feldman, and Kelman, published by *Professional Psychology* in 1988.

Broadly, research can be qualitative or quantitative. It can entail pre-experimental and quasi-experimental group or single case, as well as experimental group designs. And, as such, it can include literature reviews, analyses of social problems, assessment of individual cases, tests of novel interventions, and so forth. We advocate this expansive view of research because it allows research to meet a wide range of agency needs.

We propose a program evaluation model for research in group child care. In this approach, research is considered an internal activity, as contrasted with an activity conducted by outsiders, whose purpose is to improve programs [Koocher and Broskowski 1977].

Work conducted according to this model requires a high level of research-practice integration throughout the research process, from identification of a problem through concept formation and measurement, data collection and analysis, report writing, and review of findings. Without such integration, investigations run the risk of being irrelevant to practice, unused by practitioners, and isolated projects in which issues raised by one study are rarely pursued in the next.

Barriers to Integrating Research and Practice

Our discussions with researchers and practitioners, as well as a review of the pertinent literature, suggest a complex set of interrelated barriers to developing such integration in group child-care agencies [Wells et al. 1988]. The barriers include inadequate rationales for research program development, incompatibilities between practice and research models, flaws in research implementation, divergences in the belief systems and roles of researchers and practitioners, and a lack of long-term funding for building research capacity. Contributing to and implicated in all of these barriers is the failure of chief executive officers and boards of trustees to support research.

Inadequate Rationales for Research

Rationales for extant research program development have often been inadequate to sustain a long-term research program. Sometimes the rationale is inadequate because it remains unexpressed. It is not clear, for example, if research is intended to improve a program, to create generalizable knowledge, or to fulfill record-keeping requirements for accrediting bodies. Poorly defined rationales contribute to unrealistic expectations and ultimately undermine support for research.

At other times, the rationale for research program development is inadequate because it is political. It is a political rationale, for example, to use research to prove that services are "doing good," in order to justify continued funding of services [Jacobs and Kotkin 1972]. Political rationales cannot sustain a research program. Research findings are often disappointing, as consequences of service involvement are rarely as positive as hoped [Rossi 1978]. And perhaps, more basically, data alone cannot prove the worth of a program, because worth ultimately depends upon values that cannot be proven or disproven by a given set of data. For example, research can document the number of children who succeed in group care; it cannot, by way of contrast, determine if that number is adequate or justifies the expense of group care programs.

Irrelevance of Research to Practice

Even when the rationales for research program development are clear and are not explicitly political, the research that is often conducted has limited relevance to practice. This irrelevance is due primarily to the mismatch between the characteristics of many group care programs and the experimental method employed to examine them. Mental health services, including group child-care services, are often poorly conceptualized [Weiss 1978]: they have inadequate descriptions of clients served; unclear or contradictory goals; and underdeveloped hypotheses about the processes through which services work to promote client change [Attkisson et al. 1974]. Milieu therapy, a therapeutic modality used by most group care facilities, for example, is a vague concept, and its meaning is rarely delineated. The classical experimental group paradigm, the prevailing research paradigm in the social sciences, requires clarity, simplicity, control, and an interest in the performance of the average subject. The effort to apply this paradigm prematurely to research in group child care can have disastrous results, with the effort often underscoring internal controversy as to the nature and goals of programs, and producing data of limited interest to practitioners who want information that will inform treatment of a particular case [Morrow-Bradley and Elliott 1986].

Flaws in Research Implementation

The incompatibilities in practice and research models discussed above can be exaggerated by the manner in which a research program is developed or a particular project implemented. Often the research-related responsibilities of administrative and clinical staff members necessary to completion of a project are unclear, and the organizational processes necessary to the development of research questions, collection of data, evaluation of findings, and dissemination of research reports are poorly defined.

This ambiguity tends to put both practitioners and research staff members on the defensive, even when researchers are also engaged in clinical work. At best, the effect is to isolate researchers within an agency; at worst, to alienate practitioners and researchers, one from the other.

Divergences in Training and Role

Practitioners and researchers have different emphases in their training, as well as different roles within an agency. Clinical training typically emphasizes understanding of a particular case and acceptance of a single treatment philosophy, whereas research training emphasizes understanding of group differences and critical examination of all approaches.

There are often difficulties in negotiating these differences in perspective. And failure to do so frequently produces secondary problems, with practitioners using the ready availability of multiple explanations for behavior to dismiss research questions, and researchers prematurely promoting programmatic solutions to complex clinical phenomena.

Lack of Research Funds

Research programs are often financed initially by funders external to an agency who support one project. Although this type of backing has the advantage of providing funds to hire a staff and to start work, it fails to provide long-term research support. Moreover, it may create the expectation that research will be financed indefinitely by external funders, an expectation that is unlikely to be realized, especially for research focusing upon service programs unique to one setting.

Some Proposed Solutions

The hindrances to integrating research and practice in group child-care agencies suggest, however, an organizational approach to solving the problems posed [Wells et al. 1988]. That is, the solutions will depend upon developing sustaining rationales for integrating research and practice, selecting a focus for the research program, and instituting organizational practices to promote a continuing research program.

Sustaining Rationales for Research

One sustaining rationale for integrating research and practice is that integration is crucial to agency accountability, broadly considered; that is, integration is necessary for an agency to evaluate adequately the effectiveness of its services. The integration, moreover, is a logical extension of the licensing and accreditation activities to which agencies (and the field) are already committed. Indeed, "the most important and creative form of setting standards is evaluation" [Mayer et al. 1978: 247]. Furthermore, in a system of accountability, "there is one line leading from licensing to accreditation to evaluation and research. The closer we come to completing this line, the more securely and successfully will the field of group care be able to operate" [Mayer et al. 1978: 250].

Specifying a Research Program

Specifying or providing a focus for a research program begins with identifying a rationale for the activity. Rationales can be drawn from an agency's mission, program goals, or treatment theory. The most sustaining rationale may be one in which there is a convergence of all three. For example, a residential treatment center serving children may want to alter its definition of clients as children to include children's families and to abandon a child-centered for a family-centered approach to treatment. The rationale for the research program could be to contribute to effective functioning of a family-based treatment program. Within this framework, individual research projects could progressively investigate the characteristics of child clients' families, parents' views of existing treatment approaches, family and organizational impediments to family involvement in treatment, and modifications of treatment programs, and so forth, based on family systems theory.

In other words, it is wise to tie the rationale for research to an agency's mission and to focus investigations so that they provide data relating to questions with which practitioners are struggling in the here and now. In that way, research can play a role in organizational development and learning. Expectations for research, however, should be modest, because the accumulation of useful answers through clinical research is an incremental process.

Creating Organizational Roles

Commitment to research-practice integration needs to be translated into facilitative organizational roles and processes. Of primary importance is the appointment of a director of research and clear identification of the research responsibilities of the service delivery staff. The individual selected as director of research should have some clinical experience, participate in one or more of an agency's major policy-making committees, report directly to the agency's chief executive officer, and have authority comparable to that accorded staff members in charge of service delivery programs. In this way, the individual responsible for research is clearly designated, and he or she has access to the sources of organizational power necessary for success of the effort.

Additional research staff members can be drawn from within the agency or from local universities. In both cases, however, it is important that their research-related responsibilities be clearly specified and arrangements pertaining to their supervision detailed. Research conducted on an ad hoc or overtime basis tends not to be completed.

Developing Research Work Groups

Groups within and without the organization can be created to support research. One useful internal group is a research committee of the board of trustees. This group can communicate the board's research interests to the director, communicate and interpret research to the board, and support the research process, as a whole, by endorsing modest goals for beginning efforts and by recognizing the necessity of a long-term commitment to research.

Another useful internal group is a project work group, composed of individuals from all levels of an agency, committed to a particular research question. Project work groups discuss theoretical issues that pertain to the question under investigation and explore the clinical relevance of proposed projects.

A useful external group is a research advisory board, which can profitably review the merits of a given research design, its implications for the organization, and its probable contributions to the field. In addition to yielding technical improvements in the research design, external review can generate internal support for the research issues. These forms of review, however, must be planned with the support of key administrative and clinical staff members at the earliest stages.

Implementing Organizational Policies

Organizational policies and practices are needed to support the building of a research capacity. Policies must identify the political and programmatic conditions under which a service program will or will not engage in a particular research project. A program whose funding is unstable, for example, or whose philosophy is under internal debate, may be too vulnerable for involvement.

Once a program is selected for research, policies should be developed to ensure staff involvement in the research design and implementation. It is important to pursue questions of concern to the service delivery staff, acknowledging the impossibility of capturing the complexity of clinical phenomena in one study. It is important to avoid unwarranted intrusion of research activities into service delivery, while also acknowledging the importance of continual monitoring of data collection efforts throughout the life of a project. It is also important to consider at the onset of a project the implications of its possible findings. Staff members should consider the consequences of a failure to confirm expectations and the programmatic and political uses to which the data might be put. Early project review, moreover, paves the way for a reasoned consideration of findings at the end of a project and helps refine proposed study questions.

Finally, a productive review of research data at the conclusion of a project can be facilitated by carefully setting forth the points of view of both researchers and practitioners and the limitations and implications of the study, making clear the collaborative nature of the project.

Procuring Research Funds

The development of a program of research and the integration of research and practice require long-term funding. Funds can be obtained from within or without the organization, efforts can be made to reduce research-related costs, and creative organizational arrangements can be tried to obtain research resources free.

The agency can fund its own research positions, drawing upon its endowment, if the board and/or outside sources or third-party payers are willing. For research directed at improvement of services, it can build research expenses into the cost of service. It can seek funds from private foundations, state departments of mental health, and from the federal government. If externally produced research funds are obtained, the agency can also place the overhead procured in a restricted research fund to pay research costs when money for research is low. Some funders may, however, place restrictions upon how funds are to be used.

Efforts can also be made to reduce expenditures by hiring part-time research staff members, sharing research staff members with other organizations, or employing staff members with university connections and access to libraries, computer facilities, and technical advice [Stiffman et al. 1984].

Creative arrangements for research can be made with other institutions. For example, an agency might develop, in collaboration with a university, a research-practice center in which faculty members develop projects pertinent to an agency's mission, with faculty and service staff members implementing them, affording training opportunities for both organizations in the process.

Framework for Research Program Development

The accountability framework for research-practice integration promoted in this paper suggests a broad research agenda for both individual agencies and the group child-care field: to improve group child-care services.

Programs can be improved in many ways through research. Irrespective of the approach taken, the enterprise is best viewed:

> as a learning process with the focus of interest being an analysis of *why* a program is failing or succeeding . . . [and that the] evaluative problem, accordingly, must be formulated not as one of success or failure but rather of stop, go back, revise, or continue. The objective . . . is one of constant program assessment and improvement. [Suchman 1970: 101, 109]

The answer to why a program fails or succeeds can reside in the nature of the population served, program attributes, effects sought, or larger contexts in which the children and the programs are functioning. Research in group child care should examine all of these possibilities. Moreover, research programs should be constructed so that these issues are examined in a logical order, with the first stage focusing upon client description, the second on program implementation, the third on treatment outcomes, and the fourth on treatment effectiveness. Data collected in one stage can then inform studies conducted in the next and ultimately allow for an ability to interpret outcome and effectiveness data in terms of the initial characteristics of children and their experiences in treatment.

Phase 1: Describing Children in Care
and Their Families

The first stage involves assessing the client population: the demographic characteristics of children and their families, their home and neighborhood environments, their previous treatment experiences, and their functioning in areas believed crucial to differential program assignment and success in treatment. This information plays a key role in describing the client population, in identifying client needs, and in assessing risk of failure in treatment.

These assessments can depend upon routinely gathered clinical data or can be built into computerized management information systems. One group child-care agency, Boysville of Michigan, has developed an innovative management information system to compile information on children and families and to track family contact and other child-related behaviors routinely once a child is in care [Whittaker, Fine, and Grasso, in this volume]. On a larger scale, the California Association of Services for Children has assessed the demographic and other characteristics of children in care of its member agencies [Fitzharris 1985]. Systems such as these serve to inform agency practice, as well as public policy, as it affects children in care and their families.

Two cautionary notes are in order. Existing clinical records can rarely be used; they are frequently inadequate for research purposes and are often incomplete. Data generated by a computerized system produces, in theory, better data than clinical records, but the system requires development of simple standardized data collection forms, training of staff members to use them, and implementation of procedures for monitoring data collection.

Phase 2: Documenting Service Delivery

Documenting what evaluators sometimes call level of effort (cf. Koocher and Broskowski [1977]) is a critical and often neglected stage in the evaluation process. Level of effort refers to measuring the extent to which the planned program is actually carried out.

Level of effort can be conceptualized in terms of program functioning, program involvement, or program investment. Program functioning refers to factors such as client-staff ratio, staff turnover, staff credentials, staff use of time, and staff consistency in child treatment or response to child problems.

Program involvement refers to factors such as involvement of children in activities, involvement of families in treatment [Fanshel 1982], or length of stay of children. Research has documented, for example, the importance of such factors as involvement and support of parents to success of children in treatment [Whittaker and Pecora 1984]. And other research in progress [Whittaker et al. 1988] is exploring differential patterns of family involvement during placement and their relationship to outcomes for children.

Program investment refers to factors believed to represent the programmatic variables critical to success of children in treatment. Identification of program investment variables is aided by a well-developed theory of how a program promotes change in children. Indeed, a theory of how the program works is necessary to identify factors to study in any phase of a research program, since group care programs are too complex to study all at once. For example, at the Bellefaire/Jewish Children's Bureau a study is currently under way to assess the extent to which children have positive relationships with their prime workers, because an attachment of that kind is considered crucial to remediation of a child's problems and promotion of a child's development.

Level of effort often cannot be completely understood without observing the larger context in which a program is operating. Attention to contextual variables (e.g., control an agency has over accepting or discharging clients) may be crucial to understanding both program implementation and client outcomes—the next phase in research.

Phase 3: Documenting Client Functioning in Treatment and After Discharge

With an adequate description of the client population and service implementation in hand, the next phase in research program development is the evaluation of the progress of children and families in treatment and in functioning after discharge. Though descriptive studies do not address directly whether the program caused the effects found, the work can provide useful information to the clinical staff and can further the conceptualization of outcomes.

Defining progress in or success after treatment has occupied group child care throughout recent history [Matsushima 1965], in part because the definition adopted requires that one take a position regarding such complex questions as:

Is the client the child or the family?

To what extent are treatment goals the same for all children or families?

How much progress is required for a child to be labeled a success (or failure) in care?

To what extent does group child care claim responsibility for growth and development of children, as contrasted with amelioration of presenting problems?

If child development is a desired outcome, is it acceptable to compare the developmental status of children treated in care with children who have had more stable lives?

At what point in the child's group care and life experience should success be determined, and how should the child's variability in functioning be interpreted?

Who determines success, and how can differing views of a child's functioning be reconciled?

How can we disentangle the effects of treatment from the effects of growing up?

As difficult as these questions are, they can be addressed, though the assessment is rarely accorded the time and attention it deserves before evaluating outcomes. A critical first step is to examine pertinent questions within the context of the children's situations at intake, the agency's mission, the agency's control over intake, the type of treatment program, the aftercare provided, and the situations to which children are discharged. This last assessment is especially important and will serve as a corrective to what Koocher and Broskowski [1977: 584] call the single-input fallacy—"the belief that a single service or treatment, in isolation from others, is sufficient to restore a multi-problem child or family to an effective level of functioning."

Evaluating the questions listed above will focus and limit the outcomes selected for investigation. Recent work by the authors of this paper [Wells 1986; Whittaker et al. in press] demonstrates that the focusing can be done. Indeed, we have identified at multiple points in the placement process different indicators of success that are being evaluated at large agencies. The availability of computerized management information systems enables even small group care agencies, however, to document client functioning in treatment and after discharge. (It is more productive for agencies beginning research programs to focus upon a few consensually validated outcomes than to assess all the expected ones. In the early years of research program development, research productivity is more important than comprehensiveness of projects undertaken.)

Phase 4: Evaluating Treatment Effectiveness

The ability to state with some degree of certainty that a group child-care program causes children to improve requires an experimental investigation. The investigation demands specification of the population treated, random assignment from the target population to an experimental or control group (or some form of matching the two), participation of the experimental group in a well-defined treatment, and comparison of outcomes for the two groups studied. The model illustrates the difficulties of conducting experimental investigations in group care practice and serves as a caution against overstating the certainty with which effects found by non-experimental studies are caused by the program under study. And, in some instances, the investigations can be profitably employed.

Variants of this model are called quasi-experimental designs [Campbell and Stanley 1963] because they fail to control all the extraneous events that might influence the outcomes found. These designs can be used to assess, for example, the relative contribution of various components of a program—individual therapy, family therapy, concrete services—to various outcomes, to the progress of children in treatment, or to the interaction between child and treatment variables and their influence upon child outcomes.

If agreement can be reached on common criteria for success, enough variation exists in practice in agencies serving similar populations that useful comparisons can be made, employing quasi-experimental designs.

Summary

This paper's effort to illuminate the problems of integrating research and practice in group child-care agencies and to propose solutions makes clear that there are no easy answers. A major positive force for integration lies in the promise of help that evaluation brings to efforts to improve group care programs [Suchman 1970].

The four stages of research program development that we outlined are intended to aid the integration process as well as to frame an agenda for research in group child-care agencies. Our proposed approach, however, is not the only one and, in the end, success will depend upon the strength of commitment to the effort.

Where such a commitment exists, the actual commonalities between the practice and research enterprises can emerge:

Ideally, both require over-riding intellectual curiosity, efforts to pose ever-better questions, systematic ordering of important observations, departures from oft-tried solutions, and willingness to subject cherished assumptions to empirical test. [Harty 1977, as noted in Wells et al. 1988: 67]

It is to this commonality of purpose that this paper is dedicated.

References

Attkisson, C.C., McIntyre, M.H., Hargreaves, W.A., Harris, M.R., and Ochberg, F.M. A working model for mental health program evaluation. *American Journal of Orthopsychiatry* 44: 741–753, 1974.

Campbell, D.T., and Stanley, J.C. *Experimental and Quasi-Experimental Designs for Research.* Chicago, Illinois: Rand McNally & Company, 1963.

Fanshel, D. *On the Road to Permanency: An Expanded Data Base for Service to Children in Foster Care.* Washington, D.C.: Child Welfare League of America, 1982.

Fitzharris, T.L. *The Foster Children of California: Profiles of 10,000 Children in Residential Care.* Sacramento, California: Children's Services Foundation, 1985.

Jacobs, L., and Kotkin, J. Fantasies of psychiatric research. *American Journal of Psychiatry* 128: 1074–1080, 1972.

Koocher, G., and Broskowski, A. Issues in the evaluation of mental health services for children. *Professional Psychology* 8: 583–592, 1977.

Matsushima, J. Some aspects of defining "success" in residential treatment. *Child Welfare* XLIV: 272–277, 1965.

Mayer, M.F., Richman, L.H., and Balcerzak, E.A. *Group Care of Children: Crossroads and Transitions.* New York: Child Welfare League of America, 1977.

Morrow-Bradley, C., and Elliott, R. Utilization of psychotherapy research by practicing psychotherapists. *American Psychologist* 41: 188–206, 1986.

Rossi, P.H. Issues in the evaluation of human services delivery. *Evaluation Quarterly* 2: 573–599, 1978.

Stiffman, A.R., Feldman, R.A., Evans, O.A. and Orme, J.G. Collaborative research for social service agencies: Boon or bane? *Administration in Social Work* 8 (1): 45–57, 1984.

Suchman, E.A. Action for what? A critique of evaluative research. In R. O'Toole (ed.), *The Organization, Management, and Tactics of Social Research.* Cambridge, Massachusetts: Schenkman, 1970, pp. 97–130.

Weiss, C.H. Improving the linkage between social research and public policy. In L.L. Lynn (ed.), *Study Project on Social Research and Development, Volume 5. Knowledge and Policy: The Uncertain Connection.* Washington, D.C.: National Academy of Sciences, 1978, pp. 23–81.

Wells, K. Client applicant study methodology. In M. Blotcky (chair), *Inpatient Treatment Assessment: Research, Design, Methodology.* Symposium conducted at the meeting of the American Academy of Child Psychiatry, Los Angeles, California, October 1986.

————, Feldman, R., and Kelman, S. Toward institutionalization of a research capacity in mental health service organizations. *Professional Psychology* 19: 63–67, 1988.

Whittaker, J.K., Fine, D., Grasso, A., and Caley, J. *Differential Patterns of Family Involvement in Residential Youth Treatment: An Empirical Analysis.* Unpublished manuscript, 1988. University of Washington, School of Social Work, Seattle.

————, Overstreet, E.J., Grasso, A., Tripodi, T., and Boylan, F. Multiple indicators of success in residential youth care and treatment. *American Journal of Orthopsychiatry* 58: 143–148, 1988.

————, and Pecora, P. A research agenda for residential care. In T. Philpot (ed.), *Group Care Practice: The Challenge of the Next Decade.* Surrey, U.K.: Community Care—Business Press International, 1984, pp. 71–87.

21

*Program Evaluation: A Blueprint for
Program Excellence*

MARTIN L. MITCHELL
CHRISTINE A. AMEEN

RESIDENTIAL CARE FACILITIES TODAY ARE under more pressure than ever before to produce information concerning outcomes of services provided by child-care agencies. With the cost of residential services escalating annually, the public being served is most anxious to know what it is receiving for each dollar spent. This phenomenon is primarily a positive movement, since it makes all youth-serving residential treatment programs increasingly responsive to the issues of supply and demand. A competitive market has emerged, in which available public and private dollars are sought by many private and public treatment institutions. In addition, voluntary agencies appear to be on a collision course with proprietary organizations, competing for the same limited and, sometimes, shrinking resources.

Aside from the competitive and financial considerations, there are many altruistic reasons for providing the highest quality of care possible. The primary reason should be to serve children and families in the most efficient and effective ways known to this field.

How can organizations meet these demands for accountability and productivity? A comprehensive evaluation effort is essential now and will become increasingly important in the future. As res-

idential care agencies continue to move from less formally structured operations to reasonably well-funded, business-like child-
care institutions, the need for a sophisticated evaluation methodology heightens. The development of such a methodology for the
field of child care is in its early stages. The task is to foster its
growth.

Major Needs to Consider

Eight major needs emerge that must be dealt with if evaluation
is to become an integral part of planning and managing programs
for children and families: (1) more effective program evaluation
techniques and methodology; (2) uniformity and consistency of
evaluation methodology to permit replication; (3) a universal evaluation language; (4) professional evaluation standards designed
specifically to serve the residential care field; (5) accurate client
descriptive information; (6) a multidimensional evaluation approach to show trends in outcomes; (7) agency self-evaluation; and
(8) collaborative evaluation efforts in order that data can be shared
and compared. This paper offers recommendations as to how each
of these needs can be addressed and describes the benefits the field
of residential treatment will derive from adopting program evaluation as a management strategy.

Building Effective Program Evaluation Practices

The principal purpose of program evaluation is program improvement, and, as such, the rationale for engaging in evaluation
is improved decision making. The evaluation model developed by
Stufflebeam et al. [1971] and Stufflebeam and Shinkfield [1985]
provides evaluation techniques for each of four major decisions
involved in developing a program. The model, referred to as the
CIPP model (an acronym for Context, Input, Process, and Product
evaluation) is suitable for the residential care field. The components
of the model are described in Table 1.

At the planning stage, organizations determine what objectives will be served by the program. The type of evaluation that
occurs at this initial stage is called "context evaluation" and the

TABLE 1

Basic Decision-Making and Evaluation Procedures

Four Basic Decisions	Evaluation Procedure Used
Planning decisions	Context evaluation
Structuring decisions	Input evaluation
Implementing decisions	Process evaluation
Recycling decisions	Product evaluation

basic methodology used is the needs assessment, when the needs of a target population are assessed to determine what program objectives may best serve those needs.

At the next (structuring) stage, the concern is to design procedures that will result in attaining objectives. "Input evaluation" is required. It may involve reviewing the professional literature or securing expert consultants to assist in the generation of alternatives; staff input regarding how the program ought to be designed is also incorporated at this stage. The primary purpose of this phase is to find out what the best approach seems to be, and to assess the capabilities of the organization to adopt that approach.

In the third phase of implementation, procedures are fine-tuned and a basic question is asked: "Did you implement what you planned to implement?" To answer this question, "process evaluation" is used. This methodology usually includes survey instruments, forms, and logs, to monitor the compliance of implementation with the original program design. If it is discovered that the original design is not feasible, it is during this phase that changes are made to assure accomplishment of program objectives. At this stage, the staff members have the task of providing feedback about how the original design may be improved upon.

In the last (recycling) stage of any project or program, three questions are asked: (1) Should the program continue as is? (2) Should the program be discontinued? (3) Should the program continue with modifications? It is at this time that judgments are made about how effective the program has been. To respond to these questions, "product evaluation" is engaged. Using surveys, tests, attitude measures, and observations, usually in a pre-post test design, the data that describe program effectiveness are gathered. This information is collected from staff members, families, referral agencies, community contacts, and the resident children themselves, all of whom have an opportunity to indicate what they think about the program.

The essence of the model is that for every kind of decision that must be made during the course of a program, there is a methodology for collecting the information that facilitates the quality and timeliness of the decision.

The Need for Uniformity and Consistency

Because of the immense pressure to establish viable evaluation procedures in residential care settings, many organizations begin the process of data collection before making a comprehensive assessment of their actual evaluation needs. This "shoot-from-the-hip" approach results in poorly designed evaluation procedures and frustration with the information, which, in all probability, is neither valid nor particularly useful in answering questions about program influence and effectiveness.

Similarly, the residential care field as a whole is entering into the evaluation arena with little forethought about the need for uniformity and consistency in data collection efforts. Little cooperation appears to exist at the state level. On the national scene, there is little, if any, movement toward establishing a nationwide database representing the field of residential care.

There is a need for collective state and national efforts in the evaluation of residential care—a need to compare information from agency to agency, state to state, and nation to nation. At some point, it is not inconceivable that an international database describing the clients served and the outcomes of services provided to them will be a reality. If the field of residential care is to be successful in this effort, however, uniform and consistent data collection methodology is a prerequisite.

The Need for a Universal Evaluation Language

Just as data collection methodology must be consistent, so the language used to describe program evaluation must also be consistent. For example, many professionals use the terms "research" and "evaluation" interchangeably. From our perspective, these terms clearly imply quite different concepts. Fundamentally, research focuses on the study of the relationship between phenomena. Evaluation, however, is the collection and use of information to make decisions about programs. For example, researchers would be interested in the relationship between a family's economic base and any symptoms of family system dysfunction. Evaluators would be interested in what program interventions address the dysfunction. And, in this connection, there are also differences in evaluation models. The model presented in this article, Stufflebeam's CIPP model, is one of many.

As the field of residential care program evaluation develops, it will be necessary to establish definitions and terms to describe the evaluation components. A common language will facilitate communication about what we do, how we measure outcomes, and how we articulate those outcomes to each other and to our publics.

The Need for Professional Evaluation Standards

As an agency begins exploring program evaluation for possible implementation, it is imperative to understand that there are professionally accepted ways to do program evaluation. For example, professional guidelines have been established for performing evaluation in the field of education; in 1981, the Joint Committee on Standards for Educational Evaluation developed "Standards for Evaluation of Educational Programs, Projects, and Materials." These guidelines are easily adaptable to the field of residential care and provide an overview of what good program evaluation is. Reviewing these or other credible evaluation standards enables an agency to understand what the commitment to program evaluation entails.

The educational evaluation standards encompass four major issues that are worthy of consideration by professional evaluators during the development of evaluation projects in the residential care field. The organization of these four areas is displayed in Table 2.

The eight utility standards are designed to ensure that the research or evaluation activity will provide useful and practical information. *Audience identification*, for example, requires that the persons involved in the evaluation or affected by the results be

TABLE 2

Standards for Evaluations of Educational Programs, Projects, and Materials
(The Joint Committee on Standards for Educational Evaluation, 1981)

Utility	Feasibility	Propriety	Accuracy
Audience identification	Practical procedures	Formal obligation	Object identification
Evaluator credibility	Political viability	Conflict of interest	Context analysis
Information scope and selection	Cost effectiveness	Full and frank disclosure	Described purposes and procedures
Valuational interpretation		Public's right to know	Defensible information sources
Report clarity		Rights of human subjects	Valid measurement
Report dissemination		Human interactions	Reliable measurement
Report timeliness		Balanced reporting	Systematic data control
Evaluation impact		Fiscal responsibility	Analysis of quantitative information
			Analysis of qualitative information
			Justified conclusions
			Objective reporting

identified so that their information needs can be addressed in the evaluation. *Information scope and selection* requires that only the information pertinent to a specific evaluation question be collected, thus eliminating the collection of information that is "nice to know" but not useful in answering specific questions. *Evaluation impact* requires that the evaluation be planned and conducted to facilitate the use of the findings of the study; in other words, it is necessary for an evaluation to have an effect; if it will not, the evaluation should not be conducted.

The three feasibility standards are designed to make sure the evaluation will be realistic, prudent, and diplomatic. For example, the *Practical procedures* standard requires one to be sensitive to the amount of disruption that evaluations can create and to minimize those effects in conducting evaluations. *Cost effectiveness* requires that the findings of the evaluation be of sufficient worth to justify having performed the evaluation in the first place.

The use of propriety standards ensures that the evaluation activity will be conducted legally and ethically, with regard for the welfare of those who are involved in the activity as well as those affected by its results. *Full and frank disclosure* requires that all reports generated from an evaluation will be open, direct, and honest and will include a description of the limitations of the study. *Rights of human subjects* requires that the evaluation respect and protect the rights of clients and client records. *Balanced reporting* requires that all reports present a discussion of both the strengths and the weaknesses of the program being evaluated.

The accuracy standards are designed to ensure that the evaluation will provide technically sound information. For example, *Defensible information sources* requires that the sources of information for the study will be fully described so that their adequacy can be assessed by those using the evaluation results. *Systematic data control* requires that the data used in the study be error-free. *Justified conclusions* requires that the conclusions drawn from the evaluation will be reported clearly, with full demonstration of how the conclusions were developed.

Consistent with the intent of professional standards, all evaluation activities should be able to withstand scrutiny by other professionals and to provide like and sound results. Standards make us mindful of the issues that arise during the course of an evaluation and encourage the planning for those issues in the initial development of evaluation procedures. In addition, standards are used to train staff members about what is proper and useful evaluation. Since staff members ought to be involved in giving continual feedback about evaluation plans, it is imperative that they understand what quality evaluation is.

The Need for Accurate Client Descriptions

Probably one of the most critical components of an effective evaluation system is the collection of in-depth and accurate client description information, because it plays an integral role in the discussion about what outcomes the programs are capable of producing. It is imperative that the public understand the nature of the children served in residential care truly to appreciate what can be achieved with children and families. In most cases, these children and their families have been failed by other placements and settings or have themselves failed. Yet the public we serve has, at times, unreasonably high expectations. To some degree, unfortunately, the residential care field itself is responsible for these unreasonable expectations. To convince the public that we have viable programs, inflated success rates—quite often unverifiable—are reported. In some cases, the criteria defining success are purposefully made easily achievable, thus allowing programs to cite high rates.

By reporting accurately the demographic information concerning our clients, public expectations can be gradually molded into a more reasonable level, consistent with the difficult nature of the clients served. At The Starr Commonwealth Schools, for example, we know that only 15 percent of the children we served in 1986 came from homes where both parents were still part of the family constellation. We know that one-third of our clients had been abused by at least one of their parents, as documented in case files. We have discovered that, on the average, the children we serve have been in three other placements before coming to us. This kind of information, when shared with our publics, can help in the formulation of realistic expectations about what we are able to accomplish. Through accurate client descriptions and bona fide outcome measures, it is possible to show that residential care is effective in many cases and makes a significant contribution to society.

Descriptive information about our clients serves yet another purpose: to identify the treatment needs of children and families. For example, the majority of clients at Starr have marked deficits in basic reading and math skills; over two-fifths of the older clients habitually use marijuana and/or alcohol; half of the population come from single-parent families, most often headed by the mother. These findings have significant implications for the types of interventions Starr uses both with the children and the families. As trends in the demographic characteristics indicate changes in the kinds of clients served, so must programs be adjusted to meet those new needs.

The Need for a Multidimensional Approach to Evaluation

One of the most difficult tasks for any residential care program is to show success. In broad terms, success can be defined as the achievement of desired goals. Two major issues arise in defining success in the human services field. First, it is often difficult to detect when goals have actually been achieved; many of the indicators of change in clients require subjective evaluation. For example, determining when a child has actually experienced a change in values or behavior is a subjective judgment made by treatment staff members. Has the child really experienced the changes necessary to allow him or her to be successful after having left the residential setting? Does behavior change while in a residential setting serve as an indicator of a positive posttreatment experience?

The second issue, even more critical than the first, is defining what outcomes we expect. We are unclear about what we expect a young person coming into residential care should experience. Clear and concise definitions of program goals are absolutely imperative. If we have not decided what outcomes we desire, it is certainly difficult to ascertain whether we have achieved them.

An effort being piloted at The Starr Commonwealth Schools uses a multidimensional approach to evaluation. A variety of desired outcomes have been defined, and measures of those outcomes have been implemented. Developing the specific program goals entailed reviewing contract performance standards, listening to what our funding agencies expected, and discussing, within the agency, what our expectations ought to be. The measures were developed by either identifying valid instruments already available in the field or by developing our own instrumentation. This approach is delineated in Figure 1.

Some of the measures are straightforward and easy to determine. For example, completion rate is simply the percentage of the client population who completed their treatment programs. The length of stay is the average number of months clients are in program. The truancy dismissal rate is the percentage of clients who were dismissed from the program because of excessive truancy. Other measures require the use of instruments to collect specific information. Educational achievement, for example, is measured, on a pre-post schedule, by administering the Woodcock-Johnson Psycho-Educational Battery [1978]. This test measures math and reading achievement. By comparing clients' scores when they first come into program and, again, just before they leave, it is possible to measure achievement gain. Changes in self-esteem are detected by the use of the Piers-Harris Children's Self-Concept Scale [1984]. Both of these instruments are available from test publishers who have expended considerable resources to develop technically sound data collection devices.

Other measures being used have been designed specifically for Starr schools. The quality of the administrative and treatment climate created in the program is assessed by the Mitchell-Ameen Treatment Environment Survey [1987], which is administered to staff members and clients. The survey contains questions about the quality of administrative support, communication, problem solving, conflict resolution, team and group relationships, treatment effectiveness, and relationships with families. Given twice a year, the survey provides feedback to staff members and administrators about the climate in which treatment is delivered and how that climate can be improved.

The final component in this multidimensional approach is the measurement of postplacement adjustment. Three months after each client is released, staff members are asked to assess the quality of the placement the client is in and the level of productivity that is being maintained (i.e., is the child in school, working, both, or neither). The same assessment is again made 12 months after release.

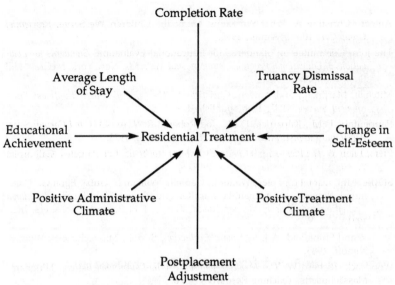

Figure 1. A Multidimensional Approach to Evaluation

By measuring several indicators of success, and then studying the trends of each indicator over time, one can determine the consistency with which specific programs are able to achieve stated program goals. A program that meets many or all of its goals justifies confidence in referring to it as successful; however, a program that fails to meet its goals, or that lacks consistency in doing so, warrants concern about its effect; the various measures being taken help to indicate the issues that the program needs to address.

One of the major concerns that arises in designing evaluations for programs is the establishment of the goals and the standards for their performance. It is important that an agency not make these decisions in a vacuum but, instead, seek the input of appropriate internal and external sources. This method will ensure that the performance standards address the expectations of the program staff and administration, the board, referring agencies, and the public. The standards established at The Starr Commonwealth Schools are displayed in Table 3.

TABLE 3

Performance Standards

Statistic	Standard
Completion rate	75%
Average length of stay (in months)	12.0
Truancy dismissal rate	10%
Educational achievement gain (in years)	1.5
Self-esteem change (raw score gain)	10
Three-month follow-up	
Positive placement rate	90%
Productivity rate	90%
Twelve-month follow-up	
Positive placement rate	70%
Productivity rate	70%

The Need for Agency Self-Evaluation

The field of residential treatment needs to adopt program evaluation as a mechanism for agency self-evaluation. The methodology is available to assist agency administrators and staff members to make more informed and timely decisions about planning and managing programs for children and families. The field of education has adopted evaluation, but only after federal guidelines required school districts to do so. The field of residential treatment need not wait for external forces to mandate program evaluation. Rather, leadership ought to be given to move all agencies with programs for families toward adopting program evaluation as a method for program improvement. Doing so will result in more effective and better-managed programs for clients.

The Need for Collaborative Evaluation Efforts

If the field of residential care is to improve the pace of which it is capable, multiple evaluation efforts will be necessary. As agencies refine their evaluation efforts, the decision-making information derived will undoubtedly be useful. The ultimate utility of this information for the field as a whole will be limited, however, unless it can be shared and compared to the work of other similar residential care settings.

A starting point for collaborative evaluation efforts might be to compare information regarding basic demographic findings of clients and families served. The work of Pappenfort et al. [1973] is a step in the right direction, in terms of using census data to describe what populations are served in out-of-home placements. Taking that a step further, however, would require building a database from actual individual client records. By means of this process, the field of residential treatment would be able to answer the question of whom it serves.

Beyond client description, it is necessary that the field more clearly define the unmet needs of the clients it serves. The use of survey research makes it possible to assess client perceptions of those unmet needs. An example of such an effort is the national study of adolescence, conducted by the Search Institute. This study surveyed 8,000 adolescents and parents, from 13 child-care groups, about their attitudes toward family life and how it can be improved. The National Association of Homes for Children participated in this research project (see Ameen [1985]) as well, to use survey research as a method for assessing needs of clients for services.

Another collaborative effort is the Peer Influence Project, managed by the Institute of Social Research at the University of Michigan. This project, a joint effort of both public and private agencies, will soon be providing valuable information about how the use of peer influence in residential group care of delinquent adolescents affects the adjustment of those youths in treatment and after release. All agencies involved assisted in the development of the project's hypotheses, data collection instruments, and data analysis, again emphasizing that it is possible to collaborate to learn more about how residential group care interacts with the youths and families served.

The ultimate collaborative effort would be a national study, which would necessarily involve agreement on how to measure outcomes and, undoubtedly, would be a stressful process. Nonetheless, it is a necessary step in the development of the field of residential treatment, and in its ability to advocate, at a national level, for the needs of the children and families it serves.

References

Ameen, Christine A. What We Know About the Children We Serve. *Residential Group Care* 10 (1): Winter, 1985.

The Joint Committee on Standards for Educational Evaluation. *Standards for Evaluations of Educational Programs, Projects, and Materials.* New York: McGraw-Hill Book Company, 1981.

Mitchell, Martin L., and Ameen, Christine A. *The Mitchell-Ameen Treatment Environment Survey, 1987.* To be published.

Pappenfort, D.M., Kilpatrick, D.M., and Roberts, R.W. (eds.). *Child Caring: Social Policy and the Institution.* Chicago, Illinois: Aldine, 1973.

Piers, Ellen V. *The Piers-Harris Children's Self-Concept Scale.* Los Angeles, California: Western Psychological Services, 1984.

Stufflebeam, Daniel L., Foley, Walter J., Gephart, William J., Guba, Egon G., Hammond, Robert L., Merriman, Howard O., and Provus, Malcolm M. *Educational Evaluation and Decision-Making.* Itasca, Illinois: F.E. Peacock Publishers, Inc., 1971.

————, and Shinkfield, A.J. *Systematic Evaluation.* Boston, Massachusetts: Kluwer-Nijhoff, 1985.

Woodcock, Richard W. *The Woodcock-Johnson Psycho-Educational Battery.* Hingham, Massachusetts: Teaching Resources, 1978.

22

Development of Quality Care Indicators in Group Care

SUSAN B. PRICE
FRED CHAFFEE
GERRY MOZENTER

Quality . . . you know what it is, yet you don't know what it is. But that's self-contradictory. But some things *are* better than others, that is, they have more quality. But when you try to say what the quality is, apart from the things that have it, it all goes *poof*! There's nothing to'talk about. But if you can't say what Quality is, how do you know what it is, or how do you know that it even exists? If no one knows what it is, then for all practical purposes it doesn't exist at all. But for all practical purposes it really *does* exist. What else are grades based on? Why else would people pay fortunes for some things and throw others in the trash pile? Obviously some things are better than others . . . but what's the "betterness"? . . . So round and round you go, spinning mental wheels and nowhere finding anyplace to get traction. What the hell is Quality? What *is* it?

—R.M. Pirsig,
*Zen and the Art of Motorcycle Maintenance:
An Inquiry into Values* (1974)

IF QUALITY IN GENERAL IS HARD TO DEFINE, attempting an authoritative definition of quality in a group care setting could very well

preclude any further action on the subject. Are structural characteristics of an agency enough to satisfy the quest for quality? That
is, is it enough to have licensed social workers, low resident-to-
staff ratios, and buildings that satisfy local codes and regulations?
It is a start, perhaps. But what if the social workers hate to do
discharge planning, and the child-care workers play gin rummy
all day? Thus we find that process measures are also important:
are the children actually involved in the program activities, and
are the service providers doing their jobs? But aren't outcomes what
matter in the final analysis? Well, yes—but who can agree on a
widely applicable definition of successful outcome?

Overview and Guiding Principles

Why Have a Quality Assurance Program?

Then why make the effort to measure quality at all? In plain
language, quality assurance is good administration. A commitment
to quality (beyond being a good public relations slogan) has many
practical advantages. Among them are the following:

> An active commitment to quality monitoring satisfies
> licensing and accrediting agencies. Even if they do not
> require an organized quality assurance (QA) program, ag-
> gressive QA activities can demonstrate that the agency
> takes its accountability duties seriously.
>
> Third-party payers feel confident about making re-
> ferrals to an agency with thorough internal monitoring
> procedures. If these external agencies also retain some
> case management or custodial responsibilities, they can
> feel confident that their clients are in good hands and that
> they will be promptly notified of problems and discharge
> plans.
>
> QA is an integral part of risk management—the pro-
> cess of minimizing lawsuits and other claims against the
> agency. QA programs facilitate prompt problem identifi-
> cation, as well as thorough investigation, documentation,
> and remedial actions.

Agencies with a reputation for high-quality service, active self-evaluation, and aggressive problem resolution have a way of attracting new dollars for program expansion and diversification.

Program administrators are systematically kept aware of the status of clients and subsystems in their programs. Frequently, through trend and pattern analysis, QA information helps to identify problem areas before they reach crisis proportions.

QA information can help identify and document client needs that are not being met by the program. This information may form the basis of a case to increase funding for a client or group of clients or may lead to other types of client advocacy, including new programs in the community.

But, as the foregoing references to documentation imply, commitment to quality requires a commitment to the measurement of quality. In addition, once we have decided what to measure, we have to implement the management systems that will assure adequate follow-up of possible problem areas. We also must confront the reality that we possess limited resources with which to tackle the dual challenge of quality measurement and quality assurance. Therefore, we have to decide what monitoring and assessment efforts will offer the greatest reward for the agency, the service providers, and the clients served.

Quality Cues

This paper describes monitoring systems developed at Hillside Children's Center, Rochester, New York. Hillside has been committed to internal monitoring systems of various designs since 1979, when a quality assurance position was established. Several systems now exist and are still rapidly evolving; they include the incident-reporting system, the concurrent review of treatment plans, and the Monday Monitors. New systems are continually under development.

All these systems are subsumed into a model called Quality Cues—a euphonious term for a quality assurance program that guarantees close communication between those who compile assessment information (the quality assurance analysts) and the service delivery staff (the clinicians).

The distinguishing organizational characteristic of the Quality Cues model is a formal two-tier system for evaluating quality of service information. Once the quality assurance committee approves the monitoring of a specific service feature and agrees on explicit criteria and standards, the QA staff applies the criteria and standards to identify the cues. These cues are signals to the program clinicians that a service delivery problem may exist. The clinical supervisory staff and the QA staff then conduct regular meetings (Cue Reviews) to provide a second level of review. Here, more sophisticated judgments are made by using additional case information and clinical experience (also referred to as "implicit criteria" because they are not well articulated), and these judgments determine whether administrative intervention is required.

Operational Definition of Quality

Hillside's operational definition of quality has three major dimensions. The first is appropriate utilization of the programs and services: the right client in the right service at the right time. This dimension includes the ability to change services when necessary and to arrange for appropriate follow-up services. The second dimension is system performance: the ability of the agency to organize its policies and procedures to maximize efficient and effective service to its clients. The third dimension is provider performance: the ability of direct-service providers and line supervisors to carry out competently their professional duties within the context of agency policies and procedures. In general, then, how do all parts of the agency work together in behalf of the clients, to stabilize their problems and improve their functioning?

Given this definition of quality, each service feature monitored may generate up to three types of cues.

Client cues address the global condition of the children (or their families). Are they responding to treatment? Are they making adequate progress? Is the condition of a particular child deteriorating? Are the children sufficiently engaged in the program? Is any child at risk of failing the placement? These cues also directly address the quality dimension of appropriateness. Is the resident still appropriate for Hillside's program? Has he or she made sufficient progress to start thinking about discharge? Does his or her condition require consideration of a higher level of care or a different kind of facility?

Service cues take up the issue of system performance. Do specified service features of residential units compare poorly to similar units? Is the client mix in a living unit too unbalanced to allow adequate behavior management? Do certain classes of service providers require additional in-service training? Are procedures and expectations clearly stated? Are there conflicts between regulatory requirements and good clinical practice and, if so, do they require administrative advocacy?

Provider cues zero in on possible problems in individual provider performance. Where there are absolute performance standards (e.g., suspected child abuse must be reported 100 percent of the time), do individuals fail to meet them? Where the standards are relative, do certain individuals appear to perform at a level significantly lower than their colleagues? If this situation is the case, are there extenuating circumstances that might justify this performance? (For example, a worker whose cases, on the average, are more severely disturbed than those of his or her colleagues might be expected to have a higher number of unstable discharges.)

Provider cues are understandably the most delicate area to monitor. Care must be taken to safeguard the privacy of individual service providers and to process information fully with the program director and/or supervisor (according to prearranged procedure). Hillside is often asked whether cue data are put into the worker's personnel file. This action occurs only when the supervisor and program director agree that the information clearly reveals a problem in performance. In such cases, personnel policies regarding employee notification, grievance procedures, and so forth are followed, as in any performance problem.

Identifying Quality Indicators

How did Hillside decide what specific bits of information (or "service features") to monitor? From the outset, the approach was frankly more pragmatic than theoretical. Amid the tons of paper that were generated and the external standards and regulations that had to be complied with, we thought there must be enough to assemble a reasonable set of quality-of-care monitors. Gradually a significant quantity of data already collected in one way or another emerges, ripe for incorporating into a quality-monitoring system. Of course, this approach occasionally has resulted in efforts to make quality judgments based on information that simply does not lend itself to firm conclusions. These indicators eventually are mustered out of the monitoring system and replaced with more useful ones.

Thus, not only have we been opportunistic in using available data, but we also recognized early that the process would be incremental. The hallmark of a good quality indicator is that it readily yields information about possible or potential problem areas. It quickly becomes a waste of time to review continually an area that consistently yields either positive or equivocal information. It is not always clear, however, when one starts out, what the potential for problems are in a given area, especially if one has never before analyzed any data from that area. Therefore, it was necessary to allow ourselves a spirit of experimentation and a willingness to keep upgrading systems that will gradually result in a nucleus of efficient, high-yield indicators. This set of indicators is still evolving, and we do not pretend to have finished the developmental work.

Once the quality indicators are identified, there remains the process of defining, writing criteria and standards, and gaining staff commitment to participate. These aspects of the process are explored in other articles [Price 1985; Price et al. 1986]. It is important, however, to make a point about staff involvement. It is easy for an august quality assurance committee to determine provider performance standards. (For example, social workers will be "cued"—that is, flagged for further review—if they consistently fail to hold treatment conferences within a week of the required due date. Child-care workers will be cued and subsequently tracked if they are involved in more than three restraints in a month.) But if these providers have not previously agreed that they should be held accountable to these standards, subsequent plans to change their job performance based on these indicators are unlikely to work. Therefore, it is important to commit time to explaining proposed cues and developing a consensus of support before the information rolls off the computer. Staff members involved in quality assurance programs do not score high in popularity polls. They can engender respect, however, if they take time to develop fair and objective assessment procedures and if they appreciate how service providers interpret their responsibilities.

A Sampling of Quality Indicators

The following is a partial listing of indicators currently in use at Hillside. The information is collected primarily from incident reports, weekly monitoring reports, and treatment plans. The source documents are generated by line staff (usually social workers and child-care workers) and sent through the quality assurance unit for computerization and analysis. They cover the following general areas: gross safety; security and supervision adequacy; service planning appropriateness; client's engagement in services; and discharge appropriateness.

Gross Safety

Accidental injuries: Accidents due to recreational activities, other activities, or environmental hazards

Missed medications and medication errors: Problems in administering medications either by sociotherapists or nurses

Environmental hazard surveillance: A monthly checklist procedure carried out by the Campus Supervisor and followed up by Maintenance

Security and Supervision Adequacy

Runaways from residence: Unaccounted absences for longer than two hours (less in high-risk cases), and for which the police are called

Drug or alcohol intoxication by residents

Self-inflicted injuries or mutilations

Assaultiveness: Behavior that results in injury to staff members or peers or is severe enough to require police intervention (either for immediate security or to file criminal charges)

Need for intensified supervision: Two levels monitored: "adult" (child must be within constant view of a staff member) and "strict adult" (child must be within arm's length of a staff member)

Need for suicide alert procedures: Includes self-inflicted injuries; also includes ideation without actual gestures or injury; the procedures include not only intensifying supervision but also appropriate notifications, consultations, and clearing the child's room of any objects that could be used for self-harm

Need for physical restraint: Refers to the holding of a child by one or more trained staff members to minimize an immediate risk of self-harm, harm to others, or harm to property

Possession of a weapon: Various forms of knives are the typical problem

Assault by non-agency persons: Occasionally a problem for children who are able to spend time unsupervised in the community; a child's vulnerability to such encounters must be considered in the decision to allow community excursions

Service Planning Appropriateness

Admission and continued stay appropriateness: Child's record is reviewed at admission and at three- and six-month intervals to determine if the child's needs could be adequately met in a less restrictive or less expensive setting. If the case does not pass the initial screening by the Quality Assurance staff, then a full review is conducted by the Utilization Review Committee (a specialized cue committee, dealing exclusively with appropriate utilization of programs and services)

Quality and timeliness of assessments: To ensure that treatment plans are based on adequate assessments, all assessment material is reviewed for timeliness (according to predetermined schedules) and quality (according to prescribed content)

Reflection of assessments in treatment plan: To ensure that assessment material is appropriately dealt with in the treatment plans

Level of contact between social worker and clients: Units of service rendered in behalf of a client and family—both direct and indirect

Conferencing between school and social workers/sociotherapists (child-care workers): Refers to the expectation of regular discussion between teachers and other principal team members on the activities and progress of children—over and above crisis calls

Regular treatment conferences: A tracking system maintained by Quality Assurance and Clinical Records assures that regular treatment plan reviews are held within the time line established for each program

Regular medication reviews: Physicians must renew all psychotropic medication orders every 30 days, in light of mandated feedback from the living units on behavioral changes and side effects

Client's Engagement in Therapeutic Services

Refusal to take medication

Involvement in structured recreation activities (currently used only by group homes): Recreation activities permeate residential treatment to such a degree that this question yielded no useful information

Adherence to house rules (group homes)

Worrisome behaviors (group homes): Contrasted with critical behaviors that require incident reports and are behaviors that may be leading up to failure or disruption in the treatment plan. They include changes in level of anxiety or depression, sexual acting out, suspected drug involvement, unhealthy community interactions, or bizarre behaviors

Achievement and/or maintenance of short-term behavioral expectations (residential treatment): The "honors" system combines generic behavioral expectations with expectations specifically tailored to the child's treatment plan. These expectations are expected to be calibrated in such a way as to allow children to achieve weekly honors status at least once a month

Failure to be maintained in classroom setting: Need to be sent to crisis intervention room; need to be sent back to living unit; need to be suspended from school

Weekly progress recorded in treatment objectives: Social work with child; social work with family; sociotherapy with child. At this point only progress in one objective in each of these areas is required. (At some point we will computerize the entire treatment plan and monitor all objectives.)

Quarterly and annual progress in Individualized Education Program (IEP): At this point, the areas of Socialization and Behavior Management of the IEPs are beginning to be computerized

Discharge Appropriateness

Review of length of stay beyond normal limits: Length of stay norms are based on the average length of stay of planned discharges from each program. If children have stayed or are going to stay more than one standard deviation beyond the average, their stay is considered protracted and is reviewed by the Utilization Review Committee for appropriateness of services and plans

Discharge of client in a stabilized condition (usually a planned discharge)

Information Processing

The collected information reviewed above is entered into an IBM-AT compatible microcomputer, using ENABLE™ software (The Software Group). ENABLE™ is an integrated database, spreadsheet, word-processing, and graphics package in which the database is not only powerful but also is easily used by the dedicated amateur. The evolutionary nature of Hillside's monitoring has required the computer software to be flexible and highly adaptable, without need for expensive programming consultants.

The information is entered regularly by a clerical worker, who is also trained to generate printed reports on a monthly or quarterly basis, according to a predetermined schedule generally planned to coincide with relevant committee meetings. Specific committees may have responsibility for reviewing the data to determine whether a problem exists and if remedial action is needed, such as the Cue Review meetings mentioned above. Other committees involved may be the Safety Committee, the Risk Management Committee of the Board of Directors, the Utilization Review Committee, or the Health and Infection Control Committee.

The remainder of this paper is devoted to detailed descriptions of how some of the monitoring systems can be used beneficially.

The Incident Report: A Quality-of-Care Indicator, with Case-Specific and Programmatic Implications

Impetus for Development of an Incident-Reporting System

All agencies involved in delivering children's services, particularly on an inpatient basis, are faced with meeting a plethora of standards. Often these standards are from outside organizations— either licensing and regulatory bodies, or those regional and national accrediting organizations such as the Council on Accreditation of Services for Families and Children or the Joint Commission on Accreditation of Hospitals (JCAH).

Meeting the multitude of standards from a variety of sources requires copious documentation, which the staff uniformly views as burdensome. Thoughtfully organizing the required information into an efficient system can, however, yield an internal monitoring system with enormous utility to the staff. Individual pieces of information can be significant, but the aggregation of the data, along with pattern analysis, often results in dramatic indices that may suggest programmatic changes.

Hillside's two major licensing bodies—The New York State Department of Social Services and the New York State Office of

Mental Health—require extensive documentation of untoward incidents. To make the best of this requirement, the agency constructed an incident report form that not only met the standards of the licensing bodies but also provided internally useful information.

The Incident Report Form

The report form itself required a long evolution. The document now used captures three main categories of information: high-risk client behavior, untoward results, and special interventions. Under high-risk client behavior, for example, are included assaultive behavior toward staff members or others, self-destructive or suicidal behavior, running away, substance abuse, possession of a weapon, and refusing medication. High-risk behavior may also lead to untoward results. For example, assaultive behavior toward a staff member might result in an injury to another client or to other staff members. In addition to high-risk client behavior and untoward results, the incident report also documents special interventions that per se require review, such as physical restraints, room searches, or suspensions from school. In general, these are interventions that carry an element of risk of injury or abuse, that should be used only under carefully prescribed conditions.

The report form is set up not only to capture the type of incident, but also to elicit the circumstances leading up to the event, how the staff member responded or tried to avoid the special intervention, and how the staff member followed through to prevent recurrence. Procedural details are also included: who was notified when, by whom, and what kinds of input each had in the related decision making either before, during, or after the incident. In other words, the incident report is in itself a quality-of-care monitoring tool as it encompasses, for a single event, an accounting of gross safety, security, and adequacy of supervision, as well as service planning and its effectiveness. It also gives some indication of a client's involvement in the therapeutic service offered.

Usefulness of the Individual Incident Report

Since the incident report is routinely reviewed by a number of supervisory, administrative, and clinical staff members, as well as receiving a final check by the quality assurance department, it can be used to ascertain whether actions taken were appropriate and whether further action is needed.

For example, a new staff member may have inappropriately become involved in a physical restraint with a youngster because that staff member had not used some of the other nonphysical intervention techniques and tools at his or her disposal. In this circumstance, the supervisor can use the incident report as a starting point for helping the staff member to gain insight into treatment techniques and the use of self in the treatment process.

Usefulness of Aggregate Incident Data

While individualized use of the incident report is helpful for immediate concerns, a more dramatic use of the reports can be seen when they are compiled over a period of time. This longitudinal aggregation provides insights into individual and group treatment to both clinicians and administrators.

Behavior Patterns of Individual Children
(Client Cues)

For example, it can be postulated that the child with borderline personality disorder often goes through a classic series of phases of engagement and disengagement in the treatment process. The most critical phase usually occurs after the client has been in treatment for anywhere from six months to one year, has apparently begun to make a real investment in effort, and is undergoing significant change. This phase is called the resistant phase and is usually manifested by symptomatic behavior that is at least as severe as the behavior that initially brought the child into treatment.

This phenomenon often engenders great disappointment within the treatment team and a call for immediate discharge: "The child is no longer profiting from treatment," or the child is "disruptive to the group." These calls for discharge are often the result of countertransferential feelings on the part of the team that has invested a great deal in the child. Insight into what the behavior really signifies can often be gained through a review of the pattern of incidents over time: The hard evidence often allows the staff to see that a youngster has indeed been able to follow routine and not act out for significant periods of time. The staff members' feelings of disappointment are recognized for what they are, and the course of the disorder and its treatment can be put in perspective.

There have also been instances where seductive children have engaged staff members so manipulatively that the latter are unable to see the deviant behavior patterns. Incident reports aggregated over a period of time enable staff members to see graphically the number and type of problem behaviors and to enlarge their understanding of the child. This larger picture encourages staff members to proceed with better treatment planning. Case-specific data can also reveal other, idiosyncratic behavior patterns. Some patterns are readily evident (e.g., frequent restraints before or after home visits). But a longitudinal study of incidents may reveal evidence of more subtle motivators for negative behavior, as in a particular time of the week that may be connected to a seemingly nonthreatening situation such as a physical education class or a music therapy session.

Indicators of Need for Living Unit Reorganization
(Service Cues)

Aggregate information collected from incident reports is also extremely useful and can result in a different deployment of staff members, as well as programmatic changes. Two examples come to mind, both of which concerned a unit of 15 latency-age children in the residential treatment center.

1. Examining incidents by time of day, we graphed instances where physical intervention (i.e., restraints) had been required to control behaviors that were dangerous to self or others. The graph in Figure 1 was drawn for one cottage for the month of September 1984 and presented a clear picture of major difficulties for the unit during transition times. Such a graphic depiction of a problem prompted the administrative and supervisory staff to respond with alacrity. Staff members were rescheduled, and transition times were restructured to meet more adequately the needs of the children in treatment. Although the problems may eventually have come to light, the graphic use of restraint data was an important aid.

2. A second major use of the aggregate data generated by incident reports involved the same latency-age group and same

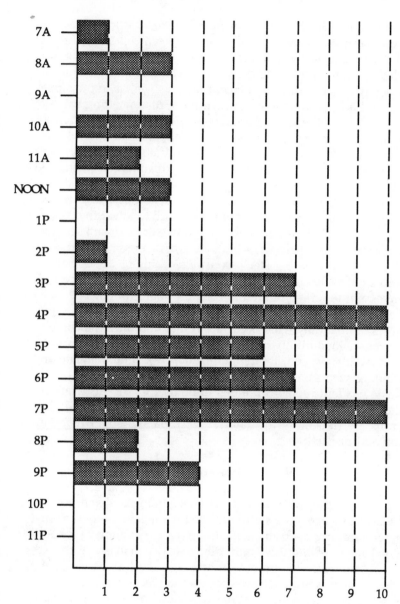

Figure 1. Restraint by time of day—Cook Cottage (one-month period).

treatment unit. For a number of months, that particular unit led the agency in the number of incidents in which children exhibited out-of-control behavior to the extent that physical intervention was needed for the safety of the clients, as well as for others. This fact was highly disconcerting to the clinicians, as well as to the supervisors and administrative staff. Even more disconcerting was the observation that the rate continued to climb month after month, even after the addition of extra staff members in the unit.

Research and experience have shown that a small group size is an important variable in the effective treatment of disturbed children, resulting in more individualized attention, more stability, less stress, and therefore a significant reduction in acting-out behavior. The Hillside program could not afford to lower the cottage occupancy, but dividing the 15 boys into two groups with separate living areas and staggered schedules was a possibility. It was, nevertheless, a fairly big step—considered only because restraint data so far had shown that less radical interventions had not worked. The restraint report continued to be a key source of objective data and a primary indicator of the success of the intervention. Figure 2 shows dramatically what occurred in that unit once the children had been divided into two subgroups of nine and six youngsters. As can readily be seen, the reorganization was an immediate and continuing success.

The incident report continues to be used as an important indicator of the status of the cottage milieu. Unfavorable trends and patterns are frequently the catalyst for thoughts about reorganization and rescheduling.

Response of Line Staff

It is interesting to note that in the beginning of this process—over five years ago—the staff perceived the incident report as just another burdensome form—a means by which administration and external agencies interfered with direct-service delivery. Although the staff members still are not enthusiastic about paperwork, the incident report is now perceived as an integral component of service delivery. Because of the series of reviews on each report, staff members get regular feedback on the quality of their interactions with children. They are continually reminded that the quality of

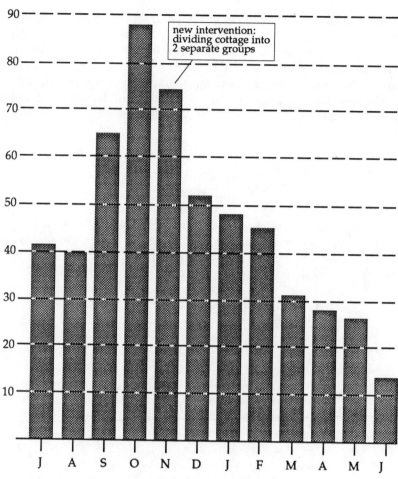

Figure 2. Monthly restraints for Cook Cottage.

the documentation will ultimately protect them from allegations of abuse, neglect, or procedural lapses.

Cottage supervisors, in particular, request both aggregate and individual monthly data to ascertain whether their treatment approaches are having an effect on individuals or groups in their care. They also use the information regularly to double-check their concern about a particular child or about the status of the cottage as a whole. The QA staff members have organized both computer files and hard-copy data to permit rapid access for special requests. This "Same Day Service—with a Smile" encourages supervisory staff members to use the database to answer specific questions about clients, services, or staff members. Their frequent requests for information have also led to modifications of the database and regular reports to maximize the usefulness of the reporting system.

Monitoring: Helping or Hindering the Clinical Social Worker?

The incident reporting system has been found to be especially useful in managing residential units and thus is most meaningful to child-care workers. Other systems have their biggest effect on the clinical social worker—the treatment coordinator at Hillside.

"Why do they want to collect this seemingly useless information?"

"How is this information gathering going to help the children anyway?"

"This paperwork exercise is too time-consuming—it takes away from my direct-service time; my clients need all the time I can give them."

"This information gathering is probably being done to satisfy some funder's need for statistics—it has no relevance to my work."

"This information gathering and monitoring is just another way of checking on me—I wish they would try to find ways to help me do a better job."

In this age of institutional accountability, service providers often perceive any attempt to monitor service process or progress as an impediment to service delivery. The statements above—along with their overtones of resistance, resentment, suspicion, and confusion—are typical of initial remarks from the social workers in response to requests by QA staff and program administration members to provide more frequent and specific information about their clients' behavior and their own efforts to provide service.

It should be understood that the social workers employed by the group care programs (residential and group home levels of care) are charged with the challenging task of clinical direction and coordination and must set priorities on their time and energy to deliver individual, group, and/or family counseling services; to coordinate and focus the efforts of other treatment team members (sociotherapists, teachers, and so on); to document treatment effort and progress; and to maintain liaison with external service delivery systems and funding sources.

These tasks are all the more formidable when multiplied by a caseload of up to 13. It is, therefore, not altogether surprising to hear the sounds of resistance from social workers. At least initially, they view a request for additional documentation and information gathering as a demand for additional time and energy without apparent reward. Nevertheless, this asumption, that the systematic monitoring of data gathered from clinical social workers creates an atmosphere that impedes service, can be defeated. *With purposeful and structured handling* of collected information, the social workers are, in fact, given feedback that can enhance their ability to provide effective and efficient service.

It is paramount for the social workers to be able to integrate an understanding of historical case material with more current behavioral information. They need to relate this integrated understanding clearly to the client, the client's family, and other team members so that appropriate treatment strategies can be carried out. This process calls for access to relevant information and the ability to identify and focus quickly on significant behavioral events, patterns, and trends.

At Hillside, several QA monitoring mechanisms provide to the social worker, social work supervisor, and program director information that can be instrumental in the identification of individual and group treatment issues. The incident report discussed earlier is one such monitoring tool, but two other mechanisms effectively aid the clinical hierarchy in ongoing treatment planning.

Treatment Plan Audits

It was stated earlier in this paper that two primary indicators of quality care are (1) the degree to which treatment team members effectively construct appropriate treatment plans and diligently try to implement them, and (2) the degree to which a client is willing and/or able to engage in this treatment effort. In large part, the appropriateness and/or effectiveness of a treatment effort can be assessed by the client's response over time. Effective feedback regarding a client's response to treatment planning and implementation can modify or reinforce current efforts. Thus, assessment and treatment remain two intertwined and dynamic processes.

Current QA monitoring systems ask social workers regularly to submit information that (1) represents their treatment planning and diligence of effort and (2) reflects their client's response to service. In return, the QA department so organizes this information as to make the social workers' tasks of assessment and treatment planning more focused and effective.

The social workers' efforts to construct appropriate and effective treatment strategies are most readily seen in the written treatment plans that are entered into the clinical records at the agency and in many cases forwarded to funders who retain some case management responsibilities. These plans are also routinely reviewed by accreditors when they try to assess the quality of care. The social workers' planning and review efforts are examined by the immediate supervisor to help assure that clients' treatment needs are being met. This work is, in general, an effective process, but due to the sheer volume of complex cases involved, there is still room for error and fuzzy planning or reporting, with less than optimum treatment. Therefore, to ensure appropriate and effective treatment planning and service delivery, the QA audit system is utilized.

After supervisory review, social workers are required to submit their treatment plans to the QA department for a more systematic technical review. The QA staff reviews these planning forms before they are included in the record or sent out to funders. The auditors may return the forms to the supervisory staff with recommendations for correction or clarification if the treatment plans are in any way internally inconsistent or inappropriate. For example, QA may find that goals and objectives fail to flow from discharge criteria or assessment recommendations, are unclear or vague, or do not delineate clear roles or tasks for treatment team members. Although the original intent of the treatment plan audit was to ensure that funding and accrediting guidelines for timeliness and format were met (all the i's dotted and t's crossed), it has proven to be a valuable tool of clinical thinking in the supervisory process. When treatment planning forms are returned, social workers and their superviors must rethink and sharpen their approach to treatment before resubmitting plans.

Program directors are informed quarterly of the rate of treatment plan return. They can use this information to identify planning or assessment weaknesses on the part of any one staff member, the staff as a whole, and/or the supervisor. Appropriate plans for intensified supervision and/or in-service training can easily flow from this information. It has been particularly helpful to both program directors and social work supervisors to obtain a list of the most common reasons for return of forms from QA so that needed improvements can be more easily identified.

"Monday Monitors"—The Weekly Overview

To obtain a clear and more frequent reading of treatment effort and client response to these carefully constructed treatment plans, the QA department asks the treatment team (headed by the social worker) to fill out a weekly monitoring sheet for reporting on (1) aspects of each client's behavior that might indicate the presence of stress (e.g., unscheduled return from school, AWOL behavior, drug use, verbal or physical acting out), (2) documented progress or lack of progress toward stated goals and objectives, and (3) assorted indicators that have been previously found to be present in successful treatment efforts (e.g., frequent contact between educational staff members and other team members, structured contact between child and family members, documented progress toward stated family goals and objectives, participation in supervised and structured recreation activities).

It might be noted that the task of gathering this information is, in itself, a self-monitoring or sensitizing process. The weekly sheet—dubbed the "Monday Monitor"—is routinely filled out at the cottage or group home staff meeting at which one usually finds the coordinating social worker and strong representation from the child-care staff. It is apparent that the staff members must communicate with one another in a focused manner, to be able to submit complete, accurate data both for each child and for their own efforts. Completing the form also necessitates a review of the residents' records (especially progress notes) either at or before the staff meeting. This review process, if done conscientiously, provides a climate for systematic, ongoing assessment of treatment effectiveness and yields information critical to future treatment planning.

The completed forms are forwarded to QA. The QA staff aggregates and analyzes a month's worth of information, flagging cases based on the Quality Cue criteria alluded to earlier. The information is printed out in such a manner as to make it possible to raise pertinent questions and concerns about individual residents, a particular grouping of residents, a particular treatment milieu, or a particular treatment team's approach.

Aggregated feedback might raise questions such as:

"Why is John Doe being sent back from school so frequently?"

"Why hasn't Joe Smith demonstrated any progress toward his treatment objectives this month?"

"Why hasn't Sue Brown had any contact with her parents this month?"

"Why haven't 75 percent of all residents at Group Home "A" participated in any structured recreation activity this month?"

"Why is there so little contact between the team at Group Home "B" and the educational staff?"

"Why are the residents seen by worker "C" having a significant decline in family contact this month?"

"Why has the frequency of AWOL behavior at Cottage "D" increased this month, while decreasing significantly at Cottage "B"?"

The patterns learned from the weekly monitoring sheets are shared monthly with the program directors. The data and the issues raised are discussed by the Cue Review Committee, consisting of QA staff, program director, and other agency representatives. The program director may be well aware of the issues raised at this meeting and already involved in implementing corrective or investigating action—or the meeting's dialogue may help him or her to initiate the needed follow-up. The program director can use this information to highlight queries to the social work supervisory staff and/or line social workers and to proceed with action that results in a better understanding of treatment issues and how to deal with them. The implication here is that the process involved in the weekly monitoring system assists the coordinating social worker to focus on specific indicators of treatment progress and plays a part in involving all levels of the program hierarchy in identifying issues and solving problems.

Conclusion

This paper has provided an overview of the quality assurance system at Hillside Children's Center. It concludes with a synopsis of the principles that appear to underlie the system's success.

Active commitment of program staff is not a new concept, but there is a difference between lip service to this principle and genuine involvement. The staff can be sold on the idea of using the data only if the QA staff continues to rework it until it is genuinely useful; therefore active commitment of the QA staff is equally or even more important. Although program staff members can generally be expected to become involved in data collection and evaluation if they feel the hot breath of the regulators at their back, the commitment of the QA staff to active use of the data will create the richest, most interactive quality assurance environment.

The first corollary of this principle of mutual, interactive commitment is the necessity of carefully defining the evaluation elements. In the case of restraints, the process of definition itself resulted in a clarification of procedures and subsequent improvement in the quality of care. Vague definitions result in vague information and cripple the ability of both the supervisors and the QA staff to make useful interpretations. A supervisor or administrator simply will not take action if he or she always has to go through a process of clarifying what the information really means.

The second corollary is that it is the responsibility of the QA staff to provide timely feedback from the data submitted or collected and to do so in such a form that it is readily comprehensible to the program staff (who, one can assume, are not used to dealing with aggregated data). The Hillside QA staff tries to do as much screening and data interpretation as possible before distribution. Whenever feasible, they incorporate graphs and charts into the work, since these can be more readily comprehended.

The last corollary is that a truly interactive system is never static. A graphic presentation of data might fascinate the staff the first time around, but the fourth or fifth time they are jaded and may hardly glance at it. A new stimulus must be invoked to keep them involved with the information, with immediate utility, of course, always the best stimulus. Most monitors have a life cycle of usefulness; then they require continual evaluation and reworking to remain useful and stimulating. They should be quickly cycled out when they no longer provoke or reveal.

Where the quality assurance staff members have been most creative and interactive, the program staff members have become correspondingly more interested in getting more and better data. They are better able to articulate what they need, and they can also be more perceptive and straightforward about requesting revisions on reports that no longer meet their needs.

References

Pirsig, R.M. *Zen and the Art of Motorcycle Maintenance: An Inquiry into Values.* New York: Bantam, 1974.

Price, S. Quality assurance monitoring in children's residential care: changing paradigms. *Quality Review Bulletin* Vol 11: 242–245, 1985.

Price, S., Chaffee, F., and Comstock, C. Clinical incident monitoring. *Residential Group Care and Treatment* 3(3): 37–51, 1986.

23

Project Cope: Agency-Based Research—
The Process, the Pitfalls,
and the Payoffs

NANCY B. RONQUILLO

P ROJECT COPE WAS AN INQUIRY INTO the perceptions of former residents of children's residential treatment centers regarding their experience in residence, and of themselves at admission and six months to a year after discharge. Launched in 1982, it was one of many evaluation research programs stimulated by a spiraling interest in the 1970s about the effectiveness of social services, particularly through follow-up information. This emphasis on follow-up emerged as a legacy of War on Poverty legislation, which required the evaluation of all federally funded programs for social intervention. As the decade of the 1980s opened, interest in long-term program outcomes was bolstered further by a demand for accountability. Agencies were asked by authorized bodies, and felt obliged to ask themselves, whether benefits were sufficiently maintained to justify their cost. The high cost of residential treatment drew special attention.

These are among the influences that led Lawrence Hall Youth Services to enlist the support of Chicago foundations and the corporate community for undertaking Project Cope, which was an immensely valuable learning experience. This paper describes the process of designing and implementing an agency-based research effort, presenting the problems and pitfalls, and making recommendations for future efforts.

The Process of Developing Project Cope

Funding

The purpose of the project was to determine how well, or how poorly, former residents of residential treatment facilities were doing after discharge. Obtaining funding for this purpose, however, emerged as a critical component in designing the project, because a major foundation invited Lawrence Hall to submit a proposal that would incorporate the following elements:

The project would preserve a service/program threatened by the first wave of Reaganomic federal cutbacks.

The project would be time-limited (a three-year limit was established).

The project would involve interagency collaboration.

The project would use volunteers who would constitute the bulk of the personnel.

Therefore, although the primary purpose of the project remained a telescopic view of residents returned to community life, the project was also committed to three ancillary goals:

To field test a model program for the systematic evaluation of residential treatment outcomes that is both replicable and cost-efficient

To modify agency programs as necessary to increase agency effectiveness

To demonstrate that volunteers can play a viable role in a follow-up program

The major funder provided full funding for the first year and a partial commitment for two additional years, contingent upon our success in garnering additional support from other corporations and foundations. The initial commitment from the major donor was extremely influential in obtaining support from other sources, but, in the final stages of the project, it became increasingly difficult to obtain funding to extend the time period. The three-year limit was stretched to three years and eight months, but the project had to be concluded at that point.

Establishing and Managing a Collaboration

Recruiting Agency Partners

When first invited to develop a collaborative project, the executive director of Lawrence Hall met with several residential agency executives to explore their interest in the project. Four agencies (Allendale School for Boys, Mercy Boys Home, Lutherbrook Children's Center, and Park Ridge Youth Campus) subsequently agreed to participate. An initial meeting of the five collaborating agencies was held to discuss the concept for the project and some of the known design elements, such as the time limitations and the necessity for using volunteers. This group formed a core steering committee that expanded once funding was assured and a project director was hired.

The Steering Committee Composition and Role

The steering committee was composed of each agency's executive director, a designated agency project liaison staff member, and the Project Cope director. Its role was to assist in both the design and execution of the project. This task included the development of the questionnaire instruments, assuring access to clients for interview purposes, eliciting support of their respective agency staffs, and disseminating progress reports internally. Each agency handled these activities in its own way. Some involved a number of staff members in the project; others relied solely on the designated liaison to manage all their project commitments and responsibilities. This committee also provided a forum for resolving operational problems, as well as a forum for debate on the issues the data began to yield.

Obtaining Consultation

Project Cope was undertaken without the central involvement of a research expert, a consequence of the agencies' strong desire to know how the former residents of their facilities were doing, without recognizing that the best way to gain the information was to develop a sound, rigorous research undertaking. The project was not viewed as a research effort, per se; hence it was designed and conducted for the most part by the social work practitioners, administrators, and volunteers. We expected to rely on a statistician in the final stages of the project, and we relied upon a computer expert to set up a program at the University of Chicago for collection and analysis of the data. The latter was referred by a professor of social work who was consulted in the early stages simply to review the project plans.

Although the agencies clearly wanted to know how their former residents fared after discharge, formal hypotheses were not developed. It was only in retrospect, toward the end of the project, that we realized the strong desire to determine what interventions were or were not helpful; at that point the role of a research expert emerged as a critical missing element.

Staffing the Project

The full-time position of project director was funded by the foundation grants, to bring the project to life from the conceptual stages, to manage the data collection, the collaboration, the recruitment and training of volunteers, and to produce a final report.

The agency liaison staff members were responsible for identifying clients and their families as candidates for the study, recruiting and supervising their volunteers, arranging for the interviews, and, in some cases, conducting the interviews as well. This responsibility was an addition to the full-time jobs of these individuals, and it became clear that the time demands for the project responsibilities were not negligible. One of the early lessons was that a study that relied heavily on volunteers still required a significant commitment of staff time.

The agency executives had an active role in the early months of the project, but once the staff and liaison members had been designated, the executives assumed an oversight function, meeting at least once a year to review progress and to discuss the data that were being collected.

Use of Volunteers

Volunteers were a central and crucial resource of the project. They conducted the majority of the resident and parent or guardian interviews, entailing hundreds of hours of work. About 25 volunteers were drawn from agencies' board members, former residents, and other friends of the cooperating agencies. At midpoint, recruitment became more difficult, and during the time period, there was some attrition within the original group. In future longitudinal studies, the recruitment of volunteers should take turnover into consideration so that continuity and consistency can be maintained. The volunteer effort required a commitment of staff time from each of the collaborating agencies. Any agency that would consider using volunteers to carry out a study should recognize that staff support is essential to the effectiveness of volunteers.

Extensive training of the volunteers was undertaken. A model kit and training manual included the questionnaire, instruction on techniques of interviewing to protect from contamination, and administrative matters (e.g., volunteer meetings, functions of their liaison). Volunteers were convened monthly to discuss their experiences with the interviews and any questions they had regarding their work. In 1984, Project Cope was selected by the Voluntary Action Center of the United Way of Chicago for outstanding achievement in effectively and creatively involving volunteers to meet community needs.

The COPE Questionnaire

Before Project Cope, Lawrence Hall had gained an initial experience in using a telephone follow-up questionnaire designed by Dr. Stephen Magura and Beth Moses, then of the Child Welfare League, for use with residents of children's treatment centers and a parent/guardian six to 12 months following discharge.[a] The in-

[a]Magura, Stephen, and Moses, Beth. Developing a follow-up interview for residential treatment. *Residential Group Care and Treatment* 5 (1): Fall 1985, p. 33–48.

terview questions focused on the respondent's satisfaction with the residential experience, as well as problems related to school, work, family, delinquent behavior, conduct, and emotional life.

Project Cope expanded this concept in two ways: two pretest instruments were developed, one for the child and one for the parent, to create a pretest and posttest research method; and two additional instruments to be used by the agency staff, one at the point of intake and one at discharge. In all, six separate questionnaires were completed for each resident who participated in the full study. The steering committee discussed the questionnaires, and modifications were made based upon the consensus of this group. Dr. Magura also reviewed the changes, as well as the new parallel pretest questionnaires that were developed. In essence, the steering committee assumed that the questionnaire was a comprehensive and field-tested instrument that needed little fine tuning.

At no point were the agencies asked to review their client files for common elements in program, type of resident, or even client case record elements. There was little preliminary planning in terms of comparison of forms, intake/discharge process, or length of stay. The steering committee dealt with the framework and mechanics of the project as it was initially conceived. All the five agencies were inexperienced in this type of undertaking, and so a great deal was taken for granted or learned along the way.

The issue of time was particularly frustrating for the agency that served the youngest residents. It was known that the project was not to extend beyond three years. This particular agency's average length of stay was three years, which ultimately prevented its inclusion in the follow-up sample. Yet there was a strong desire to participate in the project and a great deal of unrealized hope and faith that, collectively or individually, the agencies would find a way to extend the period.

Instruments for Parent and Child

The baseline questionnaire was conducted by a volunteer; it was given within the first few weeks of placement to the child and to his or her parent or guardian. There were 11 sections in the baseline questionnaire, which collected the following data (the list is not all-inclusive):

Cover sheet: Client description—age, sex, ethnicity, date of the interview

Previous residences: Their nature and number

Problem status: The problems that led to referral for placement at the center[b]

Academic information: School attendance and problems in school functioning (e.g., failing classes, annoying teachers)

Employment: The level of work experience and any job problems (getting fired, being criticized)

Involvement with authorities: Arrest record and types of offenses

Conduct problems: Behavior problems such as using drugs, running away, lying, being destructive

Symptomatic behavior: Anxiety, suicidal thoughts, enuresis, for example, and their frequency

Family and social relationships: How the child was getting along with family members, and also with peers

Previous services: Any medical care or therapy

Debriefing form: The interviewer's assessment of the truthfulness of the subject, the frequency of distractions, questionable responses—in essence, the quality of the interview itself

The follow-up questionniare was typically given by a volunteer over the phone. The former resident and the parent/guardian (when possible the same person as the baseline) were interviewed separately. The interviews were conducted after the resident had been discharged for a minimum of six months.

There were 13 sections in the follow-up questionnaire. The first three varied from the baseline and collected information regarding:

Residence: Number of moves since discharge and type of placement, if any

[b]Hereafter, "center" refers to the agency where the respondent/child was placed for residential care.

Current living situation: Location and degree of satisfaction

Satisfaction with center: Helpfulness of staff, overall satisfaction, satisfaction with distinct program elements

The other ten sections covered the same content areas as the baseline.

The Agency Staff Questionnaire at Intake

This instrument comprised questions similar but not identical to those on the resident and parent instruments. There were six sections, which covered residence, referral problems, school problems, conduct problems, symptomatic behavior, and chronicity of problems. At discharge, the agency staff members were asked to complete another questionnaire that included 11 sections:

Discharge circumstance
Presumed location at discharge
Educational program during residence
Educational progress
Type of work experience during residence
Success of the work experience
Problems during residence
Conduct problems during residence
General behavioral progress
Type and frequency of family contacts
Family cooperation with service

The Sample

Baseline Sample

At baseline, 217 residents were interviewed, ranging in age from six to 19, with 6 percent nine years old or under, 20 percent between seven to nine years old, 18 percent between ten and 12 years of age, 50 percent from 13 to 17 years old, and 6 percent from 18 to 19 years old. The mean age of the baseline sample was just under 14. Only 19 of the 217 residents were female. Whites accounted for 59 percent of the sample; Hispanics, 7 percent; and blacks, 34 percent. Parents or guardians of the residents were interviewed at baseline and follow-up. Of the 202 parents or guardians who were interviewed, 141 were biological parents, three were stepparents, 13 were adoptive parents, and ten were foster parents. Other relatives, social workers, and other staff members completed an additional 35 interviews. The agency questionnaire was completed at intake by a staff member, usually the Cope liaison staff designate, although the staff person was not always the same person, depending on the agency's staff availability.

Follow-Up Sample

Of the baseline group of 217 children, about half were not discharged soon enough to be included in the follow-up sample. Another 25 percent of the baseline group were not interviewed at follow-up because they could not be located, refused to be interviewed, had been re-placed in an institution where an interview was not obtainable, or for other such reasons. Fifty-four former residents were located and interviewed. The mean age of the follow-up group was 14½ years, about six months older than the baseline group. Only two girls were among the follow-up sample. The proportion of white to black children changed from two-thirds to one-third, respectively, at baseline, to more nearly equal at follow-up.

Of the 52 families responding at follow-up, 45 were members of the respondent's biological family. The remaining seven were members of foster or adoptive families. One hundred twenty-one discharge questionnaires were completed. Ninety-six (44 percent) of the residents had not yet been discharged at the time the project had to conclude its interviewing activities. The five agencies listed 40 percent of the discharges as planned, and four as planned but abrupt. Of those planned, 28 were judged to have made no progress, and 41 were judged to have made progress.

The Pitfalls

Although the project had faced a number of logistical and operational problems during the course of conducting the study, none was more daunting than the task of data synthesis, analysis, and interpretation. It was only at this final phase that the nature and scope of the data, as well as the limitations in some of the design elements, became fully apparent.

The project director worked with the computer input operator and a university professor to determine what data should be examined and how (i.e., what statistical measures were to be used). The goals were to issue a final report and offer a model for agencies to conduct outcome studies. When a first draft of the report was ready, a meeting of the Cope agency executives and their designated liaisons was convened to review the findings and obtain their views for the final draft of the report.

The Time Frame

The first pitfall was the time frame. About half of the baseline sample residents were still in residence at the time the interviewing had to end. It is important to note that the center from which the youngest children came was not likely to discharge clients in fewer than three years. This fact accounted, in part, for so few girls in the follow-up sample. One could reasonably argue that some of the most fruitful data were not collected. Children who remained in care for over two years were likely to provide a more complete picture. Although the questionnaire did not permit interferences about how improvements might have been effected at the centers, there may have been opportunities to gather data for this more complete picture. The follow-up sample of 54 former residents represented about half of the potential sample. Possibly significant conclusions could not be drawn from so small a sample. Extending the study for one more year could have doubled the size of the sample. Time constraints prevented an in-depth analysis and interpretation of the parent questionnaires. These separate perspectives might have been illuminating, but we were unable to correlate these bodies of data because of flawed questionnaires.

The Questionnaires

The questionnaires became our Gordian knot. Four problems prevented clear conclusions from being drawn from the data:

The response categories varied from question to question and included such options as "Maybe," "Not sure," and "Don't know," which inhibited the determination of possibly significant differences.

There was no weighing for severity; for example, under the emotional problems category, loss of appetite would carry the same weight as talking about wanting to die.

The agency staff questionnaires were not constructed parallel to the resident and parent questionnaires or even to the agency intake questionnaire. Hence, correlations between the respondents' views were impossible.

The questionnaires did not permit inferences to be drawn about the influence of the residential experience on a resident's changed behavior, because it did not ask the agency or the child and parent to identify what programs or treatment interventions had been used for the resident.

Essentially, what could be studied was information about how the children are doing, from their viewpoint, at the time of intake and six months after their discharge. We were unable to study what we, the residential centers, did to help our residents change for the better. This inability points to the final pitfall, the lack of adequate consultation. Hindsight tells us that a research expert should have been involved from the inception of the project. The inclusion of such a person on the steering committee would have helped the agency practitioners to (1) articulate more concisely the questions and hypotheses that they wanted the project to answer, (2) modify the questionnaires in light of key questions and in a way to ensure that correlations could be made between instruments and conclusions drawn from responses, and (3) flag the too-tight time frame from the outset, enabling the agencies to undertake a broader fund-raising effort.

Sample Bias

Although three of the original five project agencies served girls, females comprised only 9 percent of the baseline sample and 4 percent of the follow-up sample; the information that was yielded described only a male population. For years it was generally held that boys constituted two-thirds of the residential care population and girls the remaining one-third. The disproportionate representation of boys in this sample raises questions about how children are selected for residential care. Is there a gender bias that causes society to choose institutional care more frequently for its boys than its girls? Is there, in fact, a decline in the proportionate placement of girls in residential care?

The Payoffs

Despite limitations of funding, time, and data collection methods, a great deal was learned about children who require residential care. The responses of the children raised many questions that need to be examined in more rigorous research projects. Although it is not the intent of this paper to provide a detailed report of the findings, an overview of the most provocative issues raised is appropriate.

Resident-Reported Change

It is important to remember that the small size of the follow-up sample restricts the scope of the conclusions one can draw about the changes reported by this group. Nonetheless, each of the areas of data on change provides thought-provoking information. As an example, the section Change in Respondent Report of Conduct Problems from Baseline to Follow-up shows that every item except three reveals a reduction in problem behavior. The three problem behaviors that increased are drinking, drugs, and pregnancy. This finding mirrors three of the major problems society faces with respect to its youth today and raises questions for discussion as agencies determine what programs and services they offer to current residents and aftercare clients. Are substance abuse counseling and sex education classes offered? What additional supports can be provided for those youths exiting the protected residential facility to enable them to cope with the tremendous environmental pressures they will face?

Satisfaction Survey

The follow-up survey attempted to assess the residents' view of the helpfulness of the staff, their satisfaction with their agency's services, and their current satisfaction with their lives. In retrospect, despite the adjustment problems reported, most of the former residents looked back upon their experience with some degree of satisfaction.

Patterns of the Residential Youths in the Workplace

The various items of information that relate to employment point to a need that exists but may be difficult for the youths to recognize or articulate.

Thirty-seven of the 54 in the follow-up sample responded to the work category. Seventeen reported that they were self-supporting, and 20, that they were receiving welfare or unemployment compensation. The remaining 17 may well have comprised those who were not of employment age. Few work problems were reported. Within the six-month time frame, 14 of the 37 had had one job since discharge; 12 had had two jobs, and 11 had had three or more jobs. This information parallels job-retention information for a group of 93 youths of the Illinois Department of Children and Family Services: 33 percent were able to retain the same job for three months and 23 percent for six months or longer.

The data suggest that the child who receives residential care may lack significant work experiences when compared to peers. Given the other indications of lack of stability in the lives of these youths, does that pattern then carry over into the workplace? Recognizing the minimal social and financial supports available to discharged residents, should work experience and vocational programs receive increased attention and emphasis within the residential service continuum?

Life Patterns of Children in Residential Care

Perhaps one of the most startling and disturbing pieces of information that the project produced pertains to the transient life patterns of the children who enter residential care. The baseline population (217) reported, on the average, two moves in the year previous to placement. Of the 96 children who were admitted from their own or foster homes, 141 placements in the previous year were institutional in nature.

As the length of the study indicates, many of the children were in residence for little more than a year. This finding is particularly true of the follow-up population. The total number of children discharged from the Cope agencies was 121. Forty (approximately one-third) were identified as unplanned discharges. At follow-up, only seven of the 54 (or less than 13 percent) were living in the same place to which they had been discharged just six months before. Twenty had moved two or more times during that period.

Hence, the profile pattern for the residents reveals a patchwork quilt of placements and interventions. The likelihood (46 percent) is that the typical Cope boy is being referred from his own or foster family, but in the year before placement at the Cope agency, in addition to having lived in a familial setting, he has also lived in one or more institutional settings. He successfully engages in treatment at a project agency for about 12 months. His discharge is probably planned (66 percent), and he will have been judged as demonstrating some progress. Yet, just six months after this 14½-year-old boy has left the Cope agency, he will probably have moved twice from the planned discharge placement.

Consider this pattern within the context of current public policy and current trends to shorten stays in residential group care. It is critical to know whether this pattern is typical of the majority of children in residential care. The most widely recognized and accepted public policy relating to children is that of permanency planning. Yet five or more placements in a two- to three-year period for a 14-year-old child is a far cry from a permanency-based intervention approach. Does this finding portend a placement merry-go-round of increasing velocity?

Agency Growth as a Result of the Research

The five Cope agencies have gained a great deal from this pioneer inquiry. While describing the perceptions of the residents constituted the major part of this undertaking, the Cope collaboration was fruitful in terms of providing guidelines for the development of future program evaluation, in stimulating program modifications to enhance agency effectiveness, and in demonstrating a viable paraprofessional role for volunteers.

Several agency changes were instituted during the course of the project. One agency established a new aftercare service, and another found justification for the continuation of its aftercare program. A family outreach program was created by one agency to involve families more intensively in the treatment process. One agency inaugurated a program evaluation system incorporating elements of the Project Cope design and instruments. A more thorough intake process was instituted, as well as a more thorough follow-up study, for another agency when it incorporated elements of the Cope questionnaire into its regular operations.

The project would not have been possible without the volunteer cadre. We learned that people from various backgrounds and educational levels could be trained to conduct interviews effectively; however, a substantial commitment of staff time was an essential ingredient in the effectiveness of the volunteers. Undertaking a longitudinal study cannot be done with a strictly volunteer contingent.

The information Cope generated was suggestive rather than definitive. Nonetheless, each agency gained a picture that helped it in addressing questions of accountability to donors, board members, and funders.

Guidelines for Future Research Efforts

The following guidelines may be helpful in developing a service outcome project:

Expert research assistance should be obtained initially and continued through the project's term.

The instruments should be tailored to the questions raised by the agency.

Although there are advantages to collaboration, it is important to recognize that within the realm of service outcomes, the task of analysis becomes increasingly complex as collaborators are added. In a multiple-agency collaboration, careful attention should be given to identifying similarities and differences in agency service programs, particularly as they concern the questions that are to be answered. For example: Does each of the agencies offer a private special-education school? If educational needs are met in a variety of settings, both within and without the agency, then how can changes in academic performance be viewed in aggregate? Second, the commitment to the collaboration must come from the top. The executive directors should be involved at the outset and periodically brought together to discuss progress and to aid in its implementation.

The time frames should correspond to a sound longitudinal effort.

An agency that undertakes a longitudinal study, be it independent or collaborative, must be willing to commit ample staff time. In addition, resources must be available to support continuing consultation.

Volunteers can play a vital role in an agency's follow-up research. Two ingredients are essential to the effectiveness of volunteers. They should receive a thorough orientation to the overall project and intensive training on conducting interviews for research, and regular meetings should be held at least monthly to answer questions the volunteers raise as they gain more experience in their role and to refresh their skills when a period of time elapses between interviews. Staff support is necessary to help volunteers perform their duties (such as locating the clients, having ample forms, and dealing with client behaviors or reactions to the interview process). The greater the staff support, the more likely the volunteer will function for the longer term. Staff support is also necessary to manage the recruitment effort for volunteers, for there is typically a level of turnover with every volunteer effort.

Conclusion

For the five partner agencies, Project Cope was an important first step in addressing the question of service outcomes. The children's perceptions provoked thought and provided the agencies with information that was used for planning and treatment. The lessons taught by the project enhanced the partner agencies' capabilities in the area of service outcomes. Much of the value of an undertaking such as Project Cope is to provide the stimulus for more thorough agency internal examination and to provide the information that enables agencies to play a forceful role in shaping national policy for the benefit of children.

Contributors

Christine A. Ameen
Starr Commonwealth Schools
Starr Commonwealth Road
Albion, Michigan 49224

Myrtle Astrachan, Ph.D.
Associate Director
Beech Brook
3737 Lander Road
Cleveland, Ohio 44124

Edwin A. Balcerzak, Ph.D.
Associate Director
Child Guidance Center
2525 East 22nd Street
Cleveland, Ohio 44115

Stephen L. Buka
Sweetser-Children's Home
50 Moody Street
Saco, Maine 04072-0892

Fred Chaffee
Hillside Children's Center
1183 Monroe Avenue
Rochester, New York 14620

Elizabeth S. Cole
R.D. 2, Box 105
New Hope, Pennsylvania 18938

Mary Jo Cooke
New England Home for Little
  Wanderers
161 South Huntington Avenue
Boston, Massachusetts 02130

Nan Dale
The Children's Village
Dobbs Ferry, New York 10522

Jack K. Daniels
Methodist Home
1111 Herring Avenue
Waco, Texas 76708

Margaret DiCori
New England Home for Little
  Wanderers
161 South Huntington Avenue
Boston, Massachusetts 02130

Joan DiLeonardi
Children's Home and Aid
  Society of Illinois
1122 N. Dearborn Street
Chicago, Illinois 60610

Richard G. Doiron, Ph.D.
Neuropsychology Consultant
Sweetser-Children's Home
50 Moody Street
Saco, Maine 04072-0892

Christine H. Donnorummo
Three Rivers Youth
2039 Termon Avenue
Pittsburgh, Pennsylvania 15212

Martha M. Dore
University of Chicago
969 East 16th Street
Chicago, Illinois 60637

421

David C. Droppa
Three Rivers Youth
2039 Termon Avenue
Pittsburgh, Pennsylvania 15212

Roderick Durkin, Ph.D.
Childhaven
316 Broadway
Seattle, Washington 98122

David Fanshel, Ph.D.
Columbia University
School of Social Work
622 West 113th Street
New York, New York 10025

Stephen J. Finch
Columbia University
School of Social Work
622 West 113th Street
New York, New York 10025

David Fine
University of Washington
School of Social Work
4101 15th Avenue, N.E.
Seattle, Washington 98195

Timothy L. Fitzharris
California Association of
*   Services for Children*
P.O. Box 2769
Sacramento, California 95812

Michael Forster
Director, Clinical Services
Ullich Children's Home
3737 N. Mozart Avenue
Chicago, Illinois 60618

Robert L. Gass
Deputy Director
New England Home for Little
*   Wanderers*
161 S. Huntington Avenue
Boston, Massachusetts 02130

Anthony Grasso
University of Washington
School of Social Work
4101 15th Avenue, N.E.
Seattle, Washington 98195

John F. Grundy
Columbia University
School of Social Work
622 West 113th Street
New York, New York 10025

Gerald G. Hicks
Executive Director
Michigan Federation of Private
*   Child and Family Agencies*
230 N. Washington Square #200
Lansing, Michigan 48933

Jeffrey M. Jenson
Graduate School of Social Work
University of Utah
Salt Lake City, Utah 84112

Earl Kelly, Ed.D.
Executive Director
Orchard Place
925 S.W. Porter Avenue
Des Moines, Iowa 50315

Thomas E. Linton
University of Illinois
*   at Chicago*
College of Education
2136 North Hamlin Avenue
Chicago, Illinois 60647

Judith S. Michael, Ph.D.
Program Supervisor
Three Rivers Youth
2039 Termon Avenue
Pittsburgh, Pennsylvania 15212

Martin L. Mitchell, Ph.D.
Vice President of Program
Starr Commonwealth Schools
Starr Commonwealth Road
Albion, Michigan 49224

Contributors

Gerry Mozenter
Hillside Children's Center
1183 Monroe Avenue
Rochester, New York 14620

Donnell M. Pappenfort
University of Chicago
969 East 16th Street
Chicago, Illinois 60637

Susan B. Price
Director of Quality Assurance
Hillside Children's Center
1183 Monroe Avenue
Rochester, New York 14620

Nancy B. Ronquillo
Lawrence Hall
4833 N. Francisco Avenue
Chicago, Illinois 60610

Dorothy Seward
New England Home for Little
  Wanderers
161 S. Huntington Avenue
Boston, Massachusetts 02130

Lorraine Siegel
DSW Director
Nannahagen School Day Treatment
  Program
Box 237
Pleasantville, New York 10570

Susan S. Stepleton,
  Administrator
Salvation Army
The Hope Center
3740 Marine Avenue
St. Louis, Missouri 63118

Edmond R. Stolkner
Sweetser-Children's Home
50 Moody Street
Saco, Maine 04072-0892

Jake Terpstra
Specialist in Residential
  Care and Licensing
U.S. Children's Bureau/DHHS
P.O. Box 1182
Washington, D.C. 20013

Owen Tucker, Jr.
Methodist Home
1111 Herring Avenue
Waco, Texas 76708

Kathleen Wells, Ph.D.
Director of Research
Bellefaire
22001 Fairmount Boulevard
Cleveland, Ohio 44118

James K. Whittaker
University of Washington
School of Social Work
4101 15th Avenue, N.E.
Seattle, Washington 98195

Thomas Young, Ph.D.
Research & Training Center
Regional Research Institute
P.O. Box 751
Portland, Oregon 97207